LIVING JUDAISM

The Complete Guide to Jewish Belief, Tradition, and Practice

RABBI WAYNE DOSICK

HarperSanFrancisco

An Imprint of HarperCollins*Publishers*

HarperCollins®, ☰ ®, and HarperSanFrancisco™ are trademarks of HarperCollins Publishers Inc.

FIRST EDITION

Library of Congress Cataloging-in-Publication Data
Dosick, Wayne D.
   Living Judaism : the complete guide to Jewish belief, tradition,
and practice / Wayne Dosick. — 1st ed.
   ISBN 0–06–062119–2 (cloth)
   ISBN 0–06–062179–6 (pbk.)
   1. Judaism.   I. Title.
BM561.B65   1995
296—dc20   95–22260

   96   97   98   99   RRD(H)   10   9   8   7   6   5   4   3

CONTENTS

הנסתרות לה׳ אלהינו
והנגלת לנו ולבנינו עד עולם...

Hanistarot la-Adonai Elohanu, v'haniglot lanu ul'vananu ad olam . . .

The secret things belong to the Lord our God, but the things that are
revealed belong to us and to our children forever . . .

DEUTERONOMY 29:28

ACKNOWLEDGMENTS

I take great pleasure in extending deepest thanks and gratitude to those whose teachings and influence are reflected in this book:

The rabbis of my youth, Rabbi Ralph Simon and Rabbi Benjamin Daskal ז"ל, in whose synagogue, Congregation Rodfei Zedek, Chicago, Illinois, I learned to love Judaism.

The seven modern masters to whom this book is dedicated: Dr. Irving H. Skolnick, Rabbi Dr. Jakob J. Petuchowski ז"ל, Dr. Yehuda Shabatay, Rabbi Dr. Abraham Joshua Heschel ז"ל, Rabbi Shlomo Carlebach ז"ל, Rabbi Dr. Zalman Schachter-Shalomi, and Rabbi Jack Riemer. Each guided and taught me—some from intimately near, some from afar—in a unique way; each profoundly affected my mind, my heart, and my spirit. Those who remain in this life continue to teach me every day; the voices of those who have gone to the Great Beyond echo deeply within me.

My teachers, who brought down to me the greatness of Jewish learning, and my *rebbes,* who inspired me to the goodness of Jewish living.

Four sweet singers of Israel, who—each in his own very different way, and each at the exactly right cosmic moment—taught me to "sing new songs unto the Lord" (Psalms 96:1)—Cantor Maurice Goldberg ז"ל, Rabbi Shlomo Carlebach ז"ל, Cantor Paul Zim, and Rabbi David Zeller.

The men, women, and children of the congregations in which I have served and taught: Congregation Beth Shalom, Wilmington, Delaware; Congregation Beth El, La Jolla, California; Congregation Beth Am, Solana Beach, California; and especially, The Elijah Minyan of Greater San Diego. I am particularly grateful to those who studied from this ever-developing text: the hundreds of people in the Introduction to Judaism classes who came seeking their heritage; the eighty-six people of the most recent Adult B'nai Mitzvah classes who affirmed their future by finding their past; and the scores of remarkable people who learned and chose Judaism—exploring the past in order to embrace their future. I am most humbly and eternally grateful to five precious human beings who have learned with me continually for more than twenty years: Abe and Paula Kassam; Florence and Dr. Sheldon Kronfeld; and Dr. Gary Hartman—fellow seekers, all.

The students of the University of San Diego, who have given me the honor of sharing Judaism with them, and whose genuine curiosity, probing questions, and lovingly critical reactions have helped hone and sharpen this, their ever-evolving text; and the members of the administration and faculty who have welcomed me so warmly, especially the chairs of the Department of Religious and Theological Studies: the Rev. Dr. Robert Kress, the Rev. Dr. Ronald Pachence, Dr. Kathleen Dugan, and Dr. Gary Macy. I am profoundly grateful to my cherished friend, the Rev. James J. O'Leary, S.J., for the gift of his sacred spirit.

I express deepest thanks to the Jewish Chautauqua Society and its indefatigable San Diego representative, my long-time friend, Richard Stern, who originally made it possible for me to come to USD.

Colleagues and friends who read all or parts of the manuscript of this book and enriched it immeasurably with their wisdom and insight: Dr. Lawrence Baron, Rabbi Marc Berkson, Dr. David Ellenson, Dr. Barbara Gereboff, Dr. Joel Gereboff, Rabbi Michael Gotlieb, Rabbi Roberto Graetz, Dr. Steven Helfgot, Rabbi Menahem Herman, Rabbi Ellen Lippmann, Rabbi Jack Moline, Rabbi David Posner, Rabbi Deborah Prinz, Rabbi Arnold Rachlis, Rabbi Dennis Sasso, Alvin Schultzberg, Rabbi Elie Spitz, and Cantor Paul Zim.

I am, once more, deeply grateful to three of the men to whom this book is dedicated for sharing the depths of their learning by extensively reviewing the manuscript, and thus continuing to teach me Torah: Rabbi Jack Riemer, Dr. Yehuda Shabatay, and Dr. Irving H. Skolnick.

My extraordinary literary agent, Sandra Dijkstra, and her talented assistant, Rita Holm, who keep the faith and work their magic; and the good folks at Harper San Francisco, especially Tom Grady, Steve Hanselman, Laura Galinson, and Mimi Kusch whose company commitment is to the opening and unfolding of the world of the spirit. I am particularly grateful to my outstanding editor, Kandace Hawkinson, who brings to her work a sharp blue pencil and her great big heart and soul.

My parents, Hyman and Roberta Dosick, and my parents-in-law, Clarence and Anna Kaufman, who live Judaism with "all their heart, all their soul, all their might" (after Deuteronomy 6:5); who took us to *shul,* who made Shabbas, who guided us to God's ways, and whose faith inspires us and sustains us.

My sons, Scott and Seth. Their love envelops me always.

המלאך הגאל אתי מכל רע יברך את הנערים . . .

HaMalach hagoel oti mekol ra, y'varech et han'arim . . .

"May the angel who guards me from all evil bless these young men, and may my name be blessed in them, along with the names of my ancestors, and let them grow to greatness in this world . . . " (Genesis 48:16).

Ellen—precious wife, cherished partner, spiritual guide, planetary healer. She is a woman "in whom the spirit of God lives" (after Genesis 41:38). "By her faithfulness, she has proven to be a worthy prophet; by her words, she is known as a trusted visionary" (after Ben Sirah: 46:15).

The spirits who guide us; the guides who fill us with their spirit. Miriam: "And all the women went out after her with timbrels and with dances. And Miriam sang to them . . . " (Exodus 15: 20–21); Aaron: "And Aaron spoke all the words which the Lord had spoken . . . " (Exodus 4:30); Elijah: "And Elijah went up to heaven in a whirlwind" (2 Kings 2:11); and Jonah: "And the word of the Lord came to Jonah a second time . . . " (Jonah 3:1).

And, above all, to the One Who is above—and below, and within:

יתברך שמך בפי כל חי תמיד לעולם ועד
Yitbarach Shimcha b'fi kol chai, tamid l'olam va-ed.

"May Your name be praised, O God,
by every living soul
always and forever."

BIRCAT HAMAZON

IN THE BEGINNING

An old Jewish legend:

In the beginning—before the beginning—God's light filled the entire universe.

When God decided to create the world, He had to withdraw some of His light from the universe, so that there would be space for the land and the seas, the trees and the corn stalks, the butterflies and the lions, the ladybugs and the sea otters.

So God breathed in some of the Divine light, so that there would be room for all the things He wanted to create.

But what was God to do with the light—with the light of His Being that had filled the whole universe—now that He had breathed it in?

God put the light into jars, heavenly vessels that would hold His radiance.

And then God began to create: the sky and the earth, the dry lands and the waters, the fiery sun, the shimmering moon and the twinkling stars, the forests and the deserts, the creepy crawly things and the birds of the air, the fish of the seas and the animals roaming from here to there.

Everything was going so well. Creation was shaping up just perfectly. God was having a wonderful time!

But in the heavens, there was trouble.

God's light, which He had put into the vessels, could not be hidden away. For no vessel—not even a heavenly vessel—could contain the radiant light of God. The glory of God's splendor was accustomed to filling the universe, not being hidden away in little jars.

So it wasn't too long until—with a blazing flash—God's light burst out of the heavenly vessels.

The force of the mighty impact caused the jars to shatter into millions of little pieces.

And the light itself splintered into billions of little sparks.

The broken pieces of the vessels fell to the newly formed earth and became the ills and the evils that beset the world—little pieces of anguish and travail that, one day, will have to be collected, repaired, and made whole again.

And what happened to the billions of little shards of light?

Each of the little shards of light, the sparks of God, became the soul of a human being.

That which makes the lump of clay that is a human body into a living, breathing, person—a person capable of thinking and knowing, reasoning, and remembering, a person capable of doing justly and feeling compassion—is the soul. And the human soul is a tiny piece of God, a tiny fragment of God's light, a spark of the Divine that burst forth from the heavenly vessels and showered the universe.

God declared that the crowning works of creation were these human souls—man and woman, created in His image, created with a spark of His Divine Being. And to man and woman, God assigned a divine task and a sacred mission.

Each person, then and now, is to joyfully share the universe with God, to be His companion and helpmate, His resident caretaker and earthly steward.

And each person, then and now, is to be a partner with God in healing and transforming the universe: picking up the little pieces of the shattered vessels, repairing them, and making them—and the world—healthy and whole.

In every generation, in every time and place, human beings have developed religious and philosophical systems to seek and find God, to understand and fulfill God's word, to share with God in the ongoing process of the daily re-creation and transformation of the world, to enrich and ennoble their own lives.

For almost 4,000 years, Judaism has been—and continues to be—a wise and rewarding pathway to God; a clear channel for understanding and doing God's will, and for enhancing cosmic and personal existence. Judaism is a religion that is intellectually honest, emotionally satisfying, and spiritually uplifting. And Judaism creates a faith community that is deeply rooted, strongly bonded, and passionately loyal.

This book is your invitation into the world of Judaism.

Here you will learn about Judaism's basic beliefs and practices—the ideas and the observances that shape and mold Jewish life and lifestyle.

Here you will learn how an age-old community in contemporary garb understands and follows God's mandate to make life personally satisfying and fulfilling, and undertakes God's mission to bring the world toward justice, righteousness, and peace.

Here you will celebrate the greatness and the grandeur of the Jewish experience: being a child of God—created with a spark of the Divine—seeing God's light in every encounter, reflecting God's light at every moment.

Here is Judaism.

THE FOUNDATIONS OF JUDAISM:
GOD, TORAH, AND ISRAEL

Religion is a system of thought and belief operating not only from philosophical reason, but from intuition and faith. It acknowledges and celebrates the existence of the highest power, a Supreme Being (or Beings) who created, ordered, and controls the universe.

Religion developed out of the human need to seek answers to the mysteries of existence: to help people understand and somehow tame the mighty forces of the universe; to help people define their place and purpose, by putting them in touch with their primordial beginnings, by finding a connection to creation and the Creator.

Religion helps people to face the unknown, to find meaning and value in daily existence, to understand pain and suffering and evil, to live life and to confront death.

In ancient times, people sought to influence and control the diverse elements that affected their everyday lives. So they paid tribute to and prayerfully worshiped the sun, the moon, the mountain, the tree, the river, or the rain. They fashioned idols out of stone and precious metals, and imbued them with extraordinary powers. They offered sacrifices of animals, of grains, of first fruits, and of firstborn sons, in the hope that the forces to whom they ascribed divinity would deal kindly with them—giving them food to eat, water to drink, sun and rain in their seasons, protection from danger and harm. Each tribe, each locale, each household, had one or many gods, to whom awe-inspired homage was exaltingly and often lovingly proclaimed.

The ancient world may have been theologically naive, but it was far from unsophisticated.

The recorded history of humankind—which begins some 6,000 years ago—documents advanced civilizations growing up and flourishing: the Sumerians in Babylon, the Egyptians, the Phoenicians, the Akkadians in Mesopotamia, the Chaldeans, and the numerous kingdoms scattered throughout the region that is now called the ancient Near East. Advanced societies were also developing and flourishing throughout the known world: in China, in Asia Minor, along the Mediterranean, in Crete and Greece, in Europe, in settlements in India and Japan. These diverse societies created highly sophisticated agricultural settlements, built ships and wheeled vehicles for transport and trade, crafted pottery and wove cloth, made metal coins as legal tender, and metal mirrors to reflect beauty.

They developed not only pictographic signs, but early forms of alphabet and writing; they amassed large collections of prose, poetry, and epic tales, played finely crafted musical instruments, and made precise calendars and maps. The Babylonian king Hammurabi, in setting out laws for his kingdom, established the first systematic legal code.

The firm foundation of civilization was already well in place when, in approximately 1800 B.C.E.—when the now-6,000-year-old recorded history of humankind had already passed its one-third mark—a man named Abraham entered the world stage. He came into this world in ancient Mesopotamia, the area of the Tigris and Euphrates rivers that came to be called the Fertile Crescent, the modern-day Middle East of Syria, Iraq, Iran, Saudi Arabia, Jordan, Lebanon, Israel, and Egypt.

THE DATING OF HISTORY

The secular calendar that is currently in use throughout most of the world is based on a Christian counting of time.

In this system, there are two major periods of time: A.D., meaning anno Domini, the Year of our Lord, designating the period of time counting forward from the birth of Jesus (using the popular designation of the year of the birth of Jesus as year 1); and B.C., meaning Before Christ, designating the period of time counting backward from before the birth of Jesus.

By this calculation, 800 years before the birth of Jesus is known as the year 800 B.C. This book is being published in the year A.D. 1995, meaning 1,995 years since the birth of Jesus.

Judaism, not wanting its time designations delineated by Christianity, and modern academic scholarship not wanting its designations influenced by any one religious motif, changed the designations: B.C. is identified as B.C.E., Before the Common Era, and A.D. is identified as C.E., the Common Era.

For a concise timeline and a fully annotated reference-listing of the most important events of Jewish history, see chapter 9, Highlights of Jewish History.

GOD

In the midst of this ancient world—a world that was still primarily pagan, recognizing and venerating thousands of different gods—Abraham revolutionized the concept of religion and the idea of deity by proclaiming his belief in one God.

Abraham declared that the sole Creator and Ruler of the universe is יהוה YHWH, the Lord God. (The actual pronunciation of the proper name of God has been lost for millennia. Today YHWH is pronounced אדוני Adonai, literally, "our Master," the recognized and accepted substitute pronunciation.)

When Abraham found the one Lord God, he taught that all the other gods worshiped by the pagans were mere pretenders to divinity.

This system of thought is now called monotheism, the belief in the one and only God.

Abraham's declaration marked the beginning of the religion that would come to be called Judaism. Through Abraham, Judaism introduced to the world one of its core tenets: the belief in the one Lord God.

TORAH

The source for our knowledge of the beginnings of Jewish thought and history is the תורה Torah, the first five sections of the Hebrew Bible, the books of Genesis, Exodus, Leviticus, Numbers, and Deuteronomy.

The Torah relates the Jewish understanding of the creation of the universe and everything in it.

It relates the encounter between Abraham and God that resulted in the covenant of faith.

It recounts the revelation at Mt. Sinai, when God began to give the commandments, the מצות mitzvot, providing the moral values, the standards of behavior, by which God wants people to live. Along with the ethical commands, God gave ritual law, the instrumentality by which the ethical mitzvot are remembered and observed, and which serve to order, rhythm, and enrich everyday existence by raising ordinary acts to the level of holiness.

The mitzvot guide Jews to fulfill life's purpose and mission: to work to end all the ills and the evils that beset the world; to transform and perfect the world under the Kingdom of God; to anticipate the day when Jews—and every human being on earth—will welcome the messianic era of harmony and tranquility, peace, and perfection.

To further enhance life, the Torah mandates the commemoration and celebration of special times and days. Throughout the year, celebrations of holidays mark the seasons, commemorate historical events, and sanctify time.

The central observance of Jewish life—from its beginnings in the Torah until today—is שבת Shabbat, the Sabbath. Commemorated from sundown on Friday to sundown on Saturday (a Jewish day, following the soli-lunar calendar, begins and ends at sundown), Shabbat is a time of physical relaxation and spiritual rejuvenation. Imitating God—who rested on the seventh day following the six days of creation—on the Sabbath, the Jewish People rest from the everyday world, dedicating the day to

God, family, and personal renewal. Observing the Sabbath and holidays has kept the Jewish People strong in belief and practice and united in common purpose.

ISRAEL: THE PEOPLE AND THE LAND

The Jewish People, sometimes called the People of Israel, are linked by a shared faith in God and observance of God's commands. Yet Jews remain so deeply connected and united because Judaism is more than a religion, more than a set of theological beliefs. Judaism is also a *peoplehood*—people linked by a common history, language, literature, land, culture, and destiny.

As part of the original covenant with Abraham, God promised the Jewish People an eternal homeland, the Land of Israel.

When Joshua led the Jewish People into the Jewish Land (ca. 1200 B.C.E.), the Jewish nation established itself and created its religious and political institutions. The next 1,000 years and more were marked with high drama, trauma, and challenge: the split of the kingdom, the destruction of the largest kingdom, the destruction of the Holy Temple, exile, return, and the reestablishment of political and religious sovereignty.

With the destruction of the second Holy Temple in 70 C.E., the Jews began an odyssey of wandering that would last for almost 2,000 years. In exile, in the Diaspora, without their homeland, Jews were always guests in host countries. Without their coreligionists, they were odd strangers of different religion, ethnicity, culture. Without independence, their freedoms were often curtailed; they were easy targets for bigotry, discrimination, and persecution.

Through it all—with enduring faith, everlasting unity, boundless resilience, and their unwavering allegiance and claim to their spiritual homeland—the Jewish People and the Jewish religion may have been bruised and battered, but they persevered, adapting to meet crisis, and always emerging stronger than before.

With the establishment of the modern State of Israel in 1948, all of Judaism converged once again: the Jewish God and the Jewish People together in the Jewish Land.

This, then, is the enduring Jewish reality: that *God, Torah and Israel*—the People Israel everywhere and the Land of Israel—together form Judaism's three-pillared foundation.

This is Judaism.

> We begin at the very beginning . . .
> . . . with God.
> For, "in God's light do *we* see light."
>
> (after Psalms 36:10)

1

JEWISH BELIEFS

1.   GOD

Other religions and philosophical systems begin by giving proofs for the existence of God. Judaism begins with the *assumption* of the existence of God.

Judaism has two clear and concise statements about the existence of God: "In the beginning, God . . . " (Genesis 1:1) and "Hear O Israel, the Lord is our God, the Lord is One" (Deuteronomy 6:4). This second statement has become such an integral part of Jewish belief that it has become one of the central prayers of the Jewish worship service (שמע ישראל "*Sh'ma Yisrael*" "Hear O Israel"), recited by Jews each day as the "Declaration of Faith."

What does it say?

"Hear, O Israel" means, "Listen—pay attention—Jews."

"The Lord is our God": In English there seems to be little difference between the meaning of the word *Lord* and the meaning of the word *God*. But in Hebrew there is a significant difference. *God* is the generic, the common noun. The ancient world had many gods, each worshiped and venerated by one or more nations or tribes in one or more places. But *Lord* (in Hebrew יהוה YHWH) is the proper noun, the specific name of the God whom Abraham found.

The Hebrew root word from which YHWH is derived means "to be." Thus the very name YHWH implies both the existence and the timelessness of God: God "was," "is," and "will always be."

So the phrase "the Lord is our God" means that YHWH—not the sun or the moon or the idols made of stone, but YHWH—is *our* God.

But, there is more. YHWH is not in coequal existence with all the other gods. YHWH is not just one god among many. "The Lord is One."

The word *one* has several meanings, all of which are commingled here and are equally important.

7

1. "One" means *unique.* When this statement was first articulated, it was understood that other nations worshiped a variety of gods, and it was understood that those nations would not throw down their beliefs in their gods in a day or a year or, perhaps, forever. But no matter. YHWH is unique, the real God. YHWH is God with a capitol "G." All the others are mere pretenders.

2. "One" means *singular.* Some nations had two, three, four, or more gods with coequal status; or one chief god with a number of assistant or deputy gods, each with his or her own domain. YHWH is not one of many. YHWH is God alone.

3. "One" means *indivisible.* One God cannot be broken into parts or divided into entities. No concept of duality or trinity can exist, for YHWH cannot be separated into sections.

4. "One" is also a *mathematical formula.* If YHWH is one and not two or three or seventeen, then, YHWH is also one and not zero. Mathematically, YHWH is "not not." Since two negatives make a positive, YHWH is. YHWH was, is, and will always be. YHWH exists.

With the assumption of the existence of God, Judaism concerns itself with who God is, what God does, and what the relationship between God and humankind is and can be.

THE NAMES OF GOD

A modern prayer-writer has said that the names by which God is called "create an image in minds and hearts, an image which souls can understand and touch." These names reflect the developing Jewish ideas about God and His attributes.

In the Torah (the first section of the Hebrew Bible, the Five Books of Moses: Genesis through Deuteronomy) God is acknowledged as Creator, Redeemer, Law-Giver, and Ruler. In addition to the name YHWH, God is called by three other proper names: אלהים Elohim, אל Eyl, and שדי Shaddai. Later in the Bible, and still later in rabbinic and medieval philosophical and mystical literature, God is called by names that reflect His nature and His role in the lives of His people:

God is called צור Tzur, Rock, to characterize His firm steadfastness. He is called מלך Melech, King; דיין Dayan, Judge; and אדון Adon, Master. These are all names of power within the earthly society and presumably in the Kingdom of God.

He is called names of love and protection—אב Av, Father, and רועה Roeh, Shepherd.

He is called אבינו שבשמים Avenu Shebashamayim, Our Father who is in Heaven; רבונו של עולם Ribono Shel Olam, Master of the Universe; and המקום HaMakom, the Place. These are names that acknowledge His eternity and His power throughout the universe.

He is called הרחמן HaRachaman, the Merciful One, reflecting His care and compassion; and He is called הקדוש ברוך הוא HaKadosh Baruch Hu, the Holy One, Blessed is He, acknowledging His greatness and His glory.

In the kabbalah, the Jewish mystical tradition, God is called אין סוף Ein Sof (meaning, Infinite), Without End.

All of these names for God are masculine, both in their title or role and in their Hebrew grammatical formulation. Since Judaism was born and developed in a rigidly patriarchal society that was dominated and controlled by men, the names of God generally reflect this masculine power structure. But there is one name for God that acknowledges and celebrates God's feminine characteristics.

The name שכינה Shechinah, The Presence, is used to reflect God's all-enveloping presence, which protects from harm, nurtures, and cradles in love. When the Jewish People are sent off into exile, the texts say that it is the Shechinah who goes with them, to comfort and care.

Throughout Jewish history, God has always been referred to as Him, not Her; He, not She; Father, not Mother. Any intimation that God might have feminine characteristics was strongly dismissed at the beginning of Judaism. This was done for two reasons: first, to distinguish Judaism from the nations and tribes that worshiped a goddess, and second, to establish that God is one, without any duality; and certainly, at the time of the rise of Christianity, to declare that God is one, not divisible into any parts.

However, the idea of one God, with both masculine and feminine characteristics, remains. This concept not only gives egalitarians and modern-day feminists of both genders a role model in God, but compels each person—created in the image of God—to recognize and be in touch with both the masculine and feminine qualities within. If language would permit, it would be much better to refer to God as He/She or Him/Her. But For practical purposes, we refer to God as He or Him.

THE EVOLVING RELATIONSHIP OF GOD
AND THE JEWISH PEOPLE

The Jewish view of God is not static or frozen in any time or place. It is constantly growing, changing, expanding. For even though God is constant, people are forever growing and developing. So each person, in each generation, must discover, understand, describe, and relate to God in his or her own way, out of his or her own life experiences.

The *amidah,* one of the central prayers of the Jewish worship service, recited by traditional Jews three times each day, teaches this very lesson. The prayer begins with the words, "Praised are You, O Lord, our God and God of our ancestors, God of

Abraham, God of Isaac, and God of Jacob . . . ." Why the repetition? Hebrew is a concise language; it does not use words that it does not need. But in this prayer, instead of saying, "God of Abraham, Isaac, and Jacob," it repeats the word *God* three times: "*God* of Abraham, *God* of Isaac, and *God* of Jacob."

The prayerbook writers understood that each of these "founding fathers" of Judaism had to create a separate, individual, personal, relationship with God—each in his own time. Isaac's world was not the world of his father; Jacob's world was not the world of his father or his grandfather. Each man had to discover God for himself, for each man had his own needs and expectations of God. Because each lived at a different moment and in different circumstance, each had a unique relationship to establish.

The very name ישראל *Yisrael*, Israel, by which the Jewish People is known, means "to wrestle with God" (Genesis 32:29), indicating that each and every person must seek and find God in his or her own way.

So at various periods of history—often in response to the political situation or philosophical climate of the moment—the strivings with God of a particular person—or of a group of people, reflecting the collective consciousness—demonstrate the ever-evolving, ever-developing relationship of the Jewish People with God.

A BRIEF OVERVIEW
OF THE JEWISH IDEA OF GOD

Jewish theology begins with the assumption of the existence of God, and Judaism has always been more concerned with how people relate to God and respond to God's word and will than with what people believe about God.

Yet, as the prayerbook teaches, "The beginning of wisdom is the awe of God." For the individual Jew and for the Jewish community, the religious quest begins with God: in the formation of an individual, personal, intimate relationship with God, and then with the establishment of an ongoing communal relationship between God and the Jewish People.

The Jewish view of God has never been stagnant or fixed, but has been ever-developing, from the time of the Bible until the present day.

This brief overview outlines what various Jewish thinkers, at various times in Jewish history, have thought about God. The overview shows how the historical, philosophical, political, and social settings in which each thinker lived influenced his thinking, and how often the Jewish theological approach to God has alternated between faith and reason.

The Bible assumes the existence of the one and only Lord God, and chronicles the covenant of faith between God and the Jewish people.

Over and over again, through God's direct communication and revelation, the personal relationship between God and humankind is demonstrated.

Because of this clear exhibition of God's abilities and powers, the confident biblical premise is that future generations will affirm God through faith, and accept the biblical assertions (1) that each individual can have a personal relationship with God; (2) that God and the Jewish People have a special covenantal relationship; (3) that God gives each person free will, making each individual responsible for his or her actions; and (4) that God's will is manifest in the commandments, and that reward or punishment for observing or transgressing the law takes place in this lifetime.

In the Rabbinic Period (ca. 200 B.C.E.–600 C.E.), the sages responded to challenges to faith with rational explanation. To counter newborn Christianity's claim that God had walked the earth in human form, the sages offered proof for the existence of God (the "argument from design": Just as the house needs a builder, the world needs a builder—God) and attributed human emotions to God.

To counter the claim that the relationship between God and humankind is based primarily on faith, the sages reaffirmed the primacy of covenantal law, and expanded God's scope as Law-Giver to include continuing revelation through Oral Law.

Reflecting ever-expanding human consciousness, and responding to the political domination of the Greeks and Romans, the sages introduced the concept of an afterlife, with God's reward or punishment for earthly behavior given in a world to come.

During the Rabbinic Period, **Philo** (20 B.C.E.–50 C.E.), a Jewish thinker who lived in Alexandria, Egypt, borrowed heavily from the Greek philosophers in an attempt to synthesize Judaism and the dominant Greek culture.

Affirming (through faith) the oneness of God, Philo taught that proof for God's existence is the universal mind: Just as human beings have a mind, the universe has a mind—God; and that the best way for rational human beings to reach God is through reason.

In the ensuing 800 years, strong and diverse forces had an affect on Judaism: traditional Jewish thought; the tremendous growth of Christianity; the birth and rise of Islam; the continuing influence of Greek thought; and within Judaism, the fundamentalist challenge of the Karaites, who insisted that only the Written Law and not the Oral Law was binding.

Saadya Gaon (892–942; Egypt, Israel, Syria, Iraq, and Babylonia), the head of the great Academy of Jewish learning at Sura, attempted to balance these many and significant forces by setting out to prove that there is no conflict between faith and reason. Saadya taught that while the one God created the world, the inadequacy of language makes it impossible to describe God in any human terms, but that God's goodness is manifest in the law given to humankind: rational law, where human reason recognizes the difference between right and wrong, and law is neither inherently right or wrong, but is accepted through faith, just because God gave it.

Yehuda HaLevi (1080–1142; Spain), a philosopher and poet, rejected Saadya's attempt to balance reason and faith, and passionately advocated traditional Jewish belief and faith. After watching the often fierce conflict for supremacy and territory between Christians and Moslems in his native Spain, HaLevi wrote the *Kuzari*, claiming that Judaism is spiritually superior to all other religions. HaLevi affirmed that God is to be known not through reason but through spiritual insight; that the personal relationship between God and each Jew is established through the love-gift of Torah; and that the God-given Land of Israel is central to the Jewish spiritual quest, so the Jewish People must return to Israel from wandering exile.

Moses Maimonides (1135–1204; Spain, Morocco, Israel, Egypt) was a rationalist thinker—a legalist and a philosopher—who built his Jewish views on the teachings of the Greek philosopher Aristotle. His theology is clear indication that Jews had fully "arrived and entered into" the world, and felt compelled to explain and defend (and sometimes bend) Jewish beliefs in response to popular philosophical systems.

Maimonides taught that the proof for the existence of God is the "cosmological argument": that every object in the world is moved by another, but that God is the "unmoved mover" who set the whole process in motion. He contended that God created the world out of pure intellect and does not interfere with the ongoing process of the universe. Therefore the highest human good is to strive for intellectual perfection.

The Kabbalists (beginning in the thirteenth century) were Jewish mystics who countered the rationalism of Maimonides by developing a highly spiritual approach to God. They called God Ein Sof, meaning "Without End," claiming that God is limitless and infinite, and thus unknowable to the finite mind. They taught that the distance between God and humankind is bridged by ten *sefirot* (steps, spheres, or emanations), and that the way to come into intimate relationship with God is to ascend these *sefirot* through meditation and prayer.

Baruch Spinoza (1632–1677; Amsterdam) was a Jewish pantheist. He maintained that since everything comes from God, God, the universe, and nature are one. Being one, God did not create the universe or establish the laws of nature, but the universe and natural law *are* God.

Questioning the Divine authorship of Torah, and thus the authority of Torah law, Spinoza contended that Torah law cannot take precedence over natural law. "God's will" is nothing more than the acts and events of nature, all functioning in a predetermined manner, so humankind must accept the universe as it is. God is not personal and cannot be approached—or prayed to—by humankind, and certainly cannot change the predetermined acts of the natural universe. This philosophy of determinism is in direct conflict with the concept of free will advocated by all other Jewish theologies.

With Spinoza, the pendulum of Jewish theology swung further than ever before. For his radical thought, Spinoza was shunned and eventually "excommunicated" by the Jewish community (an extraordinarily rare act of public censure), proving that while there was great tolerance for differing points of view, there was a place where a thinker could finally step outside the spectrum of Jewish belief.

The Chasidim (beginning in the eighteenth century) were led by Israel ben Eliezer, a mystical teacher who would come to be known as the Baal Shem Tov, the

Master of the Good Name. Completely rejecting the teachings of Spinoza, the chasidim renewed the kabbalistic spiritual, mystical tradition—adding fervent, joyous prayer to meditation and contemplation as the pathway to God.

The modern era has produced many events that have had a profound and diffuse effect on the Jewish view of God: the Enlightenment, with its emphasis on scientific scholarship; the emancipation, with its political and territorial freedoms—especially for Jews; global warfare, with its threat of mass destruction; the rise and growth of a highly creative American Jewish community; the devastation of the Holocaust; the rise and growth of political Zionism and the establishment of the modern State of Israel; the quantum leaps of science and technology; and the recent deep concern about ecology and the preservation of the planet.

Reform Judaism (established in the mid-nineteenth century), in conjunction with modern scholarship, challenged the concept of the Divine authorship of Torah. It declared binding only the ethical but not the ritual laws of Torah.

Martin Buber (1878–1965; Vienna, Berlin, Frankfurt, and Jerusalem), a great Jewish thinker whose post-Holocaust teachings were warmly embraced by Christians as well as Jews, sought God in a nonreligious, nonsectarian, but deeply spiritual way. He called God the "Eternal Thou," an eternal presence that cannot be proved, defined, or described. Yet, by coming into genuine, intimate, mutual relationship, God can be met. For Buber, God is ever-reachable, and revelation is ever-continuing.

Mordecai Kaplan (1881–1983; Lithuania, New York, Jerusalem), reflecting the rationalism of an age of reason, was the founder of the Reconstructionist movement, whose central teaching is that Judaism is an "evolving religious civilization," enabling Jews to manifest and express their Judaism ethnically and culturally, as well as religiously. He contended that (rather than an individual or national relationship with God) it is the collective consciousness of the Jewish People that has made Jewish civilization distinct and unique. He was a "naturalist," rejecting the concept of a supernatural God and claiming instead that God is a Power or a Process—the sum of the forces that give life meaning and worth. Thus belief in God is really belief in the reality that spurs humankind to its own "salvation," to achieving its highest needs.

Abraham Joshua Heschel (1907–1972; Warsaw, Berlin, Cincinnati, New York), saved from the Holocaust to become one of modern Judaism's preeminent scholars, teachers, and political activists, believed that "God is of no importance unless He is of supreme importance." Reflecting the position of the kabbalists and the chasidim before him, Heschel sowed renewed seeds of faith into a rational age by teaching that each person can have a close, personal, intimate relationship with God, achieved through contemplative meditation and joyous prayer. He asserted that each human being can manifest God in the world by working to bring God's ethical mandate to a troubled universe; to work for a better, a more just, a more perfect world.

In contemporary times there is a wide variety of Jewish belief, reflecting almost every historical God-idea, placing contemporary Jews at virtually every point on the theological spectrum.

- Some Jews continue to affirm God through *faith.*
- Some Jews find God through *reason and intellect.*
- Some Jews claim that *reason and intellect causes them to reject or deny God:*
    some call themselves "atheists"—*denying the existence of God.*
    some are scientists who claim that there is *no existential or empirical proof for the existence of God.*
    some call themselves "agnostics"—*waiting for personal proof of the existence of God.*
    some claim that *God is dead,* made irrelevant by His silence to the horrors of human suffering.
    some are best described as "humanists," who claim that the *concept of God is merely a characterization of the highest human values,* who view Judaism as a peoplehood, with its rituals and celebrations as but natural expressions of collective history and contemporary unity.
- Some Jews *attempt to balance faith and reason* in finding God. **Harold Kushner** (1932–; New York and Natick, Massachusetts), author of the best-seller *When Bad Things Happen to Good People,* affirms God through faith, but uses rational argument to explain the existence of evil in the world by contending that God is all good but not all powerful. Like a loving parent, God cannot keep people from experiencing pain, but can bring comfort and love.
- Some Jews *turn back to the spiritual, mystical tradition to find God through contemplative meditation and joyous prayer.* Led by, among others, **Zalman Schachter-Shalomi** (1924–; Poland, Vienna, Brooklyn, Boston, Manitoba, Philadelphia), these modern-day seekers work—through personal and communal Jewish renewal—to recapture the intimate, spiritual relationship with God that they lost in the rationalist age.
- Some Jews, like generations of Jews before them, *struggle daily to meet and to know God,* and to carve out or deepen a meaningful, personal relationship with God.

This, then, has been the Jewish journey, from the time of Abraham until today: to define God and explain God's attributes—sometimes with faith, sometimes with reason, sometimes with an attempt to synthesize the two.

Each of these theories is the product of the thought processes of the mind, yet the individual, personal quest to find and experience God—the real way to touch and be touched by God—best comes from fullness of the human heart and depths of the human soul.

For each and every Jew—for each and every human being—the journey to God ever continues.

While belief in God is central to the Jewish religious quest—and, is for most, an uplifting, enriching, highly satisfying, integral part of being a Jew—there are no doctrines, dogma, or creeds of Judaism to which a Jew must adhere.

While it is very possible that Jews can set themselves outside the mainstream of Jewish thought, the spectrum of Jewish belief throughout the centuries has been very wide and very tolerant.

There are a few basic Jewish concepts about God on which most Jewish thinkers throughout history agree (although there is significant disagreement over even some of these tenets): that God exists; that God is One; that God created and, to a greater or lesser extent, supervises the events of the universe; that God gave humankind free will; that while God is the God of all humanity, God and the Jewish People have a special covenantal relationship; and that each human being can approach God in an individual, personal way and create an intimate relationship with God.

Still, Judaism requires no profession of faith (other than the personal choice to recite the prayer and the declaration: "Hear, O Israel, the Lord is our God, the Lord is One"); no examination of faith; no demand for any certain level or demonstration of faith; and exacts no penalty nor imposes any consequence for lack of faith. Rather, each Jew is free to believe in God and to form a personal relationship with God as he or she chooses.

The contemporary Jewish thinker Elie Wiesel has taught that Jews can argue with God, fight with God, or be angry with God, but cannot ignore God. Since the Jewish concept of God and the relationship with God has changed, developed, and grown throughout Jewish history, the task of contemporary Jews now is to take their place in the ongoing process of the Jewish quest to find and know God.

Like the Jews of old who "wrestled with God" in order to create a relationship with God, contemporary Jews—who are called by the name "Israel"—are to strive, to wrestle with God, to seek and find God in this time and this place.

2.   ברית   BRIT

is the covenant between God and the Jewish People.

When Abraham declared his belief in the one Lord God, God promised Abraham that he and his descendants would become a great nation, as numerous as "the stars of the heavens and the grains of sand on the seashore." God further promised Abraham that He would bring him and his descendants to dwell in a special land, the Land of Israel. God promised to make Abraham's name great and to bless him and his descendants (Genesis 12:2, 17, 22). This spiritual covenant forms the basis of the relationship between God and the Jewish People.

The spiritual covenant was sealed with a physical covenant—the covenant of circumcision מילה ברית *brit milah.* Abraham circumcised himself and his sons, Ishmael and Isaac, and this physical covenantal sign has been renewed with every male Jew in every succeeding generation.

When the Children of Israel, freed from Egyptian slavery, came to Mt. Sinai (in approximately 1250 B.C.E., some 550 years after the time of Abraham), the everlasting covenant between God and the Jewish People was legislated through the giving of God's law, the Torah. This covenant was conditional: "*If* you hearken to My voice and keep My covenant (commandments) *then* you will be My own treasure from among all people; for the earth is Mine. And you shall be to Me a kingdom of priests and a holy nation" (Exodus 19:5–6).

The covenant requires Jews to affirm faith in God, and to follow His commandments. In turn, Jews expect that God will fulfill His promise to make the Jewish People a great and holy nation, dwelling in the Promised Land, the Land of Israel.

God made the covenant with "those who stand here with us on this day and with those who are not here with us today" (Deuteronomy 29:14). Thus the covenant is made not just with those who were present at Sinai, but it is renewed with every Jew in every generation. According to one Jewish legend, the souls of all Jews who would ever live were present at Sinai.

For some, the if-then nature of the *brit* is disturbing, for it seems that the personal relationship between God and His people should be unconditional, not dependent on behavior. If God's love is conditional, what happens if a person fails to meet the conditions? Is that person, then, unworthy of God's acceptance and love? While understanding the requirement of observing God's commandments and fulfilling God's will, people still want a relationship with God that is based in faith and love.

This idea of an unconditional covenantal relationship is found in the Bible, more subtle but just as powerful and profound as the concept of *brit*. The late scholar-archaeologist-rabbi Dr. Nelson Glueck explained in his book *Hesed in the Bible* that the concept of חסד *chesed,* which is most often translated as "lovingkindness," really means "covenantal love."

Going beyond the conditional nature of *brit*—which is a contract based on the notion that each side agrees to a certain level of performance, with reward or consequence for meeting or failing to meet the commitment—*chesed* is the unconditional love, the providential care, the ultimate forgiveness, the grace, that each person wants, needs, and expects from God. *Chesed* is God saying, "It does not matter what you do, how you behave, how many mistakes you make, I am your God, and you are My child. I love you always and forever, with a deep, abiding, unqualified, absolute love."

These two concepts—*brit* as the if-then contract and *chesed* as the unequivocal promise—together create the unique covenantal distinction of the Jewish People as God's selected nation.

3. THE CHOSEN PEOPLE

Throughout the centuries, detractors of Jews and Judaism have pointed to the concept of chosenness as an attempt by Jews to flaunt supposed superiority and greatness. In reality, just the opposite is true.

The concept of chosen people means *not* that Jews were chosen for special privilege, but for sacred responsibility: to be אור לגוים *or la'goyim,* a "light unto the nations" (after Isaiah 42:6, 49:6), a faith community reflecting God's light of love and law.

The sacred Jewish responsibility is to receive, learn, live, and teach God's word and will.

Receiving and transmitting the "yoke of the Kingdom of God" is no easy task; it is a heavy burden, but one that is willingly and even joyously, but always humbly, accepted.

AN ESSAY ON GOOD AND EVIL

For many—throughout the centuries and today—the greatest impediment to belief in God is the existence of evil and suffering.

How can a loving God permit little children to be born deformed and disabled? How can I believe in a God who permits young fathers to die of cancer; young women to be mugged, raped, and murdered? How can a just God exist if thousands are swept away to their deaths by earthquake and flood? How could God sit idly by while 6 million innocent Jews, and millions of others, were slaughtered in the Holocaust?

There are two kinds of evil: evil caused by human beings, and evil that occurs by random chance.

HUMAN EVIL

The evil that is caused by human beings occurs because God gives each human being *free will*. We are not puppets on a string, controlled by a God who determines our every move. We can use the free will that God gave us to do anything we choose.

So much of the evil in our world comes from people choosing—often purposely or unwittingly—to use their free will to do devastating evil instead of great good.

God doesn't cause a car to go out of control or an airplane to crash, killing innocent people. A driver, a pilot, a mechanic, or an air traffic controller—a human being—creates that evil through careless or poor performance.

But what if the evil is not caused by "human error," but by mechanical failure—a brake that fails, a steel bolt that breaks?

Here, too, the responsibility belongs to human beings, not to God. Brakes and bolts are made by people who may not do a good job.

But even if the mechanical part were manufactured and maintained without a flaw, no product lasts forever; eventually, everything wears out. Tragically, sometimes a brake or a bolt wears out in the middle of a drive or a flight. There are no God-given guarantees to parts made of rubber or steel.

THE EVIL OF "NATURAL DISASTER"

Earthquakes, floods, hurricanes, and other natural disasters—and the suffering they cause—are more difficult to understand, since they seem to come directly from

God's governance of the universe. They are even called (especially by insurance companies) "acts of God."

Our biblical ancestors believed that human conduct had a direct causal relationship to God's use of the elements of nature. "If you hearken diligently to My commandments . . . I will give you the rain of your land in its season. . . . Take heed lest you worship other gods; the displeasure of the Lord will be aroused against you and He will shut up the heavens so that there will be no rain . . ." (Deuteronomy 11:13–17). They believed that natural upheavals such as earthquakes and floods were God's severe punishment for serious transgression of His commandments.

Few people today believe in this direct correlation between human conduct and Divine regulation of the elements of nature. Our conduct has little, if any, effect on whether or not the rains fall; our transgression of God's commandments has little, if any, consequence on whether the crops grow, or if there is bread on the supermarket shelves.

Once God created the universe, He set its functions in motion and permits it to take its own "natural" course. Earthquakes, floods, and hurricanes are simply part of the natural order, part of the original plan for the unfolding of the universe. The earth continues to move on its plates; the waters and the winds continue their natural ebb and flow.

Yet many are still bothered by the nagging feeling that God, who created all nature, must have *something* to do with how the elements of nature behave, with how those elements unleashed can bring about great suffering and evil.

Some contend that while God still controls the acts of nature, we human beings, using our own free will, upset the natural order. When we strip the land of its precious minerals, pollute the waters with waste, choke the sky with smog, bombard the ozone layer with spray cans, and cause acid rain to fall, we topple the delicate balance of God's carefully constructed environment and threaten our place and our planet with ecological ruin.

Others contend that a natural disaster is not inherently evil, but morally neutral. When no one lives in the path of the hurricane, when the earthquake heaves up totally uninhabited land, there is no sense of evil. What makes a natural disaster is how human beings are touched and affected.

Over the centuries, we have become wise enough to learn the natural order—that, at certain seasons, rains cause rivers to overflow their banks and flood surrounding land; that faults in the earth, which will shift and cause earthquakes, are located at certain specific places.

Once God has clearly shown us where the natural order will be played out, it would be sensible not to go back to the places where disaster is likely to occur again. But after the flood, we use our free will to choose to replant our crops on the river bank. After the earthquake, we choose to rebuild our homes right on the fault line. It may be convenient to live on the Mississippi, and it may be beautiful to live in San Francisco, but it may not be smart.

The alternative, of course, is to use our free will to choose to tame the unleashed elements of nature. Instead of fleeing in resignation or fear, we can learn to build the dams and the dikes that will contain the onslaught of the rushing waters, the kinds of houses, skyscrapers, and bridges that have a chance of withstanding the brutal forces of suddenly shifting landscapes.

Either way—by ignoring the signs and warnings of impending disaster, or by creatively struggling against them—we are exercising our free will. God is not responsible; we are.

When we think we see the hand of God at work in what we call natural disaster, it is often the work of our own hands that determines not the event, but the outcome.

THE ULTIMATE HUMAN EVIL

One instance of evil and suffering is so horrific that it has come to personify for the world the most unspeakable evil ever imagined.

The memories of the Holocaust—the systematic attempt to wipe the entire Jewish People off the face of the earth, resulting in the deaths of 6 million Jews and more than 10 million others—still pain our days and haunt our sleep. The ache of loss is still not healed; the empty void is still not filled; the anger and sadness is still not lifted. And the questions, born of anguish and bewilderment, give us no peace.

How could this happen? How could God let it happen? Where was God? Why didn't He intervene? How could a caring, loving God permit millions of good, righteous, innocent people to suffer and die? These questions, surely, challenge belief and faith.

To some, after Auschwitz, God is dead. In His silence, He became insignificant and irrelevant.

To others, as distasteful as this may seem to most, God is seen as punishing the Jewish People for its transgressions. According to this theory, so much of European Jewry had forsaken Jewish belief and practice and had assimilated into the secular culture that God was, in this generation, fulfilling the promise He had made in biblical times: "And this people will rise up and go astray after the foreign gods of the land where they go to live, and they will forsake Me and break My covenant which I have made with them. Then, My anger will be kindled against them on that day, and I will forsake them and hide My face from them, and they shall be devoured, and many evils and troubles will come upon them . . ." (Deuteronomy 31:16–17).

Not only does this argument ignore the millions of pious people and innocent children who died, but it makes God uncaring, vengeful, and brutal. Except to a few holier-than-thou, self-righteous proponents, this idea is absurd and obscene.

For others, even through the agony and the horror, the explanation is plausible if not comforting: God gave each human being free will to do good or evil. Here, that free will was used to do the ultimate evil. But even if He wanted to, God would not change His own rules for the universe by intervening to take away free will. So people of ill will perpetrated their evil on others, and millions suffered tremendously. Eventually, however, men and women of peace and good will used their free will to do good, to overcome the evildoers; and though 6 million died, many millions more were saved from destruction and death.

But where was God all this time? Why didn't He do something?

When the President of the United States, John F. Kennedy, was assassinated on November 22, 1963, Bill Mauldin, the political cartoonist of the *Chicago Sun Times*, drew a deeply moving portrait that appeared in his newspaper the next day. It was a drawing of the Lincoln Memorial in Washington, D.C., with Abraham Lincoln slumped over, head in his hands, weeping. This is the image that many have of God during the Holocaust—sitting on His heavenly throne, head in His hands, weeping at the folly His children wrought. He gave us free will, but He grieves when we use it so foolishly.

There is one more way to view God's role in the Holocaust. For, if we wish, we can see Him "dipping His finger into history," intervening to save His people as the heroic Redeemer.

When we read in the Bible of the exodus from Egypt, we do not learn how many of the Hebrew children were drowned in the Nile. We do not know how many tens of thousands, hundreds of thousands, suffered and died at forced labor and under the whip of the taskmasters. We do not ask why God sat idly by in silence while His people were enslaved and tortured. Instead we see God, the Hero, listening to His people's cries, saving them from destruction by redeeming them from their captivity, delivering them from the hand of the despot, and bringing them to freedom.

If we wish to see the God of the Holocaust in heroic biblical terms, then we can sing praises unto the Lord who redeemed His people from the slavery of the tyrant and executed judgment upon their oppressors. The story—a modern-day version of the biblical account—goes like this:

There arose a new Chancellor over Germany who remembered not the great contributions to the political, economic, and cultural life of his country that the Jews had made. He said, "The Jews are becoming strong and mighty in our midst. They have become haughty and arrogant, thinking that they are just like us. We must rid ourselves of these Jews amongst us, lest they ally themselves with our enemies and weaken our country from within."

And so the Chancellor decreed that all little Jewish children be put to death in the Nile, which he called crematoria. And he ordered that all the people be put to work at forced labor, giving up their possessions, toiling for the state, herded together in concentrated areas, which he called ghettos or camps; that husbands and wives be separated from each other, that children be taken from the arms of their parents, that they all be given but the most meager of food to eat. And he ordered that the weak, the infirm, the elderly, be put to death immediately, and that all the others work or starve to death slowly and painfully, until, finally, he decreed that all the Jews be killed, either shot with bullets or suffocated by poison gas in rooms he called gas chambers. And he ordered their remains to be burned in ovens.

And the pain and the suffering of the Children of Israel was great, and they called out to the Lord God. And God heard their cries, and He spoke unto Stalin, Churchill, and Roosevelt, and He said, "Go to Germany and tell the Chancellor, 'Let My People Go!'"

And Stalin, Churchill, and Roosevelt—flawed and reluctant though they were—went unto the Chancellor and they said, "We come to speak in the name of the Lord, the God of Israel, the God of these people you have enslaved, saying, 'Let My People Go!'"

But the Chancellor hearkened not unto the voice of Stalin, Churchill, and Roosevelt, and he increased the work of the Hebrew slaves, and their lives became even more bitter and their suffering became greater, and many, many more died at the hand of the despot.

And so the Lord God brought plagues upon the Chancellor and upon his land. The first plague was called a naval blockade; the second plague was called battleships; and the third plague was called carrier-borne aircraft equipped with radar. The fourth plague was called infantry troops, and the fifth plague was called tanks and armored vehicles. The sixth plague was called fighter planes, and the seventh plague was called bombers. The eighth plague was called paratroopers, and the ninth plague was called commando troops.

But after each plague, the heart of the Chancellor was hardened and he hearkened not unto the word of the Lord, and he refused to permit the Children of Israel to go out from their slavery.

And so the Lord God brought the tenth plague, which was called the D-Day invasion, and from the D-Day invasion came V-E Day, the day on which the power of the Lord was felt throughout the land. For, on that day, there was not a house in all of Germany that was not touched by destruction and death. The most humble in the countryside, the rich and mighty in the cities, the troops of the Chancellor's armies, the leaders of government and the ruling party, and even the once-powerful Chancellor, who lay dead in his bunker, all saw the greatness and the might of the Lord, who had come to redeem and deliver His people.

And so God opened the gates of the concentration camps. And with a mighty hand and an outstretched arm, He brought forth the Children of Israel from their bondage.

And the Children of Israel wandered in the desert of Europe for four years, until the Lord brought them into the land that He had promised to their ancestors, Abraham, Isaac, and Jacob—the Land of Israel.

And you shall gather every year, in remembrance of the Exodus from Germany, and you shall taste of the bitterness of oppression and you shall rejoice in your liberation. For you shall tell your children on that day, saying, "This is what the Lord God did for our ancestors and for us when He brought us forth out of the land of Germany, from the house of bondage, and delivered us from slavery unto freedom. Hallelujah. Praise the Lord."

RANDOM-CHANCE EVIL

Because there is evil caused by human beings, it is far easier to explain the death of six in a car accident, or of 600 in an earthquake, or even of 6 million in the Holocaust, than it is to explain the death of one innocent child from a debilitating disease.

For there is a second kind of evil, an evil that seems to defy any rational explanation. This evil seems to have its source not in any act or omission of any human being, not in the free will choice to do good or evil, but in random, capricious happenstance.

This is the suffering and evil of children born damaged and defective, of debilitating, pain-wracked illness, of sudden, inexplicable death.

What role does God have in these tragedies? Is He involved or dispassionate, responsible or blameless? Where is God's fairness, His compassion, His love, when, in the words of Rabbi Harold Kushner's book title, "bad things happen to good people"? And many may ask conversely (without the same sense of urgency but with more than mild curiosity), where is God when good things continue to happen to bad people?

Throughout human history, different cultures, traditions, and faith communities have attempted to respond to questioning, uncertain, and troubled hearts and minds:

Science says that the universe is neutral; it is neither good nor evil. It just *is*. Therefore no moral judgment of good or evil can be made. And thus God surely has no involvement in the disinterested, impartial works of the natural universe.

The ancient Greeks saw a stark dichotomy between God, whom they viewed as perfect, and the finite world, which they viewed as imperfect and flawed. Since the imperfect, finite world could not possibly achieve the perfection of the infinite God, the evils of this world have nothing to do with God

Hinduism teaches that confronting evil during this lifetime is part of the soul's evolution toward ultimate perfection. In order to achieve eternity in the presence of God, the soul strives to become more and more perfect during each lifetime, by meeting and overcoming the challenges of evil and suffering.

Buddhism says that we experience evil and suffering because of unrealistic expectations. If, for example, you expect that your child will live, but he does not, you experience pain and suffering. But if you held no expectation that your child would be healthy and well, then when he gets sick, your expectation is not disappointed and you do not feel pain.

Christianity teaches that there is a reward in the world to come, in heaven, for all who profess belief in Jesus Christ. Therefore sixty or eighty years of pain and suffering on this earth is of little consequence in anticipation of eternity with God. No matter how great the evil and suffering in this lifetime, eternal reward awaits the true believer.

Islam contends that any evil and suffering is the "will of God." Those who endure pain are doing so for the greater glory of Allah, who will provide reward in the life to come.

Secular humanism says simply that the existence of evil in the world comes through the acts of people, and through random happenstance.

So what does **Judaism** say about the existence of random suffering and evil?

There is no single response, no one Jewish answer. Some Jewish responses are variations of the positions offered by other religions: Some would say that "It is God's will"; some would say that it is a prelude to Heavenly reward; some would say that it is *bashert*, preordained. But the bottom-line Jewish response is that *we just do not know.*

This is not a very comforting answer, but it is intellectually honest. For in the end, all other responses are mere speculation. No one knows for sure; no one has a definitive, irrefutable answer.

Rather than adding to the speculation, Judaism says simply and plainly: We do not know, because we are not God. We do not know God's ways, for they are beyond our understanding. We do not know God's plan for the universe or how the universe is to unfold.

GOD'S ROLE

Yet, after all this, we are left with the same old question: Where is God when His children suffer? How can a just God permit such devastating, hurtful evil?

A story called "Footprints," by Margaret Fishback Powers, has been circulating for many years. It has become so popular that it has been printed on cards, laminated plates, and refrigerator magnets. Despite the commercialism that surrounds it, its message is both profound and moving. It helps answer our question.

One night, I dreamed a dream. I was walking along the beach with my God. Across the sky flashed scenes from my life. For each scene, I noticed two sets of footprints in the sand, one belonging to me and the other belonging to God.

When the last scene of my life flashed before me, I looked back at the footprints in the sand. There was only one set of footprints. I realized that this was at the very lowest and saddest times of my life.

This really bothered me, so I questioned God.

"God, You told me when I decided to follow You that You would walk and be with me all the way. But I have noticed that during the most troublesome times of my life, there is only one set of footprints in the sand. I don't understand why, when I needed You the most, You would leave me."

And God said, "My precious child, I love you and will never leave you. During your times of trial and suffering, when you see only one set of footprints, *it was then that I carried you.*"

When evil and suffering engulf you, when pain and anguish threaten to destroy you, do not blame God or think that He has abandoned you.

God is not in the problem. He is in the solution. God is not in the challenge. He is in how we respond to the challenge.

When you are in deepest need, when all seems lost, when the pain is overwhelming and you cannot bear it any longer, when all your resources are gone and you cannot make it alone, it is then that you come to God for consolation, for comfort, and for strength.

The biblical psalmist put it this way:

When evil men try to destroy me,
it is they, my enemies and my foes,
who stumble and fall.

If an army would besiege me,
my heart would not fear.

If war were waged against me,
I would still be confident. . . .
Even if my father and mother forsook me,
the Lord would take me under His care. . . .

[For] the Lord is my light and my help;
whom shall I fear?
The Lord is the stronghold of my life;
of whom shall I be afraid?

(PSALMS 27:2–3; 10; 1)

An army besiege you? War waged against you? Who can think of anything more frightening? Your father and mother forsake you? Who can imagine anything worse?

Yet even at these most unthinkable moments, when everything seems gone, God is still there for you, offering help and hope.

God is not in the desolation; He is in the consolation. God is not in the destruction; He is in the rebirth.

God is not in the accident, the plane crash, the earthquake; He is in the heroic acts and courageous deeds of those who rescue and rebuild. God is not in the torture and the genocide; He is in the commitment and the determination of those who rise up to conquer the despot. God is not in the sickness and disease; He is in the hearts and minds of those who seek out cures and find healings.

God imbues a community of friends with helping hands and sharing hearts, to embrace you in concern and surround you with love. He gives you the power, the wisdom, the strength, the fortitude, and the courage to face the worst and not merely to endure, but to be transformed.

The human heart and soul—though scarred and saddened and sorely tested—will ultimately prevail, for we are all empowered by Godly sparks of goodness, compassion, and love.

Where is God when you need Him most? Where is God when "bad things happen to good people"—to you?

God is not the source of evil. God is not the cause.

God is the response and the solution, the restoration and the growth.

When you need God most, confront Him with your bewilderment and your anger; cry to Him in your anguish and in your pain.

When you need God most, call to Him and He *will* answer you.

God is right beside you, right with you, right within you, giving you a full measure of Divine care and comfort, support and sustenance, grace and blessing.

He will envelop you in His compassionate concern; He will wrap you in His protecting love; He will give you from His strength; He will lift you up from out of the depths of despair.

When you need God most, you will feel His nearness, holding you tight and catching your tears. You will be touched by His goodness, whispering to you gentle words of comfort and solace. And you will hear His voice singing to you, sweet songs of healing and tender love.

4. קדושה KEDUSHAH

is holiness.

To be a Jew is to strive to be holy.

The word *holy* means "separate" and "unique"—chosen and designated from among all other similar things for special purpose or use.

For example, the Hebrew word *holy* (in its many grammatical formulations) describes Shabbat, the Sabbath. It is called "the holy Sabbath." There are six other days of the week, but *this* one day is like no other. It is separate, unique: dedicated to physical rest and spiritual rejuvenation.

Another example: The cabinet that holds the Torah Scroll in the synagogue is called "the Holy Ark." There are many other cabinets that hold clothes or books or food or medicine or paper. But *this* one cabinet is like no other. It is separate, unique: dedicated to holding the precious Torah Scroll with the word of God.

Another example: The blessing recited over wine on the Sabbath and festivals is called "holy." There are many other glasses of wine, many other times that wine is consumed. But *this* wine is like no other. It is separate, unique: dedicated to heralding and celebrating the special Sabbath or festival day.

A final example: the marriage declaration, which is traditionally recited from man to woman (and in modern liberal Judaism, from woman to man) at the moment of commitment in the wedding ceremony, says, "Behold, with this ring you are made holy unto me . . ." There are many other women in the world, but *this* one is like no other. She is separate, unique: dedicated to this man, to this relationship. She is permitted to no other man; he is permitted no other woman.

What could be more holy than God? God is unique in all the world—separate and distinct from every other entity. And this supremely holy God has commanded, "*You* shall be holy, for I, the Lord your God, am holy" (Exodus 19:2).

How is humankind to be holy—to be separate and unique in being and behavior? Certainly, as human beings, we are distinct from the animals, for, like God, we have the power to know, to reason, and to remember. But that is not enough.

To imitate God, to reflect God's holiness, to be holy like God, we need to develop God's ability to form relationships of unconditional, covenantal love—to make the life of another as precious as our own.

We need to exhibit God's capacity for demanding justice and righteousness, for feeling compassion, for acting with grace and mercy, for pursuing peace.

We need to have a unique role and a special mission. We need to share with God in the task of transforming and perfecting our world.

To be a Jew means to act—each and every day, each and every moment—to achieve *kedushah,* holiness: to make God-like our every thought, our every word, our every deed; to become, in the words of the Bible, "just a little lower than the Divine" (Psalms 8:6).

5. מצוה MITZVAH

(plural, *mitzvot*) is a commandment (of God).

The Torah contains 613 *mitzvot,* commandments. The most famous of the commandments are the עשרת הדברות *Aseret HaDebrot,* the Ten Commandments (sometimes known as the Decalogue; literally, "the ten Divine utterances/sayings"). These are the commands given by God to Moses at Mt. Sinai, which Moses brought down the mountain engraved on two stone tablets (Exodus 20:1–14; 32:1–19; 34:27–35; and Deuteronomy 4:13 and 5:1–30). These ten are the best known of all the commandments because they were the first commandments given during the theophany at Sinai, and because in a brief, pithy way, they address the central issues of human behavior toward God and with fellow human beings.

Just as they appear on the tablets—with five commandments on each of the two tablets—the Ten Commandments are designed in two equal parts. The first five commandments regulate conduct between humankind and God—how human beings are to relate to God. The second five commandments regulate conduct between people—how human beings are to relate to each other.

1. *"I am the Lord your God, who brought you out of the land of Egypt . . ."* This commandment establishes God's authority as Law-Giver. The people had just witnessed and experienced God's power in bringing them out of Egyptian slavery. Now they are told to accept God's power and authority in giving them His law.

2. *"You shall have no other gods before Me. You shall not make a graven image . . ."* The ancient world was filled with a multitude of gods, all claiming Divine authority. This commandment instructs the people to ignore the claims of all the other gods and to know that the Lord God is One—singular, unique, alone. And unlike the other nations that make symbols or idols of their gods, the people are instructed not to make any image, picture, or physical representation of the (physically invisible) Lord God.

3. *"You shall not take the name of the Lord in vain . . ."* The people are told: If you are called upon to give testimony in a legal proceeding, and if you swear—in the name of God—to tell the truth, then, tell the truth. Do not invoke God's name, through which people will believe you are telling the truth, and then lie.

4. *"Remember the Sabbath day to keep it holy . . ."* The rag-tag band of recently freed slaves—who had labored day after day, year after year, without rest—are told to set aside one day a week for physical and spiritual rest and rejuvenation.

5. *"Honor your father and your mother . . . "* The people are told: Honor and respect those who gave you life and give you love. Always remember from where you have come.

This commandment seems out of place in a series of laws that are between humankind and God, for the relationship between children and parents is a relationship between human beings. However, this commandment is considered the "bridge" commandment between the laws on the first tablet (the laws between God and humankind) and the laws on the second tablet (the laws between people) for honoring parents is like honoring God. The Talmud (BT Kid. 30b) teaches that at the moment of conception, *three* are present—the mother, the father, and *God*. So the commandment insists, remember and honor your origins, the equal partnership of three: your father, your mother, and God.

6. *"You shall not murder."*
7. *"You shall not commit adultery."*
8. *"You shall not steal."*
9. *"You shall not bear false witness . . ."*
10. *"You shall not covet . . ."*

In a few simple yet profound words, these second five commandments regulate relationships between human beings, by insisting on the highest level of holiness— that people recognize and value the sanctity of human life in themselves and in each other; that they treat each with honor and respect, integrity and faithfulness, decency and dignity.

These five commandments are listed in descending order of the importance of what one person can take away from another.

"Do not take away another person's life."

"Do not take away the extension of another person's life—his or her spouse."

"Do not take away another person's material possessions."

"Do not take away another person's honor, reputation, or good name."

"Do not even *think* about taking away anything that belongs to another person."

The commandments were given directly to the people who stood at Mt. Sinai with Moses, and also "to those who are not standing with us here today" (Deuteronomy 29:14)—every Jew, every human being, in every future generation. They belong to—and are to be followed by—every one of God's children throughout the generations as the sign and the seal of the covenant of faith, law, and love between God and humankind.

There are 603 more Torah commandments. But in giving these ten—with their wise insight into the human condition—God established a standard of right and wrong, a powerful code of behavior, that is universal and timeless. Enduring throughout the millennia, these injunctions are as relevant today as they were more than 3,200 years ago when they were first articulated.

Because they contain universal precepts and enduring truth, these Ten Commandments have been adopted by most of the Western world as basic religious and moral law.

Of the 613 commandments, 248 are positive commands ("You shall . . .") and the remaining 365 are negative commands ("You shall not . . ."). (The best way to remember the number of negative commandments is by remembering the number of days in the secular calendar year: 365.)

There are two main categories of *mitzvot* in the Torah: ritual and ethical. Ritual *mitzvot* revolve around ceremonies and rites of Jewish life, such as observing the Sabbath and festivals, eating kosher food, and participating in public worship. Ethical *mitzvot* demand a certain standard of behavior; that life be conducted in a moral manner. Examples of ethical *mitzvot* include honoring parents, not stealing, not exploiting others, feeding the hungry, and dealing fairly and honestly in business.

During the Rabbinic Period (200 B.C.E.–600 C.E.), when the Oral Law (the post-biblical law expounded by the rabbinic sages) was articulated, hundreds more *mitzvot* were inferred from the Torah. These *mitzvot* דרבנן *d'rabbanan,* "of the rabbis," had the same import as the *mitzvot* דאוריתא *d'orita,* "of the Torah," and were to be followed and obeyed with the same precision and sincerity—except in the case of a possible conflict between the two, when the Torah law always supersedes the rabbinic law.

In modern times, at least 200 of the 613 Torah *mitzvot* cannot be observed, for they are concerned with the duties of the priests (who no longer function), the Holy Temple (which no longer exists), animal sacrifice (which is no longer offered), and living in the Land of Israel (which many Jews do not). However, the *mitzvot*—both those of the Torah and of the rabbis, form the basis for Jewish ethical and ritual conduct and behavior. They are the laws by which Jews are to live.

Because *mitzvot* require a high level of ethical behavior, a *mitzvah* is popularly defined as a "good deed." This definition captures the spirit, but not the intent, of the concept of *mitzvah.* A "good deed" implies the free choice of the doer to perform a meritorious act. A *mitzvah,* however, is a requirement, an obligation, a commandment, a law. Doing a *mitzvah* is not left to whim or chance, but is the sacred responsibility of every Jew.

Nevertheless, the sense of "doing a good deed" conveys the ultimate goal of "doing a *mitzvah*"—to make the world a better, more holy place, through word and through deed.

For a Jew who has been immersed in Jewish life since infancy, following the law, observing the *mitzvot,* is as normal as breathing. For a Jew to whom Jewish law is not the norm, the sheer number and scope of the *mitzvot* can seem overwhelming. Yet, since the performance of *mitzvot*—following the law—is central to leading a Jewish life, the contemporary Jewish thinker Rabbi Arnold Jacob Wolf has offered this suggestion to those who would like to explore and try *mitzvah* observance:

> Think of each *mitzvah* as a beautiful, precious jewel. All of the jewels—all of the *mitzvot*—are on a path on which you are walking.
>
> Some of the jewels are so deeply embedded in the ground that you will not be able to dig them up, no matter how hard you try. These are the Torah *mitzvot,* which can no longer be observed because of time, place, or circumstance.
>
> Some of the jewels are just lying on top of the ground, waiting for you to pick them up and put them in your pocket. Almost every Jew who walks on the path picks up these jewels and carries them. These are the *mitzvot* that are easy to observe, like lighting Chanukah candles, attending a Passover *seder,* and reciting *kaddish* for a deceased parent.
>
> The most challenging of the jewels are the ones that are partially embedded in the ground. They are partially visible to you, with their shiny facets poking up through the earth. These are the *mitzvot* that are central to Jewish life—observance of Shabbat and the festivals, *kashrut* (the dietary laws), prayer, and ethical behavior according to Torah law— the *mitzvot* that define and shape Jewish life, but which require commitment and persistence.
>
> To pick up these jewels requires some work, some digging. It is the job of each Jew walking on the path to try to dig up some of these partially embedded jewels one at a time.
>
> Try one. You may dig and dig to no avail. This jewel may not be for you.
>
> Try another. Dig it up and walk with it along the path (observe it) for a while. This jewel may appeal to you, and you will put it in your pocket (of observance), and then start to dig up another. Or you may carry it with you for a while, decide that it is not for you, and put it back down on the path for someone else (perhaps even your own child) to pick up.
>
> Then start digging another.

The late nineteenth- to early twentieth-century Jewish thinker Franz Rosenzweig taught that there are only two answers to the question, "Do you observe the *mitzvot?*" The first answer is, "Yes." The only other answer is, "Not yet."

By walking along the path—by digging up, by trying, one *mitzvah* at a time, adding it to your life, and then trying, digging up, another, your answer to the question, "Do you observe the *mitzvot*?" moves slowly but assuredly from "Not yet" to "Yes."

Observing the *mitzvot*—following God's law—is a lifetime commitment. Those who were shown and taught *mitzvah* observance from infancy were given a great birth-gift. Those who come to *mitzvah* observance on their own, later in life, discover that observing the *mitzvot* is hearing God's word, doing God's will, and working with God to enrich and ennoble existence.

When the Children of Israel received the *mitzvot* at Sinai, they responded by saying, נעשה ונשמע *"Na'aseh v'nishma,"* "We will *do them*, and *then* we will come to *understand them*" (Exodus 24:7). You need not know the reason or the rationale—or even the benefits—of each *mitzvah* before you begin doing it. You just need to do it. For out of doing comes understanding.

When you were two or three years old, and first learned to brush your teeth, your parents did not first explain to you the philosophical reasons and practical benefits of dental hygiene. They put a toothbrush in your hand and taught you how to brush. Only later, when you were older and able to comprehend—when tooth brushing was already an ingrained habit—did you come to understand *why* brushing your teeth is so important.

So it is with *mitzvot.* You do them; and when you are able to comprehend, you come to understand and reap their great benefits.

Even after God's awe-inspiring revelation at Sinai, no one asked Moses what his people believed, only what *mitzvot* they performed.

For while it is rooted in faith, in *creed,* Judaism is not a religion dependent on profession of belief. It is, far more, a religion of action, of *deed,* of *mitzvot*—at each and every moment, at each and every opportunity—waiting to be done.

6.   ETHICAL MONOTHEISM

Judaism's ethical *mitzvot* are standards of human behavior that lead people to lives of decency, kindness, righteousness, justice, goodness, and compassion. They serve to elevate and ennoble human relationships and inspire people to strive for the highest good.

Many ethical codes have similar goals. These codes derive their standards of authority from a variety of sources: from human reason (this kind of behavior makes rational sense); from human emotion (this kind of behavior makes me feel good);

from societal norms (the consensus of our society agrees on this kind of behavior); and from intuition (this kind of behavior seems right in my "gut," at the deepest core of my being).

All of these codes have many positive aspects as determiners of human behavior, but each is equally flawed. Human reason, human emotion, and human intuition can fail to think, feel, or sense the ultimate good; we can be swayed to, convinced of, or rationalize away the darkest evil. Societal norms can be distorted by evil people with evil purpose (Nazi Germany being the prime example). All of these ethical codes are subject to situation, circumstance, whim, or caprice.

The Jewish ethical code is based on the *authority of the Author.*

This code is called ethical monotheism—for the ethic, the standard of behavior, comes from the One Lord God. God, who created humankind, has declared how His children are to behave. God's ethical commandments are not affected by time or place. They are eternal and universal—for all time, for all people, for everywhere.

Right is right; wrong is wrong—*because God said so.*

While other ethical codes have come and gone, while other ethical codes have given way to the fad of the moment, Judaism's ethical code—ethical monotheism—has endured because it comes from God, the Creator and the Commander.

By following Judaism's ethical code, and by continually striving to ingrain and observe its principles and moral mandate in our lives, we come to understand and act on what God expects from us—to be truly human and humane.

7. ETHICAL RITUALISM

Just having God's ethical mandate is not enough. For, even with all their flaws, other ethical codes (and, certainly, ethical codes that have been developed by other religions and faith communities, based on Divine authorship) are valid and worthy.

But Judaism has not only the ethics by which to live, but also the *system*—called ethical ritualism—by which to pass on and perpetuate those ethical values from generation to generation.

Since it is Judaism's goal to lead people to lives of holiness through ethical behavior, it might be assumed that the ethical *mitzvot* of Torah are more important than the ritual *mitzvot.*

But rituals are performed to bring people to a deeper place in the human psyche than words can touch. Rituals are without words, before words. They provide a physical experience—a "felt-sense"—that goes beyond intellectual "knowledge" to metaphysical intrinsic "knowing."

So the Torah gives no indication that one kind of *mitzvah* is more important than the other. Ethical and ritual *mitzvot* stand side by side and Torah commands to "remember and do *all* the *mitzvot* of God" (after Numbers 15:40). Thus the Torah not only teaches the ethical and ritual *mitzvot,* but implies the system by which the *mitzvot* are to be observed and perpetuated.

From the earliest age, for example, a child watches parents light Shabbat candles (a ritual) *and* deal fairly in business (an ethic); participate in synagogue worship (a ritual) *and* treat a stranger with kindness (an ethic); conduct a Passover *seder* (a ritual) *and* give food to the hungry (an ethic). Simultaneously, by imitating parents, a child learns the habit of Jewish ritual *and* the habit of Jewish ethics.

There is no distinction between the actions. Both the ritual observances and the ethical actions are done for the same reason: The command to do them comes from the same source—God.

Jewish ritual is thus both a way for Jews to connect with God, and the instrumentality through which Jewish ethics are conveyed, learned, and observed.

Other ethical codes—wanting to convey an enduring ethical standard—must rely on the hope that parents and great grandchildren will have the same, continuing, definitions of "good;" the same, continuing, feelings and commitments; the same, continuing, circumstances and situations.

When it comes to ethical behavior, Judaism does not rely on hope. Rather, Judaism depends on the two-pronged simultaneous approach to Jewish law: Observe Jewish rituals—because they are God's law; *and* observe Jewish ethics—because they are God's law.

There is, of course, the danger that the ritual will be treated as paramount, and that the ethic will be ignored. But when Jewish rituals and Jewish ethics are intertwined and inseparable, Judaism's inherent confidence is that generations from now, if Jewish great-grandchildren perform Jewish rituals—not only faithfully, but in good faith—they will almost certainly observe Jewish ethics.

Ethical ritualism is a system that makes sense. It is a system that works.

8. תקון עולם TIKKUN OLAM

is repairing/healing/balancing/transforming/perfecting the world.

To be a Jew means to have a special role and purpose, to have a sacred mission.

The prayerbook states simply but profoundly that the Jewish mission is to "perfect the world under the Kingdom of God" (the prayer, *Alenu*).

Created in the image of God, Jews—and all human beings who follow the Jewish model—are not to be mere spectators, mere bystanders, in the unfolding process of creation and daily existence. We are not here on earth just to breathe and live out a measured number of days and then die.

Rather, we are here on earth to be active participants, partners with God, in the task of building up the world and making it into the best place that it can be.

How do we fulfill such an awesome task?

An old Jewish story: When God created the world, He knew that we human beings were going to eat bread as the staple, the sustenance, of life. So if God knew that we were going to eat *bread,* why did He make *wheat* grow up out of the ground? Why didn't He just arrange to have neat little loaves of bread, already packaged in their colorful plastic wrappers, come up out of the ground?

The answer to this fanciful but very important question explains the partnership between God and humankind.

God provides the basic plan: that wheat is the essential ingredient of bread. And then, with the spark of life that only He can produce, God provides the raw material: the wheat growing up out of the ground. Human beings then take the resource and do with it what we must, in order to sustain ourselves. We add the imagination, the creativity, the sweat, to make what we need.

That is the basis of the partnership between God and humankind: God provides the wheat; we make the bread. Each partner has a unique and indispensable role.

In partnership with God, the Jewish mission is to take this magnificent and grand universe that God has created and to work to combat the ills and the evils that beset our world; to work to move the world, step by step, closer to transformation and perfection.

How do we go about it? How do we human beings bring balance and perfection to our world?

Picture a ladder: The very bottom of the ladder is the beginning of the universe and of humankind, with all its possibilities and all its potential. At the very top of the ladder is perfection (which we will call "Sky Blue," a term from the childhood game of hopscotch, designating the goal, the ultimate achievement). At Sky Blue is a world without hatred and bigotry and war, a world without disease and hunger and poverty and illiteracy and pain, a world of peace and serenity, of harmony and tranquility, of goodness, righteousness, compassion, and love.

The rungs of the ladder are the steps that humankind must climb, from the moment of creation to the moment of perfection. This is the journey of discovery and accomplishment that brings the world from its beginnings to its ultimate destination.

The very first human beings (let's call them Adam and Eve), conscious and aware of their place in the universe, began the climb up the ladder. They stepped up a few rungs, went as far as they could go, but then time ran out for them.

Then their children began their own climb. But they did not have to begin at the beginning, at the bottom rung. They were able to start from where their parents had finished. They stood on the rung of their parents' discoveries and accomplishments and climbed new rungs of the ladder, moving ahead into as yet unexplored territory.

That is why, in the ongoing history of the world, we do not have to "reinvent the wheel in every generation." Each generation benefits from all the accomplishments of the generation before.

To use this modern example, when our grandparents or great grandparents were children, tens of thousands of people died from smallpox. Then someone reached up into the unknown and plucked out the cure, and now no one who has access to smallpox vaccine dies of that disease anymore.

Not long ago, tens of thousands died of polio. Then someone reached up into the unknown and plucked out the cure, and no one who has access to the polio vaccine dies from that disease anymore.

Now, in our children's generation, tens of thousands die of cancer. No one has yet reached high enough into the still unknown to pluck out the cure—yet. But using the accumulated wisdom of the ages, someone will. And perhaps in our great-grandchildren's generation, no one will die of cancer.

The problem is, of course, that the ills and evils that beset the world are not finite in number. Even as we cure one affliction, new ones crop up. These new afflictions arise for one of two reasons: either because we have reached the place in the ongoing process of exploring the universe where those challenges lurked, just waiting for us to reach them; or because of our own behavior or our own misuse of the resources we have been given.

When we despoil the environment, choke the air with smog, pollute the rivers and streams, strip the land of its precious minerals, and deplete the ozone layer, we derail the naturally evolving path toward perfection. While we may have learned to limit the ways of warfare, at the same time we discovered how to make a new, completely devastating, instrument of war—completely unknown just a few decades ago. And while we may have discovered the cure for smallpox and polio and be working toward the cure for cancer, we have discovered a new, completely devastating, disease. This generation faces challenges that no generation before could have contemplated: finding the cure for AIDS, and saving ourselves from nuclear destruction. The trek up the ladder is sometimes littered with shattered dreams.

In our climb up the ladder, we benefit from all the wisdom and all the work of the people who came before us. We stand on their shoulders, stretching our fingertips as far upward as they will go. We rise higher and higher and higher on the rungs of the ladder, climbing rung by rung, step by step, reaching toward Sky Blue, toward the perfection of the world.

Notice that as we climb, we do not "invent" or "create" anything out of nothing (only God has the ability to create out of nothing). Everything that we need to make our world a perfect place is already out there, created by God at the very beginning of the beginning. It is all out there just waiting to be discovered, waiting to be found. It is all out there, waiting to be plucked out of its hiding place, waiting for the minds and the spirits of human beings to grow and mature and expand enough to reach up and grab it.

Here may be the definition of "human genius."

Shakespeare, Mozart, and Da Vinci had tremendously creative minds—minds that some would say were Divinely inspired, gifts from God, just as other people have incredible physical attributes or skills that are gifts from God. These people did not follow the normal step-by-step process of the unfolding universe: moving one step at a time up the ladder of discovery. Instead, they leaped over a number of steps of future generations in expressions of music, art, and literature that were far beyond their own times.

Moses and the people of the desert did the same thing with a code of moral behavior. By skipping over the normally unfolding generation-by-generation process of discovery, these people found forms that would be recognized and appreciated, and would last for centuries.

Human genius is making the leap far beyond the regular step-by-step process to discover answers and forms that might not have been found for hundreds of years and that will last in the human consciousness for hundreds of years more.

Bringing our world to Sky Blue, to perfection, is no easy task; there are so many ills to be cured, so much evil to be confronted, so many new challenges that arise. To truly reach the perfection of our world, we must bring an end to poverty and illiteracy, to disease and destruction, to conflict and strife, to hatred and warfare. We must bring peace and harmony to people and nations, healing and comfort to the disturbed and afflicted, faith to the faithless, hope to the hopeless, and ultimate redemption to every person on this planet.

The task seems overwhelming, impossible for any one person in any one generation. And it is. That is why an ancient sage taught, "It is not your task to complete the work, but you are not free to desist from it" (Avot 2:21).

So each person, in each generation—each of us in our time and place—takes one or two more steps up the ladder, and makes a contribution to bringing the world that much closer to perfection.

If we each try hard enough, if we each reach up and stretch just as far as we can, then—every once in a while—the members of an entire generation can witness the end of one more impediment, one more ill or evil, that blocks the way toward the Sky Blue of perfection.

Happily, there is one blight, one stumbling block on the way to perfection for which we, in our time, have found the cure—if only we would use it wisely.

We have the ability to wipe out human hunger, to make sure that no human being on the face of this earth is ever hungry again.

We have the fields, we have the seeds, we have the knowledge, to grow enough food so that every single person on this planet can eat. Clarence Birdseye discovered the technique of freezing food in order to preserve it, and Wilbur and Orville Wright discovered the airplane, the way to transport food from place to place.

Tragically, we do not use the knowledge and the technology we have. We let money and politics get in the way.

The population of the world is 5 billion people. We have the ability to feed 7 billion, but we are still feeding only 4 billion. One billion people go to bed hungry every single night (if they have a bed to go to), and more than 14 million children die each year of hunger or hunger-related disease.

We, in this generation, may not be able to reach the ultimate Sky Blue. We may not be able to stop all warfare, cure all disease, or bring everlasting peace. But here is one thing we *can* do. If only we would act swiftly and courageously, millions of human beings would live, instead of starving to death. Then one of the horrors of our planet would be gone and our children would have one less problem to solve when it comes their turn to stand on our shoulders, when it becomes *their* turn to make *their* contribution to the process of perfecting the world.

The Jewish concept, the Jewish name, for Sky Blue is ימות המשיח *y'mot haMasheach*, the days of the messiah. According to Jewish thought, the perfection of the world will have arrived when the messiah—for some, a person; for others, a time or an era—comes, to herald it and to preside over it.

To bring *masheach*, to bring the messianic age, every Jew—joined, hopefully, by every human being—must embrace the mission of *tikkun olam*—to work and strive and make a contribution to the ongoing process of bringing the world toward transformation, healing, and perfection.

It is a mission, a daily commitment, that we must accept gladly and sincerely. For the very fate of the world—its original purposes, its continuing advancement, and its ultimate future—is at stake.

Jews—and all human beings—in partnership with God, *can* and *must* make this world into the place where perfection is not only the goal, but the reality.

AN ESSAY ON THE DAYS OF THE MESSIAH

One of Judaism's fondest hopes and most fervent prayers is for the coming of the messiah.

The messianic age is humankind's ultimate goal and reward—the time when there will be eternal reward for everyone who has ever lived, and when all the ills and evils that beset the world will be gone, replaced by complete peace and perfection.

Judaism yearns for the messiah who will bring both personal and communal reward, whose coming will touch and affect individual Jews, the whole of the Jewish People, and all of humankind.

Judaism's quest for the messiah is deeply rooted in Jewish history, shaped and affected by the religious and political conditions in which Jews lived.

PERSONAL REWARD

The Hebrew Bible is concerned with how people live here on this earth, how obeying God's law and observing the *mitzvot* enhances and enriches earthly existence. The Bible teaches that reward and punishment are to be meted out here on earth, in this lifetime.

The Bible does not discuss the concept of obeying God's law here on earth, for the sake of receiving a reward after death. It contains no concept of afterlife, no mention of a heaven or hell where reward or punishment might be granted. Heaven, in the Bible, is simply the place where God dwells, as contrasted to earth, the place where humankind dwells.

Without in any way describing it, the Bible mentions a place called שאול *sheol,* a nebulous netherworld where souls descend after earthly existence. The biblical implication—undefined and unexplained—is that the soul has an eternal life.

To the people of the Bible, immortality was achieved simply through living a good life, leaving behind a good name and reputation, and most important, by having children—progeny who will carry on the good deeds that parents taught and left as their legacy.

Thus biblical Judaism focuses on how we behave, and the consequences of that behavior while we are alive.

Only later in Jewish history was a concept of reward and punishment in an afterlife introduced into Judaism.

By the beginning of the Rabbinic Period (200 B.C.E.), human awareness and sophistication had grown far beyond its place in the biblical world. A millennium of continued human growth and experience gave people the cognitive and spiritual abilities to understand ideas and concepts that had still been closed off to their desert-dwelling ancestors. This emerging human consciousness caused people to look beyond what they could empirically see, beyond the material world into the world of the spirit. Intuitively, they sensed the greater wholeness of God's universe and their place in it.

The people turned to their rabbis and sages, asking for elucidation and illumination, for the explanation of the world beyond theirs, for a map of their soul's journey after life as they knew it.

At the very same time—in these last two centuries before the Common Era—the Jewish People, living in the Land of Israel, faced increasingly intense political pressure and tyranny—first from the Greeks and then from the Romans—challenging their core beliefs about earthly existence and life's ultimate meaning and rewards. The foreign occupiers increased their influence in the land and over the people by systematically denying basic rights to the Jews. Slowly, religious freedoms and political independence were taken away. The less sovereignty the Jews enjoyed, the greater the power the occupier held.

The Jews grew restless and they came to their rabbinic sages with piercing questions: "Why," asked good, observant Jews, "should we continue to do *mitzvot,* to obey God's law, when there seems to be no reward for our faithfulness? Instead, we are being persecuted and tortured by these Romans. And, at the same time, we watch the Romans, who seem to follow no civilized code of behavior and certainly do not obey God's law, seem to be enjoying themselves very much, with 'wine, women, and song.' It is not fair. It doesn't make any sense. Perhaps we should just stop obeying the *mitzvot.*"

At first, the rabbis tried to respond with theological arguments. They taught, "Do not be like servants who minister to their master for the sake of receiving a reward. But be like servants who minister to their master without the condition of receiving a reward. And let the awe of God be upon you" (Avot 1:3).

But theology paled in the face of everyday reality, and the people continued to complain. So the rabbis—realizing that they could be facing a theological revolution—used brilliant human psychology. Instead of continuing to dismiss or counter the arguments, *they agreed with them.*

In essence, they said, "You are right. It is very unfair that you should follow the *mitzvot* and suffer, while the Romans, who obey no higher authority, seem to prosper. But do not worry. God is watching over you and He knows how well you are behaving, how diligently you are obeying the *mitzvot* in הזה העולם *haolam hazeh,* in this world, the world of life as we know it. So continue to follow the *mitzvot,* continue to obey God's law, and God will remember all the good that you did during your lifetime. And after you have died, God will reward you in הבא העולם *haolam haba,* in the world to come.

In one master stroke, the rabbis responded to their people's new-found longing to know their fate and destiny after death and, at the same time, quelled the theological rebellion they were facing. The rabbis introduced a totally new concept into Judaism—the idea of a world to come, an afterlife, where God metes out reward or punishment for earthly behavior.

The rabbis and the Jewish teachers of the time (including, eventually, a traveling preacher from the Galilee, named Jesus) immediately took up this new concept and began teaching it as mainline Jewish thought. It began to take hold and be accepted by the people, and presumably satisfied their needs to be rewarded by God for their faithful behavior—even if the reward would not come until after they had died.

Later, when newfound Christianity adopted the concepts of afterlife, reward and punishment, and eternal salvation as guiding principles of its new religion, Judaism—where the ideas were still fairly new—stepped back from them in an attempt to draw a clear distinction between Judaism and Christianity. However, the idea of reward in a world to come is still part of traditional Jewish teachings and is accepted and believed by many Jews.

Thus the concept of reward and punishment after death came into Judaism at a particular time, in response to a specific set of political and theological circumstances. It was part of an evolving Jewish theology (some of which has evolved beyond this concept). Yet despite its purposeful and political origins, this concept has brought much solace to many Jews throughout the ages. It is Judaism's clear belief that God watches over each and every one of us individually, and cares about our lives. It is the concept that assures us that God does not abandon our souls at the grave, but cradles us in His love for eternity. It is a concept of comfort and continuity.

COMMUNAL REWARD

It was not only individual reward that the persecuted Jews of the Roman period sought. They wanted relief for their besieged land and nation. They wanted an end to persecution and tyranny. They wanted tranquility and peace restored to their people, their homeland, their world. They wanted the messiah!

The Hebrew word for messiah is משיח *masheach*, which means "anointed one." In the meaning of the Hebrew word lies the original Jewish concept of the messiah.

The concept of *masheach* entered Judaism after the death of King Solomon (ca. 931 B.C.E.). A fellow named Jeroboam led a rebellion against Rechoboam, the son of Solomon, which resulted in a schism, a split in the Jewish People. Jeroboam became the king of ten of the twelve tribes (which came to be called the Kingdom of Israel), while Rechoboam ruled over the remaining two tribes (which came to be called the

Kingdom of Judah). In 722 B.C.E. the Kingdom of Israel was defeated in war by the Assyrians, and disappeared from history.

It became the hope of every Jew that one day the kingdoms would be reunited under the leadership of a descendant of King Solomon (and his father, King David). This "anointed one" (that is how kings were designated in those days—by being anointed with oil), this *masheach,* would restore the Jewish People to wholeness and reaffirm the tranquility and greatness of earlier days.

That hope was not realized; but the concept of an anointed one, a *masheach,* who would lead the Jewish People toward a time of peace and restoration, took hold in the Jewish consciousness.

Later, when the Greeks and the Romans began to dominate the Land and the People of Israel politically and militarily, denying rights and freedoms to the Jews, the memory of the hope for an annointed one, a *masheach* who would lead a free Jewish People in time of peace came to the fore once again.

Thus, at exactly the same time that the rabbis were creating and introducing the concept of reward and punishment in an afterlife into Judaism, the oppressive political climate led the people to revive the concept of *masheach,* an anointed one, who would herald national unity, tranquility, and peace, a world without pain and strife, a world healed of its ills and evils, a world transformed into perfection.

Many of the people began to believe that the days of *masheach* could not be far away, for how much worse could the lives of the Jews become than they already were under Greek-Roman oppression? When was *masheach,* when was salvation from worldly pain, ever more needed than at this moment?

TIMELESS REWARD

This hope—and, for many, firm belief—that the arrival of *masheach* was imminent, led to the establishment of another brand-new theological concept by the sages. The people said: We will do as you say. We will continue to observe all the *mitzvot,* knowing that even if life here on earth is difficult and painful, we will, nevertheless, receive God's reward in the world to come. But even anticipating an eternity of God's reward, what happens if, the day after we die, *masheach* comes? We will miss out on all the goodness, harmony, tranquility, and peace right here on earth. We will miss out on the "Perfect World" party that *masheach* is going to have.

The rabbis responded by creating another new theological concept: When *masheach* comes, every person who ever lived will be literally physically resurrected, and will return to Jerusalem to be present at the moment when the perfection of the world is announced.

Thus, in response to a particular political-theological need, at this specific time and place, it became a well-known and well-accepted Jewish concept that physical resurrection of the dead would be an integral part of the coming of *masheach*.

It is no accident, then, that at the very heart of newly forming Christianity was the belief that Jesus, as messiah, had physically risen from the dead. If simple experience showed that all who had ever lived had *not* been resurrected with the coming of Jesus as messiah (potentially harming the Jesus-as-messiah claim), then at least a cornerstone of Christian theology would be that Jesus, the messiah himself, had returned through resurrection.

Since the concept of resurrection became such a dominant aspect of Christianity, Judaism—where the concept was still fairly new—stepped back from it, again in an attempt to draw a clear distinction between Judaism and Christianity. Nonetheless, the concept of physical resurrection is still a part of traditional Jewish teachings and is still evident in many areas of Jewish thought and practice.

The second blessing of the *amidah,* one of the central prayers of the Jewish worship service, concludes by praising God, מחיה המתים *mechayyeh hammaytim,* "Who gives life to [resurrects] the dead."

Jewish law forbids any kind of mutilation of the body—such as tatooing—and requires that an amputated limb be buried in a cemetery and then be reburied with the person when he or she dies. Jewish law further requires ground burial and forbids cremation at the time of death. All these laws serve to keep the physical body unblemished and intact so that God can properly restore it at the time of resurrection. Jewish tradition even requires that a body be buried in the cemetery with feet facing east, so that when *masheach* comes and resurrection takes place, the person will have a "running start," headed in the right direction toward Jerusalem.

THE COMING OF THE MESSIAH

For Jews and Judaism, the *masheach,* or the age that *masheach* will herald, has not yet come. One look at the world in which the concept was first articulated (the time of the splitting of the kingdoms) or at the time when the concept was revived (the time of the Greek-Roman occupation), or at all the time since, is proof enough that the time of peace and perfection has not yet enveloped our world.

For Christianity, of course, the messiah has come in the form of Jesus—God on earth, bringing forgiveness for sin, salvation, and everlasting life.

Then and now, Judaism rejects the notion of Jesus as the messiah.

While it is hard (and sometimes lonely) to argue with the beliefs and faith of more than a billion Christians throughout the world, and while the rejection of Jesus as messiah-savior-God has led to persecution and death for millions of Jews throughout the centuries, the theological rejection of Jesus as messiah is really very simple.

The "job description" of the messiah contains two tasks. The first is that the messiah is supposed to bring or announce (in the words of the famous Christmas carol) "peace on earth, goodwill toward men." In this role of the messiah, Jesus clearly failed, because neither his world nor ours is a world of peace and perfection. So Jews and Judaism do not acknowledge Jesus as the messiah heralding a world of perfection here on this earth—because simple evidence shows that it is not.

Christianity seems to have realized this failure of Jesus to fulfill this job of the messiah. So, in response, Christianity developed the concept of "the second coming." Why didn't Jesus herald a world of peace? Because, concedes Christianity, the people of the world had not done their share to move the world toward peace. When we have all done our job to bring perfection to the world, when we truly deserve peace and tranquility, then Jesus will be back—in the "second coming"—to announce the peace we have earned.

Jews and Judaism do not acknowledge Jesus as messiah in hopes of the "second coming," because the concept of *tikkun olam,* the ultimate perfection of the world, through the works of our hands, has been the Jewish mission from the very beginnings of Judaism. When the perfection of the world is achieved, *masheach* will come to herald it, for the first and only time.

The second thing a messiah can do is offer the promise of a world to come to those whose life on earth merits eternal reward from God. Jesus, loyal teacher of Jewish theology that he was, began teaching this concept just as the rabbinic sages introduced it into Judaism. Jews and Judaism do not acknowledge Jesus as messiah to promise reward in life everlasting, because it is a concept right out of Judaism.

Thus the answer to the oft-asked question, "Why don't you Jews believe in Jesus?" or "Why don't you Jews celebrate Christmas or Easter?" (the Christian commemoration, respectively, of the birth and the resurrection of Jesus) is clear. We don't believe in Jesus as messiah (or celebrate the holidays commemorating him) because he did not do the job of messiah.

Yet the Jewish hope for the coming of the messiah still burns brightly, with passion and with fervor. In the words of the prayer *Alenu,* the Jewish hope of a world "perfected under the Kingdom of God," a world where "on that day, the Lord will be recognized as One and His name as One," remains central to Jewish faith and practice.

Throughout Jewish history—and, most probably, today—there have been some Jews who have hoped that the messiah will simply arrive, and that somehow all the strife and horrors of the world will just disappear. But most accept the idea that

Judaism calls us not to wait passively, but to work actively to bring *masheach*. Most agree: God will not just impose *masheach;* no one person will be able to wipe out all the ills and the evils that beset us.

Instead *masheach*—be it one individual or an era—will come when we human beings have done what it takes to bring healing, transformation, and perfection to our world. We don't sit and wait; we go out and act: for by the works of our hands, *we* bring glory.

And even when *masheach* comes, our own responsibilities for taking care of our world will not end. The rabbinic sage Yochanan ben Zakkai went so far as to say, "If you are planting a tree, and you hear that *masheach* has come, finish planting the tree and, then, go greet him" (Avot de Rabbi Natan 31).

When will *masheach* come?

The Talmud (BT Shabbat 118b) teaches, "*Masheach* will come if every Jew observes the Sabbath twice in a row."

This is not a simple statement of religious practice (although continuing commitment to religious observance certainly creates a climate conducive to bringing about worldly perfection). Rather, this is a statement that proves how very much human behavior affects and determines the path toward worldly perfection. For Shabbat is considered to be a "foretaste of the world to come," a weekly model-example of harmony, tranquility, and peace that reflects—for a short twenty-four hours—what eternity in a perfect world will be. Thus if every Jew tastes worldly perfection two weeks in a row—and presumably in the days in between, for how could that glorious a feeling be shattered?—then *masheach* will come.

When will *masheach* come?

When we are ready.

The Talmud (BT San. 98a) says that Rabbi Joshua ben Levi found Elijah the prophet (who, according to tradition will be the one to announce the coming of *masheach,* and will formally lead him into the gates of Jerusalem) sitting, disguised as a beggar, at the gates of Rome. He asked, "When will you come to proclaim the messiah?" Elijah replied, "Today, if you will only hear his voice."

Perhaps *masheach* will not come in our lifetime.

But perhaps he—or she—will.

How do we bring *masheach?*

Each one of us must do his or her small part—creating, exploring, growing, participating, producing, repairing, healing, giving, caring, sharing, loving, transforming—because each act, each word, each moment, brings us closer to a world of perfection, closer to *masheach.*

Ultimately, *masheach* is in each and every one of us—in you, in me.

How do we bring *masheach?*

The modern poet Danny Siegel translates a *rebbe*'s proverb that tells us how:

If you will always assume
the person sitting next to you
is the messiah
waiting for some human kindness,

You will soon learn to weigh your words
and watch your hands.

And if he so chooses
not to reveal himself
in your time,

It will not matter.

9. PEOPLEHOOD

Like Christianity, Islam, Buddhism, Hinduism, and all the others, Judaism is a religion. It has its own unique theology, beliefs, laws, rituals, and observances.

But Judaism is more than a religion.

Picture a pie: For most religious groups, all the slices of the pie are labeled "religion." What unites the adherents of a particular religion is a shared system of belief about God, the universe, and humankind, and the interrelationship among the three.

For Judaism, the pie is very different. Religion is the crust of the pie, that which holds it all together. But the slices of the pie are many other things. For in addition to being a religion, Judaism is much more.

Judaism is a shared history.

All Americans share a history, which includes the Boston Tea Party, the Fourth of July, the Civil War, the Rough Riders, World War I, the Great Depression, World War II, Korea, Viet Nam, the Peace Corps, the Civil Rights movement, and putting a man on the moon.

All Jews share a history, which includes Abraham finding God, standing at Sinai to receive the commandments, the battle of Jericho, the building of the Holy Temples, the exile, wandering from land to land, the sword of the Crusades, the alleys of Spain, the ovens of Auschwitz, and Israel reborn.

What has happened to one Jew—anywhere, any time—has happened to all Jews. Each and every Jew has a part, a stake, in Jewish history.

Judaism is a shared language.

Not every Jew speaks modern Hebrew, but Hebrew has been the Jewish language since Judaism's beginnings. The Bible is written in Hebrew; most of the literature of Jewish law and legend is written in Hebrew; the prayerbook is written in Hebrew.

Wherever Jews have gone, whatever everyday languages Jews have spoken, Hebrew has been the one continuing and uniting language. Any Jew—surrounded by thousands of other Jews, or isolated and alone—can open the Bible or prayerbook, read, speak, or hear the words, and be linked to all Jews everywhere.

Because most of Judaism's holy texts are written in Hebrew—and because, following the exile to Babylonia in 586 B.C.E., most Jews adopted the ancient Semitic language of Aramaic as their spoken language—Hebrew came to be considered a "holy language," reserved for texts but rarely used in everyday conversation.

During these past 2,500 years, Hebrew continued to be the language in which most of the legal and literary texts were written, but for the most part, Jews have spoken the language of the lands in which they lived.

The revival of Hebrew as a spoken language began in the 1880s, initiated by Eliezer Ben Yehuda in Palestine. Modern Hebrew—based on biblical Hebrew, but including tens of thousands of new words fashioned to define and describe contemporary life—is the predominant language of the modern State of Israel.

Throughout the ages, Hebrew has had many slightly varying pronunciations, based on regional and geographical speech-pattern differences. The two major pronunciations that remain today are called Ashkenazic, with its roots in central and eastern Europe, and Sephardic, with its roots in Spain, the Mediterranean, and Arab and Asian countries. The most noticeable difference between Ashkenazic and Sephardic pronunciations is that the Hebrew letter ת is always *tav* (pronounced with a "T" sound) in Sephardic, but it is sometimes called *sav* in Ashkenazic (pronounced with an "S" sound). Thus the Hebrew word שבת, meaning Sabbath, is pronounced Shabbat in Sephardic, and Shabbas in Ashkenazic. Modern Hebrew pronunciation, for the most part, follows the Sephardic pronunciation, so modern Israeli Hebrew is known as Sephardic Hebrew.

Throughout Jewish history, there have been three other languages that have been uniquely identified with the Jewish People. While not as pervasive or dominant as Hebrew, each has played an important part in Jewish life.

Aramaic, a common language of the Semitic Near East, was spoken by Jews beginning during the Babylonian exile. It was the everyday language of the Rabbinic Period (including the time of Jesus). Hebrew, then, was reserved as the "literary language," used only for learning and reading Torah, and for prayer. Major portions of the biblical books of Daniel and Ezra, large parts of the Talmud (the major compendium of Jewish law), the Jewish marriage and divorce documents, and a number of prayers (including the famous doxology, the *kaddish*), are written in Aramaic, and remain part of Jewish life today.

Ladino, a combination of Hebrew and Spanish, was developed by the Spanish Jewish community of the Middle Ages. A vast and rich Ladino literature was composed, and many outstanding works remain. A small number of Jews of Spanish-Mediterranean descent still speak Ladino (often as a second or third language) today.

Yiddish is a combination of Hebrew and German (with a liberal sprinkling of Russian, Polish, and in America, in this century, English—depending on the linguistic influences of the country of the speaker's residence). The origins of Yiddish go back some 1,000 years to the beginnings of the Jewish sojourn in eastern Europe. Yiddish is familiar to American Jews because so many of the Jewish immigrants to the United States in the late nineteenth and early twentieth centuries were Yiddish speakers from eastern Europe. Yiddish literature is vast, and many Yiddish stories (particularly those of Sholom Aleichem, Y. L. Peretz, and Nobel Prize winner Isaac Bashevis Singer) have been popularized in American theater and film. Many richly expressive Yiddish words have entered into the English language and are used and understood by Jews and non-Jews alike.

All Jews share Hebrew as a literary and as a restored spoken language. Many Jews share a familiarity with Aramaic, the language of the Talmud, and with Ladino and Yiddish, the languages developed over the centuries in the many lands in which Jews have lived.

Judaism is a shared literature.

Jewish communal and private library shelves throughout the world hold the same books—the Bible, the law literature of the Mishnah, the Talmud, and the Shulchan Aruch, the legends of the Midrash, and the praise and petition of the prayerbook.

Wherever Jews have gone, whatever other languages Jews have spoken, these books have been with them—telling the Jewish story, shaping Jewish values and behavior, and remaining as the enduring and continuing record of Jewish religious and communal life. To this day, literature unites all Jews everywhere.

Judaism is a shared land.

The Land of Israel is the Jewish homeland. It is the land God promised to Abraham and his descendants as an "everlasting possession" (Genesis 17:8). It is the Holy Land.

Joshua led the Children of Israel across the Jordan River to claim it; the ancient kingdoms imprinted it with uniquely Jewish characteristics; the Holy Temples were built there as God's earthly dwelling place. Israel—and especially the city of Jerusalem—became the center of the Jewish universe, for "from out of Zion comes Torah, and the word of the Lord from Jerusalem" (Isaiah 2:3 and Micah 4:2, quoted in the prayerbook).

Even when Israel was conquered by invading armies, even when the land was laid desolate, even when the people were sent off in exile to wander the earth, even during the almost 1,900 years of dispersion, the Land of Israel was never, even for a moment, out of Jewish thought and Jewish longing. Three times a day, every day, traditional Jews prayed "In Your mercy, O God, return us . . ." (the *amidah*).

With the establishment of the modern State of Israel, Jewish sovereignty has been restored, and Israel is once again physical homeland for millions of Jews. For every Jew, Israel is spiritual homeland; for Israel is not only a place, but it is a mystical attachment to everything Jewish that ever was and ever will be. All Jews, wherever they live, share the Land of Israel.

Judaism is a shared culture.

To be sure, there are many differences, regional variations, and varying customs, but millions of Jews share similar food, music, dance, modes of celebration, and rhythms of everyday life. Cultural similarities often demark and define, and thus

Jews know how to find each other by what they eat, how they sing, and even what makes them laugh and cry.

Judaism is a shared future.

Just as all Jews share a common history, all Jews share a common destiny.

There is an interconnectedness among all Jews, wherever they live—sometimes imposed by others; sometimes acknowledged, sometimes not—so that what happens to one Jew happens to all Jews. In today's world, that is both a heavy burden and a great glory, and a Jew's life is liberally sprinkled with both pain and gladness.

Jews have and continue to contribute mightily to the multihued fabric of civilization, to the intellectual, cultural, artistic, spiritual, and ethical development of humankind. Yet Jews are forever on guard, for it is no secret that there are those who would use their power to try to wipe out Jewish tomorrows.

As with every Jewish generation that has come before, the Jewish future is now this generation's to deny or give, destroy or mold. How each and every Jew acts, each and every day, will determine how the Jewish debt to history is paid and how the Jewish future is forged.

Judaism is much more than a religion. It is also a *peoplehood*—a group of people linked, much like any other nation, by history, language, literature, land, culture, and common destiny. Judaism is a group of people sharing an identity and sense of belonging, rootedness and authenticity, mutual responsibility and mutual benefit.

Note well, however, that *Judaism is not a race.*

Race is an anthropological designation based on physical characteristics such as skin color, facial structure, eye cast, and hair texture. There are Jews of all colors, Jews of all physical characteristics, Jews who are members of all races.

So Hitler's obscene call to wipe out the "Jewish race" was an impossibility, even in its basic proposal. He might have advocated killing all the adherents of the Jewish religion; he might have advocated killing all the members of the Jewish People. But his plan to murder all Jews in order to have a racially pure society was—in addition to its inherently horrific and preposterous premise—patently impossible, because Judaism—and Jews—is not a race.

Religion *and* Peoplehood combine to form the Jewish "pie," the totality of Judaism.

Religion is the "crust" that gives the pie of Judaism shape, definition, and purpose. The shared experiences of Peoplehood are the "slices" of Judaism's pie, giving it its sweetness and spice.

It is this interdependence of religion and peoplehood that has given Judaism its unique greatness and has sustained it throughout the generations.

2

THE JEWISH PEOPLE

1.   JEWISH NAMES

Jews and Judaism are called by a number of names. The first name-designation, applied to Abraham and his descendants, was עברי *Ivree,* best translated as "Hebrew."

The word *ivree* means to "cross over" or to "migrate," for in his many journeys, Abraham crossed over rivers and migrated from land to land. Even in their earliest designation, the Jewish People were known as "wanderers."

In the Bible, the descendants of Abraham—those who would be enslaved in Egypt, be redeemed, journey in the desert for forty years (stopping along the way to receive the commandments at Sinai), and enter into the Promised Land—are called בני ישראל *B'nai Yisrael,* "The Children of Israel," or the "Israelites."

Israel means to "wrestle with God." It was the name given to the patriarch Jacob after he spent a night in a semi-awake/semi-dream state, struggling with what is alternately understood as a man/an angel/the image of his twin brother Esau/himself/his conscience/God. Jacob prevailed, and in the morning he was told, "You shall no longer be called Jacob, but Israel, for you have wrestled with God and with man and you have won" (Genesis 32:29).

The name Israel implies the intimate relationship between God and the Jewish People—a relationship based on the continual struggle to find and know each other in mutual responsibility and love.

Israel is also the name given to the land of Canaan, the land that God promised to Abraham and his descendants, the land that became the Jewish homeland.

The names יהודי *Yehudee,* Jew, and יהדות *Yahadut,* Judaism, come from the Hebrew word יהודה *Yehudah,* Judah, one of the twelve sons of Jacob.

In 931 B.C.E., at the death of King Solomon, the Israelites split into two kingdoms. The larger kingdom, consisting of ten of the twelve tribes, was called Israel.

The smaller kingdom, consisting of the remaining two tribes, was called Judah. In 722 B.C.E. the kingdom of Israel was conquered by the Assyrians, and the people of the kingdom of Israel were exiled from the land. They seemingly assimilated into the surrounding nations, disapppeared, and became known as the "ten lost tribes."

The kingdom of Judah remained and flourished, and eventually its name became the name by which the entire people and the religion of the ancient Hebrews/Israelites would be known: Jews and Judaism.

2. WHO IS A JEW?

According to Jewish law, a Jew is a child born of a Jewish mother, or a person who converts to Judaism.

This is called matrilineal descent—having the religious heritage determined through the mother. If the mother is Jewish, the child is Jewish—whether or not the father is Jewish.

If the father is Jewish but the mother is not, then the child is not Jewish.

Why, especially in an ancient patriarchal society, was the mother's religion designated to be the religion of the child? First, the sages reasoned that there may be doubt as to who a child's father is, but there is rarely any doubt as to who the child's mother is. As well, it is traditionally the mother who cares for and nurtures a baby, giving a child its first introduction to religious teachings. Thus determining a child's Jewishness through matrilineal descent assures that the Jewishness or non-Jewishness of a child is certain.

In recent years, in addition to accepting the traditional law regarding matrilineal descent, the Reform and Reconstructionist movements have also decided to accept patrilineal descent, having the religious heritage determined through the father. Thus for Reform and Reconstructionist Jews, if either the mother *or* the father is Jewish, then the child may be considered Jewish. If the mother is not Jewish but the father is—and the father and child take certain proactive steps to publicly declare the decision that the child is Jewish—then the child is Jewish.

The Reform and Reconstructionist movements' decision to accept both matrilineal and patrilineal descent is understandable in the contemporary world, where the father of the child is almost always known; where both mother and father care for and nurture their baby; and where, with so many interfaith marriages, the Jewish spouse—whether mother or father—has the right and the desire to determine the religious heritage in which a child will be raised.

The problem with the decision to accept patrilineal descent is that the other movements within Judaism have not accepted and embraced the decision, and this has caused a serious rift within the Jewish community.

For example, a child of a Jewish father and a non-Jewish mother, who is reared in a Reform or Reconstructionist synagogue, receives a Jewish education, has a Bar Mitzvah, and considers himself completely and legally Jewish, may grow up and fall in love with an Orthodox or Conservative Jewish woman. After a lifetime of being Jewish (according to the Reform or Reconstructionist movements' definition), he will be told by an Orthodox or Conservative rabbi that he is not Jewish according to Jewish law, and may not marry the young woman unless he formally converts to Judaism.

This widely differing view within the modern Jewish community over the issue of patrilineal descent needs to be addressed and solved by a consensus of the entire Jewish community, so that there is a clear and widely accepted contemporary definition of "who is a Jew."

3.   שבטי ישראל   SHIVTAY YISRAEL

are the Tribes of Israel.

In biblical times, the ancient Jews were grouped according to twelve tribes.

These tribes originated from the sons and grandsons of the patriarch Jacob. Jacob's sons each received a fatherly blessing (Genesis 49), and each became the progenitor of one of the tribes of Israel. These sons were Reuben, Simeon, Levi, Judah, Zebulun, Issachar, Dan, Gad, Asher, Naphtali, Benjamin, and the favorite son, Joseph.

When the tribal units were eventually formed, Joseph's two sons, Ephraim and Manasseh, *each* became the progenitor of a tribe. This effectively gave the favorite son, Joseph, a double blessing and a double portion.

During the 400 years in which the descendants of Jacob lived in Egypt, there must have been some memory and acknowledgment of the tribal groupings; for when the Children of Israel were freed from slavery and journeyed through the desert, they encamped according to tribes, and the leaders of each tribe formed an advisory council to Moses.

During the sojourn in the desert—when the Tabernacle was built, the priesthood established, and regular sacrificial worship begun—the members of the tribe of Levi were assigned to be the priests and their assistants. Because of this special role,

Levi was no longer considered a tribe, thus reducing the number of tribes from thirteen (remember: the two sons of Joseph each had become a progenitor of a tribe) back to twelve.

When the Children of Israel entered the Promised Land, each tribe was assigned a geographical location. The Levites, the religious functionaries, were assigned to Levitical cities—interspersed throughout the land—where they were supported by the rest of the tribes as they carried out their sacred functions.

This loose confederation of tribes constituted and governed the Jewish People in the Land of Israel during the period of the Judges until the beginning of the monarchy.

After the reign of King Solomon (931 B.C.E.), when the kingdom split in two, ten of the tribes aligned together as the northern kingdom of Israel, and the other two tribes (Judah, Benjamin, and a tiny remnant of Simeon) aligned as the southern kingdom of Judah.

In 722 B.C.E., when Assyria defeated the kingdom of Israel, some of the inhabitants were taken into exile; others remained in the land and assimilated into the conquering nation; some made their way south to become part of Judah. The ten tribes of the northern kingdom lost all unique identity, and vanished from the world. To this day, they are known as the "Ten Lost Tribes."

The two remaining tribes—the kingdom of Judah—made up the whole of the Jewish People. That is why the names by which the religion and people are known until this day are "Jews" and "Judaism."

Each tribe had a symbol, based on the blessing given by Jacob. For example, Benjamin is called "a ravenous wolf" (Genesis 49:27), so the symbol of the tribe of Benjamin is a wolf. Of Zebulun it is said, "Zebulun shall dwell by the seashore; He shall be a haven for ships" (Genesis 49:13), so the symbol for Zebulun is a sailing ship. Judah is called "a lion's whelp" (Genesis 49:9), so the symbol for Judah is a lion.

These symbols of the twelve tribes have been part of Jewish ritual art for millennia. In contemporary times, they have been immortalized by the world-renowned artist Marc Chagall, whose depictions of the symbols of the twelve tribes are magnificent, towering stained glass windows in the synagogue of the Hadassah Hospital in Jerusalem.

The tribes of Israel constitute the first formal structure of the Jewish People, and remain as an enduring legacy of origins and peoplehood.

4. כהן KOHEN לוי LEVI ישראל YISRAEL

are the three ancestral groupings of the Jewish People.

The Jewish People are divided into three ancestral groupings, based on ancient role designation in regard to religious functions—first in the Tabernacle in the desert, and then in the Holy Temple in Jerusalem:

• A Kohen is a descendant of the priestly tribe—the elite of the tribe of Levi—those who officiated at the sacrificial rites at the sanctuary and at the Holy Temple.

• A Levi is a descendant of the assistants to the priests.

• A Yisrael is any other member of the Jewish People, a descendant of neither a Kohen or a Levi.

The designation of being Kohen, Levi, or Yisrael is passed from father to child (son or daughter) because in the patriarchal society of ancient times, it was the men who took part in religious rituals.

Today—when the Holy Temple no longer exists, when sacrifices are no longer brought, and when priests are no longer the ritual officiants—the ancestral groupings are of less practical importance. However, they are still recognized and used in Orthodox and much of Conservative Judaism for certain ritual purposes, most notably the order in which people are called to participate in the reading of the Torah by reciting the blessings over the reading.

5. GEOGRAPHICAL AND CULTURAL GROUPS

Since the Middle Ages, there have been three major groups of the Jewish People, designated by the geographical areas from which they come: Ashkenazim, Sephardim, and Edot HaMizrach:

• The word Ashkenaz means "Germany." It is used to designate Jews who are descendants of the Jewish communities of Germany, central Europe, and eastern Europe, including Poland and Russia.

• The word Sepharad means "Spain." It is used to designate Jews who are descendants of the Jews of Spain, and those who fled from Spain (in the expulsion of 1492) to Mediterranean, Arab, and Asian countries, and some eventually to countries in South America, Central America, and North America.

• Jews who come from Persia, Yemen, Ethiopia, and other eastern countries are classified as neither Ashkenazic nor Sephardic, but as Edot HaMizrach (literally, "the eastern community"). They constitute a smaller but equally important separate ethnic and cultural grouping of the Jewish community.

Ashkenazic, Sephardic, and Edot HaMizrach Jews share basic Jewish beliefs and follow and observe the same *mitzvot*, the same religious regulations, because Jewish law applies equally to all.

Most of the differences between Ashkenazim and Sephardim (with the Edot HaMizrach most always reflecting the Sephardim) revolve around מנהג *minhag*, custom, stemming from the cultural influences of the countries and communities of origin.

For example, in prayer, while the basic structure and most of the words are the same, there is a *nusach Sepharad* and a *nusach Ashkenaz*, a *mode* of prayer that differs between Sephardic and Ashkenazic Jews. While the differing modes means that the prayerbooks of the two groups contain a few different prayers and slightly different wording of some of the other prayers, the biggest difference is in the musical motif by which the prayers are chanted. The Ashkenazic melodies are influenced by the music of Russia and eastern Europe, and the Sephardic melodies are influenced by the music of the Mediterranean.

Other major differences between Ashkenazim and Sephardim are cultural—food, dress, music, song, dance, and customs within the home—which come from and reflect the very different countries and cultures in which the two groups have lived. For example, that which is considered "Jewish food" amongst Ashkenazim is really Russian and eastern European food, adapted to Jewish dietary laws. For Sephardim, "Jewish food" is the food of the Mediterranean countries—Greece, Turkey, Morocco, and the others—adapted to Jewish dietary laws.

Not only are there different *minhagim* within the large groupings of the Jewish People, but there are differing *minhagim* from country to country and from community to community. Sometimes Jews within the same community will have widely differing *minhagim* of synagogue and worship practices, melodies of prayer, and modes of celebration.

When there is no law regarding a particular observance or ritual, *minhag*—through practice, loyalty, and constancy—takes on the force of law. So what is comfortable and customary for members of one Jewish community may be acceptable but very foreign to the members of another Jewish community. Yet, in background and *minhag*, the differences between groups of Jews create the rich, multihued fabric of Jewish life—the brilliantly colored individual strands that make up the solid, sturdy whole of the Jewish People.

The majority of American Jews are of Ashkenazic descent.

Throughout most of its existence, the majority population of the modern State of Israel was Ashkenazic. In the late 1980s, the Sephardim, along with Edot

HaMizrach, became the numerical majority. But with the large Russian immigration in the early 1990s, the majority is once again Ashkenazic.

While there are many wealthy and powerful Sephardic and Edot HaMizrach Jews in Israel, the real financial and political power base of the country has been the Ashkenazic population. For decades, many Sephardic and Edot HaMizrach Jews considered themselves—and were treated—as the lower class of Israeli society. But in recent years, with the army as the ultimate "leveler" and so many marriages taking place in Israel between Ashkenazic, Sephardic, and Edot HaMizrach Jews, the three cultures are beginning to blend, with the best and most enriching of each culture combining in the newly forming families.

6.   MODERN DENOMINATIONS

Throughout Jewish history, there has been no one monolithic, unilateral approach to Jewish life. There have been the conservatives and the liberals, the strict interpreters of the law and the lenient interpreters of the law, the supernaturalists and the rationalists, the legalists and the spiritualists. For almost every position on the spectrum of Jewish life, there have been proponents and opponents. Sometimes the disagreements have been friendly; but just as often, they have been hostile and violent. In modern times it is no different. There are a number of approaches to and interpretations of Judaism, known as branches or wings or denominations or movements, each with its passionate advocates and followers.

ORTHODOX JUDAISM

Orthodox Judaism is the contemporary name-designation for what has been mainstream Judaism throughout the centuries. It is based on the fundamental belief in the direct revelation of Divine law—recorded in the Torah—that is eternal, unchangeable, and the sole guide for everyday life and behavior. Later compilations of Jewish law are considered reorganized versions of the original Torah law. Orthodox Jews carefully and strictly observe the commandments as the direct will of God.

Since the mid-nineteenth century, there have been several strands of modern Orthodox Judaism. For the most part, mainstream Orthodoxy has adopted a positive attitude to the prevalent culture, and has encouraged its followers to acquire the education and skills necessary for participation in everyday life. More traditional elements—sometimes characterized as "ultra-Orthodox"—maintain that only complete separation from secular society can assure Jewish survival.

The best known of these right-wing Orthodox are the Chasidic Jews, recognized by their distinctive dress—long black coats, round black hats, beards, sidelocks. Founded by Rabbi Israel ben Eliezer—who came to be know as the Baal Shem Tov—Chasidism grew up in eastern Europe in the early eighteenth century as a way to approach God with both contemplative meditation and fervent joy. Many towns became centers of Chasidic life with the *rebbe,* the rabbi of the town, being the leader of that town's Chasidic sect.

Since the destruction of eastern European Jewry in the Holocaust, Israel and the United States have become the centers of Chasidic life. The best known of the contemporary Chasidim in America—especially for their outreach programs on college campuses—are the Lubavitch Chasidim, also known as Chabad.

REFORM JUDAISM

Reform Judaism was born in the early to mid-nineteenth century in Germany, in response to the Enlightenment and the emancipation in western Europe, and was brought to the United States by German immigrants later in the century. In the light of scientific scholarship, Reform Judaism rejected the concept of Divine revelation, and instead attributed the authorship of Torah to Divinely inspired human beings. Therefore, for Reform Judaism, the law is considered instructional and inspirational but not binding—except for the ethical laws, which the early reformers still understood as an expression of God's will.

Early Reform modernized the worship service by eliminating much of the Hebrew of the service in favor of the vernacular, and by eliminating many ritual practices—all in an attempt to remove many of the distinctions and differences between Jews and their non-Jewish neighbors.

In contemporary times, Reform Judaism has reintroduced a number of ritual customs and practices, has increased the use of Hebrew in worship, and has actively affirmed its commitment to egalitarianism and issues of social justice.

CONSERVATIVE JUDAISM

Conservative Judaism was founded as a response to Reform Judaism in the mid- to late nineteenth century in Europe, and was transplanted to the United States in the very late nineteenth and the early twentieth centuries. The movement's founders accepted the Reform notion that change in Jewish belief and practice is necessary in an ever-changing world, but they felt that Reform Judaism had eliminated too many basic Jewish practices. They therefore wished to *conserve,* to retain, some of the theology and rituals that Reform had eliminated.

The Conservative movement's motto became "tradition and change," indicating the principle that Jews are still bound to observing the ritual law, but that the interpretation and application of the law is ever-evolving—based on a careful study of its origin and historical development, and its function in modern circumstance and situation.

RECONSTRUCTIONIST JUDAISM

Reconstructionist Judaism was first articulated by Rabbi Mordecai Kaplan in the early 1920s in the United States. Its organizational structure became formalized in the 1950s and 1960s. Reconstructionist philosophy rejects the idea of a supernatural God—understanding God instead as a Power or Process that is the sum of all the forces that give life meaning and worth. Reconstructionism (which takes its name from the desire to *reconstruct* Judaism and Jewish life) asserts that Judaism is not merely a religion, but an "evolving religious civilization," a peoplehood, a culture, as well as a faith community.

Each movement is far from internally monolithic. Each denomination has its center, its conservative right wing, its liberal left wing—and everything in between. Thus each movement has its own internal disagreements and ever-dynamic debate, and the need to accept and incorporate the differing views of its adherents.

In contemporary days, at the far left wing of liberal Judaism are Jewish Humanists, who reject any notion of God and are attached to Judaism through peoplehood, history, collective consciousness, and communal celebrations.

Most recently, there has been a movement toward Jewish Renewal, characterized by Jews seeking a deep spiritual connection to God, to the higher self, and to a community of friends, through fully participatory, egalitarian worship—often combined with ancient meditative practices—intense study, and joyous celebration. The "grandfather" of Jewish Renewal is Rabbi Zalman Schachter-Shalomi, and it has best been described by writer William Novak as a "new Judaic impulse fed by the best qualities in each of the recognized branches of Judaism: the authenticity of Orthodoxy, the liberalism of Reform, the scholarship of Conservative Judaism, the social awareness of Reconstructionism, [and] the excitement of Chasidism."

There is a great theological distance between the far-right-wing Orthodox and the far-left-wing liberal Jews.

It might seem that with so many divergent views, many contemporary Jews have little in common. Yet the Jewish "house" has wide doors and an even taller roof. There *is* a place for everyone.

While it is true that many Jews (most notably the right-wing Orthodox) reject the notion of pluralism, and insist that their interpretation of Judaism is the only valid one, most Jews understand that contemporary Judaism is a multi-hued fabric, made up of many beautiful strands reflecting the reality of Judaism through the ages.

Most Jews find a place on the Jewish spectrum that is comfortable for them, and gladly accept the places others find for themselves, knowing that the words of the ancient sages are true today: "*These and these* are *both* the word of the living God" (BT Erubin 13b).

For, ultimately, as the contemporary Jewish thinker Dennis Prager teaches, Jewish "labels" mean very little. It does not matter if a Jew calls himself or herself Orthodox, Conservative, Reconstructionist, or Reform; religious or secular; a "good Jew" or a "bad Jew."

There is only one designation that really counts: a *serious* Jew.

Serious Jews continually struggle to define their relationship with God; to accept Torah and fulfill its *mitzvot;* to embrace the ethical mandate of Judaism; to regulate existence to Judaism's life-enhancing rituals and observances; to support Jewish causes; to be a devoted member of the Jewish community; to maintain a bond and a sense of mutual interdependence with the Jewish Land; to feel a connection to Jewish history; and to be committed to the creative survival of the Jewish future.

By this definition, there are serious Jews in every movement, in every denomination of modern-day Judaism—just as there are nominal members of every movement who are not yet serious Jews.

Thus whatever the "label," whatever the variety of approach or interpretation, whatever the internal disagreements, the unity of the Jewish People—linked by history and by destiny—is paramount.

If, in the midst of internal squabbles, Jews sometimes seem to forget this unity, others—for good or for evil—are often quick to remind.

For example, in sending Jews to the gas chambers, Hitler did not ask, "Do you believe in God? Are you religious? Do you attend synagogue? Do you keep kosher?" Hitler had only one question: "Are you a Jew?"

The United Jewish Appeal—the international organization that raises funds to support Jewish needs in local communities, in Israel and around the world—has as its slogan the simple but powerful phrase, "We Are One."

That has always been both the Jewish hope and the Jewish promise.

This collective oneness of all Jews—in both reality and in desire—is called כלל ישראל *klal Yisrael,* the unity of the Jewish People.

7. גרות GERUT

(from the word גר *ger*, literally, "stranger/foreigner/resident in a foreign land,"
having come to also mean "convert/proselyte") is conversion to Judaism—
becoming Jewish.

A person who is not born Jewish may become a Jew by converting to Judaism.

At the very beginning of Judaism, the only Jews were the direct descendants of Abraham and Sarah—part of their extended family. Pagans could become Jewish—most often through marriage—by declaring belief in the one Lord God, and loyalty to the ever-growing tribe of the Jewish People.

From the time of Abraham until the birth of Christianity—a period of more than 1,800 years—Judaism accepted, incorporated, and welcomed anyone willing to pledge allegiance to God and the Jewish People.

From the Hebrew word meaning "stranger" or "resident alien," a convert is called a גר *ger* (male) or גיורת *giyoret* (female). A person who converts with pure motives and without reservation, out of complete sincerity and conviction, is called a גר צדק *ger tzedek,* a righteous proselyte.

The best-known and most notable example of a person embracing Judaism is found in the biblical book of Ruth, when Ruth the Moabite woman refuses to leave her mother-in-law, Naomi. She says, "For wherever you go, I will go; wherever you lodge, I will lodge; your people shall be my people, and your God, my God" (Ruth 1:16).

To this day, Ruth is considered the prototype proselyte—adopting the Jewish God and the Jewish People as her own with sincerity, determination, and joy.

After the rise and growth of Christianity, Judaism became reluctant—and afraid—to seek out converts. No longer was it a matter of taking in pagans who rejected idolatry and sought God. Rather, it was Judaism as one religious option, with Christianity as another formidable religious choice.

As Christianity grew more and more powerful, both religiously and politically—and as Jews were spurned for denying the alleged divinity of Jesus and slandered as Christ-killers—it became unwise, if not dangerous, for Judaism to seek out converts in "competition" with Christianity.

For the better part of the next 2,000 years, with some exceptions now and then, Judaism never missionized or actively encouraged non-Jews to convert to Judaism. When a person approached a rabbi about the possibility of converting to Judaism, it became the custom for the rabbi to reject the request and to send the person away. Only if the person returned again and again—displaying sincerity and conviction—would the rabbi agree to offer instruction in Judaism and eventually conversion.

With the Enlightenment, and especially with the new political freedoms granted by the American Revolution in 1776 and the French Emancipation in 1792, Judaism achieved a never-before-held status. Jews could be treated as citizens of a country while at the same time maintaining their own religious beliefs and practices. Although this new status did not lead to any sweeping conversions to Judaism—and surely did nothing to forestall the horrific, systematized murder of 6 million Jews in the Holocaust, just for being Jews—it nevertheless established Judaism as a credible religion in the modern world.

In the open society of the contemporary world, even with its lingering and all-too widespread anti-Semitism, Judaism now enjoys a recognition and an acceptance that is rare in Jewish history. More and more people are attracted to Judaism for its intellectual honesty, its spiritual passion, its ethical values, its life-enhancing rituals, and its deeply connected community.

Some come to convert after their life's philosophical and spiritual search leads to Judaism. Some come, initially, out of a desire to marry a Jewish man or woman. Still others grow to Judaism after having been married to a Jew for a number of years.

While some rabbis reject prospective converts—especially those whose original motivation is marriage to a Jew—unless intent and sincerity is unquestioned, most modern rabbis are willing to welcome and accept for instruction all prospective converts who wish to explore and grow toward Judaism.

Reasoning that converts—now often called Jews by Choice—are a great source of renewed numerical strength and spiritual vigor and commitment, the liberal denominations of modern Judaism sponsor programs of "outreach," actively promoting Jewish faith, beliefs, practices, and community, and encouraging prospective converts to embrace Judaism.

The preparation for conversion to Judaism is a multilayered, multidimensional process:

1. *A person must learn about Judaism.*

To learn about Judaism means to study Jewish history, beliefs, philosophy, theology, texts, liturgy and worship practices, calendar and holidays, ethics and rituals, and to learn Hebrew, the language both of Jewish literature and prayers and of the modern Jewish State of Israel.

To be a Jew means to know about Judaism. But knowledge is not enough. Any intellectually curious person can learn about Judaism by reading books and taking classes, without wanting to become Jewish. To be a Jew, there is much more.

2. *A person must come to believe as a Jew.*

There are certain undebatable and unalterable beliefs, which in order to be a Jew, a person must embrace.

Some—but not all—of these beliefs include: the belief in one and only one God; the belief that God is singular and indivisible into two or more parts; the belief that each person is given free will by God; the belief that people are not born into a state of "original sin," but that each person follows or transgresses God's commandments through personal choice; the belief that there are consequences for moral behavior or misdeed; and the belief that each person is responsible for his or her actions.

A person converting to Judaism must completely reject all previously held theological beliefs that are contradictory to Judaism and totally accept Judaism's core beliefs and tenets.

That is why the process of becoming Jewish is called "conversion."

It is not enough to add new knowledge about Judaism to the convert's store of already accumulated knowledge. The prospective convert must reach deep inside soul and psyche and throw out, change—*convert*—one set of beliefs and replace it with another.

3. *A person must come to behave as a Jew.*

A Jew leads a unique lifestyle that is characterized by observance of Jewish ethics and rituals.

Many, many non-Jews already follow basic Jewish values and ethics in their lives, but converting to Judaism means recognition of the *source* of those values. It is not enough to do good and be good simply out of a sense of right and wrong. The Jewish ethical mandate is based in ethical monotheism—that the ethical law comes from God, who is both Author and Authority. Being a Jew means accepting and living this ethical system as God's word and will.

The Jewish lifestyle is also defined by daily ritual practices. For example, a serious Jew observes the Sabbath and Jewish holidays, attends synagogue and participates in community worship, and gives to those in need. Many Jews keep kosher and observe other Jewish laws and customs. A serious Jew reads Jewish books, subscribes to Jewish periodicals, and has Jewish art and artifacts in the home. And a serious Jew continually learns more about Judaism through classes and study.

Preparing for conversion to Judaism means slowly but assuredly adopting these observances and practices.

One of the reasons that the process of conversion to Judaism usually takes at least nine to twelve months is that a prospective convert needs to live through one entire Jewish festival and ritual year, experiencing and participating in the observances of each holiday.

A person converting to Judaism must observe more and more Jewish rituals, until those rituals are a familiar, full, and comfortable part of everyday existence.

From his or her daily life, lifestyle, conduct, and behavior, anyone observing the prospective convert should be able to say, "This is a Jew."

4. *A person must come to belong to the Jewish People.*

Since Judaism is not only a set of religious beliefs and practices, but a peoplehood as well, a person converting to Judaism must "join" the Jewish People by feeling a connection to Jewish people and places, concerns and issues, passions and causes.

A Jew belongs to a synagogue and participates in its activities because the synagogue is the central institution of Jewish life—the place where Jews gather to express their unity and their collective longings.

While there are myriad worthy organizations and programs that deserve and should receive generous support, a Jew recognizes that his or her *first* obligation is to Jewish causes—because if Jews don't take care of Jews, who will? So a Jew joins and contributes to Jewish communal organizations, which support fellow Jews by providing for education, recreation, caring for the ill, the infirm, the elderly, the troubled, the needing. At the same time, a Jew knows that responsibility to other human beings is not determined by religion, race, or creed, so a Jew also supports the needs of the greater community.

Since many of the organizations that provide for Jewish needs depend on volunteer help to do their work, a Jew gladly gives personal time and effort to the needs of the community. While there is great sympathy and empathy for any human being in difficulty or need, there is a special familial connection, affinity, and responsibility between Jews. So when any Jew anywhere is in trouble—oppressed or imprisoned, under verbal or physical attack—every Jew who is capable gives aid and comfort.

A Jew has a deep spiritual connection to the Land and the People of Israel, personally sharing the sorrows and joys, the tragedies and triumphs, of Judaism's physical and spiritual homeland. Therefore a Jew contributes to Israel, and buys Israel Bonds (whether or not the interest rates are competitive with other financial investments) because the money goes right to work in Israel. In the midst of winter, a Jew sends money to buy a little sapling that will be planted in the soil of Israel, because it is Israel's planting season, and Israel needs trees.

A prospective convert who truly wants to be a Jew must feel and be part of the Jewish People.

Even in this modern age, it is both a glory and a burden to be a Jew.

The burden is felt by a prospective convert by no longer being part of a majority faith and culture, but in becoming part of a tiny minority. The burden is felt in the special connections, responsibilities, and obligations that must be assumed; in both overt and covert anti-Semitism that still abides; in deep-seated anti-Zionism that still poisons so much of the world. The burden is felt in the knowledge that if a

Hitler again walked the world, the convert is in mortal danger, along with all other Jews.

Yet, for most Jews, any burdens of being Jewish are greatly outweighed by the glories of being Jewish—being part of an ancient people in contemporary times with a special, intimate relationship with God, chosen for the responsibility of living and teaching God's will; living according to life-sustaining values and ethics, and to the rhythms of life-enhancing rituals and celebrations; and being a partner with God in shaping Jewish destiny, in transforming and perfecting the world, and in anticipating the grandeur of ultimate redemption.

A person converting to Judaism must be ready to accept membership in the Jewish People—with all its responsibilities and burdens, with all its gratification and glory.

When a prospective convert has learned about Judaism, come to believe and behave as a Jew, and feel a sense of belonging to the Jewish People, there are a number of rituals that make the conversion official and complete.

Since the physical sign of being part of the covenant with God is *brit milah*, ritual circumcision, a male converting to Judaism must be ritually circumcised while the proper blessings are recited. Circumcision for an adult male can be a very painful procedure, so a prospective convert who accepts the requirement of ritual circumcision demonstrates sincere commitment to the process of conversion and to Judaism. In modern times, many adult males who convert to Judaism were already circumcised shortly after birth. For these men, Jewish law has a procedure called *hatafat dam* (literally, "drawing of blood"), which legally transforms the surgical circumcision into a ritual circumcision.

Both male and female converts immerse in a *mikveh*, a ritual pool of collected waters, as a symbolic act of ritual purification. In the waters of the *mikveh*, a proselyte is spiritually "reborn." The proper blessings are recited, making the immersion a ritual act of conversion.

Following the rituals, the prospective convert comes before a *beit din*, a rabbinic court, usually comprised of three rabbis. The members of the *beit din* question the prospective convert about intention and sincerity, and establish that he or she has basic Jewish knowledge and an abiding commitment to Jewish beliefs, ethics, ritual observances, and peoplehood. The members of the *beit din* then conduct a conversion ceremony to officially accept the prospective convert as a Jew.

Some modern Reform and Reconstructionist rabbis may not require one or more of these rituals of conversion. Some Orthodox rabbis require a solemn pledge from the prospective convert to observe the ritual laws, such as Shabbat and holiday observance and keeping kosher.

This difference in requirements for a person converting to Judaism is reflective of the differences between the modern denominations of Judaism. Most accept the differences as part of the pluralist nature of contemporary Judaism. Some—most notably the right-wing Orthodox and the Israeli religious establishment—insist that only their method is correct and acceptable, and reject converts whose learning, conversion rituals, or ritual observance is not according to their standards.

These differences in who is recognized and accepted as a Jew have led to serious division within the contemporary Jewish world. They are differences that need to be addressed and resolved for Jewish unity, the common good of the Jewish People, and the well-being of the Jewish future.

The conversion ceremony can take place anywhere, but it is often held in the synagogue, in front of the open Holy Ark, which contains the sacred Torah Scrolls. This creates the image that the convert is standing to accept God's Torah, just as the Children of Israel stood at Mt. Sinai to receive the commandments.

Prayers and blessings are recited, and the convert is given a Hebrew name. Throughout Jewish history, it has been the custom to give male converts the name אברהם Avraham, Abraham, after the very first Jew; and to give female converts the name רות Rut, Ruth, after the prototype convert. In modern times, in the liberal denominations, those converting to Judaism are invited to pick a Hebrew name that has special meaning or significance to them.

Hebrew names do not have a last or family name, as names are used in contemporary secular society. Rather, one is known by one's name followed by "the son of" or "the daughter of" one's father's name, and in modern times one's mother's name also. Since a convert to Judaism does not have a Jewish father or mother, all converts are known as "the son of" or "the daughter of" Abraham and Sarah, the first Jews.

The conversion ceremony concludes with the rabbis of the *beit din* signing a certificate formally and officially recognizing this person as a Jew, and offering a warm welcome into Judaism and the Jewish community.

From that moment onward, the convert is considered a full and complete Jew.

Jewish law forbids any discrimination against a converted Jew.

Sadly, this law has not always been meticulously followed, and many converts have felt uncomfortable and even embarrassed within the Jewish community. Recently, however, more and more "native born" Jews are recognizing and appreciating the great commitment that it takes to convert to Judaism.

Converting to Judaism is an awesome, exciting, and often scary experience. For the convert, it means reaching to the depths of heart and soul. It means real or imagined confrontations with parents, priests, and persona. It means dredging up childhood, and breaking away from cherished memories. It means critically evaluating lifelong assumptions, throwing away long-held beliefs, and slowly carving out new commitments. It means rejecting and accepting; shutting off and opening up; walking out and coming in—often all at once. Converting to Judaism is a highly charged emotional transition that requires gentle assistance, unwavering support, and the promise of warm acceptance on the other side.

Happily, more and more Jews are recognizing the great and invaluable contributions that converts make to Judaism.

Converts to Judaism seek and find God. They eagerly create Jewish homes, participate in Jewish observances, and bring their children to synagogue and Jewish schools. They increase Jewish numbers, and bring a new spirit to the Jewish People.

The Midrash (Tanchuma Lech Lecha 6) tells just how precious converts to Judaism are. "Dearer to God is the proselyte who has come of his [her] own accord than all the crowds of the Israelites who stood at Mt. Sinai. The Israelites witnessed the thunder, lightning, quaking mountains, and the sound of trumpets. But the proselyte, who saw not one of these things, came and surrendered himself [herself] to God and took upon himself [herself] the yoke of Heaven. Can anyone be dearer to God?"

Converts to Judaism honor Jews and Judaism by choosing to become part of the Jewish People.

They are Judaism's new strength and an important part of its future.

3

JEWISH LITERATURE

1. תורה TORAH

(from the root meaning "teaching/instruction/law") is the first section
of the Hebrew Bible.

The Torah contains the story of the creation of the universe and of humankind. It contains the history of the Jewish People and the ethical and ritual laws given to the Jewish People by God.

The Torah consists of five books; it is sometimes called the Five Books of Moses. In Hebrew, it is sometimes called the חומש Chumash, because that is the Hebrew word for five. The five books of the Torah are Genesis, Exodus, Leviticus, Numbers, and Deuteronomy:

1. בראשית Bereshit, Genesis: The book of Genesis contains the story of the creation of the universe and of humankind. It records the establishment of the covenant between God and the Jewish People. It tells of the lives and the stories of the patriarchs and matriarchs.

2. שמות Sh'mot, Exodus: The book of Exodus contains the account of the Children of Israel in Egyptian slavery, the exodus from Egypt, and the receiving of the Ten Commandments at Mt. Sinai.

3. ויקרא Vayikra, Leviticus: The book of Leviticus gives God's ethical and ritual laws, and specific instructions to the priests on how to perform their duties.

4. במדבר Bamidbar, Numbers: The book of Numbers recounts the journey of the Children of Israel through the desert, and gives more of God's ethical and ritual laws.

5. דברים Devarim, Deuteronomy: In the book of Deuteronomy, Moses reviews the laws, and the people prepare to enter the Promised Land.

For all its length, brilliance and complexity, Torah can be summarized in three words:

• *Creation:* God created the universe and everything in it. The covenant of faith was created between God and humankind, and specifically between God and the Jewish People.

• *Redemption:* The Children of Israel were redeemed from bondage in Egypt, in order to experience revelation.

• *Revelation:* God gave His commandments, his *mitzvot,* as a blueprint for human conduct, a standard of behavior—a moral code enhanced by ritual observance—by which humankind is to live.

The Torah Scroll, called in Hebrew ספר תורה *Sefer Torah,* is the handwritten parchment containing the text of the Torah. The *Sefer Torah* is handwritten, with quill and ink, by a סופר *sofer,* a highly trained and highly skilled scribal writer.

In modern times, the Torah is read from the scroll during synagogue services four times a week—Saturday afternoon, Monday morning, Thursday morning, and Saturday morning.

The Torah has been divided into fifty-four portions. One portion is read each week throughout the year. The first part of each portion is read on Saturday afternoon and repeated on Monday and Thursday mornings. The entire portion is read on Saturday morning. Sometimes two portions are combined so that the entire Torah can be read in the period of one year.

The completion of the yearly Torah-reading cycle and its new beginning take place on the holiday of Simchat Torah (literally, "rejoicing in the Torah"), which follows the last day of the festival of Succot, in the fall.

On Jewish holidays—Rosh HaShanah, Yom Kippur, Succot, Pesach, Shavuot, Chanukah, Rosh Chodesh (the first day of each new month), and on fast days—the Torah is also read. Specially selected sections of the Torah have been chosen as the holiday readings for their thematic connection to the particular holiday. For example, on Passover, the section about the exodus from Egypt is read.

The continual process of reading Torah demonstrates the centrality of Torah in Jewish life, and Judaism's commitment to learning and observing the ethical and ritual laws given by God. Because Torah is the core source of everything Jewish, the word Torah has come to be used not just literally, as the name for the biblical books, but also as a way of describing the entirety of Jewish knowledge and interpretation, continuing teaching and learning.

2. נביאים NEVI'IM

(literally, "prophets") is the second section of the Hebrew Bible, Prophets.

A biblical prophet is not a soothsayer, fortuneteller, or mere predictor of the future. A biblical prophet is a spokesman for God. He hears God's word (or has it revealed to him in a dream) and then speaks on behalf of God—as a messenger of God—to the people.

The biblical prophets, in the name of God, admonished the Jewish People for forgetting and forsaking God's commands. They called on the people to examine their lives and their conduct. They demanded social justice—honest, decent, righteous dealings between people, with special concern and care for the needing, the poor, the hungry, the homeless, the widow, and the orphan. They warned of the dire consequences of God's punishment for those who ignore His demand for ethical lifestyle enhanced by ritual observance. They called on the people to repent their ways before it was too late. And they always held out the promise of God's forgiveness for the individuals—and for the whole Jewish People—who mend their ways, seek God's forgiveness, and return to observing God's commandments.

Nevi'im is divided into two sections, the N'evi'im Rishonim and the N'evi'im Acharonim. נביאים ראשונים N'evi'im Rishonim, the Early Prophets (or the First, or the Former Prophets), describe the history of the Jewish People in the Land of Israel, from the conquest of Canaan (ca. 1200 B.C.E.) until the destruction of the Holy Temple (586 B.C.E.).

The Early Prophets are:

1. יהושע Y'hoshua, Joshua: The book of Joshua describes the conquest of Canaan, the division of the land among the twelve tribes, and the beginning of Jewish life in the Promised Land.

2. שופטים Shoftim, Judges: The book of Judges records the history of the tribes during a period of civil rule.

3. שמואל Shmuel, Samuel: There are two books of Samuel—א Alef and ב Bet, or 1 and 2. These books describe the life of Samuel, who anoints Saul as the first king of Israel. They continue by describing the anointing of David as Saul's successor and the rule of King David.

4. מלאכים Melachim, Kings: There are two books of Kings—א Alef and ב Bet, or 1 and 2. These books describe the end of David's rule, the anointing of King Solomon, and the building of the Holy Temple. The description continues with the division of the kingdoms after Solomon's death and the individual histories of the

separate kingdoms. The books conclude with the description of the destruction of the Holy Temple and the exile of the people from the land.

THE LATTER PROPHETS

The second section of Nevi'im is נביאים אחרונים Nevi'im Acharonim, the Latter Prophets. The Latter Prophets lived between the eighth and the fifth centuries B.C.E., thus spanning the last centuries of the Early Prophets. They were literary men. They, or their scribes, collected their speeches and wrote their own texts.

Nevi'im Acharonim is subdivided into two sections, the Major Prophets and the Minor Prophets. Three prophets are known as the Major Prophets, not just because of the importance of what they said, but because of the length of their books.

The three Major Prophets are:

1. ישעיהו Yeshayahu, Isaiah: Isaiah, a book of sixty-six chapters, is actually comprised of two distinct sections, attributed to two different authors who lived at two very different times. The first thirty-nine chapters are attributed to Isaiah, the son of Amoz, who lived in the last half of the eighth century B.C.E. The remaining chapters—known as Deutero-Isaiah, or Second Isaiah—are attributed to an unnamed author or authors, who lived during the Babylonian exile (586 B.C.E. and later). While it would make much more sense for the two distinct sections to remain separate from each other, at a certain point in the history of the making and the editing of the Bible, the two sections were merged and are arranged as an uninterrupted whole.

The book of Isaiah is filled with prophecies concerning the behavior of the Jewish People and the promise of Divine retribution for transgression. Isaiah calls for spiritual and political independence from surrounding nations, for the end to idolatry, for the purity of religious observance, and for social justice. The chapters known as Deutero-Isaiah envision a time when there will be an end to warfare, when harmony and peace will prevail among peoples and nations. This time will come when God's people observe and follow God's law.

2. ירמיהו Yirmiyahu, Jeremiah: The book of the prophet Jeremiah foretells and witnesses the destruction of the Holy Temple, the Land of Israel, and the exile of the people. It teaches God's demand for ethics and human morality. It contains deeply moving lamentations over the fate of the Jewish People and offers consolation and hope in exile.

3. יחזקאל Yechezkel, Ezekiel: The book of the prophet Ezekiel contains prophecies in Babylonian exile. It is filled with lamentations over the transgressions of the people and the destruction of Jerusalem, and offers consolation and injunctions for the future. Ezekiel is a visionary prophet, telling of visions of God and the restoration of the land and the people. The book emphasizes the importance of the

Temple, the priests and sacrificial worship, and their renewed centrality when the people are restored to the land.

There are twelve Minor Prophets. Collectively, they are known by the Aramaic phrase תרי עשר *Tray Asar,* which means "twelve."

The twelve Minor Prophets are:

1. הושע Hosheah, Hosea: The book of the prophet Hosea teaches that ritual worship is meaningless unless it is accompanied by ethical lifestyle. Hosea combines opposition to the monarchy and pessimism about the future of the Jewish People with stirring passages of consolation.

2. יואל Yoel, Joel: The book of the prophet Joel urges the people to repent their errant ways. It reminds the enemies of Israel that they will one day be punished for their opposition to the Jewish nation, and tells them that they will be defeated, and that the Jewish People will live in peace.

3. עמוס Amos, Amos: The book of the prophet Amos teaches the need for kindness and compassion among people and between nations. It anticipates the return of the exiles.

4. עבדיה Ovadyah, Obadiah: The book of the prophet Obadiah prophesies the downfall of the nation of Edom.

5. יונה Yonah, Jonah: The book of the prophet Jonah calls on the inhabitants of the city of Nineveh to repent their errant ways, and dramatically illustrates how an entire city can save itself through repentance.

6. מיכה Michah, Micah: The book of the prophet Micah prophesies about the destruction of Jerusalem because of its corrupt leaders, and spells out God's requirements for humankind—"do justice, love mercy, walk humbly with your God" (Micah 6:8).

7. נחום Nachum, Nachum: The book of the prophet Nachum prophesies the downfall of Assyria (the biblical symbol of an evil nation) and the joy that will come to Israel when Assyria is defeated—celebrating the victory of Divine justice.

8. חבקוק Chabakuk, Habakkuk: The book of the prophet Habakkuk asks the question, "Why do the innocent suffer and the wicked prosper?" and replies that God's answer is that the fall of the wicked will come.

9. צפניה Zephanyah, Zephaniah: The book of the prophet Zephaniah prophesies the destruction of the wicked and the destruction of the land. It contains exhortations to repentance in order to avoid the destruction, and foretells the redemption of the remnant of the Jewish People in an era of harmony and peace.

10. חגי Chaggai, Haggai: The book of the prophet Haggai reprimands the people for living comfortably in exile and contains exhortations to rebuild the Holy Temple.

11. זכריה Zecharyah, Zechariah: The book of the prophet Zechariah uplifts the spirits of the disheartened with prophecies of victories over their enemies, future redemption, and visions of restoration and rebuilding.

12. מלאכי Malachee, Malachi: The book of the prophet Malachi contains admonishments for neglect of the ritual and ethical laws by the people and particularly by the priests. It prophesies the coming of the messianic era, the days of judgment, and ultimate peace and harmony.

During the Greek and Roman occupations of the Land of Israel, leading up to the destruction of the Holy Temple and the exile of the people in the year 70 C.E., a reading from Prophets was added to the Sabbath and holiday worship.

Some scholars contend that the prophetic reading was added because the Torah reading was censored from the service by the foreign oppressors, and that a selected reading from the Prophets—the second section of the Bible—maintained a scriptural reading as part of the service. Other scholars contend that the prophetic reading was added to the end of the service as an inspirational conclusion to the worship.

The reading from Prophets was called the הפטרה *haftarah*.

The scholars who think that the prophetic reading was added to take the place of the censored Torah reading contend that this word comes from the Greek, meaning "addition." Those who think that the prophetic reading was an inspirational conclusion to the service contend that this word comes from the Hebrew, meaning "dismiss" or "discharge."

Much later, when the weekly Torah reading was formally fixed by verses, chapters, and portions, specific sections from the Prophets were selected and assigned for each Torah reading, based on a thematic connection between the Torah reading and the chosen prophetic passage.

The *haftarah* remains as part of the worship service, for it adds depth of meaning and understanding to the weekly Torah lesson.

A *haftarah* is recited each Sabbath and festival morning, immediately following the Torah reading. It is preceded and followed by special *haftarah* blessings.

3. כתובים KETUVIM

(literally, "writings") is the third section of the Hebrew Bible, Writings.

Ketuvim contains wisdom literature, poetry, songs, narrative, history, religious philosophy, and love hymns. It consists of twelve books.

1. תהלים Tehillim, Psalms: The book of Psalms is a collection of 150 prayers, many attributed to the authorship of King David. They include soul cries of anguish and joy, and poems and songs of praise to God.

Many psalms have been made part of Jewish worship services and appear in the prayerbook, for they embody the religious quest to praise, thank, and confront God. Other psalms are used as part of the liturgy during Jewish life-cycle ceremonies such as circumcisions, weddings, and especially funerals, for the ideas in the psalms reflect the thanksgiving, joy, anguish, bewilderment, and faith that are felt and expressed at such moments.

2. משלי Mishlei, Proverbs: The book of Proverbs contains short statements that teach a value or give advice about how to live.

3. איוב Iyov, Job: The book of Job tells the story of a man confronted by great suffering and how he responds with faith. It is a sublime essay on the meaning of good and evil.

Writings also contains five more books, known, collectively as מגילות *megillot* (singular, *megillah*), the scrolls. Each *megillah* is read in the synagogue on a particular Jewish holiday or commemoration. The five *megillot* are:

1. שיר השירים Shir Hashirim, Song of Songs: Song of Songs is a passionate love poem, telling of a man and a woman in the throes of spiritual and physical union. It is a symbolic metaphor for the love between God and the Jewish People.

Song of Songs is read in the synagogue on Passover, because Passover celebrates the exodus from Egypt, the time when the Hebrew slaves became the Jewish People. Tradition teaches that God manifests His love for the Jewish People by giving the gift of Torah. The commemoration of the giving of Torah is celebrated on the holiday of Shavuot (seven weeks after Passover), so Passover marks the beginning of the "love story"—the period of the "engagement" between God and the Jewish People, which will culminate in the "wedding" at Mt. Sinai, when the Torah is given. In addition, Passover is the springtime festival, when thoughts turn to renewal and love. Since Song of Songs is the love poem of the Bible, it is read on Passover.

2. רות Rut, Ruth: The book of Ruth is a testament of faith, a commitment to God and Torah.

Ruth is read in the synagogue on Shavuot, because the main events of the story take place during the Shavuot harvest season, and because Shavuot commemorates the giving of Torah at Mt. Sinai—the time when God gave law to the Jewish People, and they accepted it and made the commitment to live and to teach it. Since Ruth tells the story of a non-Jewish woman who sincerely and joyously accepts belief in God, observance of Torah law, and membership in the Jewish People, it is read on Shavuot.

3. איכה Eichah, Lamentations: The book of Lamentations bemoans the destruction of Jerusalem and holds out hope for restoration and return through repentance. Lamentations is read in the synagogue on Tishah B'Av because Tishah B'Av (the ninth day of the Hebrew month of Av) commemorates the destruction of the Holy Temple and the city of Jerusalem by the Babylonians in 586 B.C.E., and the exile of the Jewish People from the Land of Israel. (The rebuilt Temple was destroyed again on the ninth day of Av in the year 70 C.E. by the Romans.) Since Lamentations is the eyewitness account of the destruction of the Temple and Jerusalem, and the lament over the fate of the people, it is read on Tisha B'Av.

4. קהלת Kohelet, Ecclesiastes: The book of Ecclesiastes is a rather pessimistic and sometimes cynical essay on the meaning of existence and of the need for a plan for living with the highest purposes.

Ecclesiastes is read in the synagogue on Succot because Succot is the fall harvest festival, when the land gives up its produce and when planting for the next harvest is done. Succot celebrates and commemorates the never-ending cycle of life, death, and rebirth, and the continually unfolding process of creation and recreation.

Ecclesiastes is read on Succot because it speaks of the power of God and the place of humankind within the universe; of the purpose and the meaning of existence; and says that while "there is nothing new under the sun" (Ecclesiastes 1:9), "to every thing there is a season" (Ecclesiastes 3:1).

5. אסתר Ester, Esther: The book of Esther tells the story of loyalty to God and the strength of the Jewish People in the face of an oppressive tyrant.

Esther is read in the synagogue on Purim because Purim celebrates the happy and joyful victory of the Jewish People over the plot to destroy them at the hands of the evil Haman, chancellor of King Ahasuerus of Persia in (approximately, for the exact dates are impossible to ascertain) the late fifth century B.C.E. Since Esther tells the story of Purim, with the beautiful queen instrumental in foiling the plot against her people, it is read, with much festivity, on Purim.

There are four concluding historical books in Writings. They tell of the return from exile, the reestablishment of independence, and the rebuilding of the Holy Temple. They record Jewish history from 586 B.C.E. until approximately 300 B.C.E., a time of national renewal and relative calm.

1. דניאל Daniel, Daniel: The book of Daniel emphasizes that God is the ruler of all and that His power will prevail. It speaks of the merit of faithful Jews who are courageous and loyal, and it tells of messianic visions.

2. עזרא Ezra, Ezra: The book of Ezra records the return of the Jews from captivity in Babylonia, and the plans for the restoration and rebuilding of the Holy Temple. It affirms the covenant between God and the Jewish People and the primacy of Torah study and adherence to God's law.

3. נחמיה Nechemyah, Nechemiah: The book of Nechemiah records the rebuilding of the Holy Temple and the reestablishment of religious (sacrificial) practices. It records the institution of religious reforms and the enforcement of the laws of the Sabbath.

4. דברי הימים Divray Hayamim, Chronicles: There are two books of Chronicles, א Alef and ב Bet, or 1 and 2. The books of Chronicles are a complete review of Jewish history, from the creation of the world and humankind until the return to the Land of Israel and the rebuilding of the Holy Temple—paralleling the historical segments of Torah, the books of Samuel, and particularly the books of Kings.

4.   תנ"ך   TANACH

is the Hebrew name for the Hebrew Bible.

The Hebrew name for the Hebrew Bible is created by taking the first letter of each of the three sections of the Bible and making a word out of those three letters. (Technically, this is called an acronym. A good example in English is the word SCUBA, made up from the first letter of each of the words: Self-Contained Underwater Breathing Apparatus.):

T: for ת Torah
N: for נ Nevi'im
CH: for כ Ketuvim

The three letters ת נ and כ together form the Hebrew word תנ"ך Tanach. Note that the כ turns into a ך when it is the final letter of a Hebrew word. It looks different, but it is pronounced and sounds the same.

5.   תורה שבכתב   TORAH SHEBICHTAV

is the Written Torah.

According to tradition, God dictated the entire Torah (except for the very last part of the book of Deuteronomy) to Moses in the Sinai desert. Moses wrote down every word as it was given to him by God. Because the Torah is the exact word of God, it reflects God's will and word, His laws and commandments to humankind. It is the basic foundation for all Jewish law.

A more liberal interpretation of the Written Torah is that, rather than being dictated word for word by God, its words and ideas were written by many different people, over the course of many years. Since the Torah contains so many brilliant ideas about how people are to behave and act with each other, the Torah writers must have been Divinely inspired. That means that they were given extraordinary insight by God to do their thinking and writing. Eventually, one or more editors took all the words that had been written and all the stories that had been told and put them together in one book called the Torah.

The traditional and liberal views of the authorship of Torah can best be illustrated by the following example. The first chapter of Genesis describes the six days of creation:

On the first day, God created light and separated the light from the darkness.

On the second day, God separated the waters from each other and separated the waters from the sky.

On the third day, God separated the dry land—called earth—from the sea, and created trees, plants and vegetation.

On the fourth day, God created the sun and the moon and the stars.

On the fifth day, God created fish and birds.

On the sixth day, God created animals, and then God said, "Let us make man in our image, after our likeness. . . ."

"And God created man in His image, in the image of God, created He them; male and female, created He them." (Genesis 1:26–27)

The beginning of the second chapter of Genesis says:

"The heaven and earth were finished and all their array. On the seventh day, God finished the work He had been doing and He ceased from all the work He had done." (Genesis 2:1–2)

Thus we learn in the first chapter and in the first few verses of the second chapter of Genesis that God created the universe and everything in it in six days. On the sixth day, man and woman—the crowning work of creation—were created *together* ("male and female, created He *them.*") Then God was finished with all His work of creating, and on the seventh day, He rested.

That would seem to be the end of the story, but the second chapter of Genesis later says:

"The Lord God took the man and placed him in the Garden of Eden. . . .

The Lord God said, 'It is not good for man to be alone; I will make a fitting helper for him. . . .' So, the Lord God cast a deep sleep upon the man and, while he slept, He took one of his ribs and closed up the flesh at the spot. And the Lord God fashioned the rib that He had taken from the man into a woman, and He brought her to the man. Then, the man said, 'This one at last is the bone of my bone and the flesh of my flesh. This one shall be called Woman, for from Man was she taken.'" (Genesis 2:15, 18, 21–23)

What is going on here?

It seems as if there are two versions of the creation story. In the first, man and woman are created together. In the second, first man is created and then woman is created, fashioned from the rib of the already existing man.

How can this be? How can the Bible—which is supposed to be the completely true word of God—have two different and seemingly contradictory accounts of creation?

Those who accept the traditional view of the authorship of Torah—that God is the sole Author—explain that the second version is simply a detailed description of what was summarized in the opening version. The first account states the simple fact of creation, while the second account fills in the specific details of how creation took place. It is as if a television announcer gives the news headline during a program break and then says, "Details at eleven."

Those who accept the liberal interpretation of the authorship of Torah—that there were many authors, writing over the course of many years, and that eventually one or more editors compiled the final version of Torah—point to the creation story as a perfect example for proving their position.

The advocates of the liberal interpretation contend that there are two differing stories of the creation of man and woman because there were two different accounts written by two different authors.

In the first account—where man and woman are created together—the act of creation is attributed to God, in Hebrew, אלהים Elohim.

In the second account—where man is created first and then woman is created from his rib—the act of creation is attributed to the Lord God, in Hebrew אלהים יהוה YHWH Elohim.

Since both accounts had achieved popularity and sanctity in the folklore of the Jewish People, the Torah editor(s) could not choose between them, and thus included both in the final version of the Torah.

This theory of the multiple authorship of Torah was offered in the late nineteenth century by German theologian Julius Wellhausen (preceded in formulation, most notably, by Karl Heinrich Graf and Wilhelm Vatke, based on the earlier work of

Witter, Astruc, and Eichhorn). Called the Documentary Hypothesis, the theory identified four distinctly different strands of Torah authorship. Wellhausen calls them J, E, P, and D:

J is for *YHWH* (the German J sounds like the English Y). These texts call God "Lord God."

E is for *Elohim*. These texts call God "God."

P is for *Priest*. These texts are attributed to writers from the Priestly family.

D is for *Deuteronomy*. These texts are attributed to a writer (or writers) who reviews and recapitulates history and laws.

The four strands are intermingled throughout the Torah, sometimes within the same sentence.

So there are two ways to look at the authorship of Torah. The traditional view is that God is the sole Author. The liberal view is that there were a number of authors and one or more editors who were all inspired by God.

Whichever view is believed and accepted, one thing is clear. The Torah is the manifestation of the will of God. It therefore offers great insight into human behavior and—through its ethical and ritual laws—shows a way to live that insures human dignity and justice, combined with compassion and love, and challenges each human being to reach the height of his or her potential.

The Written Torah is the basic, core document, the constitution, of the Jewish People.

AN ESSAY ON BELIEVING THE BIBLE

Bible stories are part of the collective consciousness of the Western world.

Religious or not, from earliest childhood, we have all heard the tales of Adam and Eve, Noah and the Ark, Abraham, Isaac, and Jacob, Moses in the Bulrushes, the Burning Bush, the Ten Plagues, the Splitting of the Red Sea, the Ten Commandments, the Golden Calf, Joshua Who Fought the Battle of Jericho, David and Goliath, Samson and Delilah, the Valley of the Dry Bones, the Fiery Chariot, Daniel in the Lion's Den.

When we are young, Bible stories fascinate and thrill us: they excite our imagination and give us larger-than-life heroic playmates. But when we get older, the same Bible stories accost our sense of reality and test our logical rationality. A bush that burned but was not consumed? A river that turned to blood? A sea that turned into dry land? A sun that stood still? A giant slain by a slingshot? A man's strength ebbed by a haircut? Hard to believe. Harder to accept.

How you relate to the Bible, what you believe, how much you accept, depends on a number of factors.

THEOLOGICAL VIEWPOINTS

If you truly believe that the Bible is the exact word of God, that God is not only Hero, but Author as well, then you have no problem with the text. Your fundamentalist view convinces you that if God wrote it, then it must be true. Belief in authorship means belief in the account. So for you, the stories and miracles of the Bible happened just as they were recorded.

The question of belief in the Bible is more complicated for those who accept the notion that the Torah was written over a long period of time by many Divinely inspired authors, and is—in some ways—an accurate account of the encounter between God and the Jewish People.

Then there are some modern scholars who claim that the Bible is *in no way* a historical document, that its stories and its lessons are wholly reflective of the imagination of its writers.

DEFINING "PROOF"

How do you *know* something? What constitutes proof for you?

Many require rational, logical, scientific evidence: You know only that which can be demonstrated, quantified, proven, and statistically confirmed through accepted scientific principles of research and study.

Some people demand existential proof: You must personally experience an event or a conversation to know that it happened. You saw it, heard it, read it, did it, so that makes it real for you.

Other people will take the word of someone they trust as proof enough. For example, you trust your mother. So if she tells you that she saw it, heard it, read it, did it, you believe her.

For many, the source of knowledge need not be personally known. A book, a newspaper article, a secondhand account, a videotape, an old newsreel, are all accepted for their reports, as long as the author is considered trustworthy and as long as possible bias and misrepresentation, manipulation, and tampering are accounted for.

In modern times tremendous advances in technology have allowed us to see and experience faraway events almost firsthand, without having to rely on secondary accounts. But modern technology has also meant a greater ability to manipulate and tamper with sources of information, so the challenge of evaluation and discernment is now greater than ever before.

Still, most of us accept sources of knowledge that are not personally known, for it would be far too limiting to demand of ourselves only experiential or firsthand knowledge. The scope of our lives would be far too narrow if we believe and accept as true only that which we can see, hear, or do.

So, if you accept portrayals of George Washington (1776) and the accounts of John Smith and Pocahontas (1620), why not also accept the accounts of Christopher Columbus (1492)? Macbeth (1057)? Mohammed (632)? Constantine the Great (337)? Nero (62)? Jesus (1)? Julius Caesar (44 B.C.E.)? Sophocles (406 B.C.E.)? Homer (900 B.C.E.)? Moses (1250 B.C.E.)?

THE PROOF OF TORAH

The only difference in how you *know* about Moses and how you *know* about George Washington is in the amount of time that has elapsed between his life and yours.

And actually, that difference should heighten your acceptance and belief rather than lessen it.

Today we "drown" in paper; we are "Xeroxed to death." Everyone with a pencil, a sheet of paper, and a copy machine calls himself an author. In ancient times, however, writing was rare and precious. Anything that was written down had to be useful or important; anything that was purposely preserved was precious and valuable.

Torah is like that: preserved and cherished, because of its importance and veracity.

If Torah had been lost 2,500 years ago, and if tomorrow archaeologists discovered a complete Torah Scroll under the sands of the desert, it would be immediately hailed as definitive history and sacred writ.

That we have had Torah for all this time—though it has been subject to our constant critical analysis and all too often taken for granted—makes it no less deserving of our acclaim and affection as historically accurate and spiritually uplifting.

TORAH'S RESPONSE TO SKEPTICISM

The Torah writers knew that we would still be skeptical.

Do you remember what the Children of Israel ate during their trek through the desert? The Torah tells that God provided manna, a sweet, sticky, seedlike substance that fell from the heavens each day. This manna, the Torah says, was enough to nourish and sustain the multitudes for forty years as they journeyed to the Promised Land.

Manna? Food falling from the heavens? Every day (except on the Sabbath) for forty years? It seems hard to believe. It stretches the imagination and calls into serious question the credibility of Torah.

But God knew that, from the distance of the millennia, we would be dubious about this report. And God knew that our doubt about manna could lead to mistrust and disbelief in all of Torah.

So God told Moses, "'Let an *omer*-ful [a measure] of it [manna] be kept throughout your generations, that they may see the bread with which I fed you when I brought you forth from Egypt.' And Moses said to Aaron, 'Take a jar and put an *omer*-full of manna in it and put it before the Lord [next to the ark in the Tabernacle] and keep it throughout the generations'" (Exodus 16:32–33).

The jarful of manna will be proof. When later generations see manna with their own eyes, all doubt will disappear, all accounts will be believed.

So where is the jar of manna? Where can we see it? When can we affirm Torah with our own eyes?

The manna is missing.

But here is what might have happened to it. If Aaron followed the instructions of Moses exactly, then he put the manna in the Ark of the Covenant, along with the Tablets of the Law. When the Holy Temple was built in Jerusalem, the ark, the tablets, the manna, and the other accoutrements of the sanctuary—including the eternal flame and the seven-branched *menorah*—were placed in the center of the Temple.

Could these sacred ritual objects have survived the Babylonian assault on the Holy Temple in 586 B.C.E.? Perhaps they were hidden away, buried deep within caverns and tunnels beneath the Temple Mount, waiting, to this day, to be discovered by modern-day explorers. But most likely the manna—along with all the other ritual objects—was lost when the first Holy Temple was destroyed.

However, if the manna and the other sacred objects did survive the Babylonian destruction, then we can well speculate about what happened to them.

In 70 C.E. the Romans sacked Jerusalem, destroyed the city and the rebuilt Holy Temple, sent the people into exile, and carried off the spoils. To commemorate their great victory and to pay tribute to their leader, the Romans built the Arch of Titus—still standing in Rome today, located between the Colosseum and the Roman Forum. Carved in bas relief on the arch are the spoils being carried off from Jerusalem—particularly a large and clear depiction of the seven-branched *menorah*.

It stands to reason that if the Romans took the *menorah* from its holy spot, they also took the other precious things. Perhaps this *menorah* was a duplicate, fashioned to replicate the original *menorah* that had been destroyed by the Babylonians. But if the original *menorah* had somehow survived the Babylonian assault, then it is possible that other sacred ritual objects had also survived the Babylonians. The jar of manna may very well have been carried off to Rome along with the *menorah*. Surely, these sacred objects were subsequently destroyed; but once they may have been carried off from Jerusalem in triumph.

MODERN SCIENTIFIC EVIDENCE

The manna is gone, but much else in the Bible has been proven—both by modern archaeological investigation and by sheer luck.

Here is the best example of sheer luck. In 1947 an Arab shepherd boy was tending his flock in the hot, dry area around the Dead Sea in the south of Israel. Trying to locate some sheep that had wandered off, he threw pebbles into the steep cliffs and caverns. A plinking sound sent him climbing and exploring, and there in the caves he discovered earthenware jars (perhaps like the one that once held the manna) containing 2,000-year-old scrolls of the Bible.

Now known as the Dead Sea Scrolls, these delicate but well-preserved parchments confirm what we already intuitively knew: The Bible text we have today is virtually identical to the text of antiquity.

The discovery of the Dead Sea Scrolls was striking and dramatic, but time and time again during these past two centuries, archaeologists digging in the sands of the desert and through the layers of Middle Eastern civilizations have found remains that absolutely confirm what the Bible says. From the smallest of objects to entire cities, the Bible is verified with precision and accuracy.

Here is one of the most intriguing stories of an archaeological find. During the summer of 1981, the most popular movie in the United States was *Raiders of the Lost Ark,* a thriller about an international search for the Ark of the Covenant, containing the Ten Commandments. Audiences flocked to see this flight of cinematic fancy.

At the very same time, a true thriller was taking place in the north of Israel, in the Upper Galilee, in a town called Nabratein, near the Lebanese border and the

Golan Heights. There a husband and wife archaeological team, Eric and Carol Meyers of Duke University, discovered an ark dated between 205 C.E. and 305 C.E., making it ten centuries older than any other ark found to date.

The Meyers's stunning find is admittedly more than 1,000 years younger than the Ark of the Covenant (and made of stone, while the Ark of the Covenant was made of more easily decomposing wood). But truth is stranger than fiction. While American film audiences got caught up in make-believe, archaeological researchers were finding the real thing.

To be sure, everything the Bible describes has not been unearthed. But nothing that has been uncovered denies or even contradicts the Bible.

Modern archaeology will not find all that the Bible describes. But if no stone is left unturned and no grain of sand is left unmoved, there is always the possibility of finding more and more. For archaeologists, the rallying cry will always be, "Not yet. We haven't found it—not yet. But if we keep digging, someday we may. And we will continue to prove that modern science reveals and confirms ancient truths."

UNDERSTANDING TORAH'S PURPOSE
MEANS UNDERSTANDING TORAH

The very best way to believe the Bible is to step out of your twentieth-century world-view. Suspend your usual intellectual demand for rational, verifiable scientific proof and see Torah through the eyes of those who originally received it.

B'nai Yisrael, the Children of Israel, were a tribe of nomads wandering in the desert. They came from hundreds of years of slavery. They were a folk-tribe, related only by stories of a great-, great-, great-, great- . . . grandfather named Abraham, who had found a new God, and by their redeemer, Moses, who purported to speak in God's name. They were uneducated, illiterate, naive.

To this unsophisticated, innocent people would be given a set of ethical laws so refined, so advanced, that human relations would be forever enhanced and elevated.

How were these people, whose very lives depended on their docile submission to human taskmasters and their recognition of gods of wood and stone, supposed to relate to the one, unique, invisible God, who tolerates no idols or images? How were these people, who as slaves were used to nearly constant labor, supposed to under-stand the concept—yet less the observance—of a day of rest? How were these beaten, downtrodden people supposed to understand the harm of envy? How were these people, who had to beg and grovel for meager food, supposed to understand the demand of sharing with others?

They had neither the intellectual capacity nor the emotional maturity to be told in direct, concise, terms what God offered to them or expected from them. So

Torah used a simple method to teach its wise lessons. It couched its momentous values and profound philosophy in easily understood stories, parables, allegories, and metaphors.

So much of literature works just this way. Aesop's fables, Grimm's fairy tales, and Mother Goose rhymes all use the same methodology. A very important lesson is expressed in an easily understandable, enjoyable story geared to the level of the hearer—a two-, five-, or nine-year-old. Rather than with intellectual, philosophical dissertation, the point is made, the moral of the story is taught, in a gentle, pleasant tale.

Torah does the same thing.

The nomadic desert dwellers would have had a hard time understanding deep philosophical discourse, so God's lessons to them were contained in engaging, exciting stories that captured their imagination and sustained their interest. The moral—not the metaphor, or even the factual account in which it is wrapped—is what is important.

Does it matter if the world were really created in six days? Does it matter if the Sea of Reeds really parted? Does it matter if the voice of God thundered over Sinai?

No.

What matters is that God *did* create the world—in the same creative-evolutionary pattern described in Torah—regardless of the exact time sequence. What matters is that *B'nai Yisrael* were on one side of the Sea, and that God brought them to the other side. What matters is that out of the desert experience, God's will was understood and articulated in the ethical and ritual laws of Torah.

And what matters is that the point is made; the moral of the story is clear.

Bible stories are just that—stories that employ all the best and most effective literary forms and devices in order to convey essential ideas. And they succeed at their purpose: From out of the compelling stories and delightful tales, we see the kernels of truth, we learn the lessons and values that Torah teaches.

Torah is about values. It is God's ethical mandate, the moral code for how we are to live. Torah stories offer those values in gentle, easy to understand, easy to digest doses.

And Torah is about God, the superhero, who does wonders for His people. Torah stories tell of God's larger-than-life accomplishments so that *B'nai Yisrael* in the desert, and we, their descendants in future generations—and the pagan world, which had yet to meet God—could know Him and come to accept His greatness.

BIBLE THEN, BIBLE NOW

The Bible is an enduring treasure.

In it is our past, for it is the record of the encounter between God and the Jewish People.

And from it comes our future, for it invites us to ongoing dialogue with God: to seek and affirm faith, to hear continuing revelation, and to add our own explanations and interpretations to the ever-unfolding wisdom of Torah.

By understanding the source of the Bible, by realizing the purpose of the Bible, by believing the truths of the Bible, we can explore all of Judaism, which was born and is rooted in the Bible.

The birth-gift of the Bible is a great inheritance.

Its message is now ours to learn.

6. THE APOCRYPHA

At a certain point in time, the Hebrew Bible had to be canonized. That means that the books that would be included in the Bible had to be chosen, the selected books had to be placed in an agreed order, and all other books—which might have had the possibility of being included—had to be permanently excluded. The Bible had to be complete, with its "back cover," its final form, fixed for all time.

The task of canonizing the Bible fell to the Rabbinic sages in the first century of the Common Era. They determined the criteria and selected what would be included in or excluded from the Bible.

They decided, first, that true prophecy had ended with the prophet Malachi, so that any "prophetic works" written after his time (approximately 450 B.C.E.) would be excluded. They further decided that the teachings of the book of Ezra would be the latest teachings included in the Bible. Thus any work written after approximately 400 B.C.E. would also be excluded. Finally, they had to decide on the validity, the sanctity, and the appropriateness of a number of books. Some met their criteria and were included; some did not and were excluded.

The canonization process was completed in approximately 90 C.E. to 100 C.E. (although some scholars contend that the canonization was not complete until approximately 250 C.E. or 300 C.E.), and the Hebrew Bible, as it is known until this day, was in its final form.

The books that were excluded from the biblical canon came to be known collectively as the Apocrypha, a Greek word that means "hidden," for these books were to be "hidden away" from the average Jew (through their exclusion from the canon) lest they be considered to have equal status with the books of the Bible.

The best-known of the books of the Apocrypha are the two books of the Maccabees. These books tell the story of the events of the Syrian occupation of the Land of Israel, the restrictions placed against the Jews, the military uprising led by the Maccabees, and the rededication of the Holy Temple—the events that would lead to the establishment of the festival of Chanukah. Since these events took place in 165 B.C.E.—well after the time of Ezra, the end point for biblical inclusion—the books of the Maccabees are not included in the Bible, and Chanukah is the only ancient festival not mentioned in the Bible.

Another well-known book of the Apocrypha is Ecclesiasticus, or the Wisdom of Ben Sirah, which contains poetry and wise proverbs. The other books of the Apocrypha are Esdras, Tobit, Judith, Additions to Esther, the Wisdom of Solomon, Baruch, the Epistle to Jeremiah, Susanna, Bel and the Dragon, and The Prayer of Manasseh.

Since the translation of the Hebrew Bible into Greek (known as the Septuagint) took place before the Rabbinic sages finally canonized the Bible, the Septuagint version of the Bible (which forms the basis for the Latin translation, the Vulgate) contains the Apocrypha. Thus the Catholic Bible (which is based on the Greek and Latin translations) contains the Apocrypha. Historically, however, Protestant Bibles (except for some study editions) have not included the Apocrypha.

The books of the Apocrypha—with the possible exception of the books of the Maccabees and the Wisdom of Ben Sirah—have had little place in Judaism. Nonetheless, their origins and their role in the process of the canonization of the Bible make them of historical interest and import.

7. תורה שבעל פה TORAH SHEB'AL PEH

is the Oral Torah.

Tradition teaches that when Moses wrote down the Written Torah, God also gave him a second Torah—one that was not written down, but was told to Moses orally. This Oral Torah was passed down, by word of mouth, to each new leader in each new generation.

According to tradition, God knew that the laws He was giving in the Written Torah would not be sufficient when the Jewish People were no longer wanderers in the desert. The laws of the Written Torah did not cover situations that the people would face once they lived in towns and villages, once they were farmers or businessmen, instead of nomads; once they would set up permanent places of worship instead of portable tabernacles in the desert. However, the people did not have the capacity to look into and understand the future, and therefore they would not understand any laws given in their time and place that applied to a future time and place. So God told Moses the laws for the future, but they were not written down.

Instead, they were told to each new leader, until the time and place came when the new laws were needed. Then the leader of the moment would tell the people the laws—the Oral Torah—and the new laws would finally be written down and preserved. Because the laws had been transmitted orally, to fallible human beings, the possibility for error—or at least differing versions—always existed. These differing interpretative versions of the oral laws became the basis for the scholarly arguments, disputes, and debates found in the later Jewish law literature.

The liberal interpretation agrees that not all the laws that were needed for the future were written in the Torah. However, this interpretation does not think that

God transmitted the Oral Torah to Moses any more than it thinks that God dictated the Written Torah to Moses.

Instead, the liberal interpretation believes that those who wrote the Written Torah gave laws and commands that were appropriate and sufficient for the time and place in which they lived. They could have no way of knowing what the future would bring. Later, when the Jewish People lived in different times and different places, and the laws of the desert no longer covered every situation or need, the great leaders, thinkers, and sages of the time came together to create and write new law. The law had to be created within the framework of the Torah, but it would address the questions and meet the new needs and requirements of the time.

The liberal interpretation of the Oral Law still keeps the Torah as the absolute constitution of the Jewish People. However, instead of seeing the Oral Law as simply an extension of the Written Law, as tradition suggests, the liberal interpretation sees the Oral Law as the amendments to the constitution and the case law that derives from it.

Both the traditional and the liberal interpreters agree that the Oral Law must not violate the Written Law, because just as in the process of law in the United States, no law can be created that is unconstitutional.

Here is an example of a question that the Oral Law would have to address: The Torah prohibits the lighting of fire on the Sabbath. In Torah times, in the desert, this meant that the huge bonfire used for light and warmth could not be lit or stoked on the Sabbath. But what happens when the people no longer live in the desert and use campfires, but instead live in houses in cities and use oil lamps? Does the law prohibiting lighting the bonfire in the desert also apply to lighting an oil lamp in a house? And what about today, when we use electric light bulbs? Does the law prohibiting lighting a bonfire in the desert also apply to turning on an electric light?

The articulation of the Oral Law marked a sweeping change in Judaism—the beginning of a whole new era of Jewish life.

Biblical Judaism—which began with the making of the covenant between God and Abraham, was highlighted by the giving of the law at Sinai and the entrance into the Promised Land, and continued with the centrality of the Holy Temple as the place of worship and the prophets as God's messengers—was over.

No longer would God's word be ascertained though prophecy, with individuals claiming Divine revelation. Instead, God's word would come only through the rabbis and the sages—who, according to their own proclamation, would be the sole inheritors and transmitters of God's continuing revelation. Judaism as it had been known in the Biblical Period was entirely overhauled and changed, and the new era—Rabbinic Judaism—began and continues to this day, characterized by the sages' articulation of ever-developing, ever-evolving law.

In addition to the vast changes revolving around the law, the early Rabbinic Period (200 B.C.E.–200 C.E.) was fraught with both internal and external challenges and upheaval that threatened Judaism's very existence.

In this 400-year period, the people were oppressed and persecuted by the Greeks and Romans, and the Holy Temple was desecrated. The Romans conquered Jerusalem (63 B.C.E.) and Jewish rule of the country ended (37 B.C.E.). The birth and death of Jesus (1 C.E. and 36 C.E.) served as the catalyst for the formation of a new and powerful religion. The Holy Temple was destroyed; the place and mode of Jewish worship was lost; any hope for the restoration of Jewish sovereignty ended; and the people were sent off into exile (70 C.E.). The final attempts to resist the enemy (Masada, 73 C.E., and the Bar Kochba rebellion, 132–135 C.E.) failed, and the last vestige of hope of regaining the Land of Israel was crushed.

Any one of these traumas might have been enough to decimate the Jewish People. But instead of being bowed and broken, they rose up to meet the challenges and reconstitute themselves as a new and stronger people and faith community.

In response to the Greek and Roman occupation, the Maccabees mounted a military uprising to conquer the enemy and restore the Holy Temple (165 B.C.E.). Their stunning victory led to the establishment of the Hasmonean Dynasty. The Hasmoneans eventually won full political independence from Syria (140 B.C.E.) and established a free and independent Jewish State—the Second Jewish Commonwealth.

For the first time in almost 450 years, the Jewish People were once again politically independent in the Jewish Land. This was a time of unprecedented geographical expansion and population growth, and of tremendous religious, cultural, and social reform and development. Later, in response to growing foreign presence, the ruling Hasmonean Dynasty invited the Romans to govern Israel, in an attempt to mollify and work with the foreign power (37 B.C.E.). The ill-conceived attempt failed, but at least they tried.

In response to the birth and growth of Christianity, the rabbis and sages (through the Oral Law) articulated new Jewish theology and newly developing ideas about God.

In response to the destruction of the more than 1,000-year mode of worship, prayer was developed to replace animal sacrifice, and the synagogue was developed to replace the Holy Temple.

In response to the loss of the priesthood—the central religious functionaries, engaged in the central religious activities—an academy of learning was established

(70 C.E.) where the study of sacred texts would become the supreme expression of Jewish life, and scholar-rabbis would take the place of the cultic priests.

In response to the exile, the rabbis and sages articulated new law (in final compilation by 200 C.E.) that would help the Jewish People survive and flourish as guests in host countries, while at the same time, the few who were permitted to remain in the Land of Israel would learn to maintain Jewish life under foreign rule.

In response to the final failures to keep their land from the control of their enemies, the Jewish People celebrated those "last stands" as the enduring symbol of the hope and promise of eventual restoration and return to their land.

In the early, formative years of Rabbinic Judaism, the rabbis and sages proved that flexibility and adaptation would be the new hallmark of Jewish survival and continuing growth. By responding with such creativity to the challenges they faced— some would say by totally revamping Judaism as it was then known—the rabbis saved Judaism from ruination and possible oblivion.

Rabbinic Judaism has served Judaism and the Jewish People well for these 2,000 years and more, by applying ongoing principles of adaptability and change to meet new and potentially threatening situations—whether caused by internal debate or external challenge.

Because of the massive changes that have taken place in Jewish life and in the secular world in the past 250 years, one of the greatest questions facing contemporary Judaism is whether Rabbinic Judaism has now played out its purposes and its effectiveness—as Biblical Judaism once did—and whether we now stand on the brink of a third major era of Jewish life.

Necessity and time will tell.

The prospects—as they were when Biblical Judaism gave way to Rabbinic Judaism—are both frightening and exhilarating.

8.   משנה   MISHNAH

is the first compilation of the Oral Law.

The laws and ideas that are in the Mishnah were compiled over a period of approximately 400 years, from 200 B.C.E. until 200 C.E. At the beginning of the third century of the Common Era, the various laws were put together in one collection by the editor, Rabbi Yehuda HaNasi, Judah the Prince.

The Mishnah, which collects all the Jewish legal material from the post-Torah era, is divided into Six Orders (major chapters) each of which is subdivided into tractates (or books.) There are sixty-three separate tractates in the Mishnah. The titles of the Six Orders of the Mishnah reflect the wide variety of issues that the Mishnah addresses:

1. זרעים Zera'im, Seeds: deals with agriculture and tithing in the Land of Israel during the time of the Holy Temple (eleven tractates). The first tractate of the Order, called ברכות Berachot, Blessings, deals with a different subject: prayer in the synagogue (which is the way God was worshiped after the destruction of the Holy Temple) and blessings for various occasions.

2. מועד Mo'ed, Festivals: deals with the laws of observing the Sabbath and the festivals (twelve tractates).

3. נשים Nashim, Women: deals primarily with the laws of betrothal, marriage, and divorce (seven tractates).

4. נזיקין Nezikin, Damages: deals with civil and criminal law. This Order contains one tractate of an entirely different nature: פרקי אבות Pirkae Avot, The Sayings (or Ethics) of the Fathers, is a collection of powerful ethical teachings that has been studied with devotion and love from the time it was first compiled (ten tractates).

5. קדושים Kedoshim, Holy Things: deals with the rules of bringing sacrifices to the Holy Temple (eleven tractates).

6. תהרות Taharot, Purifications: deals with laws of ritual purity and impurity (twelve tractates).

The Rabbinic sages who are quoted in the Mishnah are called the תנאים Tannaim, the "Teachers."

9. גמרא GEMARA

is a compilation of the discussions, interpretations, explanations, and theological arguments about the Mishnah.

In the 400-year period from the final editing of the Mishnah in 200 C.E. until about 600 C.E., new situations arose that the Mishnah had not addressed. In response, the Rabbinic sages of the time articulated new interpretations and new laws.

Unlike the Mishnah, which is straightforward statements of law, the Gemara includes legal debate, the personal stories of many of the sages, ethical insights, folklore, history, biography, theology, and homily (sermon-lessons) all woven together. The Gemara, therefore, contains both הלכה halachah, Jewish law, and אגדה aggadah, Jewish stories and legends.

Actually, *two* Gemaras developed simultaneously. One Gemara developed in the Land of Israel, compiled by the Rabbinic sages who were the descendants of those Jews who remained in Israel after the Holy Temple was destroyed in 70 C.E. The other

Gemara was developed in Babylonia, compiled by the Rabbinic sages who were the descendants of those Jews who lived in what had become the center of Jewish life outside the Land of Israel in the years following the destruction and the exile.

There is Gemara for many, but not all, of the tractates of the Mishnah. Some Mishnaic tractates have Gemara from both Israel and Babylonia. Some Mishnaic tractates have Gemara from either Israel or Babylonia, but not both.

For example, there is extensive Gemara from Israel to the first Order of the Mishnah—Zera'im, Seeds. This is because those living in the Land of Israel had to develop laws for a Jewish agricultural society based in an Israel that was no longer a free and independent state, and which was subject to the law of the ruling power. There is, however, no Babylonian Gemara for this Order (with the exception of the first tractate, which deals with a separate subject) because laws for agriculture in the Land of Israel were of less concern to those living outside Israel.

The Rabbinic sages who are quoted in the Gemara are called אמוראים Amoraim, the "Interpreters."

The Gemara in Israel was developed until approximately 350 C.E. to 400 C.E., and was compiled into a final form by 500 C.E. The Gemara in Babylonia developed until approximately 500 C.E. Discussions and debates over its final form took another hundred years. So, at its final compilation, around 600 C.E. the Gemara encompasses a 400-year period, between 200 C.E. and 600 C.E.

10. תלמוד TALMUD

is the combined Mishnah and Gemara.

The Talmud is often referred to as the ש"ס SHAS, from the first initials of the Hebrew words ששה סדרים Sheeshah Sedarim, which means Six Orders: the Six Orders of the Mishnah on which the Talmud is based.

Because there are two Gemaras, one from the Land of Israel and one from Babylonia, there are two Talmuds.

The תלמוד ירושלמי Talmud Yerushalmi, the Jerusalem (or Palestinian) Talmud, contains the Mishnah, along with the Gemara, from the Land of Israel.

The תלמוד בבלי Talmud Bavli, the Babylonian Talmud, contains the Mishnah, along with the Gemara, from Babylonia.

A tractate (or volume) of Talmud is called a מסכת masechet (plural, masechtot). The Babylonian Talmud has thirty-seven masechtot; the Jerusalem Talmud has thirty-nine masechtot.

Since, from the time of the compilation of the Talmuds, most Jews have lived outside the Land of Israel, the Babylonian Talmud is the more important of the two Talmuds, because it deals with issues that have relevance to the majority of Jews.

There are fifteen additional tractates of Talmud, known as the Minor Tractates, which were compiled after the Babylonian Talmud was completed (ca. 600 C.E.). Sometimes they are printed as an addendum to the text of the Babylonian Talmud; sometimes they are printed in a separate book.

The Talmud is a massive collection of legal interpretation, case law, and legal precedents, along with history, biography, ethical teachings, Jewish thought, and story-legends.

Sometimes the arguments in Talmud are difficult to follow because the discussions often wander very far from the starting point before returning to the original question. Also, the editors who compiled the final version of the Talmuds arranged the arguments of the Rabbinic sages according to the subject matter under discussion, with little regard for when the particular sage lived.

Thus in two succeeding lines of a Gemara in the Talmud, two sages who lived hundreds of years apart seem to be arguing with and responding to each other over a particular issue. It is as if a book discussing principles of U.S. law had President Washington's and President Clinton's statements about a particular issue following one after the other, in seeming discussion and debate, even though one president had died long before the other was born, and they lived in vastly different times and governed under vastly different circumstances.

Yet even with its apparent depth and difficulty, even with its incredible scope, even though Jewish law continued to evolve, and even though a number of other compilations of Jewish law have since been written, the Talmud remains the basic and central document of postbiblical Jewish law.

Talmud is studied for the practical applications of its laws; for its mind-expanding challenges in logic and reasoning; for its total immersion in Jewish concerns; for its wisdom and insights into the human experience; and for its own sake—for the simple love of learning and growing.

Following the compilation of the Talmud, the heads of the Talmudic Academies in Babylonia were looked to as the authorities and spiritual guides of the Jewish People. They were called גאונים *Geonim* (singular: *Gaon*), meaning "pride," "genius," or "outstanding scholar" (based on Psalm 47:5, "He chose our heritage for us, the pride/genius of Jacob whom He loved"). The period of the *Geonim* lasted from approximately 600 C.E. until approximately 1000 C.E.

11. פרושים   PERUSHIM

are the commentaries to the Bible and the Talmud.

Beginning in the Middle Ages, great thinkers and scholars wrote commentary to both the Bible and the Talmud in order to explain, interpret, and elucidate the text and its meaning.

These commentaries became so important to understanding the text, and so popular with students of Bible and Talmud, that learning commentaries is now considered an integral part of learning the text.

The best-known and most renowned commentator, who wrote massive commentary on both the Bible and the Talmud—and whose commentary is now the classical standard with which every text is studied—is Rabbi Shlomo ben Yitzchak of France (1040–1105), known as Rashi. Rashi is an acronym taken from the initials of his name: *Rav* (Rabbi) *Sh*lomo ben (son of) *I*saac (Yitzchak).

Throughout the centuries, up to and including modern times, many illustrious and distinguished commentators have added new and unique understanding, insight, and interpretation to the study of Bible. The commentaries of a number of these classical sage-teachers often appear in printed copies of the Bible along with the biblical text and the commentary of Rashi.

One of the best-known approaches to explicating Bible is called פרדס *PARDES* (literally, "orchard"), which is an acronym for a way of interpreting Bible. The invitation is to enter the "orchard," the beautiful "garden" of understanding God's word and will. Biblical interpretation is to be done on four levels:

1. פ *pay,* which stands for פשט *p'shat,* the simple, literal meaning of the text.
2. ר *resh,* which stands for רמז *remez,* the hint, the underlying, interpretive meaning of the text.
3. ד *dalet,* which stands for דרש *d'rash,* the homiletical, moral lesson of the text.
4. ס *samach,* which stands for סוד *sod,* the hidden, mysterious, mystical meaning of the text.

Taken together, these four levels of reading and commenting on the text offer the way toward deep and profound understanding of the meaning and purpose of Bible.

Other prominent commentators on the Talmud include Rashi's descendants and disciples (including his grandsons), whose commentaries are known, collectively, as טוספות *Tosaphot,* The Additions, written in France and Germany between the twelfth and fourteenth centuries.

Throughout the Middle Ages, centers of Talmud study were established throughout North Africa, Spain, and a number of places in Europe. Great talmudic scholars added—and to this day continue to add—to the commentary and explanation of the text. The great scholars and teachers from the tenth to the fifteenth centuries are known as ראשונים *Rishonim,* the First Ones. The great scholars and teachers from the sixteenth century on are known as אחרונים *Acharonim,* the Latter (or the Last) Ones.

12.   משנה תורה   MISHNAH TORAH

is a code of Jewish law,
written by the great sage Moses Maimonides, in the year 1180.

Moses Maimonides was born in Cordoba, Spain, in 1135, and died in Cairo, Egypt, in 1204. He is buried in Tiberias, in Israel. He is known as the Rambam, taken from the initials of his name, *Rabbi Moshe ben* (son of) *Maimon.* He was the greatest Jewish authority of the Middle Ages, writing not only this massive code of law, but also an intricate, far-ranging philosophical work called *The Guide to the Perplexed.*

The Mishnah Torah (sometimes known as יד החזקה Yad Hachazakah, the Strong Hand,) was written when Maimonides lived in Egypt. It was written in order to update the law of the Talmud and make it clear and concise for the Jews of the time. It consists of fourteen books, each one dealing with a separate subject in the Jewish legal system. The contents of the fourteen books can be grouped into four major subject headings: on God and humankind; on the life of the individual; on religion and ritual law; and on civil and criminal law.

13.   ארבעה טורים   ARBA'AH TURIM

(literally, "Four Rows") is a compilation of Jewish law,
written by Jacob ben Asher in Toledo, Spain, in 1475.

Ben Asher felt that most all of the rulings of Jewish law were open to differences of opinion and debate. So he sought to spell out, clearly and concisely, the laws as they were to be observed and followed by each individual Jew.

The Arba'ah Turim, known simply as the טור Tur, gets its name—The Four Rows—from its structure. There are four major books, each one dealing with a different phase of Jewish law and life:

1. אורח חיים Orach Chayim, The Path of Life deals with the laws and liturgy of prayer and festivals.

2. יורה דעה Yoreh De'ah, The Teachings of Knowledge deals with ritual laws of everyday life.

3. אבן העזר Eben Ha'Ezer, The Stone of Help deals with the laws of marriage and divorce.

4. חושן המשפט Choshen Hamishpat, The Breastplate of Judgment deals with Jewish civil law.

14. שלחן ערוך SHULCHAN ARUCH

(literally, "Prepared Table") is a compilation of Jewish law, written by Joseph Karo (or Caro) ca. 1567, in the town of Tz'fat (or Safed) in the north of Israel.

Joseph Karo was a mystic who taught that it was time for God to send *Masheach*, the messiah, to redeem the world.

Karo contended that if God had not yet sent *Masheach*, it meant that the world was not yet ready for redemption. The only way the world could become ready was for people to make the world into a better, more perfect place. That perfection would come if people—led by the example set by the Jewish People—would follow God's law with more precision and devotion.

So Karo wrote the Shulchan Aruch to make the law clear and accessible to every Jew. It is written in a very concise, straightforward manner; the laws are simply listed, without much reason or explanation given. The four volumes of the Shulchan Aruch are identical in structure, titles, and subject divisions to the Arba'ah Turim.

Karo was a Sephardic Jew, who brought the influence of Sephardic custom to the writing of the Shulchan Aruch. Rabbi Moses Isserles (known as Rama) of Poland, an Ashkenazic Jew, wrote commentary and addenda (and often dissenting opinion) to the Shulchan Aruch, based on Ashkenazic custom. The commentary of Isserles is called the מפת השלחן Mapat HaShulchan (literally, "The Tablecloth of the Table"). With the addition of this commentary of Isserles, with Ashkenazic customs, the Shulchan Aruch became acceptable to and accepted by every segment of the Jewish community, Sephardic and Ashkenazic.

The Shulchan Aruch is the last formal compilation of Jewish law. It remains, to this day, the guide to all matters of Jewish law.

Rabbi Solomon Ganzfried (1804–86) compiled an abridged version of the Shulchan Aruch, which he called the קיצור שלחן ערוך Kitzur Shulchan Aruch (literally, "The Shortened Shulchan Aruch [Prepared Table]"). He arranged the laws in the order of everyday use, and his clear and easy-to-understand style made it very popular with the Jewish community. The Kitzur Shulchan Aruch has been translated into dozens of languages—making it accessible to Jews throughout the world, whether or not they can read and understand Hebrew—and is still in widespread use today.

15. שאלות ותשובות SH'ELOT UTESHUVOT

"Questions and Answers," the Responsa Literature, is the way Jewish law
has developed since the time of the Shulchan Aruch.

Since the time of the Shulchan Aruch, no new compendium or collection of Jewish
law has been written. However, times and situations have changed greatly, and old
laws have faced new challenges and the need for new interpretation.

Employing a methodology that has been in use since the time of the *Geonim*
(as early as 600 C.E.), the law has developed through a system of "Questions and
Answers." A question of Jewish law is asked of a great Rabbinic sage. He studies the
question, researches it in the law literature, and gives his answer, or response (hence,
Responsa Literature). The question is called a שאלה *sh'elah* (plural, שאלות *sh'eylot*).
The answer is called a תשובה *t'shuvah* (plural, תשובות *t'shuvot*). How much the
answer is accepted as Jewish law depends on how great an authority the rabbi is,
how many followers he has, and how many people are willing to accept his legal
pronouncements.

Many of the *t'shuvot* are kept by the people who receive them, and eventually
the *t'shuvot* of a particular rabbi are collected into a book giving his legal decisions.

T'shuvot cover a wide range of ethical, ritual, and civil matters, and touch upon
every phase of human existence. The answering rabbi never simply gives a personal
opinion, but bases his decisions on a careful study of the Jewish law that has been
developed up until the time in which he lives.

The Torah always serves as the constitutional basis for all decisions in matters
of Jewish law. In addition, any decision given by a rabbi must also follow and conform to the (case) law that has been developed over the centuries in the Talmud, the
Mishnah Torah, the Tur, and the Shulchan Aruch.

In modern times, the Orthodox community continues to use this method to
make and give new legal decisions. Great rabbis who are recognized and accepted as
legal scholars are asked questions of Jewish law, and then they respond with their
decisions. The power of the decision, and how many people it affects, is based on
how much the responding rabbi is respected as a scholar and how many people are
willing to accept his decisions. In modern Orthodoxy, a person chooses a rabbi and
then accepts the legal decisions that rabbi makes. Once a Jew chooses a rabbi, that
rabbi's legal decisions are accepted as binding by that Jew; he or she does not pick
and choose, accepting some and rejecting others.

Reform Judaism has, for the most part, rejected the idea of binding ritual Jewish law, so the issue of how legal decisions are made and accepted is not of much concern for much of Reform Jewry. There are a few Reform rabbis who have written

t'shuvot, basing their decisions on a Reform-liberal interpretation of the law; but these *t'shuvot* are instructive rather than binding for Reform Jews.

The Reconstructionist movement has various commissions that offer non-binding principles and guidelines on issues of ritual and ceremonial practices, and personal status.

The Conservative movement has established a Committee on Jewish Law and Standards, which receives questions and renders decisions. Instead of one rabbi functioning in the role of decision maker, the committee is made up of a number of rabbis, chosen for their knowledge and scholarly abilities, who study and vote on the issues that are raised. This committee gives "majority decisions" that are supposed to be binding on Conservative Jews. But it also issues "minority decisions," which means that if enough committee members vote in a particular way, even if they are in the minority, their opinion is offered as an alternative and can be accepted as an option for Conservative Jews.

Although it is handled differently by each of the branches of modern Judaism, the Responsa Literature is the recognized and accepted way that issues of Jewish law are addressed today.

Jewish law literature is the source of הלכה *halachah* **(literally, "the way to walk/go," "the pathway")—Jewish law.**

Mitzvot, the commandments of the Torah, form the basis of *halachah*—the ethical and ritual injunctions a Jew is to follow, the standards of behavior on which to "walk" life's path.

Throughout the centuries and into modern times, Torah law has been amended, extended, expanded, and sometimes limited, in the law literature of the Mishnah, the Talmud, the Mishnah Torah, the Tur, the Shulchan Aruch, and the Responsa Literature. This law literature develops *halachah* by means of evolving case law based on prior precedent.

Halachah—the legal code of moral and ethical behavior, enhanced by ritual observances—is the basic system by which a Jew is supposed to live.

In addition to reflecting the development of Jewish law, Jewish law literature tells the story of the Jewish People—where Jews have lived, what languages they have spoken, who has ruled over them, when conditions have been good and when they have not, when Jews have been creative and flourishing, and when they have been oppressed and persecuted. The law often changed to address the challenges of time and place, and therefore the books that record the law tell the tale of the times and the places—the evolving history of Judaism and the Jewish People.

The developmental process of Jewish law also links all Jews everywhere. Not only does every traditional home, every synagogue, every house of study, every Jewish library, have a copy of the Bible, but each of these places has a copy of all the books of Jewish law. No matter where Jews live, no matter what everyday language they speak, no matter what people, conditions, or circumstances guide their lives, these books—with their ethics and rituals that give rhythm to everyday life and shape enduring values—belong to every Jew. They are the Jewish legacy and the Jewish inheritance received and given from generation to generation.

AN ESSAY ON LAW AND SPIRIT

Judaism is a religion of law.

Even though Judaism was founded on the concept of *belief,* with Abraham declaring his belief in the One Lord God, the relationship between God and the Jewish People has been one not so much of faith, but of law; not so much of creed, but of deed.

Beginning with the Torah and continuing through the Mishnah, the Gemara (and the Talmud), the Mishnah Torah, the Arba'ah Turim, the Shulchan Aruch, and the Responsa Literature, Judaism emphasizes the requirement to fulfill the *mitzvot,* the commandments of God—as they are enjoined in the Written Torah and developed in the Oral Torah.

Judaism's intricate legal framework is based on the concept of a constitutional system. The Torah is the constitution, the foundation for all law, for it is the word and will of God.

When changing time, place, and circumstance required it, the constitutional law was amended, new law was developed, and case law was established. Each new law had to conform to the law given in the Torah; it could not be "unconstitutional" by violating the Torah constitution's basic principles. And as the law developed over the centuries, it had to also follow the precedents set down in each new legal compilation.

For example, a Gemara law had to conform not only to the constitutional principle in the Torah, but also to any decision that had been rendered in the Mishnah. By the time that Joseph Karo compiled the laws of the Shulchan Aruch, those laws had to follow every preceding legal decision of the Talmud, the Mishnah Torah, and the Arba'ah Turim. Today, when a rabbinic scholar renders a *t'shuvah,* a rabbinic response to a legal inquiry, every legal precedent—all case law—on the subject must be followed as the question is decided.

For all its stringent requirements, the capacity of the Jewish legal system to develop new law on top of the old is one of the main reasons that Judaism has survived and flourished over the millennia. Rather than being static, Jewish law has been flexible enough to adapt to the challenges of changing circumstance.

THE REASONS WHY

The Jewish emphasis on law is quite understandable. Judaism was born into a pagan world of moral anarchy and ethical chaos. Those with power or wealth ruled indiscriminately and capriciously. There was virtually no sense of equality or human freedom, almost no sense of justice or fairness, little sense of tolerance or compassion.

Torah law set out to right those wrongs.

So to a world where every manner of god was worshiped and venerated, the Lord God said, "I am the Lord your God . . . You shall have no other gods before Me" (Exodus 20:2–3).

To a world where vigilante justice reigned supreme, and an innocuous injury might result in harsh and unwarranted punishment, God said, "An eye for an eye, a tooth for a tooth. The injury to be inflicted is as the injury suffered" (Leviticus 24:20).

In a world where kings ruled by power and might, where their word was law, and where they could impose any demand on their subjects, God said, "[The king] shall not keep many horses [as instruments of war] . . . or have many wives, lest his heart go astray. Nor shall he amass excess silver and gold. . . . When he is seated on his royal throne, you shall have a copy of this Torah written for him . . . and let him read it all his life, so that he may learn to revere the Lord his God and faithfully observe . . . all these laws . . . so he will not act haughtily toward his fellows" (Deuteronomy 17:16 ff).

In a world where warfare meant utter destruction and death, rape, pillage, and plunder, God said, "When you approach a town to attack it, first offer it terms of peace. . . . [And] if you besiege a city for a long time, making war against it, you must not destroy the trees. . . . You may eat of them, but you may not cut them down. Are the trees of the field human beings that they should come under your siege?" (Deuteronomy 20:10, 19).

In a world where slavery was common, and indentured servants were enslaved for life, God said, "When you acquire a Hebrew slave, he shall serve for six years; in the seventh year, he shall go free" (Exodus 20:2).

In a world where workers were exploited for their labor, and had no rights and little dignity, God said, "You shall not keep the wages of a laborer until morning"(meaning, pay what you owe as it is earned, for the worker may need the money to eat that night) (Leviticus 19:13).

In a world where work was continual, and rest a luxury only the rich could afford, God said to everyone, "Remember the Sabbath and keep it holy" (as a day separate from all others, a day of physical rest and spiritual rejuvenation) (Exodus 20:8).

In a world where the poor had to fend for themselves and depend on the goodwill of the wealthy for food and sustenance, God said, "When you reap the harvest of your land, you shall not reap the corners of your field, or gather the gleanings of your harvest. You shall leave them for the poor and the stranger" (Leviticus 23:22).

In a world of the "survival of the fittest," where individual and tribal self-interest were paramount, God said, "Love your neighbor as yourself" (Leviticus 19:18).

THE PURPOSE OF LAW

Torah law—then and now—has served the Jewish People well.

Torah law is the blueprint, the standard for moral and ethical behavior, the code of conduct for humankind. The ritual laws of Torah serve as the instrumentality, the method of remembering and performing the ethical laws.

Torah law is God's greatest gift to the Jewish People—and through the Jewish People, to all humankind. God's great love for His people is manifest through this extraordinary gift—the law by which humankind is to live and thus fulfill God's plan for His beloved children.

When it was given—and to this day—Torah law tempers freedom with responsibility, assures human rights and dignity, elevates the human spirit, and enriches and ennobles human existence.

The ultimate goal of the law is to bring the world to a place where the law is no longer necessary—a world, in the words of the prayer *Alenu,* which has been "perfected under the Kingdom of God," a world of harmony and tranquility, a world of peace and goodwill, a world of messianic perfection. "On that day," says the prayer, "the Lord shall be recognized as One, and His name as One."

The Talmud (BT Nidah 61b) goes so far as to say that "Ritual *mitzvot* will be abolished when the messiah comes." Why? Ritual commandments exist as the constant reminder, the pathway, toward ethical conduct. When the world has reached perfection, when the messiah has arrived, ethical conduct will abound and ritual reminders will not be necessary.

Thus, according to Jewish thought, the very best thing the law can possibly do is make itself obsolete.

CONTINUING REVELATION

From out of the biblical world came the law, but not the worldly perfection the law sought. So the sages who became the leaders of what is now known as the Rabbinic Period (200 B.C.E.–600 C.E.) became the keepers and interpreters of the law. They were the inheritors who first proclaimed the Oral Law, the scholars who taught the law, the judges who decided the law.

They insisted on the centrality of the law. They were quick to rebuff any challenge to their authority—not only to support their own claims that continuing revelation came through them, but to protect the integrity of the law.

The sages of each succeeding generation protected, expanded, and cherished the law. They insisted on its observance, they affirmed reward for those who fulfill the law, and warned of punishment for those who transgress. They kept the law ever-essential and ever-indispensable to Jewish life.

Yet what is often missing from Judaism's historical and contemporary emphasis on law is the attention to the original purposes of religion, the original reason for the covenant between God and the Jewish People.

Remember: Religion developed out of the human need to seek answers to the mysteries of existence; to help people understand and tame the mighty forces of the universe; to help people define their place and purpose; to find meaning and value, fulfillment and satisfaction, in existence; to help people experience good and understand evil; to help people live life and confront death; to help people seek and find God.

Judaism came into being to bring the Lord God into the world; to help people feel the connection to creation and the Creator; to celebrate the deep spiritual relationship between God and each human being; to help people feel God's presence and be enveloped in His nearness; to help people know God through faith and love; to share with the world God's word and will.

That is what law is all about. Law is the instrumentality to help people reach up to God, and the avenue for God to reach down to us. The law is a way to speak to God, and to listen as God speaks to us. The law is the way for God's light to continually come into the world, and for us to reflect His being.

Given Judaism's insistence on the observance of the law, and given the wide diversity of human nature, it is not surprising that—then and now—much of Jewish life has gotten caught up in the minutiae of the law, the petty detail, the hair-splitting interpretation. For many, the law—then and now—became the entirety of Judaism, with praise or condemnation for those who observe or violate the smallest particular.

Yet sometimes obscured, sometimes forgotten, sometimes ignored, the original intent of Jewish law remains: to foster the relationship and the spiritual connection between God and the Jewish People.

THE WORLD OF SPIRIT

In the time of the Rabbinic sages, just when Jewish law—its observance, much more than its original intent—was being ingrained into the collective Jewish psyche, a messenger came to move the world from the realm of the law back into the original realm of the spirit.

Christianity came into being contending that while the law was important, the vital component of life is the spiritual connection between individuals and God, that the belief and faith that Judaism assumes and sometimes takes for granted is really the core element of the relationship between God and humankind.

Judaism rejected the basic tenets and teachings of Christianity, because the form contained assertions that Jews simply could not accept: the coming of the messiah, God manifest in a human being, God divisible into three separate entities, humankind born into a state of original sin, one taking responsibilities for another's transgressions and dying for them.

But in rejecting the forms, Judaism ignored the substance—the lesson that was being taught the world: that God and humankind are connected through faith, spirit, and deep love; that God can be sought and found in an intimate, deeply personal relationship; that the central questions of the universe and of existence can be asked and will be answered in the midst of a personal spiritual journey.

This lesson, the substance of Christianity—then and now—is true and certain. It is a lesson that the world needs to be reminded of again and again. It is a lesson that Jews—then and now—would do well to hear and heed.

THE WORLD OF JEWISH SPIRIT

To be sure, Judaism has all these concepts. Judaism has all the ways for people to find the personal connection with God, to give life meaning and purpose, to help people achieve fulfillment and satisfaction, to lead people toward wholeness and holiness.

For many, observing the law, following the *mitzvot,* has been and is the pathway to the spiritual connection with God; for by fulfilling God's commands, the relationship with God can develop and grow.

Yet for just as many, if not more, the demand to follow the law has obscured the original purpose of the law—to create and enhance the spiritual connection to God.

At least twice in the past 2,000 years, movements within Judaism have attempted to bring Judaism back to finding the spiritual, to celebrating faith: the kabbalists, beginning in the thirteenth century, and the chasidim of the early eighteenth century. But their attempts were always stifled. The world of the spirit—especially in these last 200 years since the Enlightenment and the emancipation—has been smothered by the rationalists and the legalists.

BALANCING LAW AND SPIRIT

For many modern Jews—especially American Jews, who were brought up in a society that grants and celebrates "unalienable rights"—the requirement to follow ancient law poses an even greater dilemma: How do I balance the obligation of the law with freedom of choice? How do I accept responsibility without foregoing my rights? How do I assent to boundaries and limitations when I am autonomous and unfettered? How can I consider the common good without protecting my special interest? Why should I be bound to demands and duties when my spirit can be free and unencumbered?

In these contemporary times, Jews answer all these questions—the questions of history and the questions of modernity—in a number of different ways.

Following the model of Jews throughout the centuries, a small but passionate—and growing—minority of Jews adheres strictly and meticulously to the law. Another small group of Jews is committed to the concept of binding law, and struggles to balance legal requirements with modern circumstance.

But for the vast majority of contemporary Jews, Jewish law has little power and little relevance. The modern Jewish thinker Rabbi Harold Schulweis says of most Jews, "They will not be told what to eat, where to eat, when to eat; when to rest, where to rest, how long to rest; when to marry, whom to marry, where to marry; whom to mourn, how long to mourn, where to mourn. In short, modern Jewish consciousness is less proud in being chosen than in choosing.

"They are not," Schulweis continues, "traditional Jews in the sense that the historian Jacob Katz understands tradition: the belief that my public and private life can be regulated by law, and that my meaning and values are derived from 'total reliance on the distant past.'

"And yet," Schulweis counters, "for all their modernity . . . for all their distance from religion, they express a yearning for 'spirituality' . . . a need for guidance. . . ."

No less than Abraham who found God, and Moses who covenanted with Him, no less than the prophets who heard God calling and spoke His word, modern Jews hunger for the sacred. They long to hear the voice of God, to feel the presence of God, to know the will of God, to be wrapped in the comfort and love of God.

All they seek—the cosmic connection to the universe and a deep, personal relationship with God; a happy, more satisfying life; a richer, more noble, more fulfilling existence; spiritual certainty and inner peace—is right within Judaism today, as it has always been.

Yet the sad reality of modern Jewish life is that rabbis, teachers, and Jewish institutions have failed to convey Judaism's spiritual splendor. While contemporary Judaism is very good at creating community and doing *mitzvot*, saving oppressed Jewry and supporting the State of Israel, it has not done well what is central to the religious quest: helping people find and know God.

And the second sad reality of modern Jewish life is that when Jews do not find what they need in Judaism, they either ignore Judaism as insignificant and irrelevant, or they go off seeking: to the meditation centers and the ashrams, the spiritual retreats, the self-help groups and the cults.

THE REBIRTH OF SPIRIT

Contemporary Judaism aches for a rebirth of faith, a balancing of the world of the law with the world of the spirit.

Contemporary Jews want to know God. They do not want to be like the patriarch Jacob, who waited half a lifetime before God appeared to him in a dream and then had to say, wistfully and regretfully, "All this time, God was in this place, but I did not know" (Genesis 28:16). They do not want to be like the Children of Israel, for whom God parted the sea, but instead of seeing the miracle only complained about getting their feet wet.

Contemporary Jews long to be shown not just the way to obey God's laws, but how to hear God's voice, to feel God's presence, to be enveloped in God's love.

Contemporary Jews seek an intimacy with God; to experience God as friend, mentor, counselor, comforter, guide.

Contemporary Jews want a personal, direct, comfortable relationship with God.

The time for Jewish spiritual renewal has come.

The time has come for the symbolic rebirth: to blend and merge the world of the law and the world of the spirit—to bring together all the mutuality, all the diversity, and all of the growth the world has known: the law that brought order out of chaos, the faith that showed us God's intimacy, the spirit that brings us close to Him.

When that synthesis comes, with it will come the realization that the worlds of law and spirit are not so different after all.

Although some see law as corrosive and oppressive, demanding and restrictive, just the opposite is true.

Law is the human spirit at its finest: enlightened, empowered, and enabled; able to make choices, assume responsibility, and affect result. Law is the human spirit at its most free, for the ultimate moral courage is the freedom to say, "No."

God's law exists simply yet profoundly to celebrate the spirit: the spiritual connection between God and His people, and the human spirit of God-like holiness.

When the long-awaited union of law and spirit finally comes—may it be speedily and in our day—then each Jew—each human being—will be assured that God knows you, loves you, and is with you always.

And each Jew—each human being—will know God, love God, and be with God.

As Judaism celebrates the world of the spirit, as you go on your own spiritual journey, you will find life's deepest meaning and most profound happiness emanating from the "holy sparks" that come from your reaching up to touch God, and God bending down to touch you.

God is waiting for you to seek Him. God is waiting to answer when you call.

16. מדרש MIDRASH

(plural, Midrashim) is collections of stories, folklore, legends, interpretations, and homilies (sermonic teachings) about the Bible.

Jewish history is rich with אגדה *aggadah*, legends, parables, and folklore, stories that add depth of understanding and meaning to the Jewish experience. The greatest source of ancient *aggadah* are Midrashim, which contain stories and legends about the Bible.

There are two kinds of Midrashim: Teachings and stories based on and explaining Jewish law are called מדרש הלכה Midrash Halachah. Teachings and stories based on the narrative and ethical parts of the Bible are called מדרש אגדה Midrash Aggadah—legends and lore.

Midrashim serve to "flesh out" the Bible, to make it more understandable, to make its characters more human. They draw meaning from the simple, concise text, and teach lessons based on the text. They were created to teach the Bible in a simple, folksy way, to tell stories and offer moral lessons. They were the sermons—the ethical lessons drawn from the biblical text—of their time.

Midrashim were compiled over thousands of years, from at least as early as 500 B.C.E., until the mid-1500s C.E. The most famous of the *halachic* Midrashim (the ones dealing with law) are:

מכילתא דרבי ישמעאל Mechilta d'Rabbi Yishmael on Exodus

ספרא Sifra on Leviticus

ספרי Sifrei on Numbers

מכילתא Mechilta and ספרי דברים Sefrei Devarim on Deuteronomy

The most famous of the *aggadic* Midrashim (the ones dealing with the narrative and ethical portions) is מדרש רבה Midrash Rabbah, The Great Midrash. It has a separate book for each of the five books of the Torah and for each of the five *megillot*.

Some other famous *aggadic* Midrashim are:

תנחומא Tanchuma

פסיקתא דרב כהנה Pesikta d'Rav Kahana

פסיקתא רבתי Pesikta Rabbati

פרקי דרבי אליעזר Pirkae d'Rabbi Eliezer

מדרש תהלים Midrash Tehillim on Psalms

A number of Midrashic anthologies (collections) were compiled in the Middle Ages, including:

ילקוט שמעוני Yalkut Shemoni

מדרש הגדול Midrash Hagadol

A Midrash-like compendium of all the collected legends and stories from the Talmud is called עין יעקב Ein Yaakov.

Like the long-enduring and continually renewing Jewish experience, the telling of Jewish stories is never-ending and ever-evolving; so new *aggadah* has been created by Jewish storytellers in every generation.

In contemporary times, modern storytellers and Midrash writers continue to weave new Jewish tales, bringing new depth, new richness, and new understanding to the continually unfolding Jewish adventure.

17.   זהר   ZOHAR

The Book of Splendor, is a mystical interpretation of the Torah,
rich with spiritual inspiration.

The *Zohar* is attributed to Moses de Leon of Granada, in Spain, in the late 1200s; a generally accepted date is 1268. De Leon tried to make the reader think that the author of the *Zohar* was the second-century Rabbinic sage Shimon bar Yochai. But almost all modern scholars agree that it would have been impossible for Bar Yochai to have written the *Zohar,* and most agree that de Leon is the author.

The *Zohar* presents mystical teachings on the five books of the Torah. The teachings emphasize that the Torah contains higher truths in addition to the literal meaning of the text; that the highest goal of a human being is to reach for and understand the innermost secrets of existence; and that every human act has a ripple effect on the entire universe.

The publication of the *Zohar* began the period of the קבלה kabbalah, the mystical interpretations of the philosophies and the hidden meanings of Jewish life and teachings.

קבלה   KABBALAH

(literally, "receiving" [the tradition]) is Jewish mysticism.

Jewish mysticism is a way of looking at the universe beyond what is known or experienced empirically. It is a system of thought and a mode of feeling that seeks answers to the mysteries of the universe. It is the quest for ultimate meaning.

With roots stretching back to the Bible and nurtured throughout Jewish history, the kabbalah began to grow and flourish with the publication of the *Zohar.*

The kabbalah asks life's ultimate questions: Who is God? What is the origin of the universe? What is the purpose and meaning of human existence? How do human beings connect and communicate with God? What is humankind's destiny? What are the deepest meanings of Torah and how do they help answer life's ultimate questions?

The kabbalah seeks to explain the relationship between the infinite (God) and the finite (humankind) by means of ten steps, or powers, or emanations, called ספירות *sefirot*, between God and humankind. It teaches that there is an unbroken connection between God, the universe, and humankind. It understands prayer to be the unifying force of the universe and maintains that the moral spirit of humankind will triumph over the challenges of evil.

The great proponents and teachers of the kabbalah were Rabbi Isaac Luria (known as the Ari) (1543–1620) and Rabbis Chaim Vital, Moses Cordovero, Joseph Karo, and Solomon Alkabetz, who lived in Tz'fat (Safed) in the north of Israel, in the sixteenth century.

In the rationalism of the Enlightenment and the emancipation, the kabbalah lost much of its primacy and potency in Jewish life. Its teachings have become rather hidden and obscure during the last 250 years.

But the spiritual awakening of contemporary days has led to a rediscovery of the kabbalah by many, who understand that life's deepest and most profound meaning can be found not only in the realm of the rational intellect, but also—and even more so—from the "holy sparks" that emanate from seeking the spiritual and the mystical.

18.   סדור   SIDDUR

is the prayerbook.

The *siddur* is the structured, organized collection of Jewish prayers, recited on weekdays and the Sabbath.

When prayers with words began to replace sacrifices of animal and agricultural products as the main method of Jewish worship, a regular structure of prayer times and prayer modes began to develop.

The Hebrew word סדור *siddur* means "order." So as an agreed-on order of prayers began to be fixed, the repository of the order of prayer, the prayerbook, came to be called the *siddur.*

The first systematic *siddur* was outlined by Rab Amram ben Sheshna Gaon in the Academy of Sura in Babylonia in the year 870 C.E. Less than a century later, the great Rabbi Saadya Gaon (882–942) compiled a more complete, more logical *siddur,* which to this day still serves as the basic format for Jewish prayer.

The basic *siddur* is in Hebrew, but its words have been translated into almost every language of every country in which Jews have lived.

The *siddur* is the most flexible and fluid of all Jewish books. Some of its original prayers were taken directly from the Bible. Some were written by the rabbis and sages of the day. To its basic structure, in most generations and in most places, every group of Jews has added its own words and prayers. New prayers are written and become so popular that they are put into new editions of the *siddur*. In any given *siddur*, on three consecutive pages, may be a prayer taken from the words of the Bible, a prayer written in the 1600s, and a prayer written just a few years ago.

Throughout the ages, the *siddur* has been the formal vehicle by which a Jew could communicate with God. Its fixed structure has given format to prayer, but its openness to accepting modern ideas and words has permitted new inspiration to come from each generation and each individual.

19.   מחזור   MACHZOR

is a prayerbook for a festival.

The Hebrew word מחזור *machzor* means "return," or "cycle." Since each festival occurs once each year, the name given to the festival prayerbook reflects the return of its annual cycle, the coming again to the celebration of the festival.

There is one *machzor* for Succot (Tabernacles), one for Pesach (Passover), and one for Shavuot (Weeks, or Pentecost.) The best-known *machzor* is the one for the High Holidays, Rosh HaShanah (the Jewish New Year) and Yom Kippur (the Day of Atonement).

The festival *machzorim* (plural of *machzor*) contain the basic rubric of prayer with special changes and additions for each festival. The High Holiday *machzor* contains the basic rubric of prayer, along with the changes and additions for Rosh HaShanah and Yom Kippur, especially many special פיוטים *piyyutim* (singular, *piyyut*), which are poems written specifically for the High Holidays, reflecting the themes of the High Holiday commemorations.

The two oldest sources of the use of the word *machzor* in referring to the festival prayerbook are the *Machzor Yannai* and the *Machzor Vitry*, dating to the late 1100s and the early 1200s. Because the High Holidays are the most commemorated and most observed of all Jewish festivals, the High Holiday *machzor*, with its lofty prayers and its warm familiarity, is one of the most beloved of all Jewish books.

20. הגדה HAGGADAH

(literally, "legend" or "telling") is the book used during the Passover *seder* to tell the events of the exodus from Egypt, and how to conduct the *seder* ritual.

The name for the book used to relate the Passover story is *haggadah,* which is taken from the Hebrew word אגדה *aggadah,* meaning "legend," for the book is filled with biblical quotations and rabbinic legends, interpretations, and stories about the exodus from Egypt.

The *haggadah* is used to conduct the *seder* of Passover, to tell the story of the journey of the Hebrews from slavery to freedom, and to outline the rituals performed during the *seder.*

The oldest published version of the *haggadah* is in the prayerbook of Saadya Gaon, from the tenth century. There are now more than 2,500 separate editions of the *haggadah,* reflecting the unique customs, ceremonies, and concerns of the many and varied places and times in which Jews have lived.

The *haggadah* is the one Jewish book that has been most illustrated by artists. There are hundreds of separate editions of the *haggadah,* from Jewish communities all around the world, decorated with striking and evocative artwork.

The *haggadah* is one of Judaism's best-known and most beloved books (with most Jews having a personal familiar and favorite edition) because it is used from earliest childhood in celebration of the joyous festival of Passover.

4

JEWISH DAYS AND HOLIDAYS

1. DATING JEWISH TIME

In antiquity, the counting of years was marked in relationship to events: for example, the forty days and nights of the flood; the 175 years of the lifetime of Abraham; the forty-year journey in the desert; the twenty-year reign of King Saul.

When Christianity began counting years in chronological order, counting from the year that was considered as the birth-year of Jesus, Judaism's rabbis and sages devised a method of counting the years that would be acceptable to Jewish sensibilities.

In their simple naiveté—or their abiding faith—the sages decided to determine the actual historical date of the day of the creation of the world, and then use that date as a basis for counting the years forward.

Using all the biblical accounts, historical records, and oral tradition available, the sages of the Rabbinic Period counted backward in history to determine the moment of creation. They counted the number of years of the reigns of each of the kings; the number of years that each of the Holy Temples stood; the number of months and years of various battles and wars; the number of years of the lifetimes of all the biblical figures; the number of years of all of the events described in the Bible.

Using this method, the sages concluded that the destruction of the Second Temple had taken place 3,830 years since the creation of the world.

Since the destruction of the Second Holy Temple took place in the year 70 C.E., then the year 1 (the year popularly acknowledged as the year of the birth of Jesus) would be the year 3760 since creation (that is, 3,830 minus 70).

Each year Rosh HaShanah, the Jewish new year, celebrates the anniversary of the day of creation and one year is added to the Jewish counting of the years.

Thus, to determine the Jewish year, add 3,760 (the time from creation until year 1) to the civil year (the time since the year 1).

The Jewish year when this book is being completed—in the civil year 1995—is the year 5755 (3,760 plus 1,995 equals 5,755). Since the Jewish year changes at Rosh HaShanah, which occurs in September or October, for the time period between Rosh HaShanah and January 1, add 3,761 to determine the equivalent year.

The problem with the Jewish dating system, of course, is that while the Rabbinic sages may have truly believed the biblical accounting of the passage of time—and therefore believed that their count of the years back to the time of creation was accurate—modern science teaches that it has been millions of years—not just under 6,000—since the time of creation.

We accept the notion that the ancient sages did the best they could in devising a counting system based on the best available information at the time. But how do we—knowing what we do about scientific theory and fact—continue to count the years one by one every Rosh HaShanah, pretending that it is only some 6,000 years since creation?

Surely, we place ourselves in the continuum of Jewish history: Our ancestors believed the counting of the years to be accurate and true; we know it to be poetic and metaphorical.

But beyond that, while we recognize that the *physical* world is millions of years old, we equally recognize that it has been but some 6,000 years since humankind became aware of its place in the universe and began to tell and record its own story. So we can accurately say that on Rosh HaShanah we celebrate the new year, counting the years since the recorded dawning of human history in this multimillion-year-old universe.

2.   THE JEWISH CALENDAR

The secular calendar, by which most of the contemporary world functions, is a solar calendar.

In this calendar, which has months named January, February, March, and so on, the new day begins and ends at midnight.

One year is 365 days, the time it takes for the earth to revolve around the sun.

Because it actually takes 365¼ days for the earth's revolution, once every four years an extra day is added to the year (February 29) and the year is known as a leap year.

The Jewish calendar is a soli-lunar calendar, based on the revolution of the moon around the earth, with certain adjustments to account for the revolution of the earth around the sun.

The use of the lunar calendar recognizes the natural ebb and flow of the universe: the gravitational pull of the moon on the earth; the movement of the waters and the tides; and the process of a woman's reproductive cycle, offering the possibility of new life as each month turns into the next.

In this calendar, the new day begins at sundown and ends approximately twenty-four hours later at sundown of the next secular day. This pattern follows the account of creation, recorded in the opening chapter of the biblical book of Genesis: "And there was *evening* and there was *morning,* a first day . . . a second day . . . a third day . . . a fourth day . . . a fifth day . . . the sixth day" (Genesis 1:5, 8, 13, 19, 23, 31). Thus, for example, the Jewish Sabbath begins at sundown on Friday, and ends after sundown on Saturday.

Each month in the lunar calendar consists of 29½ days—the time that it takes for the moon to revolve around the earth. Since a month cannot have a half-day, the months in the Jewish calendar alternate numbers of days: one month, 29 days; the next month, 30 days. At the end of a full year, the 12 half days have been regarded as 6 full days—the thirtieth day of every other month.

Each 12-month lunar year has 354 days (29½ days × 12 months)—which is 11¼ days shorter than the solar year of 365¼ days.

To keep the solar and lunar calendar years in equal balance—and to keep the seasons in sync—the Jewish calendar is arranged on a 19-year cycle, with 12 years of 12 months each, and 7 leap years of 13 months each.

The mathematical formula goes like this: The number of days in 19 solar years is equal to 235 lunar months, which is 19 years, plus 7 months. Thus the extra 7 months are inserted within the 19-year cycle—in the third, sixth, eighth, eleventh, fourteenth, seventeenth, and nineteenth years—creating the leap years of 13 months each.

The leap month—called Adar Sheni, the Second Adar (Adar II)—is inserted in late winter, somewhere around February/March, thus keeping the observance of Passover in the springtime season.

Jewish holidays always occur on the same date on the Jewish calendar. For example, Yom Kippur, the Day of Atonement, is always on the tenth day of the month of Tishri; Chanukah always begins on the twenty-fifth day of the month of Kislev. But because the solar and lunar calendars do not coincide, the Jewish holidays fall on different days of the solar calendar each year. So Chanukah may be very early in December one year, and the next year begin late in December, even going over into January.

3. THE HEBREW MONTHS

There are twelve Hebrew months. The following table shows the months and their approximate dates on the secular calendar. (In a leap year, there are two Adars, Adar I and Adar II. The celebration of the holiday of Purim passes over into Adar II, in order to keep the holidays in sync with their correct seasons.)

MONTH		OCCURS
תשרי	Tishri	September/October
חשון	Cheshvan	October/November
כסלו	Kislev	November/December
טבת	Tevet	December/January
שבט	Shevat	January/ February
אדר	Adar	February/March
ניסן	Nisan	March/April
אייר	Iyar	April/May
סיון	Sivan	May/June
תמוז	Tammuz	June/July
אב	Av	July/August
אלול	Elul	August/September

The first day of each Hebrew month is designated as ראש חדש Rosh Chodesh (literally, "head of the month"). Rosh Chodesh is the day that the new moon appears in the sky, beginning its 29½-day cycle of revolving around the earth.

Since a month cannot have a half day, each year six Hebrew months have twenty-nine days and six months have thirty days—the twelve half days counting as a full day every other month.

In the months that have thirty days, the thirtieth day is designated Rosh Chodesh, along with the first day of the new month. Since half of the thirtieth day technically belongs to the old month, and the other half technically belongs to the new month, the whole thirtieth day is considered an "honorary" part of the new month.

At one point in Jewish history—before the calendar was formally fixed, and when the declaration of Rosh Chodesh literally depended on the physical sighting of the new moon—this two-day Rosh Chodesh was the insurance against being late in declaring the new month to have begun. The two-day Rosh Chodesh, occurring every other month, permitted enough leeway for slight miscalculation and kept the calendar as accurate as possible.

Since Judaism is very conscious of the need to sanctify time, the coming of each new month is recognized and celebrated.

On the Sabbath preceding the week in which the new month will begin, a special prayer called ברכת החדש *Bircat HaChodesh,* the Blessing of the New Month, is recited in the synagogue. The prayer serves to remind the worshipers that Rosh Chodesh is coming, and asks God for a multitude of blessings in the new month ahead.

On the day of Rosh Chodesh, special prayers are added to the synagogue service and a short portion is read from the Torah at the morning service, in honor of the day.

Rosh Chodesh is considered a "half-holiday." Traditionally, it has been known as a "women's holiday" because on Rosh Chodesh women would stop their work early in the day and come together to study and celebrate.

Today many women have reclaimed the spirit of Rosh Chodesh as a celebration of and for women by writing new prayers and liturgies and gathering together in prayer and study groups to mark the monthly observance.

4. JEWISH HOLIDAYS

A Jewish holiday is called a חג *chag* (plural, *chagim*). The most important and holy days of the Jewish holidays are called יום טוב *Yom Tov* (literally, "Good Day"). In Yiddish, *Yom Tov* has been contracted and shortened to be pronounced *Yontiv* or *Yontif.*

On *Yom Tov* the holiday is observed with all its worship, ritual, and celebrations, and with certain restrictions, including prohibitions against engaging in everyday secular activities such as work.

The most important of all Jewish holidays—the central observance of Jewish life—is שבת Shabbat, the Sabbath. Shabbat is the once-a-week day of physical rest and spiritual rejuvenation on which the Jewish People emulate God, who rested on the seventh day after the six days of creation.

In addition to Shabbat, the Torah describes five major holidays:

ראש השנה   Rosh HaShanah is the Jewish new year.

יום כפור   Yom Kippur is the Day of Atonement.

סוכות   Succot is the fall harvest and is a reminder of God's continuing blessings.

פסח   Pesach (Passover) celebrates the coming of spring and commemorates the exodus from Egypt.

שבועות   Shavuot marks the spring harvest and celebrates the giving of Torah at Sinai.

Rosh HaShanah and Yom Kippur are commemorated in the fall to foster personal and communal introspection and self-evaluation and to celebrate new beginnings. Together, Rosh HaShanah and Yom Kippur are called ימים נוראים *Yamim Noraim,* the Days of Awe, reflecting their solemn and most important purpose and nature. In English they are known as the High Holidays, or the High Holy Days.

The three other Torah-mandated holidays are collectively known as שלש רגלים *Shalosh Regalim,* the Three (Walking or) Pilgrimage Festivals. They were given this designation because, in ancient times, Jews would celebrate each of these three festivals by walking to Jerusalem from all over the Land of Israel, making pilgrimage to Jerusalem to bring sacrifices to the Holy Temple.

Two holidays commemorate historical events.

פורים Purim, chronicled in the biblical book of Esther, celebrates the defeat of an enemy who was foiled in his plot to destroy the Jewish People.

The postbiblical holiday of חנוכה Chanukah celebrates the military uprising that recaptured the Holy Temple from the oppressor and its rededication to God.

Other minor holidays, fast days, and commemorations fill the Jewish calendar and give rhythm to the Jewish year.

In recent years, the calendar of Jewish observances has been expanded to include יום השואה Yom HaShoah, Holocaust Remembrance Day, paying tribute to the martyrs who perished in the horrors of the Holocaust, and יום העצמאות Yom HaAtzmaut, Israeli Independence Day, celebrating the establishment of the modern State of Israel.

The Jewish holiday cycle reflects the same three themes that summarize the Torah. The fall holidays, beginning with Rosh HaShanah and concluding with Succot, reflect the theme of *creation*—the creation of the universe and everything in it, the continual creation and recreation of the human spirit, and the ongoing creation and recreation of God's gifts of nature.

Pesach, the early-spring festival, reflects the theme of *redemption*—the historical redemption of the Children of Israel from Egyptian slavery, and the hope for the ultimate redemption of the universe and humankind when the world will be perfected under the Kingdom of God.

Shavuot, the late-spring festival, reflects the theme of *revelation*—the giving of Torah at Mt. Sinai, when God revealed His word and will for all His children.

These three themes—reiterated in the Torah, in the holiday cycle, and also in the fixed structure of the Jewish prayer service—give a strong and significant unity to Judaism and the Jewish People. By linking God, Torah, and the *mitzvot* of prayer and holiday celebration, these oft-repeated themes weave the Jewish experience into a harmonious whole.

Since a Jewish day begins and ends at sundown, a twenty-four hour holiday begins at sundown of one secular day, and ends at sundown on the next secular day. For example, the Sabbath begins at sundown on Friday and ends at sundown on Saturday.

The beginning of the holiday—the evening before the full secular day—is known as ערב יום טוב Erev Yom Tov, because the Hebrew word ערב *erev* means "evening." Thus, for example, Friday night is ערב שבת Erev Shabbat, the evening of the Sabbath; and the evening when the holiday of Succot begins is called ערב סוכות Erev Succot.

The evening when the holiday ends (for example, the Sabbath ends on Saturday night) is called מוצאי שבת Motza'ay Shabbat (literally, the "going out" or "leaving" of the Sabbath), or מוצאי יום טוב Motza'ay Yom Tov (literally, the "going out" or "leaving" of the holiday) because the Hebrew word מוצאי *motza'ay* means "going out" or "leaving."

According to the Torah, Rosh HaShanah, Yom Kippur, and Shavuot are to be observed for one day each; and Succot and Pesach are to be observed for seven days each.

When the Jews were exiled from the Land of Israel, the sages mandated that an extra day be added to all the holidays except Yom Kippur.

Because the calendar was not yet fixed, and because in exile the affirmation of the sighting of the new moon (indicating the first day of each new Hebrew month) might take longer than it had in pre-exilic times, the sages were concerned that the holidays might not be celebrated on their proper days. By adding the extra day to the holiday, there would be less doubt that the holiday was being properly commemorated.

This second, extra, day of the holiday was called יום טוב שני של גלויות *Yom Tov sheni shel galuyot* (literally, "the second day of the holiday of the diaspora"). So Rosh HaShanah and Shavuot became two days instead of one. Succot and Pesach became eight days instead of seven. Only Yom Kippur remained its one original day, because adding a second day would have required extending the Yom Kippur fast to forty-eight hours.

Today—reasoning that the calendar was fixed long ago, and that there is no longer any reason to doubt that the holiday is being observed at its proper time—Reform Jews have returned to the biblically mandated one- or seven-day holiday commemorations.

Jews who live in Israel have also returned to the one- or seven-day observance (except for Rosh HaShanah, which still remains two days). Israeli Jews reason that since the second day of the holiday was for diaspora Jewry, and since they are living in Israel, the reason for the added day no longer applies.

Orthodox and Conservative Jews living outside of the Land of Israel are now the only ones still observing the second, extra, day of the holidays, although some Reform and Reconstructionist Jews observe two days of Rosh HaShanah.

The first one (or two) day(s) and the last one (or two) day(s) of Succot and Pesach are observed as Yom Tov, full holidays, with all their celebrations and certain restrictions.

The five (or four) days in between the full Yom Tov days are known as חול המועד Chol HaMo'ed, the "secular" or "intermediate" days of the holiday, when ritual observances and restrictions are lessened.

Thus, for those who celebrate Pesach as a seven-day holiday, the first and seventh days are observed as the full Yom Tov, and the five middle days as Chol HaMo'ed. For those who celebrate Pesach as an eight-day holiday, the first two days and the seventh and eighth days are observed as the full Yom Tov, with the four middle days as Chol HaMo'ed.

The observance of the holiday of Succot is more complicated.

In the Bible, Succot is a seven-day holiday. However, the Bible itself adds an additional day—called Shemini Atzeret, the Eighth Day of Assembly—onto the seven days of Succot. So, in biblical times, Succot—along with its additional Shemini Atzeret day—was observed for eight days, with the first and eighth days being the full Yom Tov and the six middle days as Chol HaMo'ed.

Much later, after the yearly Torah cycle was established and fixed, another additional day was added onto the end of the Succot holiday. This day was called Simchat Torah, the Rejoicing of the Torah, when the yearly Torah-reading cycle was completed and begun again.

Since Simchat Torah was added when the Jews were already living in the diaspora and had already established the second day of Yom Tov, the holiday became a nine-day observance, with the first two days and the last two days—Shemini Atzeret and Simchat Torah—as the full Yom Tov, and the five middle days as Chol HaMo'ed.

This is how Jews living in the diaspora today continue to observe Succot, Shemini Atzeret, and Simchat Torah.

For those who have returned to the original biblical observance, the Succot holiday is observed for a total of eight days. The first and the last days are the full Yom Tov, with the six middle days as Chol HaMo'ed. On the eighth day, the observances of Shemini Atzeret and Simchat Torah are combined.

Although the Jewish calendar is calculated with astronomical precision and fixed with exact structure, the calendar merely represents the *measure* of time. Part of the genius of Judaism throughout the ages has been the desire and the ability to sanctify time: to recognize the uniqueness of each year, month, day, hour, and moment, and to infuse time with special meaning and purpose.

5. שבת SHABBAT

(also known as Shabbas) is the Sabbath, the day of rest,
which occurs each week from Friday at sundown until Saturday at sundown.

According to the Torah, God finished the work of creation in six days; and on the seventh day, He ceased from work and rested—establishing the Sabbath, a day of physical rest and spiritual rejuvenation from labor and work (Genesis 2:1–3).

Since God rested on the seventh day, human beings—created in the image of God—are to imitate God and cease from work to rest each seventh day.

So, when the Ten Commandments were given, the Children of Israel were instructed to "remember the Sabbath day to keep it holy" (Exodus 20:8), and later were enjoined to "observe the Sabbath day throughout the generations as an everlasting covenant" (Exodus 31:16).

All manner of labor and work is prohibited on Shabbat. The Torah lists four specific prohibitions. The rabbis of the Mishnah derived a list of thirty-nine prohibitions from the Torah's original four; and based on these Mishnaic thirty-nine, later law literature extends the prohibitions even further. Shabbat is to be a day of complete rest and relaxation—for physical, mental, and spiritual rejuvenation; for refreshment of psyche and soul.

Shabbat is the central, core celebration of Jewish life because it is the weekly reminder of the creation of the universe and of humankind, and of the creation of the covenant between God and the Jewish People.

Shabbat is a twenty-four hour period each week that permits each Jew to connect with God, with family, with community, with self. In the fast-paced, complex world, where there never seems to be enough time for all that we must and want to do, Shabbat is a weekly "mini-vacation" that insists on and permits the pressures and the vagaries of the workaday world to be set aside.

Traditional Jewish law prohibits everyday labor on Shabbat—activities such as doing business, engaging in commerce, spending money, shopping, doing housework, driving, riding in a vehicle, writing, using electricity, and even using the telephone.

Yet, rather than being harsh restrictions, these prohibitions are actually positive, life-sustaining affirmations. "I have the ability and the power to control my time and my commitments. I have the ability and the power to set aside one day in seven for what is really important—to replace the tensions and demands of the everyday with physical rest and spiritual rejuvenation: time for spouse, children, parents, and friends; time for prayer, contemplation and reflection; time for leisurely meals, meaningful conversations, and soul-filling renewal; time for affirmation and celebration of the greatness and goodness of life; time for God; and time for myself."

Shabbat is the weekly time not "to do," but "to be."

Some even suggest that Shabbat is a foretaste of the messianic era, a brief but powerful weekly sample of the time of ultimate peace, tranquility, harmony, and worldly perfection.

Shabbat begins at sundown on Friday with the lighting of the Shabbat candles. One Shabbat law prohibits the lighting of fires, so originally the kindling of a Sabbath lamp—or later, candles—had the practical purpose of providing light in a darkening household between sunset and bedtime. Over the centuries, the lighting of Shabbat candles took on the religious symbolism of being the ritual ceremony that marks the beginning of the Sabbath.

The lighting of the Shabbat candles also has a mystical meaning. Shabbat is called זכר למעשה בראשית *zecher l'ma'aseh v'raysheet,* "the remembrance of the act of creation."

What was the first act of creation? God said, "Let there be light" (Genesis 1:3). The exact moment of creation was infused with God's light. On Shabbat, at the exact moment that is the remembrance of the act of creation, we imitate God's creation by "creating" light. The simple act of lighting a candle becomes a mystical moment of merging with the creation and the Creator.

A short synagogue service at sundown celebrates the beginning of Shabbat. The regular evening service (with certain insertions and changes for the Sabbath) is preceded by the קבלת שבת *Kabbalat Shabbat* (literally, "welcoming [or greeting] the Sabbath"). This is a series of prayers, mostly taken from the biblical psalms, which underscore the specialness of the day by serving as a transition from the secular weekday to the holiness of Shabbat. The central prayer of this service creates the image of Shabbat as the "queen of days," metaphorically infusing the Sabbath observance with the sense that the day should be treated like visiting royalty, with atmosphere, food and drink, and celebrations "fit for a queen."

Today many synagogues—most Reform and many Reconstructionist and Conservative—hold "late" Friday evening services, at 7:30 P.M. or 8 P.M. Because so many members of the Jewish community are unable to stop work early enough on Friday afternoon to make attendance at a sundown service possible, the later service gives many who could not or would not otherwise do so the opportunity to participate in Sabbath worship. These late services are frequently more formal in nature, often complete with choir music, a rabbi's sermon, and a time for refreshments and socializing following the worship. The social hour is most often called the ענג שבת *Oneg Shabbat* (literally, "joy of the Sabbath"), an informal time for friends and members of the community to meet and greet each other at week's end.

The Sabbath greeting and prayer is שבת שלום "*Shabbat Shalom*," "May it be a Sabbath of peace"—for you, the ones you love, the Jewish People everywhere, and all the inhabitants of the world.

The major Friday evening celebration is the Shabbat dinner, usually at home with family and friends. The table is set for a special dinner and fine foods are prepared. The meal begins with the chanting of קדוש *kiddush,* the prayer over wine. Since wine is traditionally a symbol of joy and gladness, it is used to welcome Shabbat and sanctify the day.

In some families, the husband expresses his love for his wife by reciting verses from Proverbs: "A woman of valor, who can find? Her price is far above rubies . . ." (Proverbs 31:10 ff), and the children are blessed by the parents.

The prayer for bread המוציא *hamotzee,* praising God who "brings forth bread from the earth," is recited over חלה *challah,* a braided white or egg bread that is specially baked for Shabbat.

Following the meal, זמרות *zemirot,* songs, chants, and melodies are sung, and the ברכת המזון *bircat hamazon,* the prayer of thanks for the food that was eaten, is recited. The Shabbat table is a place for good companionship, good food, and good conversation in a relaxed and joyful atmosphere.

Shabbat morning is spent at the synagogue in prayer and worship. The centerpiece of the service is the reading and studying of the weekly Torah portion. Following lunch, the afternoon is spent resting, reading, learning, taking walks, visiting with friends, and enjoying a few hours of quiet leisure.

The Shabbat afternoon service includes a short Torah reading—the first few verses of the new week's Torah portion. A light meal called סעודה שלישית *s'oodah shleesheet* (literally, "the third meal") is eaten. This is the third formal meal of the twenty-four-hour Sabbath, the first being Friday dinner and the second being Saturday lunch.

At sundown—when three stars are visible in the darkened sky—marking the end of Shabbat, the brief הבדלה *havdalah* (literally, "separation") service is recited, separating the holy Sabbath from the secular week.

Shabbat ends with the lighting of a braided, multi-flamed *havdalah* candle, indicating that it is now permissible to light fire again. And just as Shabbat began with a cup of wine, it ends with the *havdalah* cup of wine. The third ritual of *havdalah* is the smelling of sweet spices, called בשמים *b'samim,* usually held in a decorative container, the *b'samim* or spice box. Smelling sweet spices symbolically permits the sweetness of Shabbat to linger for a few moments longer, a continuing reminder of the joy and the sweetness of Shabbat.

As *havdalah* concludes, worshipers (and family members, for the brief *havdalah* service is often conducted at home) greet each other by saying שבוע טוב *"Shavu'a tov,"* "May it be a good week."

The centrality of Shabbat to Jewish life was captured by the modern Hebrew essayist Asher Ginsburg, who was known as Achad Ha-Am. He taught, "More than Israel (the Jewish People) has kept (observed) the Sabbath, the Sabbath has kept (preserved) Israel."

For wherever Jews have lived, under whatever circumstances or conditions, the observance of Shabbat has kept Jews, individually and collectively, unified and strong—committed to God and each other.

THE YEARLY HOLIDAY CYCLE

6.   ראש השנה   ROSH HASHANAH

(literally, "Head of the Year") is the Jewish new year. It occurs on the first
and second days of Tishri, in September or early October.

Some cultures and societies greet a new year with parties, loud music and raucous behavior, attempting to "blot out" the past in order to begin the future with a "clean, blank slate."

Judaism greets its new year with serious introspection, self-evaluation, and prayer—with its annual personal and collective חשבון הנפש *cheshbon hanefesh,* "accounting (or inventory) of the soul." In this way, the future can be shaped by assessing the successes and failures of the past.

Rosh HaShanah, the Jewish new year, begins a ten-day period called עשרת ימי תשובה *Aseret Y'may T'shuvah,* the Ten Days of Repentance, culminating in Yom Kippur, the Day of Atonement. The synagogue prayers for Rosh HaShanah and the next eight days revolve around evaluation of conduct and behavior in the year just ended, repentance for mistakes and transgressions, and seeking forgiveness from fellow human beings and from God.

Since honest personal evaluation and self-assessment is not an easy task, preparations for Rosh HaShanah begin far in advance of the actual holiday. In the month of Elul, the last month of the fading year—the month preceding the new year—special prayers and rituals are added to the daily worship services to remind and prepare the worshipers for the job of repentance.

On the Saturday evening before Rosh HaShanah, the סליחות *Selichot* (literally, "forgiveness") service is held. These penitential prayers set the mood and the tone for the prayers that will be recited beginning on Rosh HaShanah, and continuing through Yom Kippur.

The *Selichot* service is held at midnight—the only service during the Jewish year that is held at this unusual hour (remember: a Jewish day begins and ends at sundown). The reason that midnight is designated for the *Selichot* service is that Jews are enjoined to "get up (be eager) to do repentance." In earlier times—when most people's days began at the crack of dawn—awakening and arising four or five hours earlier than usual—at midnight—to recite the *Selichot* prayers demonstrated a Jew's willingness and eagerness to do repentance. Today, the *Selichot* service—at its special time and with its special prayers—is, in most synagogues, a very beautiful and moving entryway into the observance of Rosh HaShanah.

The various names given to the Jewish New Year reflect its themes and observances.

Actually, Jewish tradition identifies three other new years during the course of the year: (1) the New Year of Kings (1 Nisan), which was used in biblical times to determine and designate the reign of each king; (2) the New Year of the Animals (1 Elul), which was used in biblical times to determine the number of animals born in a given year for the purposes of tithing and ritual sacrifices; and (3) the New Year of the Trees (15 Shevat), the Jewish Arbor Day, when new trees are planted as part of the growing season.

In the early years of the Common Era, Jewish calendar-makers—trying to determine the number of years since the creation of the world—declared the first day of the month of Tishri as the birthday of the world. Even though the Bible lists Tishri as the seventh month of the Jewish calendar year, the calendar-makers stood by their calculations. So the first day of the month of Tishri came to be called Rosh HaShanah, the Head of the Year, or the New Year of Years. On Rosh HaShanah, the anniversary of the creation of the world is celebrated, and one counted year turns into the next.

Because Rosh HaShanah is to be the time of self-evaluation, repentance, and seeking forgiveness, Rosh HaShanah is also called יום הדין Yom HaDin, the Day of Judgment, and יום הזכרון Yom HaZikaron, the Day of Remembrance, when God is asked to remember and deal kindly with His people, while judging their deeds.

Rosh HaShanah often begins with a festive meal at home with family and friends. Candles are lit, with the proper blessing, to usher in the holiday, and *kiddush* is recited over wine. The *challah* that is eaten with the meal is often baked in a round shape. The round *challah* is to resemble a crown, acknowledging God as King.

It is customary to eat apples dipped in honey at the beginning of the Rosh HaShanah meal, symbolizing the hope for a sweet new year. Before eating the apples and honey, this formula is recited: "May it be Your will, O Lord our God, that we may be renewed for a good and a sweet new year."

In the synagogue, the curtain on the Holy Ark and the Torah covers are changed from their usual colors to the color white, symbolic of the quest for the purity of being that Rosh HaShanah represents.

A short synagogue service is held on Erev Rosh HaShanah—the evening when Rosh HaShanah begins. In some synagogues, the service is brief and takes place just at sunset, before the home meal. In other synagogues, the service is more elaborate, and takes place at a later hour, usually following the home meal.

A lengthy synagogue service is held on the morning of Rosh HaShanah.

While some liberal Jews celebrate only one day of Rosh HaShanah, holding a service on that day alone, all other Jews—including Israeli Jews—still celebrate two days of Rosh HaShanah, holding services on both days.

All of the prayers of the Rosh HaShanah (and Yom Kippur) services are chanted in a distinct, unique prayer-melody (one for the evening service; another one for the morning service) that evokes the special and awesome character of the day.

The traditional order of the service is supplemented throughout with a large number of special prayers called פיוטים *piyyutim* (singular, *piyyut;* from the Greek, meaning "poem") added to embellish and enhance the worship. The *piyyutim* reflect the major themes of the Rosh HaShanah worship: the kingship of God; repentance; judgment and forgiveness.

Many of the prayers of the Rosh HaShanah liturgy are elaborate metaphors—picturing God as king, sitting on the Throne of Judgment, on the Day of Judgment, writing the fate of each individual for the coming year in the Book of Life.

Most modern worshipers consider the ancient prayers as poetry and metaphor. Yet most readily acknowledge that human conduct—how each and every person behaves, each and every moment of existence—does determine the quality and the character of life and, ultimately, how God relates to and deals with each individual. The recitation of Rosh HaShanah prayers affirms that there is cosmic significance to human behavior.

A unique ritual is also added to the service: the sounding of the שופר *shofar*, the ram's horn. In biblical times, the shofar was used to call people together or to sound warning if danger were near.

On Rosh HaShanah, hearing the *shofar* sounded during the service serves many purposes: It acclaims God as king; it recalls the giving of Torah at Mt. Sinai (the Bible reports that the sound of the *shofar* was heard as the commandments were given [Exodus 19:19]); it serves as a warning to people to "wake up out of their lethargy," to scrutinize their deeds, to improve their conduct; it serves as a prelude to the announcement of God's judgment; and it serves as a reminder that one day, the Kingdom of God—the time of the messiah—will be announced to the whole world.

The *shofar* is blown to produce three different sounds: תקיעה *teki'ah*, one long blast; שברים *shevarim*, three short blasts; and תרועה *teru'ah*, nine short, staccato blasts. The final sound that is blown on the *shofar* is תקיעה גדולה *teki'ah gedolah*, the great *teki'ah*, a long, sustained sound.

Because of the ritual of the sounding of the *shofar*, Rosh HaShanah is known by yet another name, יום תרועה Yom Teruah, the Day of the Sounding of the Shofar.

Listening to the primitive wail of the ancient musical instrument not only reminds worshipers of Judaism's beginnings in a long-ago, far-away desert, but also touches the deepest and most basic places in the human soul—those places where each human being searches for and finds primordial beginnings and the mysteries of existence. On Rosh HaShanah, when each worshiper honestly and sincerely searches for transgression, and comes humbly seeking forgiveness, the heart-piercing and rending blast of the *shofar* is the perfect sound to lead the way toward soul inventory and to direct the path toward God.

The last part of the service for Rosh HaShanah revolves around three themes: the acceptance of God as King of the universe; the acknowledgment that God remembers the deeds of His people, rewarding good and punishing evil; and that through the sound of the *shofar*, God revealed His will at Mt. Sinai and will reveal Himself again to declare the ultimate redemption—the messianic era of the transformation and perfection of the world.

On the afternoon of the first day of Rosh HaShanah (or the afternoon of the second day, if the first day falls on Shabbat) many Jews gather at a body of flowing water (an ocean, lake, river, stream, or creek) for the תשליך *Tashlich* (literally, "casting" or "throwing") service. This quaint ceremony, begun in the Middle Ages, is the symbolic casting of transgressions into a body of water, to be carried away by the currents.

The worshiper throws bread crumbs, pebbles, or pocket-dust—symbolically representing the transgressions—into the water, and watches as they float away. While no one believes that bread crumbs are sins, or that flowing water has the capacity to carry away human transgressions, the symbolic visual effect can be very dramatic and powerful. In modern times, in many communities, the *Tashlich* service—conducted as a late-afternoon sunset service near an ocean, river, or lake—has become a beautiful way for the members of the community to gather together in observance of a Rosh HaShanah ritual and in celebration of the new year.

While the Rosh HaShanah prayers are solemn and serious, they are also filled with joy and with hope. For Judaism teaches that God is ready and very willing to forgive the transgressions of those who come in sincere repentance.

Rosh HaShanah begins the period when, as the Bible promises, each person can attain a "new heart and a new spirit" (Ezekiel 18:31). That, coupled with the large communal outpouring of identification and participation, and the gathering of family and friends to celebrate the holiday, infuses Rosh HaShanah with importance, gladness, and the spirit of renewal.

The Rosh HaShanah greeting is שנה טובה "*Shanah tovah*," "May it be a good year," or לשנה טובה תכתבו "*L'shanah tovah tikatevu*," "May you be inscribed (in God's Book of Life) for a good year." The Rosh HaShanah greeting is exchanged in cards, letters, telephone calls, and in person, as people wish each other the blessings of health, happiness, and peace in the new year.

The Shabbat between Rosh HaShanah and Yom Kippur (since this is a ten-day period, there is always one intervening Shabbat) is known as שבת שובה Shabbat Shuvah, the Sabbath of Repentance. Special prayers are added to the regular liturgy, along with a special prophetic reading, emphasizing the themes of repentance and forgiveness.

While the joy of the Sabbath is never diminished, the special additional prayers of Shabbat Shuvah serve to remind the worshiper of the solemn mood and tone of the entire ten days of repentance and of the serious self-evaluation that must be done.

7. יום כפור   YOM KIPPUR

is the Day of Atonement. It occurs on 10 Tishri,
in late September or early October.

Yom Kippur is a twenty-five-hour day of solemn prayer and repentance culminating the ten days of repentance that begin with Rosh HaShanah.

Because the task of repentance is so awesome, the usual and "normal" activities of life are avoided on Yom Kippur. Signs of comfort and luxury are prohibited, so people do not wear leather shoes or belts. (Leather was a symbol of luxury in ancient days, so traditional Yom Kippur worshipers wear sneakers or canvas shoes to synagogue.) Women often avoid the use of makeup and other beauty aids. Sexual relations between husband and wife—a sure time of joy and comfort—are prohibited.

The most forceful indication that comfort and luxury give way to full concentration on prayer and repentance on Yom Kippur is that Yom Kippur is a full twenty-five-hour fast. No food is eaten; no liquid is drunk. By not eating or drinking, the worshiper demonstrates that not only is the time for eating better spent on prayer, but that the task of prayer and repentance is so important that it supersedes even the normal physical needs for food and drink.

Many people choose to wear white clothing on Yom Kippur, a symbol of purity and cleansing. Some wear a *kittel,* a robe-like garment of pure white. As they were on Rosh HaShanah, the Torah covers and the curtain of the Holy Ark are white for dramatic visual effect as an aid to remembering the Yom Kippur task of seeking purity of soul through repentance. As the prophet Isaiah taught, "Though your transgressions be red as scarlet, they shall become white as snow" (Isaiah 1:18).

The Yom Kippur ritual begins, as the sun sets, with the כל נדרי *Kol Nidre* service. The entire service takes its name from the first prayer, *Kol Nidre,* which means "all vows." The prayer, chanted in a haunting and now very familiar melody, says that all vows that were made and not yet fulfilled are hereby canceled. The prayerful response is the acknowledgment that the transgressions of the people are great, yet God will hear prayers of repentance and grant forgiveness. The *Kol Nidre* prayer sets the tone for the Yom Kippur task of coming before God, admitting transgression, and asking for forgiveness.

Jewish tradition dictates that forgiveness can be sought from God only for transgressions of laws between a person and God. For transgressions between people, forgiveness must first be sought and obtained from the one who was offended, and then—and only then—from God.

Yet even after obtaining forgiveness from the offended person, the worshiper must still go to God in repentance, for the original law, proscribing conduct between people, comes from God. Since a person has not only offended another person, but has also broken one of God's laws, after forgiveness is obtained from the offended person, it then must be sought from God.

In some communities, immediately preceding the recitation of the *Kol Nidre* prayer, worshipers walk around the synagogue, speaking with each other and asking forgiveness from each other for offenses committed during the past year. In other communities, the conversations are more private, and take place in the hours and days preceding the *Kol Nidre* service.

One of the prayers of the *Kol Nidre* service has as its theme the continual nature of the Yom Kippur day—that prayers ascend to God on this evening, arrive by dawn, and are heard and accepted by the following evening. Many of the prayers of *Kol Nidre*—and the rest of the full day of Yom Kippur that follows (echoing the themes that were established on Rosh HaShanah)—set up the poetic, metaphorical scene of God sitting on the Throne of Judgment, watching people pass before Him in prayerful repentance. Many special *piyyutim* (poetic prayers) are interspersed throughout the service to embellish and deepen the worship.

During the *amidah* (the silent meditation) that is repeated aloud later in the service, two confessionals are recited—one short and one lengthy. These confessionals are a litany of human foibles and failings, and give the worshiper the opportunity to acknowledge a wide array of mistakes and transgressions.

Interestingly, the confessional is written in the plural: "*We* have transgressed . . . ," reflecting Judaism's notion of communal responsibility for conduct and human behavior. The theory is that even if I did not commit the particular transgression, "all Israel (the Jewish People) is responsible, one for another." So I take on a degree of responsibility for my neighbor's transgressions, just as he or she takes on responsibility for mine.

The traditional Yom Kippur morning Torah reading recalls the Yom Kippur ritual in biblical times, when the High Priest would sacrifice one goat to God, as the special offering, and send another goat—a "scapegoat"—out into the wilderness to die, symbolically carrying with it the transgressions of the people (Leviticus 16). The *haftarah,* taken from the words of the prophet Isaiah (57:14–58:14), recalls that Yom Kippur ritual is empty if it is not accompanied by the true and sincere spirit of repentance.

On Yom Kippur afternoon, the יזכור *Yizkor* memorial prayers are recited, recalling, with love and reverence, loved ones who have died, those who gave life, and whose lives formed the foundations of the lives of the worshipers.

Later in the service, the ancient Yom Kippur ritual is recalled, when the High Priest—this one and only time during the year—would enter into the Holy of Holies (the Inner Sanctum) of the Holy Temple, to recite God's great and holy name, and to pray for himself, the members of his household, and the entire Jewish People. Also, prayers are recited recalling the martyrs of the Jewish People—first during the Roman occupation, leading to the destruction of the Holy Temple in 70 C.E.; and then recalling the martyrs throughout Jewish history.

During the afternoon service, the biblical book of Jonah is read. The prophet Jonah came to the city of Nineveh to tell of its impending destruction for the continual transgressions of its people. Hearing Jonah's prophecy, the people immediately repented their ways. God forgave them their iniquity and the people and the city were saved. As the sun begins to set and Yom Kippur begins to draw to a close, the worshipers are reminded that if an entire city can save itself through repentance, then surely individuals can save themselves through repentance.

The final service of Yom Kippur—recited as the sun sets and darkness falls—is called נעילה *Ne'ilah* (from the Hebrew meaning "closing" or "locking"), which creates the metaphor of the final prayers of Yom Kippur ascending to God as the gates of the heavens are about to close. The *Ne'ilah* prayers are chanted in a slow, haunting melody, used just this once each year to create a beautiful and bittersweet atmosphere.

At sunset (actually, about forty minutes past sunset—well into darkness—making the Yom Kippur observance almost a full twenty-five hours) the worshipers chant a "declaration of faith," beginning with the שמע ישראל *Sh'ma Yisrael* ("Hear, O Israel, the Lord is our God, the Lord is One") and concluding with the words, "The Lord is God," which is repeated seven times.

One long blast of the *shofar* is sounded. The worshipers join together in saying, לשנה הבאה בירושלים "*L'shanah haba'ah b' Yerushalayim*," "Next year in Jerusalem," the Jewish hope and prayer—recited for millennia—for an end to exile and return to the Land of Israel, and at the same time, a prayer for ultimate redemption, for peace and perfection for the entire world.

The Yom Kippur greeting is, גמר חתימה טובה "*G'mar chatimah tovah*," or in abbreviated fashion, גמר טוב "*G'mar tov*," meaning "May you be sealed for good," or "A good seal." Since the Rosh HaShanah greeting is, "May you be inscribed (in God's Book of Life) for good," on Yom Kippur, when the metaphor of God writing each person's fate in a book is played out to its poetic conclusion, the greeting is now, "May you be sealed (affixed/approved/recorded) in God's Book for good."

The solemnity of Yom Kippur is followed by the satisfaction of knowing that the difficult task of repenting has been completed well, and by the joy of hearing God's forgiveness. It is customary for family and friends to gather together at the end of Yom Kippur to "break the fast" by eating a light meal, enjoying each other's company.

While Yom Kippur is observed once each year, the purpose and the spirit of Yom Kippur is observed each and every day. In the *amidah*, the silent meditation prayer that is recited by traditional Jews three times each day, there is a prayer of repentance, a prayer seeking God's forgiveness for transgression. Thus a Jew understands that while Yom Kippur is the annual communal recognition of transgression and the seeking of forgiveness, the task of evaluating conduct and striving for improvement is a daily obligation.

Because of their great power and importance in Jewish life, Rosh HaShanah, the Ten Days of Repentance, and Yom Kippur are collectively known as the High Holidays or the High Holy Days. Even more compelling is the name by which they are designated in Hebrew: ימים נוראים *Yamim Noraim,* the Days of Awe.

This name demonstrates the awesome task and the eventual joy that characterize Rosh HaShanah and Yom Kippur—the difficult and painful process of genuine self-evaluation, the honesty of humble repentance, personal growth, hoped-for forgiveness, and the ultimate satisfaction of receiving God's richest blessings.

AN ESSAY ON RIGHT AND WRONG

Judaism has no word for sin.

In English, sin means not only a violation of a religious moral precept, but is often defined as a state of being, entered into at birth, caused and imposed on each person by the "original sin" of Adam and Eve in the Garden of Eden.

Judaism has the concept of חטא *chet*. Although it is sometimes conveniently but incorrectly translated as sin, *chet* means to "miss the mark"—to be heading for the "bull's-eye" of moral and ethical behavior but to veer off course, to make a mistake. The Jewish "bull's-eye" is the proper observance of the *mitzvot*—the ethical and ritual commands of God. So *chet* means to "transgress the *mitzvot*," to fail to correctly or completely fulfill God's precepts and commandments.

The Hebrew word for repentance is תשובה *t'shuvah*, which means "to return"— to come back to the path leading to the "bull's eye" of following God's commands. When you repent and seek forgiveness, you commit to return to the path from which you have strayed, to redirect yourself to the straight path of fulfilling the *mitzvot*.

PERSONAL RESPONSIBILITY

Unlike other religious traditions, Judaism has no belief that anyone died for another's sins, no concept of anyone who takes upon himself the responsibility for another's actions. And Judaism believes that no one stands in the stead of another to admit or accept error or transgression.

Rather, Judaism believes that each one of us—created in the image of God, and given free will by God—is individually and personally responsible for our actions— for our own fulfillment or transgression of the *mitzvot*. And each of us must stand before God personally and with our own admissions, our own guilts, our own repentance, and our own request for forgiveness.

God makes seeking forgiveness a demanding but a richly satisfying task. Like a loving parent, God is quick to forgive misdeeds against Him, but He tenaciously protects the feelings of His children when they are hurt. That is why the sages taught, "God forgives transgressions committed against Him, but offenses against another human being must first be forgiven by the injured party" (BT Rosh HaShanah 17b).

To best illustrate this point, the late Rabbi Abraham Joshua Heschel was once asked if he had ever publicly forgiven the Nazis for the atrocities they had committed during the Holocaust. In reply, Heschel told this story:

The famed Rabbi Chaim Soloveichik of Brisk, the Brisker Rav, once decided to visit a sick friend who lived in a distant city. He wanted to fulfill the *mitzvah* of *bikkur cholim,* of visiting and comforting the ill.

But he wanted his trip to be personal and private rather than an official journey of a great rabbi—who would be mobbed by admirers and well-wishers all along the way. So, dressed in simple peasant clothing, he left his disciples and students at home and took a train to visit his sick friend.

The visit complete, the rabbi headed back to Brisk on the train. Not long after the train had left the station, two other travelers, young men dressed in stylish, modern clothes, entered the train car where the rabbi was sitting. They looked at him in his peasant clothes, with his threadbare carpetbag at his feet, and they began to speak.

"Poor peasant, what are you doing on this train? You don't belong here with us. Just look at your clothes! Just look at your miserable carpetbag! Don't you know that this train car is for people of means and distinction? You have no business being here. You are a disgrace. You make us ashamed to even be seen with the likes of you!"

The rabbi sat silently through the tirade, but it was to no avail. The two young men continued to tease and taunt him throughout the entire trip.

When the train finally pulled into the station at Brisk, the rabbi gathered up his carpetbag and left the train. As fate would have it, the two young men were also from Brisk, and they too got off the train at the Brisk station.

What they saw in the station house sent chills of fear up and down their spines. Filling the waiting room were hundreds of the people of Brisk, eagerly greeting their rabbi on his return from his journey. The young men realized that the old peasant they had been teasing on the train was none other than the Brisker Rav himself!

They ran up to him, and in trembling voices they said, "Rabbi, Rabbi, please forgive us. We didn't know that it was you on the train. We didn't mean to tease you or say any of those horrible things. Please, Rabbi, please. Forgive us."

The rabbi looked at them for a long, long time and then he said, "My sons, I am sorry. I cannot forgive you."

The young men were crestfallen, and they went to their homes in shame and despair.

They waited until Friday afternoon, and then they went to the home of the rabbi. They said, "Rabbi, Rabbi. Please forgive us for what we said on the train. We didn't know that it was you. We didn't mean to hurt you. Please, Rabbi. Shabbas is coming—the holy Sabbath, when our hearts are supposed to be filled with joy and happiness. But, there can be no joy for us if you do not forgive us. Please, Rabbi, please. Please forgive us."

The rabbi looked at them for a long, long time and, then, he said, "My sons, I am sorry, I cannot forgive you."

The young men spent an anguished Shabbas and their souls were in agony as the days turned to weeks and the weeks turned to months. Still the rabbi had not forgiven them.

Then it was Rosh HaShanah, the new year, when according to tradition, God's Book of Life is opened and He inscribes it for the coming year: "Who shall live and who shall die?" Only true repentance can bring God's forgiveness and avert the severity of the decree.

The young men went to the rabbi. "Rabbi, Rabbi," they said. "Rosh HaShanah is coming. We must stand before God to repent. But we cannot seek God's forgiveness for those transgressions we have committed before you. Please, Rabbi. We didn't mean to offend you; we didn't mean to dishonor you. Please, Rabbi. Let us enter this new year with cleansed souls. Please, Rabbi. Forgive us."

The rabbi looked at them for a long, long time. With great sadness in his voice, he said, "My sons, I am sorry. I cannot forgive you."

Rosh HaShanah came and went. The Ten Days of Repentance passed swiftly by. It was Yom Kippur, the Day of Atonement, the most solemn day of the Jewish year, the day when God seals the Book of Life with the fate of each and every person.

The young men went to the rabbi. They said, "Rabbi, now it is Yom Kippur. We are so afraid that God will not grant us anything good for this new year. Please, Rabbi, please. We have suffered enough already. In the name of all that is holy, on this sacred day of Yom Kippur, please, Rabbi, please. Forgive us for what we said to you on the train."

The rabbi looked at them for a long, long time, and then he said, "My sons, I am sorry. I cannot forgive you."

The young men's agony could not have been greater. They spent the twenty-four hours of Yom Kippur in utter anguish—each minute like an entire lifetime.

And then Yom Kippur was about to end. It was time for the final service of the day, the *ne'ilah,* when the prayers tell of the sealed decrees and the gates of the heavens being shut up and closed to any more supplication.

The sun was setting in the western sky, streaks of dark night had already begun to fill the universe. There was almost no more time. So, the young men walked right up to the pulpit of the synagogue, and in front of the whole congregation, they pleaded: "Rabbi, Rabbi, please. The gates of the heavens are closing. Our fates are soon to be sealed. And you have not yet forgiven us. Please, Rabbi, please. Please forgive us for the words we spoke to you on the train. We didn't mean them. We didn't mean to offend you. Please, Rabbi, please. Please forgive us."

The rabbi looked at them for a long, long time, and with great sadness, he said, "My sons, I am sorry, I cannot forgive you."

A cry went up from their throats, and an audible gasp was heard from the congregation.

"But now, my sons," said the Rabbi, "since Yom Kippur is almost over, I will tell you *why* I cannot forgive you.

"All this time," he explained, "you have come to seek forgiveness from *me,* from the Brisker Rav. But you did not offend *me,* you did not offend the Brisker Rabbi on the train. You offended the *poor peasant.* You must seek forgiveness from *him.*"

To this, Rabbi Heschel added, "The Nazis did not offend *me.* They offended the ones they shamelessly tortured and brutally murdered. *I* cannot forgive them. Let them seek forgiveness from the dead. It was *they* who were offended."

THE WAY TOWARD FORGIVENESS

Heschel's story and response are poignant and powerful, and they emphasize the Jewish way toward forgiveness:

- Know your actions and their consequences.
- Know that you, and you alone, are responsible for your actions.
- Know that you, and you alone, must come before God in repentance, seeking forgiveness for transgressions of the *mitzvot.*
- Offend God and you may go directly to God with your repentance.
- Offend another human being, and before you go to God—which you must eventually do, for God's ultimate forgiveness must be sought—you must go to the one you have offended.
- And remember: God will always listen to your plea—whatever transgression you may have committed—when you come to God in honesty and in sincerity.

SEEKING FORGIVENESS

How is repentance done? How is forgiveness sought? With what words, in what way, do you come before God to bring your confession, to seek and hear God's forgiveness?

The sages taught: "Repent one day before you die" (Avot 2:15). Since no one knows the day on which death will come, the sages meant: "Repent everyday."

Since each person can have a personal, intimate relationship with God, each person can come to God with personal, intimate words of confession—words no one else could speak, words out of the depths of pain, of anguish, of guilt, of honesty, of sincerity.

But if it is difficult or embarrassing to find the right words of confession to speak to God, the daily liturgy provides words to say: "Forgive us, O Father, for we have missed the mark; pardon us, O our King, for we have transgressed. You are merciful and forgiving. Praised are You, O Lord, who desires repentance."

Once each year, at Rosh HaShanah and Yom Kippur time, the collective thoughts of the Jewish People turn to repentance. By entering into a new year with reflection and prayer, by seriously and sincerely evaluating our past conduct, admitting past error, and seeking forgiveness for transgression, we are spiritually renewed, wholly restored, at peace with ourselves, our fellow human beings and with God.

The liturgy of the High Holidays leads each Jew to introspection and repentance: the figurative scenes of God judging His people's behavior; the recitation of the lengthy, brutally honest confessional; the scriptural reading depicting the ancient ritual of choosing one goat to be sacrificed to God and another to be sent off as the "scapegoat" representing transgression; the reenactment of the High Priest's entrance into the Holy of Holies to ask God for forgiveness; the stirring story of the city saved through repentance.

Animal sacrifice is no longer offered; no goat is sent out to the wilderness to die; the Holy of Holies no longer exists. Few people today take literally the heavenly scenes described by the prayer-writer, but understand the prayers to be metaphors, trying to capture—in word pictures that are easily understood—the awesome relationship between God and His children.

But the intent of the Yom Kippur rituals and the original High Holiday prayers remains. The Ten Days of Repentance is the time for Judaism's annual "soul inventory," for serious contemplation, sincere repentance, and joyous renewal.

Yet the prayers themselves hold far less power than the actions they inspire. That is why we match our Yom Kippur actions to our Yom Kippur words and personally ask forgiveness from those we have offended and grant forgiveness to those who seek our pardon.

GOD FORGIVES

Forgiveness from another person, if not easily requested or obtained, is at least easy to hear. We speak the same language, use the same words, understand the same meanings.

But how does God—invisible, and inaudible to many—speak forgiveness to us? How do we hear forgiveness from God? How do we know when we have been forgiven?

We know that we have been forgiven when we hear forgiveness within—when we have *changed enough* to not commit the same transgression again, or at least to be immediately aware and repentant if we make the same mistake again.

A personal example to illustrate: Not long ago, I was walking on the streets of New York City, place of striking contrasts—tremendous opulence and grand wealth side by side with deep poverty, despairing hunger, and homelessness.

The streets of New York are filled with the desperately needing, people who turn to the well-off to help them survive the bitter cold, the searing hunger, the utter frustration.

We could debate long and hard about the reasons that these conditions exist and about long-term, permanent solutions, but to a visitor to these streets, the immediate plight of the starving is more important than political debate over the causes or eventual solution. So as I walk the streets of New York, I keep dollar bills in my pocket and I give them to the "street people," the hungry and the homeless.

One night, it was very cold and wet. The strong wind was whipping the rain and chilling to the bone. As I made my way to another corner, I saw a young woman sitting near the curb. She seemed to be about my age—but she could have been twenty years younger; poverty takes an early and a deep toll. She was holding up a sign that read, "Can you help a starving artist? I don't have anywhere to live and I am hungry. Will you please help me?"

I reached through the pocket of my coat to the pocket of my trousers where I keep the dollar bills that I give out, but my pocket was empty. I had given away all the bills that I had put there. My mind worked in that microsecond it takes to make a decision. If I wanted to give her money, I would have to stop there on the freezing street corner, take off my gloves, unbutton my coat, reach into my inner pocket, get my wallet, open it in the strong wind, take out a dollar, hand the woman the money, button up my coat, put my gloves back on and continue on my way.

In the split second that it took to calculate all this, I determined that it would be too much trouble. I walked on.

To this day, the face of that young woman on the street corner in New York haunts me.

I made a mistake. I missed the mark. I transgressed one of God's most important commands—to help a fellow human being in need.

In my repentance, I hear forgiveness. For I am a changed human being. I will never again disregard a person in need, especially for my own comfort or convenience. I may not always respond in the same way, but I will always respond to those in need. And if I have not yet achieved perfection—as I surely have not—then at least if I make the same mistake again—and I surely will—I will realize it and, hopefully, do something about it, before it is too late.

It is not easy to face our foibles and our failings. Other religion's pathways to forgiveness sometimes seem much easier than Judaism's. But Judaism's demand that we take responsibility for our own actions, admit our own mistakes, confess our transgressions, and hear God's forgiveness is ultimately very satisfying. For in confronting our own errors and wrestling with our own mistakes, we emerge into the light of growth and change, and we become more human and more humane.

REASONS FOR REPENTANCE

Why do our mistakes, our transgressions of the *mitzvot,* call us to repentance and stir us to seek forgiveness?

A most compelling reason is that if we believe that the commandments came directly from God, that they are God's will for us, then as children of God, we must obey His law. The power of God calls us to follow His rules, and if we disobey them, to say, "I'm sorry."

Beyond that, the Torah repeats, time and time again, the conditional nature of the covenant. "*If* you obey My commandments and observe My *mitzvot, then,* I will reward you. *But, if* you disobey and transgress My *mitzvot, then* I will bring punishment upon you" (see, especially, Leviticus 26).

The people of biblical times truly believed that *if* they followed God's law, *then* the rains would come, the crops would grow. But *if* they disobeyed God's law, *then* they would be thirsty and hungry (see, especially, Deuteronomy 11:13 ff). The prophets take up where the Torah leaves off, foretelling severe punishment for the people and for the Jewish nation if God's commands are not fulfilled, linking transgression of *mitzvot* to the eventual conquering of the Land of Israel, the destruction of the Holy Temple and the exile of the people.

To many of us, the *if-then* covenant may seem fallacious: We see little evidence of a causal relationship between human behavior and whether or not the rains fall.

Yet we cannot deny that there is a connection between how we act—whether or not we obey God's law—and what ultimately happens to the world in which we live.

God doesn't really have to intervene, because we bring reward or punishment upon ourselves: Every action causes a reaction; every act has a consequence; every word ripples through time. Everything we do and say affects those around us—our jobs or businesses, our communities, our neighborhoods, our organizations, our spouses, our children, our relatives, our friends. Everything we do and say determines whether things will be good or bad, easy or hard, loving or alienating.

To be sure, there is random happenstance; we cannot control the actions of others who choose to do evil rather than good; we cannot tame all of the forces of nature. But we can have an effect on our small worlds: our offices, our homes, our marriages, our relationships. And since the whole world is ultimately made up of individual human beings—just like you and me—then we can and ultimately do have an effect on how our whole world works.

The 1960s campus slogan is profoundly true: "What if they gave a war and nobody came?" Not only are our most intimate relationships ours to form, but in the end, war and peace are in our hands too.

For war and peace are not made by faceless entities called "nations," but by the individual human beings who lead those nations by playing out on the world's grand stage their personal definitions of right and wrong, their own sense of transgression or adherence to God's law, and—most significantly—their own state of inner turmoil or well-being.

AT-ONE-MENT

When we know the difference between right and wrong, when we honestly admit our mistakes and our transgressions, when we repent, seek and hear forgiveness, we "get right with God." We restore balance to our lives, bring peace to our hearts and quiet calm to our souls.

Then our newfound tranquility and inner joy undulates outward to touch everyone, and eventually ripples throughout the entire world. There is no limit to the positive effect that being one with the universe, to being one with God, can have.

In coming to God with our faults and our failings, with our honesty and our humility, the words of the Yom Kippur liturgy are our daily hope and prayer, "In Your unbound mercy, O God, forgive the transgression of this people, as You have forgiven our people from the days of Egypt until now" (Numbers 14:19).

God's reply is our comfort and our everlasting salvation, "As you have asked, I have forgiven" (Numbers 14:20).

8. סוכות SUCCOT

(literally, "booths" or "huts") is the Festival of Tabernacles.
It is a seven- (or eight-) day holiday, beginning on 15 Tishri, in late September
or early October.

Succot is an agricultural festival, celebrating the fall harvest. It is therefore also known as חג האסיף Chag Ha'asif, the Festival of Ingathering. It recalls how, first during the trek through the desert and later at harvest-time each year, Jews would live in small, fragile booths or huts (tabernacles) built in the desert or in the fields.

To remember the lives of the ancestors, to identify with their journeys, and to acknowledge the harvest-time, in celebration of the festival of Succot, Jews build a

סוכה succah, a small, fragile booth/hut. During the festival, it is customary to eat meals in the succah and entertain guests there. Some even sleep in the succah each night.

The succah is to be a temporary structure. It must be strong enough to last the entire festival, but it must also be fragile and delicate enough to indicate that it is not a permanent dwelling place. It is built with a roof made of branches and leaves, so that the sun by day and the moon and stars by night are visible through the roof. The succah is often filled with fruits, vegetables, and other products of the harvest, as well as decorations made by the children.

Two ritual objects are used during the festival, both in the succah and during worship services. The לולב lulav is a palm branch, with willow and myrtle leaves attached. The אתרוג etrog is a lemon-like citron. Together the lulav and the etrog are known as ארבעה מינים arba'ah minim, the four species. The traditional explanation is that the lulav represents the strong backbone and the etrog represents the warm heart of the Jewish People. A more plausible explanation is that the lulav and etrog are ancient fertility symbols, used at harvest-time to thank God for the bounty of the current harvest, and to ask God for continued abundance in the coming planting.

At a specific point in the Succot morning worship services, the lulav and etrog are held together and shaken in all directions while a special blessing is recited. Pointing the lulav and etrog in all directions serves to reminds us that God—provider of all blessings—is everywhere, all throughout the natural world.

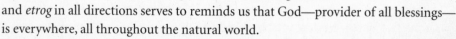

The first day of Succot (or the first two days, for those in the diaspora who celebrate the additional day of the festival) is a full Yom Tov, with all its celebrations and certain restrictions. Synagogue services are held, which—in addition to the recitation of the blessing over the *lulav* and *etrog*—include the chanting of הושענות *hosha'not*, hymns of praise to God, which are sung as the worshipers circle the synagogue carrying the *lulav* and *etrog*. *Hallel* prayers—psalms of praise to God—are recited, and the Torah reading reflects the theme of the festival.

Chol HaMo'ed, the intermediate days of the festival (either five or six, depending on the length of celebration of the entire festival) are considered "half-holidays." The festival continues, special prayers are added to the daily worship (including the *hosha'not* and *hallel*), and people continue to eat and dwell in the *succah*. But there is a return to normal, daily activities, without the celebrations and restrictions of a full Yom Tov.

During the festival of Succot, there is always at least one Shabbat—either a Yom Tov or a Chol HaMo'ed day. During the synagogue service on Shabbat Succot, the biblical book of Kohelet (Ecclesiastes) is read, sounding the theme of the power of God, the place of humankind within the universe, and the ultimate meaning of existence.

When Succot was a seven-day biblical festival, the seventh day came to be known as הושענא רבה Hoshana Rabbah, the Great Hoshana, the Great Praises. At the conclusion of the festival, God was greatly praised, and the *lulav* was beaten against the ground (most probably as a final, symbolic throwing away of transgressions at the end of the festival period that began back on Rosh HaShanah). Hoshana Rabbah was the last day of the festival of Succot, and was enhanced with all the celebrations of a full Yom Tov.

However, the Bible itself added an additional day onto the end of Succot. It is called שמיני עצרת Shemini Atzeret, the Eighth Day of Assembly—a final conclusion to the entire holiday period. Over time, Shemini Atzeret came to be considered as the final day of Succot, and took on all the celebrations of a full Yom Tov, with Hoshana Rabbah being relegated to being part of Chol HaMo'ed, the intermediate days.

A very special prayer called תפלת גשם *Tefilat Geshem*, the Prayer for Rain, was added to the liturgy of Shemini Atzeret. For those living in the Land of Israel, the prayer was a logical extension of the praise and thanks for the harvest, since rain is needed during the winter months. For those who came to live outside the Land of Israel, the prayer for rain established a bond to the Land and its needs that linked the Jews of the diaspora to the Jewish Land throughout the centuries of exile. Now, on Shemini Atzeret, in addition to all the special festival prayers, the *Yizkor* memorial prayers are also recited.

This would be the configuration of the celebration of the festival of Succot (with the two days—Hoshana Rabbah and Shemini Atzeret—most probably being treated as full Yom Tov for those in the diaspora who observe the additional day of the holiday), except that after the yearly Torah-reading cycle was formally fixed (probably some time around the third century of the Common Era); an additional day was added onto Succot. This day is called Simchat Torah.

שמחת תורה SIMCHAT TORAH

Simchat Torah (literally, "The Rejoicing of the Torah") celebrates the conclusion and the new beginning of the yearly Torah-reading cycle. It occurs on the twenty-third of Tishri, adding a ninth day to the eight-day festival of Succot.

Each year, the Torah is read in its entirety. Simchat Torah is the day when the concluding words of the book of Deuteronomy are read, followed immediately by the reading of the opening words of Genesis.

This yearly celebration—symbolizing, literally and figuratively, the unbroken continuity of the Jewish People and Jewish life—is characterized by much joyous singing and dancing.

The Torah Scrolls are removed from the Holy Ark to the chant of a series of biblical verses known as אתה הראת *Atah Haratah* ("Unto you it was shown, that you might know . . . that the Lord is God . . ." [Deuteronomy 4:35]). The Torah Scrolls are paraded around the synagogue (in at least seven separate parades) with great, happy rejoicing. Each parade is called a הקפה *hakafah* (literally: "circuit" or "circling"; plural, *hakafot*). The children join in the parades, marching with flags and banners.

Simchat Torah celebrates the satisfaction of Jewish learning fulfilled, through the completion of the yearly Torah cycle, and the joyous anticipation of the continuation of Jewish learning through the beginning of a new Torah-reading cycle. It is a time for great personal and communal happiness.

On the morning of Simchat Torah, it is customary for everyone in the synagogue to be called up to the Torah to recite the blessings over the reading of the Torah. Thus everyone can personally participate in the joyous *mitzvah* of completing and beginning the annual Torah-reading cycle. Following the Simchat Torah service, there is often a festive, communal meal or refreshments, so that the members of the synagogue community can extend the Simchat Torah celebration.

With Simchat Torah now added at the end of the festival of Succot, for those who observe the biblically mandated holiday, Shemini Atzeret and Simchat Torah are combined as a full Yom Tov on the eighth day. Thus the first and eighth days are full Yom Tov, with the six intermediate days designated as Chol HaMo'ed.

For those in the diaspora, who observe the additional day of the festival, the first two days are Yom Tov, and the eighth and ninth days—now, Shemini Atzeret and Simchat Torah—are Yom Tov, with the five intermediate days designated as Chol HaMo'ed.

For everyone, Hoshana Rabbah has now become part of Chol HaMoed.

Succot—indeed, the entire Succot, Hoshana Rabbah, Shemini Atzeret, Simchat Torah sequence—is a beautiful and deeply meaningful holiday. However, it is not observed by many modern Jews with as much devotion and enthusiasm as it once was.

Coming so soon after the observance of Rosh HaShanah and Yom Kippur, and revolving around celebrations of the agricultural harvest—with which most contemporary Jews are little involved—Succot has failed to capture the imagination and allegiance of many modern Jews. The exceptions, of course, are the Orthodox community—which observes all of Jewish life, simply because of God's mandate—and many Jews who live in Israel, who are caught up in the harvest-time nature of the festival.

Yet Succot holds an important message, which every Jew can learn and remember.

First, even though few Jews are involved in farming or other agricultural work, it is good to remember that human beings still depend on the ongoing process of nature to provide food and sustenance. God is the original source of all food—the spark of creation that is at the absolute core of everything that lives and grows. It is good to praise and give thanks to God for life and sustenance. Succot provides that opportunity.

In addition, Succot comes so closely after Rosh HaShanah and Yom Kippur for a very specific purpose. After the difficult task of self-evaluation and repentance, and after hearing God's forgiveness, some may be tempted to become haughty and arrogant. After all, it seems as if the process of repentance has worked, and that all will be well in the year ahead. Succot reminds us that the ultimate power of the universe—the power of life and death—belongs not to humankind, but to God alone. That is why a Jewish legend teaches that God will not finally "seal" the "Book of Life"—in which He records the fate of each person—until Hoshana Rabbah. Even with all the prayer and repentance of Rosh HaShanah and Yom Kippur, there is still time to come before God seeking forgiveness, all throughout the festival of Succot. Succot calls out for reverence and humility.

So, rather than being little observed, Succot can be widely appreciated and much commemorated. Its purposes speak to the minds and hearts of people who seek connection to creation and the Creator, to the purpose and meaning of existence.

The Succot greeting—as it is for Pesach and Shavuot—is חג שמח "Chag Sameach," "A happy holiday." In Yiddish, the greeting is "Gut Yontiv," "A good festival/holiday."

With its reminder of God's greatness in the universe, with its symbols—the succah, the lulav, and the etrog; with its deep connection to the Land and the People of Israel; with its celebration of Torah learning and the continuity of the Jewish People, Succot can and should be a very happy holiday.

9. חנוכה CHANUKAH

(literally, "dedication") is the Festival of Dedication, also known as the Festival of Lights. It is an eight-day festival, which begins on 25 Kislev. It usually falls sometime in December, although it occasionally begins in late November, but sometimes it begins late enough in December to run over into January.

Chanukah is the only ancient holiday that is not mentioned in the Bible. This is because the events of Chanukah took place in the year 165 B.C.E., while the last events in the Bible occurred in approximately 400 B.C.E. However, the events of Chanukah are described in books 1 and 2 of the Maccabees, which is included in the Apocrypha in some Christian Bibles.

Here, briefly, is the story of Chanukah.

Early in the fourth century B.C.E., Alexander the Great swept through the ancient Middle East—including Israel—spreading Hellenistic culture as he extended Greek political influence.

After his death, the lands he had conquered came under the control of a number of different countries and rulers. At the end of the second century B.C.E., Israel fell under the rule of Antiochus Epiphanes of Syria. Syrian troops were dispatched throughout the Middle East to pave the way for Antiochus's hoped-for conquest of Egypt. Between Syria and Egypt, Israel lay as a stepping-stone for Antiochus and his armies.

Antiochus decreed that all under his rule would be forced to Hellenize, and the Jews of ancient Israel were gradually denied more and more religious and political freedoms. Many Jews resisted Hellenization, but a number of Jews quickly adapted to Greek culture.

Aided by a faction of wealthy Jews who had gradually abandoned their own religious traditions in favor of Greek culture, Antiochus replaced the High Priest in the Holy Temple with a corrupt "puppet" priest. By 165 B.C.E. Antiochus had forbidden all forms of Jewish religious observance—including worship of the One Lord God, circumcision, and the observance of the dietary laws. The Holy Temple in Jerusalem was desecrated, and a statue of Zeus was placed on the ritual altar. The Syrian army strongly enforced Antiochus's decrees, and opposition was met with torture and murder.

It was at this point that strong Jewish resistance to Antiochus and Syrian domination began to develop. A few small bands of Jews tried to repulse the Syrians, but they were no match for the Syrian armies.

However, in the village of Modin, not far from Jerusalem, a local priest named Mattathias the Hasmonean, together with his five sons, organized a successful rebellion against the Syrian army. They defeated the Syrian troops in a number of minor skirmishes and, exuberant with victory, headed to Jerusalem to liberate the Holy Temple.

Word of their successes had spread before them, and when they reached Jerusalem, they met with little resistance. The sons of Mattathias captured the Holy Temple from the Syrians, destroyed the Greek idols, purified the ritual areas and objects, and prepared to restore the Temple to the rightful priests and its sacred purposes.

According to the book of the Maccabees, the ceremonies rededicating the Holy Temple to its sacred purposes took place over eight days—a belated eight-day Succot celebration, because the holiday had not been properly observed under Syrian control of the Temple. The celebration took its name from the Hebrew word for "dedication," חנוכה *chanukah*.

It is here that legend enters, not only to explain the eight-day dedication ceremony, but to bring an aspect of Divine intervention to the story. According to legend, the sons of Mattathias prepared to rekindle the sacred eternal lamp of the Holy Temple. However, they discovered that all but one vessel of purified oil had been destroyed by the Syrians. This small cruse contained only enough oil to last for one day, but the legend relates that a "miracle" took place. The oil burned in the Temple lamp not for one day, but for eight days—the time that it took to purify new oil for the Temple's needs.

The sons of Mattathias became known as the Maccabees, which means "hammers," for their strong resistance to the powerful Syrian armies. In fact, the Maccabees led the first recorded military uprising—not just in Jewish history, but in the history of the world—on behalf of religious freedom.

The victory in Jerusalem did not end their struggles, for the Syrian army still exhibited much power and control throughout the countryside But soon after the death of Antiochus, freedom of religious practice was restored to the Land of Israel.

Judah, the leader of the Maccabees, was killed in a subsequent battle, but his brothers ascended to the High Priesthood, establishing the Hasmonean Era. Eventually, their descendants provided the lineage for the Hasmonean Dynasty of kings.

Syrian domination of the Middle East diminished as Roman influence spread throughout the area. Later, in 37 B.C.E., internal strife led the Hasmonean leader to invite the Romans to govern Israel—the beginning of the final end to Jewish self-rule in the Land of Israel.

The holiday of Chanukah was established to commemorate the Maccabeean victory and the rededication of the Holy Temple. To recall the "miracle" of the oil burning for eight days instead of one, the holiday is celebrated for eight days; and on the evening of each of those days, oil lamps (now candles) are lit in remembrance and gratitude.

The candles are lit in a candelabrum known as a חנוכיה *chanukiah,* a Chanukah lamp. More popularly, the Chanukah candelabrum is known as a מנורה *menorah.*

The *menorah,* which can be very plain or a beautiful piece of art, has nine branches—one for each of the eight nights of Chanukah, and the ninth for the candle known as the שמש *shamash* (literally, "servant"), the candle that is used to light the others.

The candles are placed in the *menorah* (with the *menorah* facing you) from right to left. On the first night, one candle, plus the *shamash* (which is most often placed at the center of the *menorah*), is placed in the *menorah.* On the second night, two candles (plus the *shamash*) are placed in the *menorah*—one for the current day of the holiday and one for the previous day. On each succeeding night, an additional candle is added to the *menorah,* until finally, on the eighth night, the *menorah* is completely full with the eight candles, plus the *shamash.*

The candles are placed from right to left, but they are lit from left to right—that is, the current day's candle is lit first, then yesterday's, backward until the first day's.

Each night, for the eight nights of Chanukah, families gather together to light the *menorah,* reciting special blessings as the candles are lit. The first blessing thanks God for the commandment to light the lamp/candles of Chanukah. The second blessing praises God, "Who did miracles for our ancestors at this time of year in ancient days." The third blessing—which is recited only on the first night—is the traditional blessing said at the beginning of any festival, or when anything is being done for the first time: praising God, "Who has kept us in life, sustained us, and enabled us to reach this occasion."

It is customary to exchange gifts on Chanukah, small tokens of love and affection. One of the traditional gifts, often given by Ashkenazic Jews, is "Chanukah *gelt*"—money. It used to be that a coin or two would suffice, but these days "inflation" has hit even Chanukah *gelt*, and gifts (most particularly to children) not only of money, but of toys, games, and all manner of presents, are often very generous.

The time when the Chanukah candles are burning is to be a time of enjoyment and relaxation. Often, family members play סביבון *sevivon* (Hebrew) or *dreidel* (Yiddish) (often with small wagers of pennies or toothpicks) as an enjoyable game.

A *sevivon-dreidel* is a four-sided top. Each of the four sides contains a Hebrew letter: נ *nun*, ג *gimel*, ה *hay*, and ש *shin*. These four letters stand for the words נס גדול היה שם *nes gadol hayah sham*, meaning, "A great miracle happened there." (In Israel, the fourth letter on the *sevivon-dreidel* has been changed from a ש *shin*, for the word שם *sham*, meaning "there," to a פ *pay*, for the word פה *poh*, meaning "here." Thus in Israel the *sevivon-dreidel* says, "A great miracle happened *here*.")

Potato pancakes, *latkes*, are the traditional Chanukah food because they are fried in oil. In Israel jelly doughnuts, called *sufganiyot*, also fried in oil, are the favorite Chanukah food.

For all its festivity, Chanukah is actually a minor holiday on the Jewish calendar. Yet, in modern times—particularly in the United States, where the festivities of the Christmas season are all-pervasive—Chanukah has taken on great import and celebration because of its relative time connection to Christmas. Chanukah has seemingly become the "Jewish answer to Christmas," particularly for the children. That seems to be why children now receive such lavish gifts for Chanukah, and why there are so many Chanukah parties as a counterbalance to all the Christmas parties. That is why a festival as minor as Chanukah has become the best known of all Jewish holidays—to Jews and non-Jews alike.

Because of this emphasis, it is important to remember a few facts: Chanukah and Christmas have nothing in common, other than that they are celebrated at the same time of the year. Chanukah does not need to be compared to any other religious observance, or celebrated in any out-of-proportion way. Chanukah stands on its own merit and deserves its own unique reputation and honored status in Jewish life—as a celebration of the uprising for religious freedom, as a celebration of the rededication of the Holy Temple to the service of God, as a reminder to continually strive for the cause of freedom for all people, and as a celebration of the winter season and of bringing new light into places of darkness.

10.   ט״ו בשבט   TU B'SHEVAT

(literally, the fifteenth [day] of [the month] of Shevat) is the Jewish Arbor Day,
the "birthday of the trees," commemorated on 15 Shevat,
in late January or early February.

Tu B'Shevat is the biblically designated new year of the trees.

It takes its name from the day and the month on which it occurs.

שבט Shevat is the name of the Hebrew month that falls sometime around late January/February of the secular year.

The ב B' means "in" or "of."

The word ט״ו Tu is made up from a combination of two Hebrew letters, which represent the number 15.

The Hebrew letter ט tet represents the number 9, and the Hebrew letter ו vav (sometimes pronounced as a "v," sometimes pronounced as "oo") represents the number 6. The ט tet and the ו vav together, pronounced ט״ו tu ("too") is 9 + 6, which equals 15.

Therefore Tu B'Shevat is the fifteenth day of the month of Shevat, the new year of the trees.

It would seem much more reasonable to add 10 + 5, rather than 9 + 6, to get to 15. However, the Hebrew letter representing 10 is י yud, and the Hebrew letter representing 5 is ה hay; and י yud and ה hay together form the word י״ה Yah, which is a name for God.

To avoid using the name of God for the secular purposes of designating and counting numbers, Jewish tradition requires that the number 15 always be represented by the letters ט tet and ו vav, 9 + 6, rather than by the letters י yud and ה hay, 10 + 5.

Tu B'Shevat is designated as the new year for the trees because, in the Land of Israel, it is at this time of year (late January/February) that the trees begin to form their fruit. It is also an excellent time for the planting of new saplings. Thus Tu B'Shevat is a holiday that recognizes and celebrates the natural order—the annual blooming of the trees, and the necessity of planting new trees at this time of year.

For Jews living in most places in the diaspora, a holiday that falls in the middle of cold winter and celebrates new planting and new growth has little practical value or application.

However, for all the years of the diaspora, Tu B'Shevat has served as an important link to the Land and the People of Israel. Commemorating Tu B'Shevat, when the icy winds howled and the snow was still in high drifts in the lands of the dispersion, kept the connection to the Land of Israel alive, and the hope of return never-ending.

In modern times, especially since the establishment of the State of Israel in 1948, Jews of the diaspora have celebrated Tu B'Shevat by collecting money to send to Israel for the specific purpose of planting new trees in Israel's soil. The Jewish National Fund has led the tree-planting effort, and since 1948 enough money has been contributed to plant more than 200 million trees in the Land of Israel.

On Tu B'Shevat it is customary to eat fruits, nuts, and other natural produce of the land.

In honor of Tu B'Shevat, children in Jewish schools often participate in programs and activities that teach about the Land of Israel and its people.

In recent days, the commemoration of Tu B'Shevat has been used to heighten awareness of ecology, the environment, and the responsibility of each and every person to preserve and enhance the earth.

11.   SPECIAL SABBATHS

In the early winter—after Chanukah, and either just preceding or following Tu B'Shevat—comes the commemoration of a special Sabbath called שבת שירה Shabbat Shirah, the Sabbath of Song. In the yearly Torah-reading cycle, the weekly portion that is read on this Shabbat contains שירת הים Shirat HaYam, the "Song of the Sea," (Exodus 15: 1–18). This prayer of gratitude and thanksgiving was chanted by the Children of Israel after safely crossing the Sea of Reeds (more popularly known as the Red Sea) as they left Egyptian slavery. The haftarah recited on this Shabbat contains another song of triumph, the "Song of Deborah," (Judges 5:1–31). In modern times, Shabbat Shirah has become an occasion to celebrate the beauty of Jewish music and its central and powerful place in Jewish life.

In the late winter, there is a series of five special שבתות Shabbatot (plural of Shabbat) leading up to the celebration of the festival of Purim, and then leading up to the celebration of the festival of Pesach. These five Shabbatot are observed over a period of time ranging between five and eight weeks, depending on whether or not it is a leap year.

Each of these Shabbatot is marked with a special additional reading from the Torah and a special haftarah—both readings specially selected to reflect the theme of the special Sabbath.

1. שבת שקלים Shabbat Shekalim (literally, "Sabbath of the Shekels" [a *shekel* is a coin]) serves as a reminder that it is time to start preparing for the observance and celebrations of Pesach.

2. שבת זכור Shabbat Zachor (literally, "Sabbath of Remembrance") always occurs on the Shabbat of the week in which the festival of Purim will be celebrated, and serves as a reminder that, throughout Jewish history, there have been vicious enemies who have wished to destroy the Jewish People. Shabbat Zachor reminds us: Be ever cautious and vigilant.

3. שבת פרה Shabbat Parah (literally, "Sabbath of the Cow, or Heifer"), serves as a reminder of the ancient requirement for ritual purification for the observance of Pesach, and of the contemporary home preparations for the celebration of the holiday.

4. שבת החדש Shabbat HaChodesh (literally, "Sabbath of the Month") is the Shabbat that occurs at the beginning of the week when the new Hebrew month of Nisan (the month when Passover is celebrated) will begin, and serves as a dramatic and vivid reminder that Pesach is soon to be celebrated.

5. שבת הגדול Shabbat HaGadol (literally, "The Great Sabbath") is the Shabbat that occurs at the beginning of the week when Pesach will be observed. It is called the "Great Sabbath" because it precedes the great festival of Passover, with all its historical and religious significance and all its grandeur. Shabbat HaGadol has no special additional Torah reading, but there is a special *haftarah*—which ends with the words, "Behold, I will send you Elijah the prophet, before the coming of that great and awesome day" (Malachai 3:23).

According to Jewish tradition, it is Elijah the prophet who will foretell and announce the coming of the messianic age. Pesach is a reminder and a celebration of historical redemption—the coming out of Egypt—but it also encompasses the promise of ultimate redemption—the redemption that will be heralded by Elijah—when peace will envelop the earth. Shabbat HaGadol is a fitting conclusion to the series of special Shabbatot leading up to the celebration of Pesach, for it holds out the hope and the promise that the real meaning of Passover—the real meaning of redemption—can and will be fulfilled.

12. פורים PURIM

(literally, "lots") is a holiday commemorating and celebrating the historical
events described in the biblical book of Esther, when the Jewish People
were saved from death and destruction. Purim occurs on 14 Adar,
in late February or early March. In a Jewish leap year,
when there are two Adars, Purim occurs in the second Adar.

The biblical book of Esther chronicles the events that led to the establishment of
Purim as a holiday on the Jewish calendar. Though the exact dates of the events of
this biblical account are impossible to ascertain, general scholarly consensus places
them in the late fifth century B.C.E.. Here is the story.

Ahasuerus, king of Persia, ruled over a vast empire. He was served by a large retinue,
including his chancellor, a fellow named Haman. But the queen, Vashti, greatly dis-
pleased the king, so he banished her from his presence.

To find a new queen, the king held a beauty pageant. The most beautiful
women from throughout the kingdom vied to become the new queen. At the urging
of her uncle Mordecai (who will be the subject of a subplot in this unfolding story), a
Jewish woman named Hadassah, also known as Esther, entered the queen-to-be contest. She did not reveal that she was Jewish (which most likely would have eliminated
her from consideration); but because she was so lovely, Esther triumphed over all the
other women of the kingdom and became the new queen.

Meanwhile, back at the palace gates (here comes the subplot), Mordecai over-
heard two palace guards plotting to overthrow the king. He reported the plot to
Esther, who (in Mordecai's name) told the king. The plot was uncovered, the guards
were impaled, and the events were recorded in the king's journals.

Meanwhile, back at the palace, Haman—much impressed with his own power
and prestige—issued an order that all people in the kingdom were to bow down to
him. Mordecai the Jew refused, for Jews bow in reverence before no human being,
only before God. Furious, Haman decided to kill all the Jews of the kingdom. He cast
"lots," or *purim* (one lot is a *pur*), to determine the day on which all the Jews would
die. The lots fell on the thirteenth day of the month of Adar. Haman convinced the
king that the Jews—who would not obey the law of the land—should be killed, and
the king permitted an edict to be announced that all the Jews of the kingdom were to
die on the thirteenth of Adar.

Mordecai told Esther that she, and she alone, could save the Jews from death by
interceding with the king. Esther invited the king and his chancellor, Haman, to
come to a banquet, where she planned to ask the king to save the Jews.

Back to the subplot: The king could not sleep, so he asked his royal scribe to read to him from the king's journals. The scribe read of the plot against the king that had been foiled by Mordecai, and the king learned that Mordecai had never been rewarded for his actions.

Just then, Haman appeared, and the king asked, "How would you reward a man whom the king wishes to honor?" Thinking that the king wanted to honor *him*, Haman replied that the man should be dressed in the royal robe and paraded throughout the kingdom with the proclamation, "This is the man the king wishes to honor." The king then ordered Haman to do just that to Mordecai the Jew. Haman did what he was ordered, but hated Mordecai even more than before.

Back to the main story: The king and Haman came to Esther's banquet, and the king was so pleased that he offered Esther anything she desired. Her reply was that she wanted life for herself and her people.

The king was shocked, and asked who would want to destroy her. Dramatically, Esther pointed to Haman. The outraged king ordered that Haman and his sons be hanged on the very gallows that had been prepared for Mordecai.

The king appointed Mordecai to Haman's high office. The original order to kill the Jews could not be rescinded because, according to the law of the land, even the king could not rescind his own edict. So the king told Mordecai to send a message throughout the kingdom that the Jews were permitted to defend themselves against attack on the thirteenth of Adar. Many in the kingdom understood the new message and did not harm the Jews. However, many others fulfilled the original edict and attacked the Jews. The Jews defended themselves and defeated all who came to harm them.

The day following the battle—the fourteenth of Adar—was a day of great rejoicing, feasting, and celebration. In succeeding years, the fourteenth of Adar was established as a joyous holiday, in commemoration of the defeat of the enemy who tried to destroy the Jewish People. The holiday came to be known as Purim, named after the lots that Haman had cast. In celebration, Jews began to recount the story of the events of Purim with much merriment and joy.

According to tradition, the Jews of Shushan, the capital of ancient Persia, the seat of the throne of the kingdom of Ahasuerus, had to battle against the attackers for an extra day, since the strength of the kingdom was much greater in the capital than in the countryside. Thus the Jews of Shushan celebrated Purim not on the fourteenth of Adar, but on the fifteenth. The fifteenth of Adar became known as Shushan Purim, and the rabbis and sages declared that any Jews living in a walled city (as Shushan was) were to celebrate Purim on the fifteenth of Adar, on Shushan Purim. Thus in Jerusalem, which is a walled city, the Israeli Jews celebrate Purim on Shushan Purim.

For traditional Jews, the observance of Purim is preceded by תענית אסתר Ta'anit Ester, the Fast of Esther, on the thirteenth of Adar. The fast recalls the prayerful fast of the Jews of Shushan, in the three days preceding Queen Esther's audience with the king, when she was to plead for the life of the Jews (Esther 4:15–16). It also recalls that—following the king's decree—the Jews of Shushan were permitted to gather on the thirteenth of Adar, preparing to defend themselves against attack on the next day. The Fast of Esther is observed in gratitude and thanksgiving that the Jewish People were spared from destruction and death.

Purim is celebrated with the reading of the *megillah* (scroll) of Esther, the telling of the Purim story. The *megillah* is read at a service on Erev Purim, and again on Purim morning. The reading of the *megillah* is accompanied by singing, dancing, and an atmosphere of unrestrained merrymaking. During the reading of the *megillah*, children (and many adults) use a special noisemaker, called a *gregger* (or *graggor*.) Every time the name of Haman is mentioned in the reading, the *greggers* are used to make as much noise as possible, to "blot out" the name of the wicked villain.

It is customary for the children to dress up in costume on Purim. Years ago, children dressed up as the characters in the Purim story—the king, Queen Vashti, Queen Esther, Mordecai, or Haman. Now (especially in Israel) children dress in almost every kind of costume, representing any kind of character. For Israeli children, Purim costumes are like the Halloween costumes of American children. The costumes in Israel reflect the times—for a while, dressing as an American cowboy was popular. Then it was space travelers. Now it is rock and roll stars, rap singers, and popular cartoon characters. Contemporary politician masks are ever popular.

The Purim celebration always includes delicious refreshments of food and drink. The popular Purim food is little cakes, baked in the shape of a triangle, filled with fruits or poppy seeds. The cake is called a *hamantash* (plural: *hamantashen*), which means, "Haman's hat." According to legend, Haman wore a three-cornered hat, thus the three-cornered cake. Alternately, the cake is called "Haman's pocket."

It is also customary to drink liquor on Purim, because, as the Bible teaches, "wine makes the heart of a man glad" (Psalms 104:15). Since Purim is such a joyous, festive holiday, the drinking of liquor is supposed to add to the feelings of merry celebration. And while drinking liquor within Jewish ritual life is always in moderation, on Purim people are instructed to drink עד דלא ידע *ad d'lo ya'da*, "Until you do not know (the difference between Haman and Mordecai)."

This is a very strange custom within Jewish life, which otherwise counsels moderation in most every phase of human existence—especially in the use of liquor.

It seems that the instruction to drink on Purim *ad d'lo ya'da* has two purposes: First, liquor causes a person to lose inhibitions. On Purim, people dress in costume—they put on masks—and then they are told to drink enough to figuratively "take off the mask" of inhibition. People often wear figurative masks to shield themselves, to protect themselves, from real feelings. But Purim demands that they reach to the core of their beings, to the place where real joy can be felt. With drinking, inhibitions tend to fall away, false masks are stripped off, and people can and do touch their deepest feelings of joy and contentment.

The second reason that Purim calls for drinking "until you do not know the difference between Haman and Mordecai" is to serve as a warning. The line between good and evil is very thin. So, the warning is, "Be careful. See what can happen when you lose your sense of right and wrong. Never be a Haman. Always be a Mordecai." Thus even the strangest customs have an ultimate purpose and an ultimate lesson to teach.

On Purim—either at the time of the reading of the *megillah* or on a Sunday preceding or following the actual holiday—children are often treated to special fun-filled activities. In contemporary times, especially in American synagogues and Jewish schools, this activity takes the form of a Purim carnival, complete with games, booths, prizes, and gifts.

For adults, the Purim festivities often include the staging of funny Purim plays or skits, and, sometimes, include holding a "Great Purim Debate," most often over the question of which is the greater delicacy: the Purim *hamantash* or the Chanukah *latke?*

On Purim, it is customary to send little gifts of food and drink (and sometimes a coin or two) to family, neighbors, and friends. This custom is called שלח מנות *shalach manot* (literally, "sending gifts"), also known as *m'shaloach manot*. The tradition is that the *shalach manot* should contain at least two different kinds of gifts: fruit and cake, or cookies and wine, or any combination of two different "goodies." In this way, it is shown that the *shalach manot* is not just the sharing of a particular food, but a sincere, well-thought-out gift.

It is also a Purim custom to give food and monetary gifts to the poor and needing within the community. Since a holiday of such a festive nature should be for everyone to celebrate, the gifts to the needing assure that every person in the community has the means, however modest, to observe and celebrate Purim.

In the midst of the doldrums of winter, Purim time serves as a beacon for festive rejoicing. Its original purpose—to commemorate the Jewish People being saved from death at the hands of a villainous tyrant—has been enhanced with all manner of fun-filled celebration.

The talmudic sages counseled, "Be happy. It's Adar"—the month of the observance of Purim (adaptation of BT Ta'anit 29a). Modern Jews happily fulfill that ancient dictum with joyous celebrations of the festival of Purim.

13. פֶּסַח PESACH

is Passover. It is a seven- (or eight-) day holiday,
beginning on 15 Nisan, usually in April.

Pesach commemorates and celebrates the historical exodus of the Hebrew slaves from Egyptian slavery.

At the same time, it is the springtime festival, celebrating the "rebirth" of the earth after the long, cold winter. Thus Pesach is also known as חג האביב Chag Ha'A-viv, the Spring Holiday.

THE STORY OF PESACH

The events leading to the establishment of the Pesach holiday are described in the Bible (Exodus 1–15). The Hebrews were descendants of Jacob and his sons, who had come to Egypt some 400 years earlier to escape famine. They were perceived by the Pharaoh (the king of Egypt) to possess enough power that they might align with a foreign enemy to help defeat Egypt in time of war. To prevent this, Pharaoh ordered that all newborn Hebrew males be drowned in the Nile River, and that the people be enslaved—forced to work at hard labor, building whole cities out of bricks made of mud and straw.

The lives of the Hebrews became bitter and unbearable, and in their pain they cried out to the God of their ancestors to free them from their torment. God, seeing their oppression, sent His servant Moses to bring the Hebrew slaves to freedom.

Moses, the son of Hebrew slaves in Egypt, had been saved from death. When he was born, rather than throw him in the Nile to drown, his parents had put him in a basket to float down the river to safety. He had been discovered by the daughter of Pharaoh, and had been brought to the palace to be raised as the son of the princess.

When he was older, Moses saw an Egyptian taskmaster beating a Hebrew slave. In his sad fury, Moses killed the taskmaster and had to flee Egypt for his own safety. He came to Midian, where he became a shepherd, tending the flocks of Yitro, the priest of Midian. He married Yitro's daughter and led a life of relative obscurity—until God called him to his task.

From out of a bush that burned but was not consumed, God spoke to Moses, telling him to go to Pharaoh, and in the name of the Lord, God of Israel, tell Pharaoh to "Let My people go!"

Moses was a reluctant prophet; he did not want the job. But no one can escape the call of God. Moses, accompanied by his brother, Aaron—who would serve as spokesman for the rather inarticulate Moses—returned to Egypt as the messenger of God, saying to Pharaoh, "Let My people go!"

Pharaoh was hard-hearted. He did not want to release his slaves; he did not want to accede to the demand of the invisible God of Israel. So, in the name of God, Moses brought nine plagues upon Egypt, one after another: (1) the Nile turned to blood; (2) frogs invaded the land; (3) the land was filled with vermin (lice and flies); (4) wild beasts roamed the land; (5) cattle disease decimated the herds; (6) boils broke out on the bodies of all the people; (7) the land was bombarded with hail; (8) locusts swarmed; and (9) the entire country was engulfed in an all-pervasive darkness. After each of the plagues, Pharaoh seemed to be ready to free the Hebrew slaves. But, each time, his heart hardened and he refused to let them go.

God told Moses to prepare the Hebrews for the tenth and final plague. Each household was to sacrifice a lamb and smear the blood of the lamb on the doorposts of the house, as a sign of protection. During the night, God and the "angel of death" swept through Egypt. Every firstborn male Egyptian died. But God and the angel of death "passed over" or "protected" the houses of the Hebrew slaves that were marked with blood.

Thoroughly defeated, Pharaoh commanded Moses to lead the Hebrew slaves out of Egypt immediately. Moses led the people out of Egypt. The Hebrews departed so quickly that the bread they were baking did not have time to rise, but was left as flat, unleavened, cakes called מצה *matzah.*

According to the Torah story, 600,000 males of military age came out of Egypt. If this is so, then there must have been an equal number of women. Add to this number the children, the elderly, the ill and the infirm, and the "mixed multitude" that the Torah says joined in the exodus, and the number of people leaving Egypt may have come close to 2 million.

Even as the Hebrew slaves were leaving, Pharaoh changed his mind and sent his soldiers to bring the slaves back. At the Sea of Reeds (more commonly referred to as the Red Sea), with the waters in front of them and the Egyptian soldiers pursuing them, Moses and the Hebrews called out to God for help. God caused the waters of the sea to turn to dry land, and the people walked through in safety. As the Egyptian soldiers followed, the waters came crashing down, and they drowned in the sea.

Moses and the Children of Israel stood on the other side of the sea and sang songs of praise to God for their deliverance. The Hebrews had come from slavery to freedom to begin their trek, first to Mt. Sinai where they were to receive God's law, and then to the Promised Land of Israel.

The festival of Pesach was established to commemorate the exodus from Egypt, and God commanded that every person, in every generation, should feel as if he or she, personally, were redeemed from Egypt. For יציאת מצרים *yetze'at Mitzraim,* the "Going Out (or Exodus) from Egypt," is the central event that transformed a rag-tag band of slaves into a nation. From a folk-tribe, the exodus created the Jewish People.

More than any other Jewish holiday, the celebration of Pesach is filled with observances that give the opportunity for a deep level of personal participation and a sense of true involvement.

Central to the observance of Pesach is the food that is eaten (and the food that is prohibited from being eaten) during the holiday. Since the Hebrew slaves had to flee Egypt with such haste that their baking bread did not have time to rise, during the entire week (or eight days) of Pesach, Jews eat only the flat, unleavened bread that the newly freed slaves ate, called מצה *matzah*. All leaven—that is, anything that rises in baking—may not be eaten.

In Hebrew, leaven is called חמץ *chametz*. But everything—not just leavened bread—that is prohibited on Pesach is also called *chametz*. The Rabbinic sages went far in defining *chametz* when they delineated the Pesach food prohibitions. The rabbis specified five grains that are *chametz* (presumably because leavened bread can be made from them): wheat, barley, spelt, rye, and oats. To these were added rice and legumes (including peas, beans, corn, maize, lentils, millet, and mustard), which expand when cooked.

Thus prohibited on Pesach are leavened bread, cakes, cookies, biscuits, crackers, cereals, coffee (if mixed with grain), and anything else made from any one of the five grains, including beer and liquor. The only exception is the *matzah*. Although it is usually made from wheat, production is carefully supervised by rabbinic authorities who make sure that the wheat flour comes in contact with water (the process which would cause the wheat to rise) for only a specified number of minutes, precluding leavening.

Since all food that is *chametz* is prohibited during Pesach, the Rabbinic sages also prohibited the use of all utensils used in preparing and eating of *chametz*. Thus, in a traditional Jewish home, all dishes, glassware, and silverware, all pots, pans, cooking utensils, and small appliances used during the year, are put away during Pesach and are replaced with cooking and eating utensils reserved for and used solely on Pesach.

The special "Pesach dishes" (with separate sets for meat and dairy, in accordance with the laws of *kashrut*) are stored away all year (usually in boxes in an attic, basement, garage, or other storage area) and are brought out to be used for the one week of Passover. The house must be thoroughly cleaned, and all *chametz* (even the cookie crumbs that the children left under the bed) removed. All the large appliances in the kitchen—the refrigerator, the stove and oven, the microwave, the dishwasher, the sink—must be completely cleaned and scoured. All visible traces of anything *chametz* must be gone.

Preparing the house for Pesach is the ultimate "spring cleaning." It is a tremendous task to clean the house and to "change over" an entire kitchen, with all its equipment, from *"chametz"* to "Pesach" (and then back again after the holiday is over); but it is a task that is undertaken with commitment and pleasure by observant Jewish families.

The prohibition against possessing *chametz* during Passover is so strong that a number of rituals have been instituted to make sure that all the *chametz* is removed from the home. On the night before Pesach begins, a ceremonial search for the leaven, called בדיקת חמץ *bedikat chametz,* takes place. This ceremony is a symbolic "last chance" to find any *chametz* that might have been overlooked during the cleaning and preparations for Pesach. The search follows an old custom, which was undoubtedly established for its practicality but is now continued in this way for its nostalgia. The searchers use a lighted candle to illuminate the room (now, for safety's sake, a flashlight is often used) and a feather to brush the *chametz* into a wooden spoon, with which they scoop the discovered *chametz* into a napkin or bag for disposal. Actually, one of the members of the household hides some *chametz* beforehand so that at least a little *chametz* will surely be found and the blessing recited over the search will not have been said in vain. The *bedikat chametz* culminates the preparations for Pesach and is a time, particularly for the children in the family, for fun and enjoyment. (There is an interesting possibility that Christianity's annual Easter egg hunt came about as an imitation of Judaism's search for the *chametz.*) After the search is completed, this formula is recited: "Any leaven that may still be in the house, which I have not seen or have not removed, shall be as if it does not exist, and as the dust of the earth."

In the morning of the day that Pesach will begin at sundown, the *chametz* that was found in the previous evening's search is burned. This ceremony is called ביעור חמץ *bi'ur chametz,* the burning of the leaven. While only the most traditional Jewish households still observe this custom, the burning of the leaven ceremony underscores how very important it is that all *chametz* be gone from the home.

Yet even all this careful cleaning and preparation is not enough. The Rabbinic sages declared that a Jew should not even *own* any *chametz* during Pesach.

Reasoning that it would be too much of a financial hardship to dispose of all *chametz* (such as unopened bottles, jars, and cans of food that are stored away and will not be opened or used during Pesach but are nevertheless *chametz*), the sages created a legal process permitting certain items of *chametz* to be "retained" but not "owned" by Jews during Pesach. This legal instrumentality is called מכירת חמץ *mechirat chametz,* or the selling of the *chametz.* The head of each Jewish household authorizes the rabbi to sell all the *chametz* still in possession of that household to a non-Jew for the duration of the Passover holiday. On the morning of the day that Pesach will begin at sundown, just after the burning of the *chametz,* the rabbi writes a formal contract with a non-Jew, transferring ownership of all the *chametz* in his house or possession and in the homes or possession of all who have authorized him to act as agent.

The Jews need not worry about possessing or owning *chametz* during Passover because, according to this legal transaction, the non-Jew to whom the *chametz* was sold is the rightful and legal owner. At the end of Pesach, the sale becomes null and void and the ownership of the *chametz* reverts to its former owners. Legally, the non-Jew to whom the *chametz* was sold could come into each Jewish household during Passover, claim possession of his *chametz,* and take it away, but in practice this is never done.

Using this legal procedure of selling the *chametz* permits a Jew to observe both the letter and the spirit of the law, while not undergoing tremendous financial or logistical hardship. Some would consider this procedure no more than a legal fiction, but it works for Jews for whom serious observance of all the laws and customs of Pesach is vitally important.

With all the preparations (including the search for the *chametz,* the burning of the *chametz,* and the selling of the *chametz*) complete, it is law and custom not to eat any *chametz* after ten o'clock in the morning on the day when Passover will begin at sundown. This law came into being when almost all meals were eaten at home, and had the practical effect of making sure that the home would be cleaned and ready in time for Passover.

Today many Jews still eat *chametz* for lunch, as long as the meal is eaten outside the home in a restaurant owned and operated by a non-Jew, a place that does not have to be cleansed and prepared for Passover. Yet even those who eat Passover food during the day when Passover will begin at sundown do not eat *matzah* because, according to law and custom, the first *matzah* of Passover is to be eaten as part of the ritual, at the festive meal on the evening when *Pesach* begins.

One more custom is observed before Passover begins. During the day when Pesach will begin at sundown, all firstborn Jewish males are to fast. This fast is called תענית הבכורים *ta'anit habechorim,* the fast of the firstborn. In eternal remembrance that—in order to achieve and assure the freedom of the Hebrew slaves—the first-born Egyptian males were killed in the tenth plague, all firstborn Jewish males, in every generation, fast on the day preceding the beginning of Pesach. It is a fast of history and of humility.

Sometimes, however, the fast can be suspended, for if someone who is required to fast on a fast day such as *ta'anit habechorim* completes or hears another's completion of the study of a tractate of Talmud, then the celebration (complete with food and drink) that accompanies the completion of a unit of study, called a סיום *siyyum* (literally: "termination" or "end"), supersedes the fast.

Thus many synagogues arrange to have the rabbi or another learned Jew complete the study of a tractate on the morning when Pesach will begin. Following the morning worship service, the learner, in the presence of the other worshipers (including all the firstborn who wish to be present), completes learning the final few sentences of the text, creating a need for a celebratory *siyyum,* and eliminating the firstborns' requirement to fast on that day.

Finally, before Pesach begins, special *tzedakah,* a form of charity—called מעות חטים *ma'ot chitim,* (literally, "wheat money")—is given. This ensures that anyone in need will have enough money to purchase *matzah* (wheat) and other essential provisions for the holiday.

THE SEDER

The major observance of Pesach, held in the home on the first night of the holiday (the first two nights for those who observe eight days of the festival), is a festive, ritual meal called the סדר *seder* (literally, "order"). With words, songs, special food, and prayers of praise, the story of the exodus from Egypt is told, reenacted, and explained—especially to the children—and celebrated.

The book used during the Passover *seder* to relate and explain the events of the exodus from Egypt is called the הגדה *haggadah* (literally, "legend," or "telling.") The *haggadah* is filled with biblical quotations and rabbinic interpretations about the exodus. It outlines the rituals that are to be performed during the course of the *seder* meal. It explains the meaning of the symbols, objects, and foods used during the *seder* to tell the story of slavery and freedom. It contains psalms and songs of praise to God for the miracles He did in bringing the Jewish People out of Egypt.

The oldest published version of the *haggadah* is in the prayerbook of Saadya Gaon, dating to the tenth century C.E. Many different versions of the *haggadah* have been preserved in texts, from the thirteenth to the fifteenth centuries. Since the fifteenth century, more than 2,500 separate editions of the *haggadah* have been produced, coming from every country in which Jews have lived, reflecting the unique customs of the various communities. The *haggadah* has been the one Jewish book that has been the most illustrated by artists. Beautiful artwork adorns hundreds of editions of the *haggadah* from every corner of the earth.

Throughout the centuries, Jews have added to and expanded on the traditional *haggadah* text to reflect specific timely concerns and needs, based on the theme of freedom that the *haggadah* articulates.

For example, in 1945 American soldiers wrote additions to their *haggadah* for their *seder,* conducted only days after they had helped liberate Jews from the horrors of the death camps. In the 1960s, Americans wrote the *Freedom Haggadah* to express sentiments supporting the civil rights struggle and opposing the war in southeast Asia. In the 1970s, a *haggadah* was written focusing on freedom for Soviet Jews held in political bondage. In recent years, a *Women's Haggadah* has been written, reflecting the feminist struggle for equality.

In every age, freedom must be renewed, reflecting the needs of particular places, issues, and events. The *haggadah* gives Jews the opportunity to remember ancient slavery and celebrate historical redemption, while providing the framework for including the circumstances of the moment in the never-ending desire and quest for human freedom and dignity.

THE SEDER TABLE

On the *seder* table is a *seder* plate. It contains five (sometimes six) foods that symbolically tell the story of Passover:

1. ביצה *betzah*, a roasted egg. The egg has a twofold meaning: First, it symbolizes one of the Passover sacrifices that was brought as an offering to the Holy Temple. Second, it is a symbol of the wholeness and continuity of life.

2. כרפס *karpas*, a green vegetable. The *karpas*, usually parsley or celery, represents springtime and renewal. During the *seder*, the *karpas* is dipped into saltwater (symbolic of the tears which the Hebrew slaves shed) and eaten.

3. זרוע *zaro'a*, a roasted shankbone. The shankbone symbolizes the lamb that was sacrificed as the Passover offering.

4. מרור *maror*, bitter herbs. The *maror*, usually horseradish, is a reminder of the bitterness of Egyptian slavery. During the *seder*, the *maror* is eaten so that the *seder* participants can literally taste the "bitterness of bondage."

5. חרוסת *charoset*, a mixture of chopped apples, nuts (sometimes dates), and wine. The *charoset* represents the mortar with which the Hebrew slaves were forced to make bricks. During the *seder*, the *charoset* is eaten so that the participants can literally ingest the experience of slavery.

On some seder plates, there is a sixth food, חזרת *chazeret*, another bitter herb. Since bitter herbs are eaten twice during the *seder*, some Jews have the custom of putting a second bitter herb onto the *seder* plate. If horseradish is used for the *maror*, then a bitter lettuce is often used for the *chazeret*.

In addition to the *seder* plate, the *seder* table also holds a number of foods and ritual objects that have special significance in the observance of Pesach and play an ongoing role in the unfolding drama of the *seder* service.

The flat, unleavened bread called מצה *matzah* is the main food that is eaten during Passover, the remembrance that the Hebrew slaves had to flee Egypt so quickly that their baking bread did not have time to rise. The *seder* table has a stack of three *matzot*, (plural of *matzah*), representing the unity of the Jewish People—the ancestral tribes and the modern-day descendants of Kohen, the priests, Levi, the assistants to the priests, and Yisrael, the rest of the People Israel, the Jewish People.

In modern times, many families add a fourth *matzah* to the stack of three on the *seder* table, in remembrance of the Jews of the world who are still held in political captivity. This fourth *matzah* is most often called the "*Matzah* of Hope" or the "*Matzah* of Unity."

At the beginning of the *seder,* the middle *matzah* is broken in half. One half becomes the אפיקומן *afikoman,* the "official" dessert of the *seder* meal. The *afikoman* is hidden away and the children search for and "steal" it, holding it for a "ransom," usually a gift. Since the *seder* cannot be completed unless the *afikoman* is eaten, the children's ransom request is always met. This little game of stealing and ransoming the *afikoman* serves to keep the children involved in the *seder,* when they might otherwise get tired during the late-evening rituals.

It is custom during the *seder* to drink four cups of wine, corresponding to and celebrating the four statements of redemption made by God and recorded in the Torah: "I will bring you out." "I will deliver you." "I will redeem you." "I will take you." (Exodus 6:6–7). Each participant has a wine glass that is refilled four times during the course of the *seder.*

Following the four statements of redemption in the Torah is the promise, "And I will bring you (to the Land of Israel)" (Exodus 6:8).

Some of the ancient rabbis contended that this fifth statement was also a statement of redemption, and therefore five cups of wine should be drunk at the Passover *seder.* Other sages argued that only the first four statements, about coming out of Egypt, were the true statements of redemption, with the fifth statement being the promise of destination and destiny. These rabbis contended that only four cups of wine, corresponding to the four actual statements of redemption, should be drunk at the *seder.*

When the ancient rabbis could not agree, they would symbolically leave the final decision to the prophet Elijah—who, according to tradition, will return to earth to be the one to announce the coming of the messiah. When the messiah comes, the sages reasoned, all disputed issues of Jewish law will be resolved, for Elijah will not only announce the coming of the messiah, but will also announce the decisions to the disputed questions of law.

The compromise, therefore, was to declare that four cups of wine would be drunk at the *seder,* but that a fifth cup would be set out—a cup that belongs to the *seder* ritual itself and thus to every person at the *seder.* Called the Cup of Elijah, it is a reminder that one day Elijah will come to herald redemption and will then rule whether the fifth cup of wine is to be drunk at the *seder*. Late in the *seder* ritual, Elijah is symbolically and metaphorically invited into the house to join in the *seder* and to take a sip from his cup of wine.

This ceremony of Elijah has two purposes: First, while celebrating historical redemption from Egypt, it serves as a reminder of the Jewish hope for ultimate redemption, that the time of peace and tranquility on earth will come speedily and soon. Second, it is another device to keep the tired children interested and involved in the lengthy *seder* ritual. For the children are told that Elijah will visit the *seder* and drink from his cup. At a certain point in the ritual, the children go to open the door, and then carefully watch the level of wine in the cup and report when Elijah has come and taken his sip of wine.

In contemporary times, many families have adopted a new custom: They do not simply wait for Elijah to symbolically drink from his cup, but have each participant in the *seder* pour a few drops of wine from his or her own wine cup into the Cup of Elijah. This new custom demonstrates that we cannot simply wait for redemption to come, but need to be active partners in bringing redemption to our world through the work of our hands.

Every place at the *seder* (or, according to some customs, the place of the leader of the *seder*) is set with a pillow so that while sitting at the *seder,* the participant(s) can visibly recline, an ancient sign of liberty and freedom. Slaves were forced to sit rigidly at meals; free men and women had the luxury of reclining. So while much of the *seder* ritual remembers and reenacts the misery of slavery, the setting (and seating) of the *seder* is freedom.

THE ORDER OF THE *SEDER*

The *seder* service has fifteen parts, recited and performed in a specific order.

1. קדש *Kadesh:* The blessing over and the drinking of the first of the four cups of wine.

2. ורחץ *Urechatz:* The washing of hands. This is a symbolic ritual purification for the purpose of conducting the *seder* ritual, and because the green vegetable is about to be eaten. No blessing is recited. According to some customs, a pitcher of water is brought to the leader of the *seder,* who pours the water over his or her hands. In other customs, all the participants wash—either at the *seder* table with the pitcher of water, or away from the table at a sink.

3. כרפס *Karpas:* The eating of the green vegetable dipped in saltwater. Some explain that eating a vegetable at this early point in the *seder* is a way to arouse the children's curiosity so that they will ask about the meaning of Passover. Still others

explain that, since the meal will not be eaten for a while, the vegetable serves as an appetizer to satisfy hunger.

4. יחץ *Yachatz:* The breaking of the middle *matzah.* The middle *matzah,* from the stack of three (and, in modern times, four) *matzot* on the *seder* table, is broken in two. One half becomes the *afikoman.*

5. מגיד *Maggid:* The telling of the Passover story. The youngest child present asks the famous Four Questions, which create the framework for explaining the Passover story: "Why is this night different from all other nights? On all other nights, we eat either leavened or unleavened bread; on this night, why only unleavened? On all other nights, we eat any kind of herbs; why, on this night, do we eat only bitter herbs? On all other nights, we do not dip (foods) even once; why, on this night, do we dip twice? On all other nights, we eat either sitting or reclining; why, on this night, do we only recline?"

The *haggadah* text—with its stories, legends, and the interpretations of the rabbinic sages, explaining and expanding on the Passover story—forms the basis for answering the Four Questions and for delving into the meaning and the purpose of the Pesach ritual.

Highlights of the *maggid* portion of the *seder* include the recitation of the ten plagues. As each plague is recited, a bit of wine is poured off from each wine cup. A full cup is a symbol of complete joy. But because others had to suffer and die in order for the Hebrew slaves to achieve freedom, Jewish joy, throughout the generations, has been tempered and diminished. Pouring off a drop of wine with the recitation of each plague is acknowledgment of the pain and suffering of others.

Another highlight is the singing of the popular song דינו *"Dayenu,"* "It Would Have Been Enough," which enumerates all of the miracles God performed for the Jewish People. After each miracle is stated comes the refrain, *"Dayenu,"* "It would have been enough" had God done only this. But the list of miracles goes on and on, dramatizing these great and wondrous acts that God performed for the Jewish people.

Finally, the *maggid* section explains the three major symbols of Pesach—the paschal sacrifice, the *matzah,* and the *maror.*

The traditional text can and should be embellished with stories, questions, discussions and modern readings, in order to dramatize the significance of redemption and freedom, then and now.

During this portion of the *seder,* the second cup of wine is drunk, and psalms of praise to God are recited.

6. רחצה *Rachtzah:* The second hand-washing. This time, the hand-washing is done with the proper blessing, in preparation for the eating of the *matzah.*

7. מוציא *Motzee:* The first of two blessings over the eating of the *matzah.* This is the generic blessing thanking God for "bringing forth bread from the earth."

8. מצה *Matzah:* The second blessing over the eating of the *matzah.* This is the specific blessing thanking God for the commandment "to eat *matzah.*" The first *matzah* of the Passover season is eaten.

9. מרור *Maror:* The eating of the bitter herbs, a reminder of the bitterness of slavery, preceded by the recitation of the proper blessing. Some have the custom of combining the *maror* with the *charoset,* the food symbolic of the mortar with which the Hebrew slaves made bricks, thus figuratively combining the bitterness of slavery with the source of the bitterness—the brick-making.

10. כורך *Korech:* Combining the *matzah* and the *maror.* Using the bottom *matzah,* a "sandwich" is made with *matzah* and *maror* and then eaten. This is known as the "Hillel Sandwich" because the Rabbinic sage Hillel had the custom of eating *matzah* and *marror* together when he observed Passover.

11. שלחן עורך *Shulchan Orach:* The festive Passover meal is eaten.

12. צפון *Tzafun:* The *afikoman* is "ransomed" from the children who "stole" it, and it is eaten as the "official" dessert of the *seder* meal.

13. ברך *Barech:* The traditional blessing after meals is recited, in gratitude to God for the food that was eaten and for all God's many blessings.

The third cup of wine is drunk, with the appropriate blessing.

The ceremony of Elijah takes place. The door is opened and Elijah is symbolically invited to come in and visit the *seder.* This is the time in the *seder* when the celebration of historical redemption gives way to the hope and prayers for ultimate redemption, the time of the perfection of the world, and everlasting peace. Elijah is the honored guest at the *seder,* since according to tradition, it is Elijah who will announce the coming of the messiah, the era of worldly peace and perfection. The hope and the prayer is that the time will come "speedily and in our day."

14. הלל *Hallel:* Psalms of praise to God are recited: for the many miracles He performed, and for the many blessings He continually bestows. The fourth cup of wine is drunk, with the appropriate blessing.

15. נרצה *Nirtzah:* The conclusion of the *seder.* The *haggadah* is completed, with the expression of the hope that the *seder* prayers and rituals will be acceptable to God.

The concluding words recited at the *seder* ritual are לשנה הבאה בירושלים *"L'shanah ha'ba-ah b'Yerushalayim,"* "Next year in Jerusalem." This is the hope and prayer—expressed for millennia by Jews in the diaspora—that just as *B'nai Yisrael,* the Children of Israel, wandering through the desert were brought to the Promised Land of Israel, the Jewish exile and wandering will soon end and that there would be a return to the Land of Israel. In this generation, the almost 2,000-year-old prayer has been answered with the establishment of the modern State of Israel in 1948.

It is also a statement of hope for ultimate redemption. For "Jerusalem" has come to mean not only the earthly city of Jerusalem, but signifies an "eternal Jerusalem," a symbol of ultimate and enduring peace and perfection.

These are the same words recited at the conclusion of Yom Kippur, giving a natural symmetry to the Jewish festival cycle. Since Yom Kippur and Pesach are six months apart, each holiday is the other's half-way point in the ever-renewing yearly cycles of Jewish observance. These words—recited at the conclusion of these two major Jewish holidays—keep the hope for return and redemption ever present in Jewish belief and practice.

Passover songs are sung, including such favorites as אדיר הוא *"Adir Hu,"* "Mighty is He [God] "; אחד מי יודע *"Echad Me Yoda-ah,"* "Who Knows One?"; and חד גדיא *"Chad Gadyah,"* "One Little Goat."

Those who observe eight days of Passover conduct a second *seder* on the second night of the holiday.

THE EIGHT DAYS OF PASSOVER

The first day (or the first two days, for those who observe eight days) and the last day (or the last two days, for those who observe eight days) are full Yom Tov holidays. Synagogue services are held, with the recitation of the *hallel* psalms and special Torah and *haftarah* portions, reflecting the themes of the festival.

On the morning of the first day of Passover, תפלת טל *Tefilat Tal,* the Prayer for Dew, is recited. On Shemini Atzeret, at the end of the fall festival of Succot, the Prayer for Rain was recited, in the hope that the crops in the Land of Israel would have sufficient rain to grow and flourish. Now, with the coming of spring, the winter rains come to an end, and the prayer for dew is recited, with the hope that God will provide just enough moisture to keep the lands fertile and green.

On the Shabbat of Pesach (which occurs either as a full Yom Tov day or during Chol HaMo'ed, the intermediate days of the festival) the biblical book of Shir Ha Shirum, Song of Songs, is read in the synagogue.

The love poem of the Bible, Song of Songs, is dramatically and vividly appropriate for the springtime festival of renewal. It also serves as the symbolic indication of the "romance" between God and the Jewish People, which begins with the exodus from Egypt on Pesach and will be "consummated" with the "marriage," the giving of the Torah at Mt. Sinai seven weeks later, celebrated on the festival of Shavuot.

On the final day of the festival of Pesach (the seventh or eighth day, depending on observance), the *Yizkor* memorial prayers are recited as part of the synagogue service.

During Chol HaMo'ed Pesach, the intermediate days of the festival (four or five days, depending on whether the seven- or eight-day festival is observed), the full celebrations and certain restrictions of the full Yom Tov are lessened, but the eating of only foods permitted on Passover is still strictly observed.

The festival of Pesach—with all its many customs, traditions, and observances—is central to Jewish life. It commemorates the Jewish People's being freed from bondage and becoming a nation, and it celebrates the enduring human quest for freedom.

It is a holiday with great historical significance and continually unfolding meaning, for within the celebration of historical redemption is the hope and the promise of ultimate redemption, פסח לעתיד *Pesach l'atid,* the "Passover of the Future," the time when all humankind will be redeemed to live in freedom and tranquility in a world dominated by justice, filled with compassion, and enveloped in everlasting peace.

14. ספירת העומר   SEFIRAT HAOMER

(literally, "counting of the *omer,* a measure of grain") is the Counting of the Omer, a period of seven weeks beginning on the second night of Passover.

As an agricultural festival, Passover marks the spring barley harvest. Some seven weeks later, in the late spring or very early summer, newly ripened wheat is ready for harvest. At the very same time, the first fruits ripen on the vines and trees and are ready for picking.

The Bible commands a careful counting from harvest to harvest: "From the day after the Sabbath [meaning: the day of rest that is the first day of the festival of Passover], the day that you brought a measure of wheat as a wave-offering, you shall count seven weeks. They shall be [seven] complete [weeks]. Count until the day after the seventh week, [until] fifty days. Then you shall bring an offering of new grain unto the Lord. You shall bring from your settlements two loaves of bread as a wave-offering . . ." (Leviticus 23:15–17).

While the *Torah* gives no reason for the careful counting from one harvest to the other, it is likely that the ritual requirement was a method of assuring that the crop would be well tended, and that the harvest would take place at exactly the right time.

There is little evidence as to how the counting was carried out in ancient times. Some speculate on the possibility that each day, a measure of grain—an *omer*—was added to a container that held precisely forty-nine measures. When the container was filled, the counting of the seven weeks was complete and the harvest began.

Later, a prayer for the counting—which remains in the liturgy today—was made part of the evening service. As the sun sets, marking the beginning of a new Jewish day, the day is counted as a succeeding day of the *omer* period, until the full forty-nine days are counted.

From the Rabbinic Period on, the *sefirah*—the period of counting—has been treated as a period of mourning for the Jewish People. The reason for this designation is not clear. Some suggest that it is a reflection of ancient pagan and Roman beliefs about the spirits of the dead returning to earth at this time of year. Others suggest that it is because of one of two misfortunes that befell the students of second-century Rabbi Akiba: a reported plague that allegedly killed thousands, or the unsuccessful revolt of Bar Kochba against the Romans in 132–35 C.E., which Akiba and his disciples supported.

Whatever the reason, as a communal period of mourning, these seven weeks embody several Jewish mourning practices for traditional Jews: Many refrain from shaving and cutting hair, celebrations are not held, and marriages do not take place.

The mourning is suspended—with the most practical result being that wedding ceremonies are held—on Rosh Chodesh (the first day of a Hebrew month) Iyar and Sivan (the two months that begin during the *sefirah*). Since the establishment of the modern State of Israel in 1948, the mourning practices of the *omer* have also been suspended on Israeli Independence Day, the fifth day of the month of Iyar.

Mourning is also suspended on the thirty-third day of the *omer*, a day called ל"ג בעומר Lag B'Omer (which means "the thirty-third of the *omer*"). Using numerical equivalents, ל *lamed* is 30, and ג *gimel* is 3. *Lag* (30 + 3) is the thirty-third day, בעומר *b'omer*, of the *omer* period. Lag B'Omer always falls on the eighteenth day of the month of Iyar.

This day is special because, according to tradition, it was the day on which the plague that befell Akiba and his students ended, or was somehow suspended. Others contend that it is somehow connected to a temporarily successful counterattack in the Bar Kochba revolt.

Traditionally, Lag B'Omer is commemorated with outdoor activities—picnics and games. Some have the custom of playing with bows and arrows, which would be consistent with the theory of associating Lag B'Omer with the Bar Kochba revolt. Today, Lag B'Omer—a very minor point in time on the Jewish calendar—is celebrated (especially in Israel, but, also in American religious schools) with outings and sports games, particularly for the children.

In practice, it is only in the traditional community that the mourning-custom restrictions during Sefirat HaOmer—most notably the prohibition against marriages taking place—are still practiced. Some continue to observe the restrictions until Lag B'Omer, but then suspend them. Most liberal denominations—arguing that the original reasons for the period of mourning are obscure—have lifted any restrictions.

15. שבועות SHAVUOT

(literally, "weeks") the Feast of Weeks, or Pentecost. It is a one- (or two-) day
holiday that occurs on 6 (and 7) Sivan, in late May or early June.

Sefirat HaOmer, the counting of the forty-nine days, concludes with the commemoration of the fiftieth day, Shavuot.

The Bible enjoins, "You shall count seven weeks, starting to count when the sickle is first put to the standing grain. Then you shall observe שבועות Shavuot (literally, "weeks"), the Feast of Weeks, for the Lord your God, offering free-will contributions according to [the way] the Lord your God has blessed you" (Deuteronomy 16:9–10).

Shavuot was to be a celebratory conclusion to the barley harvest, which had begun at Passover, and the beginning of the early-spring wheat harvest. That is why another name for Shavuot is חג הקציר Chag HaKatzir, the Festival of Harvesting/ Reaping. In biblical times, in commemoration of this aspect of Shavuot, two loaves of bread were brought as an offering to God.

At the same time, Shavuot was to be a celebration of the harvest of the first fruits of late spring. That is why Shavuot is also called חג הבכורים Chag HaBikurim, the Festival of the First Fruits. In biblical times, in commemoration of this aspect of Shavuot, first fruits—wheat, barley, figs, dates, grapes, pomegranates, and olives— were brought as an offering to God.

When the Holy Temple was destroyed and the people sent off to exile, two things happened to the festival of Shavuot. First, as with the other festivals that were observed in the diaspora—where the calendar was not formally set—an additional day was added to the commemoration to make sure that the festival was properly celebrated. So the biblical one-day holiday became a two-day observance.

Second, Shavuot lost much of its power and popularity after the Holy Temple was destroyed and there was no longer any place to bring the offerings, and as many Jews moved out of agricultural settings into villages and towns.

What was to become of a biblically mandated holiday that was being increasingly ignored? To reinfuse Shavuot with meaning and with loyal observance, the sages taught that Shavuot is really much more than an agricultural festival.

With some "creative mathematics" in their way of counting the time in the biblical account, the sages determined that it was exactly seven weeks between the exodus from Egypt and the revelation at Sinai. Thus they linked Shavuot to the theophany—the exact moment when God gave the Torah at Sinai.

As well as its other names, then, Shavuot also came to be known as זמן מתן תורתנו Z'man Matan Toratanu, "the time of the giving of our Torah." With this designation, Shavuot regained primacy in Jewish life—for what could be more important to Jews and Judaism than the giving and receiving of Torah? Shavuot, contended the sages, is the commemoration of that defining event in the history of Judaism, and the history of the world.

With Shavuot now commemorating the giving of Torah, Sefirat HaOmer also took on new meaning also.

The sages and the mystics taught that Shavuot is the moment of eternal commitment—the marriage—between God and the Jewish People. On Pesach God and the people pledge themselves to each other. The *sefirah* is the period of the courtship and engagement, the time when trust and love grow deeper and stronger. Sefirat HaOmer thus becomes not just a time for counting toward an agricultural harvest, but a time of heartfelt emotion and excited anticipation, as the relationship between God and the Jewish People moves swiftly forward toward consummation, toward the wedding at Sinai—the time when God will give His wedding gift of Torah. Sefirat HaOmer is now a time not only to count the days, but to make the days count, in preparation for the transcendent moment of revelation.

In modern times, for Jews in Israel and for Reform Jews, Shavuot is a one-day festival. For Orthodox and Conservative Jews living in the diaspora, Shavuot is two days.

The major celebrations of Shavuot take place during synagogue services. At the morning services, the *hallel* psalms of praise to God are added to worship. In some synagogues, a medieval *piyyut*, a poem written in Aramaic called אקדמות *Akdamut* (literally, "prelude") is chanted, glorifying God and anticipating the messianic era. Since Shavuot commemorates the giving of Torah, the Ten Commandments are read as the special Torah reading of the day. As on the other pilgrimage festivals—Pesach and Succot—the *Yizkor* memorial prayers are recited (on the second day for those who observe two days.)

On this holiday (on the second day, for those who observe two days), the *megillah* of Ruth is read. It is most appropriate to hear the book of Ruth on Shavuot for two reasons. First, the central events of the story take place at harvest time, so the book is linked to the spring harvest festival. More importantly, Ruth is the story of the Moabite woman who voluntarily chooses to become Jewish, saying to her mother-in-law, Naomi, "Wherever you go, I will go; wherever you lodge, I will lodge; your people shall be my people; and your God, my God" (Ruth 1:16). On the day that commemorates the giving of Torah, it is very fitting to read the biblical book that celebrates acceptance of God and Torah.

Two customs have come to be associated with the commemoration of Shavuot—one old and one new.

Beginning with the kabbalists in the sixteenth century, it became tradition to stay up all night (the first night for those who observe two days) of Shavuot, studying sacred texts. Since Shavuot commemorates the giving of Torah, it is most appropriate to stay up all night learning Torah. The custom, called תקון ליל שבועות *Tikkun Layl Shavuot* (literally, "the prepared [texts] of the night of Shavuot"), has become increasingly popular in recent years.

In some synagogues and communities, the "prepared" texts are studied—a section from each of the books of the Bible and Talmud. In other places, other texts are chosen. While some people study from dark until dawn, others maintain the "spirit" of the *tikkun* by learning for a number of hours in the evening.

A Jewish legend teaches that at exactly midnight on Shavuot, the heavens open for a moment and God will respond favorably to any prayer that is uttered then. It is very likely that the legend was told to keep children—and perhaps weary adults—awake, alert, and interested as the studying went on through the late hours of the night.

The second Shavuot custom was established in the twentieth century in the United States, when the Reform movement created the ceremony of Confirmation. The early reformers eliminated the Bar Mitzvah ceremony from Jewish life, reasoning that it was an "unnatural" stopping point for a young person's Jewish education. Instead, they mandated an educational system that continued through age fifteen, sixteen, or seventeen, and culminated in a ceremony called Confirmation—where young Jewish men and women would "confirm" their allegiance to God and Torah. The Confirmation ceremony took place on Shavuot, not only because the holiday occurs at the end of the academic year, but because the festival celebrating the giving of Torah is the perfect time for a person to confirm loyalty to Torah teachings.

In many Reform synagogues—and in some Conservative and Reconstructionist synagogues that adopted the ritual—Confirmation was and remains an elaborate ceremony that marks academic accomplishment, spiritual commitment, and family and community celebration. Some congregations hold Confirmation on Erev Shavuot, the night when Shavuot begins; others, on Shavuot morning. In addition to the recitation of the liturgy, the singing of special songs, and the personal statements of the young people, many Confirmation ceremonies—reflecting one of the ancient rituals of Shavuot—include the bringing or "offering" of flowers and first fruits. Even after most synagogues in the Reform movement have returned to the celebration of Bar and now Bat Mitzvah, the Shavuot Confirmation service remains an integral part of the movement's educational and spiritual development for its young people.

On Shavuot, it is customary to decorate the synagogue and home with flowers and greens.

The traditional food for Shavuot is fresh fruit, representing the ancient offering of the first fruits.

It is also customary to eat dairy products on this holiday. Ashkenazic Jews, in particular, are fond of eating *blintzes* on Shavuot. While there is no clear reason for this custom, legend suggests that the Children of Israel who received the Torah at Sinai were like little babies, exposed for the very first time to the wonders of the world of Torah. Just as newborns drink only milk, legend has it that Jews, commemorating the moment at Sinai, should drink and eat only dairy.

For all the attempts to infuse Shavuot with new meaning and purpose, in modern times—except in the Orthodox community, which observes and celebrates all festivals with equal fervor—no Jewish holiday is more ignored and less observed than Shavuot. It is only a one- or two-day festival, and often falls in the middle of a busy work week. It comes at a time of year when there is little else on the calendar with which to identify or link it. It has no distinguishing rituals or rites—like the *shofar,* the *succah,* the *lulav* and *etrog;* no *menorah* and candles, no noisemakers and costumes, no family *seder* gatherings or *matzah* substituting for bread.

Sophisticated urban dwellers little identify with another harvest festival that commemorates the ebb and flow of nature.

Still, if most contemporary Jews were committed to lives of Torah learning and living, Shavuot would be a central celebration of Jewish life, since the giving of Torah is the central event of Jewish life.

Yet sadly but all too realistically for all too many Jews, Torah is no longer at the core of existence. Many take it for granted, and even more no longer feel bound by its laws. In the contemporary world, many of the descendants of the ancient "people of the Book" cannot read the Book in its original Hebrew, and rarely read it in the vernacular. For many, if not most, the "idea" of Torah may be inspirational or instructional, but the "reality" of Torah is that it is rarely read and sporadically followed.

The modern attempts to celebrate Shavuot for its agricultural importance meet with indifference, and the attempts to steer the Shavuot celebration back to its Torah-giving roots through observances such as the *Tikkun Layl Shavuot* have captured the imagination and the participation of only a few. Even the Confirmation ceremony, which tried to infuse Shavuot with the purpose of witnessing a young Jew's lifelong commitment to Torah, has become more of a school graduation exercise than a true affirmation of belief.

Is it any wonder, then, that Shavuot is the least known and the least observed of all major Jewish holidays?

What is a Jewish community to do?

Shall we just cross Shavuot off the calendar? Shall we simply relegate Shavuot to fond nostalgia and communal memory? Shall we leave its observance to just the pious few?

There are two ways that Shavuot can be reinfused with meaning and newfound popularity in this generation.

In many places, certain aspects of Judaism—creating community, supporting the State of Israel, advocating social causes, combating anti-Semitism, and more—have taken precedence on the modern Jewish agenda. Contemporary Jews need to be reminded constantly, by their rabbis and teachers, of the primacy of their personal spiritual relationship to God and of the centrality of Torah and *mitzvot* in their lives.

When Torah again becomes not just the theoretical, but the practical centerpiece of Judaism, then Jews will gladly and gratefully commemorate the anniversary of its revelation. Shavuot can be a festive and joyful birthday party for Torah.

The celebration of Shavuot can also be renewed by taking Shavuot back to its origins—in the idiom and metaphor of modern life. The Shavuot offering of the ancient Jews was the first fruits of their orchards and vineyards. While few contemporary Jews literally plant and reap the harvest of their fields, most can still acknowledge and celebrate the first fruits of their lives.

From one Shavuot to the next, many undergo new and moving life-experiences that deserve recognition and thankful expression: the birth of a new baby; a child taking first steps and speaking first words; a youngster who learns to read; a school graduation; a new job; new love; marriage; professional and personal growth, accomplishment, achievement.

Shavuot can be the celebration of the first fruits of modern life, the time to truly give thanks for the bounty of all of God's blessings. On Shavuot, happy and grateful people can express their happiness and gratitude.

The festival of Shavuot—with its ancient and enduring purposes—can prove and confirm, in the words of contemporary teacher Rabbi Eugene Mihaly, that "Sinai is ever present; not only a past event. Wherever people gather to seek God's presence, to renew the covenant, to discover His will, whenever we listen and hear, receive and transmit, we stand at Sinai."

16.   יום השואה   YOM HASHOAH

(literally, "day of the calamity") is Holocaust Remembrance/Memorial Day. It occurs on 27 Nisan, in late April or early or mid-May.

Between 1939 and 1945, the Nazi Party, led by German Chancellor Adolph Hitler, engaged in the systematic attempt to kill every Jew in the world.

In their plan to take over the world and establish the Third Reich, which would endure for a thousand years and more, their stated goal was to make the world racially pure. Their planned genocide was what they called "the final solution to the Jewish problem"—ridding the planet of every Jew, just because they were Jews.

To accomplish their goal, Hitler and the Nazis employed almost every form of persecution, torture, mayhem, and murder then known to humankind.

They wantonly destroyed homes, shops, synagogues, and schools—eventually decimating thousands of European towns and villages. They herded people into crowded ghettos, denying them food and water. They terrorized, brutalized, and killed tens of thousands in their homes. They used human beings for medical experimentation, leaving them to die like animals. They transported men, women, and children from place to place in dank trucks and railway cattle cars, leaving them to choke and suffocate to death. They established concentration camps, where hundreds of thousands of Jews were worked or starved to death. They lined up and shot thousands at a time in cold blood. They built gas chambers, where hundreds of thousands more were gassed to death. They built massive crematoria, where little children were burned alive.

By the time world armies defeated Hitler and the Nazis, 6 million Jews—one and a half million of them children—were brutally murdered, along with at least 10 million others—the gypsies, homosexuals, handicapped, communists, and citizens and soldiers of Europe and the world.

The death of 6 million—one-third of the entire world Jewish population—was, and remains, overwhelmingly devastating to the Jewish People. The real loss of 6 million human beings—and the yet unborn generations that would have come from them—the personal and communal psychological scars from being hated and tortured, the unspeakable pain of the survivors, are all deep wounds from which the Jewish People has yet to recover.

To mark and commemorate this dark chapter in Jewish history, and to pay tribute to the memories of those who died, a day has been set aside on the yearly calendar. It is called Yom HaShoah, the Holocaust Remembrance/Memorial Day.

It is not as if one day can possibly suffice as a day of remembering the horrors of the Holocaust, and it is not as if the Jewish People will ever forget. But as with any momentous event in the history of an individual or a nation, marking and commemorating a specific day as an anniversary can help to focus memory, thought, and future action—not only of the Jewish People, but of the world community.

It was never made completely clear why the Israeli Knesset (Parliament) chose the specific date of 27 Nisan as Yom HaShoah. There seemed to be some attempt to place Yom HaShoah in between the anniversary of the Warsaw Ghetto uprising, which took place on the first day of Passover (15 Nisan) and the anniversary of the establishment of the modern State of Israel (5 Iyar) for there is, in some minds at least, a connection between the destruction of the Holocaust and the rebirth of Israel.

Yom HaShoah is commemorated with solemn programs of remembrance, which often include worship and song, memorial prayers, reminiscences of survivors, multimedia presentations, and exhibits.

Yom HaShoah can do little to erase the anguish of destruction and death, but it can do much to help Jews—and men and women of peace and goodwill throughout the world—remember the victims, and pledge themselves to work toward a world where this kind of horrific genocide will never happen again.

AN ESSAY ON THE HOLOCAUST

There is no greater agony or lament in the history of the Jewish People—and no greater stain on the conscience of humankind—than the Nazi Holocaust, the systematic attempt by the German government to murder every Jew on the face of the earth.

The history of that dark and brutal time is chronicled in other places by historians, anthropologists, sociologists, psychologists, theologians, writers, poets, artists, and musicians, who have sought to record the events and understand their meaning.

Here we will focus on the human dimension—the madness of the perpetrators, the agony of the victims, the spirit of the survivors.

We begin—as we must—in trembling and in silence, for the enormity of the crime, the vastness of its effect, the immensity of its horror, fills us with ineffable rage and makes us unspeakably sad.

THE PLAN

How shall we begin to comprehend the well-planned, well-executed desire to wipe an entire people from existence?

Make no mistake: It was no accident. In his jail-house manifesto, *Mein Kampf (My Struggle)* published in 1925 and 1926, Adolph Hitler carefully laid out his intention to make society racially pure, to rid the world of the Jews and all others whose lives impeded his grand design.

His dream of the Third Reich, a thousand years and more of German world supremacy and the measures that it would take to achieve his goal were no secret when—through free, open, and democratic elections—he became Chancellor of Germany in 1933.

Hitler's monstrous plan was depraved and perverted, and his basic premise was inaccurate and unfounded. Jews may be adherents of a religion and members of a faith community, but they are not a race. Fact, however, did not matter. Hitler—like Pharaoh, Haman, Nebuchadnezzar, the Romans, the Crusaders, the Inquisitors, and the Czar before him—was hell-bent on destroying the Jews.

To do this, he built not just machines of war, not just machines of death, but machines of genocide. Kill every Jew—and every communist, every gypsy, every homosexual, everyone lame, blind, infirm.

It did not matter if they had brilliant minds, sensitive souls, creative powers. It did not matter if they were men or women, young or old, rich or poor, educated or illiterate. It did not matter if they lived in country huts or city apartments, tenements or fine mansions. It did not matter if they were streetsweepers or symphony conductors, shopkeepers or university professors, housewives, fish merchants, or newspaper editors. It did not matter if they were unknown or had friends in high places. It did not matter if they were acculturated and assimilated or if they were pious and devout.

If they were Jews, then because they were Jews—just because they were Jews—they would die.

THE DESTRUCTION

How shall we begin to enumerate the destruction?

We do not have to guess, for the Nazis were so sure of their cause, so sure of victory, that they proudly chronicled their work in meticulous records and preserved its images on film. They were saving and savoring, for themselves and their progeny—and for the posterity of the thousand-year Reich—their accomplishments and their vindication.

So we know of Poland, where before the Holocaust, more than three and a half million Jews lived a flourishing Jewish religious and cultural life. In Warsaw alone, more than fifty Yiddish newspapers were published every day. By the end of the Holocaust, no more than 300,000 Polish Jews were left alive. More than 90 percent of the Jewish population of an entire country had been murdered.

We know of the hundreds of thousands of homes and business destroyed, the thousands of synagogues left in smoldering ruins.

We know of the thousands of towns and villages—once full of life and human promise—desolated and empty.

We know of the architecture and design of the concentration camps, the dimensions of the gas chambers, the formula for the gas, the construction of the crematoria ovens.

We know the train schedules into the camps, the names and the numbers of the people herded there, the hair cut from their heads, the gold fillings pulled from their teeth, the exact day and time of their deaths.

We know of the medical experimentation: how human beings were treated as laboratory animals, and how medical doctors trained to preserve life became instead tormentors and torturers.

We know of the wallets and lampshades and banjos made from the parchment of Torah Scrolls, and the soap made from the flesh of human beings.

We know how decent people got caught up in the frenzy, and how—in their acquiescence or their silence—all but a precious few permitted the madness to go on.

The Nazis were well-pleased with what they were doing. So, as they made their way through Czechoslovakia, rather than destroying them, the Nazis kept the Jewish ritual and art objects from the synagogues and homes. For, after they had achieved their goal of killing every last Jew in the world, they were going to create what they were going to call the Museum of Jewish Extinction, displaying there the strange objects of the strange people they had slain.

We have seen the few Torah scrolls and *kiddush* cups and *menorahs* and prayer-books saved from destruction, only to serve as mute testimony to the utter desolation all around them.

THE MAGNITUDE

How shall we begin to speak of 6 million people—among them one and a half million innocent children—brutally but purposefully murdered, snuffed out forever—they and their generations yet unborn?

Six million *anything* is a hard number to grasp, much less 6 million living, breathing human beings.

How many is 6 million? How do we count to 6 million? How can we comprehend 6 million deaths? Here's how one teacher tried to help her class understand: At the beginning of the school year, a teacher announced a contest. The class that brought in the most soda and beer bottlecaps by the end of the year would win a prize.

All through the year, the students collected bottlecaps from their parents, their grandparents, their neighbors, their friends. Each week, the students brought bags filled with bottlecaps to the school. The teacher took the bags and stored them in a closet.

Near the end of the school year, the teacher brought all the bags to the school auditorium, and spilled out the bottlecaps on the floor.

For hours and hours, the students counted and counted.

At the end of the counting, the students learned that over the course of the whole year, collecting bottlecaps from everyone they knew, competing with each other to bring in the most caps, they had collected a few more than 200,000 bottlecaps.

The students understood. With their combined and enthusiastic effort, they had collected a mere 200,000 bottlecaps. That's not even a quarter of a million; not anywhere close to a half a million; very, very far away from 1 million; and incredibly far, far away from 6 million.

And these were bottlecaps—pieces of metal and cork, not human beings of flesh and blood, human beings who were husbands and wives, fathers and mothers, brothers and sisters. These were bottlecaps; not human beings who could think and love and laugh.

The enormity of the number 6 million, and the overwhelming sense of pain and loss, became just a little more real to those collecting children, and now, perhaps, to each one of us.

The teacher's little game may be silly, even inane, in trying to understand something so serious as the death of 6 million in the horrors of Hitler's hell.

Yet, consider this: In a little more than five years, kill every man, woman, and child in Wyoming, Alaska, Vermont, the District of Columbia, Delaware, North Dakota, South Dakota, Montana, and Rhode Island, and you kill just over 6 million people. It would take the deaths of the entire population of eight states and the nation's capital to equal the number of Jews systematically murdered in the Holocaust.

The death of 6 million Jews, 6 million human beings, is almost too implausible to imagine, too inconceivable to fathom. Yet die they did.

THE REACTION

How shall we begin to account for the reaction of the world—which was none too eager, and none too swift?

Who heard the cries? Who came to redeem, rescue, and save?

There were some notable and noble efforts.

In Denmark, the king put the yellow star—which the Nazis forced Jews to wear as an identifying symbol—on his own clothes, and walked the streets of his country. The message to his countrymen was clear: I am just like the Jews, and they are just like me, for we are all human beings. Permit the Jews to be killed, and it is as if you are permitting me, your own king—and yourselves with me—to be killed. Ninety percent of Danish Jewry escaped the Nazi genocide.

There were men and women of all nationalities, of all religions, of all ethnic backgrounds, who sheltered and saved Jews—sometimes at the peril of their own lives. These rescuers, now sometimes called "Righteous Gentiles"—were quiet, self-effacing, but selfless heroes, who honored and cherished the sanctity of all human life.

But from the vast majority of the world, there was apathy, ambivalence, and deafening silence.

More than 900 Jews were able to escape the clutches of Hitler's armies by boarding a ship called the *St. Louis.* They sailed the open seas, going from port to port, country to country, asking some government, any government, to take them in, to save them. Nation after nation—including the United States of America—refused them entry. They were forced to return to Germany, where almost all of the 900 passengers were sent to their deaths.

President Franklin Roosevelt was shown clear and irrefutable photographs of the train tracks leading into Auschwitz, and of the human cargo being transported to the death camp. Yet he refused to order bombing of the tracks. The trains continued to roll. The Jews continued to die.

The pope—who could, perhaps, have used his moral suasion to influence, or at least inform—sat immobile and silent.

The countries of Europe, anxious to save their lands and their freedoms, went to battle to protect themselves. But they claimed they knew little of the war against the Jews taking place in their own backyards.

Eventually, world governments—prodded by their own fear and self-interest as much or more than by men and women of conscience—acted to confront and defeat the madness of genocide.

Hitler's diabolical scheme was foiled. While 6 million Jews had died, more than 12 million Jews around the world survived the onslaught. Hitler's vision of a world without Jews failed. The Jewish People live.

But how long it took, how much suffering there was, how many died, before the world heeded the cry.

And we are left to ask why our brother was not our keeper, why so many sat idly by our blood.

THE SUFFERING AND THE SURVIVAL

How shall we begin to measure the extent of human suffering?

There are still people who walk this earth with the blue numbers of Auschwitz tattooed on their arms, people with haunted and hollow eyes, people with bruised and battered souls. They are the survivors of the camps, the ghettos, the forests where they ran to hide, the sewers where they ate rats and slept in dung.

They watched as their husbands were shot before their eyes, their wives and children led to the gas chambers. They were forced to labor to the brink of death, they were denied nourishment to the brink of starvation. They ran in fear, until their lungs were about to burst. They hid in darkness, until their eyes could barely see.

When they finally came out of the camps, they were emaciated and disoriented; when they finally came out of hiding, they were angry and afraid. Their families were slain, their towns laid waste, their homes destroyed, their lives shattered.

They live today haunted by the demons and the monsters that are with them always: the screams of anguish reverberating through their bones, the stench of the ovens filling their nostrils, the cries of infants resounding in their ears.

Yet they are the survivors left to tell the tale. They are, in the words of the prophet Zechariah, "the firebrand plucked from the fire" (Zechariah 3:2).

Their dreams were crushed; their spirits sorely tested; but their will was never completely broken. Those who survived—by will, or fate, or Divine intervention—knew with the philosopher that "That which does not kill me makes me stronger."

There is a woman who was taken to Auschwitz when she was sixteen years old. On the very night that her mother was taken to the gas chamber, she was forced to dress in fine clothes and dance a delicate ballet for the camp commander.

How did she—and the thousands like her—survive?

Holocaust survivor Dr. Victor Frankel explains: "Even in such terrible conditions of psychic and physical stress . . . man can preserve a vestige of spiritual freedom, of independence of mind. . . . Everything can be taken from a man but one last thing: the last of human freedoms—to choose one's attitude in a given set of circumstances, to choose one's own way."

This is not to imply that 6 million could have survived simply by having a positive attitude. The Nazi death machines were too powerful and all pervasive for that.

But for those few who were given the tiny possibility of physical survival, it is to bear witness to choice: either to be the victim or to become the victor.

There are those who came from the camps and the forests as perennial victims. Their physical existence was spared, but they were so wounded, so scarred, that though they were granted the gift of life, they never could really live. And then there are those who came out of the camps and the forests refusing to be the victim. Even as the curls of smoke from the crematoria chimneys still floated over Europe, they went into the Displaced Persons camps, they met and married and gave birth to babies—affirming and celebrating life.

They rose up from out of the ashes, came to Israel and the United States—and, in a few demonstrations of abiding faith, returned to the cities and homes from which they had been wrenched—and began new lives.

They would never, ever be the same. How could they be? They would never forget. Why should they? Some never forgave. Who could really blame them?

But they refused to give Hitler a posthumous victory by walking the earth in a living death, or by holding on to never-ending sorrow. They refused to be the victims any more.

Instead, they would be—they are—the victors.

They, and their faith community; they, and every Sabbath candle they ever light, every prayer they ever utter; they and their children and their children's children are the ultimate laugh in Hitler's face.

THE CAUSES

How shall we begin to grapple with the paramount question, the supreme riddle: How could the mad destruction of the Holocaust ever have happened?

Historians and theologians offer theoretical reasons.

In his classic work, *The Decline and Fall of the Roman Empire,* Edward Gibbon lists the five characteristics that led to the collapse of Rome, and that are replicated when every once-great civilization or country begins its inevitable descent from supremacy: (1) corruption in commerce and government; (2) excessive spending on amusement; (3) breakdown of family; (4) decay of religion; and (5) the buildup of offensive armaments when the real enemy is within, due to the decay of individual responsibility.

Add to these already present factors Germany's high unemployment, food shortages, and rampant inflation.

How bad was it?

A young German-Jewish woman who turned twenty-one years old in the late 1930s had been given a gift from her father when she was born. In her name, he purchased an annuity insurance policy. Every year, for twenty-one years, he paid the premium on the policy, expecting that when his daughter reached marriageable age, the policy would return enough money to provide her with a more than generous dowry.

On her twenty-first birthday, the young woman went to collect the money from the policy—the money that her father had been paying for more than two decades, and all the interest that had accumulated.

In the economic climate of the day, the money she received was just enough to pay her bus fare home.

The prescription for disaster for Germany was indelibly written.

When anger and fear—born out of a growing sense of helplessness and desperation—begin to permeate every level of society, two major things begin to happen.

First, people look for a "savior," a leader who offers hope and swift redemption, most often based not on logical political or economic solutions, but on trust in the personal charisma and power of the leader.

Adolph Hitler—whose psychological profile and personal motivations remain a much speculated but enduring enigma—took perfect advantage of Germany's hunger for a quick cure, and with his dominating personality, seized the opportunity to impose his fanatic plan.

Second, rather than taking personal or communal responsibility for their troubles, people begin to look for a scapegoat on whom to blame their woes.

And when it comes to being a scapegoat, the Jews know all too well what it is to be "the chosen people."

Hatred of Jews—which is conveniently manifest in making the Jew into the societal scapegoat—was not new to Germany in the 1930s and 40s. Hatred of the

Jews—most often called anti-Semitism—stretches back at least 2,000 years, and stretches across countries and continents.

Anti-Semitism has, at its origins, at least three major causes.

The first cause is based in religion. With the advent of Christianity—rooted in the Gospels of the New Testament—Jews were accused of deicide. The label "Christ-killers" was applied early on, and hounded Jews wherever they went—until Vatican II (1962–65), under the leadership of Pope John XXIII, absolved the Jews from any responsibility in the death of Jesus. Yet, even when not denounced for killing Christ, Jews were considered infidels. Their constant refusal to accept Jesus as Lord and Savior, and to convert to Christianity, created tension, derision, and enmity.

The birth of Islam—and the Jews' refusal to accept Mohammed as prophet, and the Koran as holy writ—added another source of bitterness, rancor, and discrimination to Jewish existence.

It is ironic—and more than sad—that the Jews, who introduced the wisdom of religious faith and the beauty of religious practice to the world, have suffered such pain and persecution because of religious intolerance.

The second cause of anti-Semitism is based in economics.

Again, irony. For most of their sojourn as guests in host countries, Jews were denied the right to own land or property, or to join the guilds. Forced to make a living with "portable" goods, Jews often became small merchants, traders, jewel dealers, and money lenders. While these sources of income were far less lucrative than owning land or developing businesses, since they dealt in highly desirable commodities such as jewels and money, Jews were perceived as being wealthy.

When a society began to fall on hard economic times—out of yearning and envy—people easily turned against those they considered to control the wealth. Those suffering without money—and without food, without a place to live, with little prospect for employment—strike out against those they think have money—whether it is true or not. They especially resent that it is the "outsiders," the Jews, who seem to have resources when they, the native citizens of the country, do not. That is why the Jew—the ultimate outsider—was always hated in difficult economic times.

The third cause of anti-Semitism is based in morality.

The Jews were chosen by God for the special responsibility of receiving, learning, living, and teaching God's ethical mandate to the world. Yet very few like to have the mirror of morality held in their faces—even though they secretly suspect that what is being asked of them is right and good. So rather than reject the moral code—and, in the process, seem to reject God too—it is much easier to sweep away the mirror and the ones who are holding it.

Through its long history, the world has seemed to employ a simple formula: Get rid of the Jews, and thus get rid of the moral mandate the Jews represent and teach.

Blend together national pride and ethnic passion—for which Germany is so well known—with the historically proven elements of the fearful and spiteful reactions of a staggering and declining society, and mix in long-established formulas for anti-Semitism. The result? Hitler and the Nazis.

THE RESPONSE

Even with all of these rational explanations of why and how the Holocaust could have happened, Elie Wiesel—chronicler of the Holocaust, conscience of a generation, Nobel Peace Laureate—teaches, "There is no answer to Auschwitz."

The realities of the Holocaust are so horrific that it is impossible to explain why even a madman would decide to slaughter a whole people, how an entire nation could embrace his folly, how industries of death were constructed and deployed, and how the whole world could not—or would not—know.

Yet, Wiesel continues, "There is a response."

The response to the Holocaust that Wiesel and we—and we hope the world with us—expect from all humanity is: "Never Again!"

A world made aware of such atrocity can never again countenance such evil. A world made sensitive to such cruelty and barbarity can never again permit such destruction and death.

How good it would be—in this half-century and more since the Holocaust ended—if the world had indeed responded humanely, firmly, and conclusively, "Never Again!"

Yet hatred has not dissipated. Ethnic pride has not given way to universal love.

How to explain the slaughter of both Hindus and Muslims when Pakistan was created in 1947? How to explain the intense hatred of Arabs for Jews and the Jewish State? How to explain the slaughter of Arabs by Arabs? How to explain the intense hatred of Catholics and Protestants in Northern Ireland? How to explain the systematic murder of more than 2 million Cambodians in the 1970s? How to explain the murder of the Afghans in the 1980s? How to explain the "ethnic cleansing" in Bosnia in the 1990s? How to react to a world still rife with bigotry and hate, still filled with racial prejudice, religious intolerance, and ethnic chauvinism, still constantly stalking a convenient scapegoat?

Auschwitz—even after Auschwitz—has, tragically, not been confined to one place and time.

Why have we—all of us—who live in the shadow of the Holocaust not come to the rescue? Why have we let it—on perhaps a smaller scale, but for so many of the same reasons—happen again, and almost continually?

We try to explain: We simply did not know of these atrocities. They were hidden away in parts of the world that are far and secret. If only we had known, we, surely, would have acted. But these rationalizations and excuses have been rendered mute by the incredible advances in technology that enable us to see the oppression, to see the slaughter half a world away—instantaneously, as it happens, right on our television sets.

We can hear the absurd claims of the so-called "historical revisionists," whose assertions that "the Holocaust never happened" are nothing more than ugly anti-Semitism garbed in the cloak of academic inquiry. We can watch the neo-Nazis in Germany brutally attack foreigners and thrust their arms sharply in the air while shouting out, "*Heil* Hitler!" We can see the random acts of vandalism and violence of the skinheads in America. And we can look on with sadness and deep concern as the United States exhibits so many of the classic symptoms—poverty, joblessness, hunger, homelessness, racial and ethnic tensions, growing fear and anger—that mark a once great country in decline, knowing that the inevitable search for a scapegoat may not be long in coming.

What happens around the globe happens right in our own living rooms.

What happens to one human being, happens to every human being.

There is no longer any plausible explanation for sitting idly by the blood of our brothers and sisters. There is no longer any valid excuse for remaining silent while hatred and bigotry go unchallenged, while ethnic genocide still drowns our earth in blood.

If the horrors of the Holocaust are to be anything more than sad and ancient history, and the occasion to build more museums and monuments, then we—and every man and woman of good will and peace in this world—must listen to these words of Elie Wiesel, "If we have learned one thing from the past, it is that to live through dramatic events is not enough. One has to share them and transform them into acts of conscience."

We must say, "Never Again!" and mean it. We must act—whenever and however we must—to stop oppression and persecution, to save and preserve life.

It is a sacred task not just for every Jew, but for every human being. German Protestant theologian and pastor Martin Niemoller—a pacifist and vocal Nazi foe—poignantly taught, "In Germany, they first came for the communists, and I didn't speak up because I wasn't a communist. Then they came for the Jews, and I didn't speak up because I wasn't a Jew. Then they came for the trade unionists, and I didn't speak up because I wasn't a trade unionist. Then they came for the Catholics, and I didn't speak up because I wasn't a Catholic. Then they came for me, and by that time, there was no one left to speak up."

THE MEANING

How shall we begin to give meaning to death, and to forge the future from out of the ashes?

Every Jew alive—today and tomorrow—is intimately and intensely bound up with the 6 million.

We have a sacred trust, and faith to keep—with them and with Jewish destiny.

In the words of the modern prayer, "We are the survivors left to tell the tale. We are the inheritors who bear witness to heaven and earth."

Our grandparents and our parents will never forget. Our children and grandchildren will never know—unless we tell them.

But stories and laments are not enough.

Again, the modern prayer: "They killed the Jews, but Judaism survives; they burned the parchment, but the words endure."

Six million who perished can be given enduring, eternal life through us. Little towns once vanquished can be reborn in us.

When we live lives that bring honor and glory to our God, His Torah and our People, when we live lives filled with decency and goodness, compassion and love, then the oppressor is defeated over and over again: "The chain has not been broken; the chain continues still."

THE AFFIRMATION

Hundreds of thousands of the holy martyrs walked calmly into the gas chambers singing centuries-old words, "I believe, with perfect faith, in the coming of the messiah. And even though he tarries, through all this, I believe."

They did not live to see their abiding belief fulfilled. But we who carry their dreams on our souls and their memories in our hearts take up their aspirations and their certainty. We hope, we pray, we work, for the day—for ourselves, and, if not for us, then for our children's children's children—when the messianic promise will come to be.

On that day, none will be afraid.

Screams of agony will be turned into shouts of gladness, and mourning will be turned into dancing. Hatred and bigotry will vanish; understanding and love will suffuse the universe. The spirit of God will fill the earth, and all of God's children will touch hands in peace.

The destination is worthy of every bit of our energy: from the black pit of the darkness of the Holocaust, to the new light of the dawn of redemption.

It is a journey waiting to be taken.

The souls of 6 million await ultimate deliverance and everlasting triumph.

They wait for us to bring them home.

17. יום העצמאות YOM HAATZMAUT

is Israel's Independence Day. It occurs on 5 Iyar, in late April or early May.

On November 29, 1947, the United Nations voted to partition Palestine, effectively permitting the establishment of both Jewish and Arab states.

On May 14, 1948——which fell on the fifth day of the Hebrew month of Iyar—the third Jewish Commonwealth, the modern State of Israel, declared independence. For the first time in almost 1,900 years, the Jews had a free and independent homeland in the biblically Promised Land.

Israel's declaration of independence was met with an immediate declaration of war by the Arab states. At the very moment of her birth, Israel was forced to fight for her freedom—and her very existence.

Against all odds, Israel prevailed in the War of Independence, and the State of Israel took her rightful place as a nation state of the world.

Each year, on the fifth of Iyar, Israel celebrates Yom HaAtzmaut, Independence Day, with joyous festivities. The Jews of the world join in the anniversary celebration with their own community commemorations: for Israel is the physical homeland of many Jews, but the spiritual homeland of all Jews.

The day before Yom HaAtzmaut is commemorated as יום הזכרון Yom HaZikaron, the Day of Remembrance, a day of memorial for the soldiers who died in the War of Independence and in all the subsequent wars, defending the land and the people of Israel.

Yom HaZikaron is a day of quiet reflection in Israel. A siren sounds, and a minute of solemn silence is observed throughout the entire country, in memory of the soldiers who have died.

Since Israel is such a small country, there is hardly a family that has not been personally affected by the death of a soldier—a son, a husband, a brother, a cousin, a next-door neighbor, a best friend. The grief of loss is deep and widely felt, and there is an abundance of gratitude to the fallen soldiers for defending Israel's existence—her lands, homes, and people.

Since 1967, the twenty-eighth day of Iyar has been celebrated as יום ירושלים Yom Yerushalayim, Jerusalem Day. During the Six Day War in 1967—on the twenty-eighth of Iyar, which fell on June 7, 1967—Israeli soldiers captured and reunited the Holy City of Jerusalem.

With partition in 1948, Jerusalem—Israel's ancient and eternal capital—was supposed to be a free and open city, with equal access for peoples of all nationalities and faiths.

However, the Arab states cut off east Jerusalem—with its holy shrines, including the Temple Mount, the ancient site of the Holy Temples—from Israeli access.

With armed soldiers, the Arab states divided Jerusalem in half and refused entry to east Jerusalem—often called the Old City—to Israelis and world Jewry.

During the ensuing nineteen years, Israel built up west Jerusalem, but never gave up the longing and hope that one day Jerusalem would be reunited into one whole city again.

The swift and decisive victories of the Six Day War gave Israel the long-awaited opportunity. Jerusalem was once again united, under Jewish control, as Israel's Holy City and capital.

Unlike the Arab states nineteen years before, Israel permitted free and open access to Jerusalem and its holy sites to peoples of all faiths, and left jurisdiction of religious sites holy to Christians and Moslems under their control.

Both Yom HaAtzmaut and Yom Yerushalayim are commemorations of the secular State of Israel. There are no special religious rituals or ceremonials associated with them, and the days—except for the celebrations marking independence—are treated as regular work days.

18. תשעה באב   TISHAH B'AV

(literally, "the ninth of [the Hebrew month of] Av) is the day commemorating the destruction of the Holy Temples in Jerusalem in 586 B.C.E. and 70 C.E. It occurs on 9 Av, in mid-July to early August.

In 586 B.C.E., on the ninth day of the month of Av, the Babylonians destroyed the Holy Temple in Jerusalem and sent the Jews into exile. The destruction and exile was witnessed by the prophet Jeremiah, who chronicled it in what would become the biblical book of איכה Eichah, Lamentations.

The ninth of Av became a day of sad commemoration and mourning for the Jewish People, who had lost their homeland, their independence, and their Holy Temple. The psalmist put it poignantly, "By the rivers of Babylon, we sat down and wept when we remembered Zion" (Psalm 137:1).

Some fifty years later, the Jews were permitted (by the Persians, who had defeated the Babylonians) to return to Israel to reestablish their independent homeland. The life of the Jewish People in their land was restored, and the Holy Temple was rebuilt, returning sacrificial worship to its rightful place.

In 70 C.E., culminating more than 200 years of Greek and Roman occupation and persecution, the Romans destroyed the Holy Temple and sent the people into exile. Once again, the Jewish People was ripped from its homeland—this time to wander the earth for almost 2,000 years, until a free and independent Israel would be reestablished in 1948.

By coincidence—or more likely, through the Romans' ironic and sardonic sense of history—the second Holy Temple was destroyed on exactly the same day as the first had been—the ninth of Av.

During the almost 2,000 years of exile, Tishah B'Av was a day of national morning and deep yearning. Wherever they were living, Jews would gather on Tishah B'Av to remember Israel and Jerusalem, weep and mourn over her loss, and recite prayers of hope for return and restoration.

To demonstrate the enormity of the calamity and the depth of communal grief, Tishah B'Av is a full fast day—with no food or water consumed for the entire twenty-four-hour period.

Traditional Jews begin preparations for the observance of Tishah B'Av three weeks earlier. שבעה עשר בתמוז Shivah Asar B'Tammuz, the seventeenth day of the month of Tammuz, marks the first breach of the walls of Jerusalem by the Romans in 70 C.E. The day is commemorated with a half-day fast, from sunup to sundown.

During the three weeks leading up to Tishah B'Av, traditional Jews refrain from participating in celebrations, particularly weddings. Some Jews do not shave or cut their hair, traditional signs of mourning.

Beginning with the first day of Av, for the nine days culminating in the observance of Tishah B'Av, traditional Jews do not eat meat or drink wine, ancient symbols of comfort and luxury that are eliminated during a period of mourning.

The Shabbat immediately preceding Tishah B'Av is called שבת חזון Shabbat Chazon, the Sabbath of the Vision. It takes it name from the special *haftarah* that is recited on Shabbat morning, which begins with the words, "The vision of Isaiah, son of Amos, which he saw concerning Judah and Jerusalem . . ." (Isaiah 1:27). The *haftarah*—which culminates three weeks of recitation of "*Haftarot* of Admonition"—is the prophet's warning to the people that their unfaithfulness to God will lead to their destruction at the hand of the enemy.

The Tishah B'Av observance begins at sundown on the ninth day of the month. If the ninth day falls on Shabbat (Friday sundown to Saturday sundown), the entire Tishah B'Av observance is moved to the next day (Saturday sundown to Sunday sundown) because no mourning takes place on the Sabbath.

On Tishah B'Av, many visible signs of mourning are displayed. Most dramatically, people sit on the floor or on low stools in the synagogue, which is usually illuminated only with low lights or candles.

The centerpiece of the Tishah B'Av evening observance is the recitation of the biblical book of איכה Eichah, Lamentations, in its haunting melody. The chanting of Lamentations is followed by the recitation of קינות *kinot* (literally, "lamentations/dirges/elegies") *piyyutim,* medieval liturgical poems, lamenting the destruction of the Temples.

At the Tishah B'Av morning service, special Torah and *haftarah* portions are read, along with *kinot*. In some synagogues, Lamentations is recited again, as it was on the previous evening.

Just as mourners would not wear *tallit* and *tephillin*—prayershawl and phylacteries—between the time of death of a loved one and the funeral, the communal mourners do not wear *tallit* and *tephillin* at the Tishah B'Av morning service. Dramatically, the *tephillin* are worn—this one and only one time throughout the entire year—at the afternoon service, the beginning of the recognition that the mourning practices of Tishah B'Av and the preceding three weeks will come to an end at sundown.

The Shabbat immediately following Tishah B'Av is called שבת נחמו Shabbat Nachamu, the "Sabbath of Comfort." It takes its name from the opening words of the *haftarah*, "Be comforted, be comforted My people, says your God" (Isaiah 40:1). This *haftarah* begins a series of seven "*Haftarot* of Consolation," leading up to the observance of Rosh HaShanah.

There are two more minor fasts—sunrise to sundown—associated with the events that culminated in Tishah B'Av, which take place during the Jewish year.

צום גדליה Tzom Gedaliah, the fast of Gedaliah, takes place on the third day of the month of Tishri, the day following Rosh HaShanah. This fast marks the assassination of Gedaliah, who was the governor of Judea, appointed by the Babylonians following the destruction in 586 B.C.E. Gedaliah's death was the final blow to any immediate hope of Jewish restoration and independence.

תענית עשרה בטבת Ta'anit Asarah B'Tevet, the fast of the tenth of Tevet, usually falls in December or early January, occurring soon after Chanukah. It marks the beginning of the siege of Jerusalem by the Babylonians.

In modern times, for many, the observance of Tishah B'Av has become much more a day of remembrance rather than a day of actual mourning. With the establishment of the State of Israel in 1948, and most particularly since the reunification of Jerusalem in 1967, many feel that Tishah B'Av should remain an historical commemoration, but that the restoration to Israel from the lands of dispersion eliminates the need for any further mourning.

While some traditional Jews continue the full Tishah B'Av commemoration, many Jews now fast and exhibit the visible signs of mourning only on the evening when Tishah B'Av begins, or at the most, through the early afternoon on Tishah B'Av day.

In Israel today, at the Western Wall—the last remnant of the second Holy Temple—on Tishah B'Av there is a liberal mixture of mourning, of remembering, and of quiet celebration. At the wall, on Tishah B'Av—and throughout the Jewish world as well—the whole of the Jewish experience comes together; and like all of Jewish history, it is a combination of tears and laughter.

The contemporary observance of Tishah B'Av reflects both the glory and the burden of the Jewish past, and, at the very same time, it leads the way into the Jewish future. It is a solemn yet hopeful commemoration of Jewish history and Jewish destiny.

5

JEWISH WORSHIP

1.   HISTORY AND DEVELOPMENT

Originally, Jews worshiped God by offering animal and agricultural sacrifices.

Priests (first Aaron, the brother of Moses, and then his descendants) officiated at daily sacrificial offerings.

When the Children of Israel were on their trek through the desert, the sacrifices were brought to the Tabernacle. When the Jewish People entered the Promised Land of Israel, various sacrificial altars were set up. Eventually, the sacrificial offerings were centralized in the Holy Temple in Jerusalem.

In English, the word *sacrifice* means to give up something in order to achieve or get something better. For example, in baseball, a batter hits a "sacrifice bunt" knowing that he will be out at first base, but also knowing that he will advance his teammate runner into scoring position.

The animal and agricultural sacrifices brought for Jewish worship had this connotation. The worshiper "gave up" something of value—the animal or the grain—in the hope of gaining something of more value: God's favor.

But in Hebrew the word *sacrifice* has a deeper, more important meaning. The Hebrew word for sacrifice is קרבן *korban,* from the root word קרב *karov,* which means "to bring close." The offering of the *korban,* the sacrifice, was intended to bring the worshiper into a close, intimate relationship with God.

There were two daily communal offerings: one in the morning and one in the afternoon. The afternoon offering was a smaller offering, consisting of fine grain or meal. Additional offerings were brought on the Sabbath and the festivals, to acknowledge the specialness of the day. Individuals could also bring special additional offerings for special occasions or reasons.

When the Holy Temple was destroyed and the Jewish People sent into exile in 586 B.C.E., prayers with words developed to substitute for animal sacrifices because the Holy Temple—the place where the offerings had been brought—was no longer in existence.

Fifty years later, in approximately 538 B.C.E., the Jews were allowed to return to the Land of Israel. About twenty years later, the Holy Temple was rebuilt and animal and agricultural sacrifices were reinstituted. But some of the prayers that had been developed during the exile had become so popular that the people continued to recite them in addition to the bringing of sacrifices.

When the Second Holy Temple was destroyed and the people sent into exile in 70 C.E., a much more elaborate set of prayers was developed. As the exile became longer and longer, the prayers became more and more ingrained and established in the life of the Jewish People. Prayers replaced the sacrifices, the synagogue replaced the Holy Temple, and rabbi-scholars replaced the cultic priests.

The format for prayer replicated the format of the sacrifices: two prayer services a day, the main service in the morning and a brief service in the afternoon. Later an evening service was added to the structure of worship, reflecting the human need and desire to seek out and communicate with God at the beginning, throughout, and at the end of the day.

This rubric of three prayer services a day follows both the structure of the Jewish day, which begins and ends at sundown (beginning at evening, continuing through morning, and concluding in late afternoon), and also the secular day (beginning with awakening in the morning, continuing through the afternoon, and concluding at night's bedtime). On the Sabbath and the festivals, additional prayers were added to reflect the additional sacrifices that had been brought on those days.

Each prayer service began to take on its own form. Some of the prayers were taken directly from the Bible. Some were written by the rabbis and the sages of the day. Each generation added prayers. Gradually, a familiar pattern for each prayer service began to emerge.

An order of the service began to be fixed. The first systematic prayerbook was outlined in the year 870 C.E. by Rav Amram ben Sheshna Gaon, in the Academy of Sura in Babylonia. Less than a century later, the great Rabbi Saadya Gaon (882–942) compiled a more complete, more logical, and better organized prayerbook. Saadya's prayerbook—called in Hebrew a סדור *siddur* (literally: "order")—serves as the model of the Order of the Service until this day.

2. ברכה B'RACHAH

(plural, *b'rachot)* is a blessing.

The basic formula of Jewish prayer is a *b'rachah,* a blessing, for it is by means of blessings that Jews acknowledge, praise, thank, and petition God.

B'rachot are the basic rubric of the communal worship service. Just as often, they are recited privately, as a personal expression of gratitude or desire.

In English, "to bless" means to "bestow favor on." That means that the one who has the "goodies," the greatest strength, power, or influence, or the best or the most desirable qualities or possessions, can offer those "goodies" (or a portion of them) to another.

Since God is the ultimate holder of life's "goodies," it is easy to understand why human beings would seek God's blessings—asking God to bestow favor by giving a measure of His strength, wisdom, compassion, and love, by granting health, prosperity, and happiness. It would thus make great sense for the formula of a Jewish blessing to be, "O God, please bless me (us) with . . ."

But the formula of a Jewish blessing is very different. Jewish blessings begin with the words, ברוך אתה ה' *Baruch Atah Adonai,* "Blessed are *You,* O Lord."

It is a curious formulation. For who are we human beings—those seeking the "goodies," God's favor—to say to God, *"We* bless *You"*? What do we have that God is lacking, that God would want?

The answer lies in the translation of the Hebrew word for "blessed," ברוך *baruch.*

According to some scholars, the ancient Hebrew word conveys not just the sense of "bestowing favor," but of "acknowledging power."

Thus rather than meaning *"We* bless *You,* O Lord" (offering our "goodies" to God), the sense of a Jewish blessing is that "We acknowledge within You, O Lord, the power to . . . ."

Since the English phrase "Blessed are You, O Lord" does not convey the real meaning of what a Jew is trying to say to God, and since the phrase, "We acknowledge within You, O Lord, the power to . . . " is a lengthy and cumbersome translation, the best way to convey what a blessing is really trying to say to God is to understand the formula to mean, *"Acknowledged* or *Praised* are You, O Lord who . . ."

TYPES OF BLESSINGS

There are three types of blessings.

1. The first type of blessing thanks God for enjoyment of the five senses. This blessing begin with the six-word formula . . . ברוך אתה ה' אלהנו מלך העולם *Baruch*

Atah Adonai, Elohanu melech haolam, meaning, "Praised are You, O Lord, our God, King of the universe." Each separate blessing then concludes with specific words thanking God/acknowledging God's power.

The best-known of this type of blessing is called המוציא *hamotzi,* the blessing for bread specifically, and all food in general. Added to the basic six-word opening formula are the words, ". . . who brings forth bread from the earth."

A complete rendition of the meaning of this blessing conveys the full sense of what a Jewish blessing says: "We acknowledge within You, O Lord our God, Ruler of the universe (and we thank You, too) who (through Your power) brings forth bread from the earth. For who—other than You, God—has the power to create the spark of life that makes the wheat grow and thus provide food for us?"

Another very well-known blessing of this type is called קדוש *kiddush,* "sanctification." It is a blessing recited when drinking wine—wine that has been specially designated, sanctified, for the special and unique purpose of inaugurating the Sabbath or a festival.

Other blessings of this type praise God for creating various kinds of foods, and for creating the awesome sights and sounds of nature.

A lengthy blessing, beginning with the same six-word opening formula, is recited after eating a meal. This blessing is known as ברכת המזון *bircat hamazon,* the blessing for food.

All of these blessings thank God for the wondrous universe in which we live, and for the sustenance of body and soul.

2. The second kind of blessing is recited before performing a *mitzvah,* a commandment of God, to acknowledge that the commandment is Divinely given, and to thank God for the opportunity to fulfill a religious precept.

To the basic six-word opening formula for a blessing—"Praised are You, O Lord our God, Ruler of the universe . . ."—four more words are added: אשר קדשנו במצותיו וצונו . . . *asher kidshanu b'mitzvotav vetzivanu . . . ,* meaning, "who sanctified us by (means of) Your commandments and commanded us . . ."

Each separate blessing then concludes with specific words acknowledging God's command of the religious precept or ritual that is about to be performed.

The best-known of this type of blessing is the blessing recited when lighting candles at the beginning of the Sabbath on Friday evening.

3. The third kind of blessing is recited to praise, thank, or petition God.

Most often, this blessing begins with the usual six-word opening formula, "Praised are You, O Lord, our God, Ruler of the universe . . . ."

The best-known blessing of this type is called שהחינו *shehecheyanu,* which means "who has kept us alive." This blessing is recited at the beginning of each festival, or when anything is done for the first time ever, or the first time in a long time, to thank God "who has kept us in life, preserved us, and brought us to this time." It is a blessing of celebration and thanksgiving.

Many blessings of this type are recited during worship services as part of the liturgy of praise and petition. Reflected in these blessings is the full litany of the needs and desires of human beings, coming before God, hoping for God's favor.

The three types of Jewish blessings that are recited to God embody the whole of the human condition: the desire and the need to praise and thank God for all His many gifts, and to ask of God continuing favor and benediction.

An observant Jew recites at least 100 blessings each and every day. Spending so much time and spiritual energy acknowledging, praising, and thanking God is recognition and affirmation that God is at the center of a person's life, that the spiritual quest for a personal, intimate relationship with God is a primary purpose of human existence.

The recitation of blessings is a constant reminder to each and every Jew—and each and every human being—of who we are, from where we have come, what we have witnessed and what we have achieved, and—with God's continued favor—what we can hope to become.

3.   דאווען   DAVEN

(Yiddish; either from the Latin *divinus,* meaning "Divine" or "of God";
or from the Lithuanian meaning "gift.") is fully engaged participation
in the act of worship.

Jewish worship—within the context of a structured worship service, recited either personally or as part of a communal group—is more than the recitation of words from a prayerbook, more than an intellectual exercise of approaching God with rational thoughts and reasoned arguments.

To really worship, to truly pray, is to *daven* (or to participate in the act of *davenen* or *davening*)—to come to God with open heart and soul, with the depths of emotional celebration or need, with soul cries of anguish or joy, with the deep desire to touch God.

To *daven* means to connect and communicate with God; to be caught up in the immediate reality of speaking to God, of knowing that God is listening, and of hearing God in return; to be deeply, emotionally involved in the process—completely engaged, fully participating, and wholly affected by the words, the music, the mood, the encounter.

Davening is like being in love—while it can be described in words and rationally defined, the only way to truly understand and fully appreciate its sublime meaning, its profound power, and its spiritual potency, is to experience it personally and be caught up in its intense and awesome life-affirming energy.

4. מנין MINYAN

(literally, "number") a quorum, the minimum number of people
necessary for public Jewish worship.

A Jew can pray to God *(daven)* in one of two ways: individually, or as part of a communal group.

Private, personal prayer can be recited either at the traditionally set times for worship services, using the fixed words of the prayerbook, or it can be offered anywhere, at any time, speaking the innermost words of mind and heart.

Public worship takes place at certain specific times—the three daily times of worship—using the structured rubrics of the prayer service.

The sages decided that it would take a minimum number—a quorum— of ten Jews to make up a "congregation" or "community" for public worship.

The choice of the number ten was based on the linkage of two biblical verses. In one place, the Bible says, "God stands in the *congregation* of Divine beings" (Psalms 82:1). In another place, it says, "How long shall I bear with this evil *congregation* that keeps muttering against me?"—referring to the ten scouts who were sent from the desert into the Land of Israel, and returned with a negative report (Numbers 14:27). Since in one case *congregation* meant ten people, and in the other case, it seems as if God is speaking (as in prayer) with the *congregation* of His heavenly assistants, the sages decided that it would take ten people to form a congregation for the purpose of public worship.

The minimum of ten people (in Orthodoxy, only men) thirteen years of age (Bar/[Bat] Mitzvah) or older, constituting the community for public worship, is called a *minyan.*

Because the *minyan*-quorum is necessary for public worship, the word *minyan* has also taken on the connotation of the worship service itself. For example, "Are you going to the *minyan* (meaning the service) today?"

THE WORSHIP SERVICES

5.   DAILY SERVICES

There are three Jewish worship services each and every day of each and every year—one in the evening, one in the morning, and one in the afternoon. Traditional Jews recite the prayers of these worship services either together in a synagogue—or in another communal setting—or individually.

מעריב   MA'ARIV

is the evening service.

The service gets its name from the Hebrew word ערב *erev*—the root word of *ma'ariv*—which means "evening."

Since a Jewish day begins and ends at sunset, the *ma'ariv* service is the first service of a Jewish day.

The *ma'ariv* service is recited after the sun has set, and can be recited up until midnight.

שחרית   SHACHARIT

is the morning service.

The service gets its name from the Hebrew word שחר *shachar* which means "dawn" or "morning."

The *shacharit* service is recited any time after dawn until about ten o'clock in the morning.

The *shacharit* service begins with a set of introductory prayers, which are called ברכות השחר *Birchot Hashachar*, the Morning Blessings, and פסוקי דזמרה *P'sukay D'zimrah*, the Verses of Song. These blessings and prayers of praise to God—many taken from the biblical book of Psalms—are the introductory, "warm-up" prayers.

They set the mood and the tone for worship, and serve as the transition from the "outside world" to the sanctuary and the purpose of the worship service.

מנחה   MINCHAH

is the afternoon service.

The service gets its name from the Hebrew word מנחה *minchah,* which means "gift" or "offering."

When sacrifices were brought to the Holy Temple, the afternoon sacrificial offering was of fine grain or meal. Since this afternoon offering was not as elaborate as the regular daily sacrifice made in the morning, the *minchah* was a much simpler ritual than the morning rites.

Reflecting that simplicity, the *minchah* worship service is a much abbreviated form of the morning service.

The *minchah* service can be recited any time in the afternoon.

Many Jews recite the *minchah* and *ma'ariv* services separately from each other—*minchah* anytime throughout the afternoon, and *ma'ariv* much later, after dark.

But for practical purposes, the *minchah* and *ma'ariv* services are most often recited one following the other. *Minchah* is recited just before sunset, and *ma'ariv* just after sunset, so that the worshipers come to the synagogue (or gather to pray) twice a day—once for *shacharit* in the morning, and once for *minchah* followed by *ma'ariv* in the later afternoon—early evening.

6.   קריאת התורה   KERIAT HATORAH

is the Torah reading.

The centerpiece of certain worship services during the course of each week is the reading of the Torah.

The Torah has been divided into fifty-four separate sections or portions, each called a פרשה *parashah* or סדרה *sedrah.* One portion is read each week (sometimes two are combined), so that the entire Torah is read from beginning to end in the course of one year, with the completion of the yearly Torah-reading cycle—and the immediate beginning of the new cycle—taking place in the fall on the festival of Simchat Torah, at the end of Succot.

The Torah is read four times each week. The first part of the weekly portion is read for the first time on Saturday afternoon (at the Shabbat *minchah* service) and is repeated at the *shacharit* services on Monday morning and on Thursday morning. The entire weekly portion is read at the Shabbat morning service.

The Torah is also read on all holiday and festival mornings, including Chanukah and Rosh Chodesh, and on fast days. The Torah reading for each festival was specially selected by the sages for its thematic connection and relevance to the holiday being celebrated.

At the Shabbat *minchah* service, the Torah is read near the beginning of the service, before the major prayers of the service are recited. At the morning services, the Torah is read following the *shacharit* service.

Following the Torah reading on Shabbat, Rosh HaShanah, Yom Kippur and festival mornings, and on Yom Kippur and other fast day afternoons, a section from the biblical prophets is read. This prophetic reading is called the הפטרה *haftarah* (from the Greek meaning "addition," or from the Hebrew meaning "dismiss" or "discharge"), and it has been chosen for its thematic connection to the particular Torah portion in order to add depth of meaning and understanding. The reading of the *haftarah* is preceded and followed by special blessings.

7.   SPECIAL SERVICES FOR SPECIAL TIMES

קבלת שבת   KABBALAT SHABBAT

(literally, "welcoming, greeting the Sabbath") are the prayers—recited preceding the *ma'ariv* service on Friday evening—for welcoming the Sabbath.

These prayers are designed to acknowledge the specialness of Shabbat and to serve as the transition between the regular weekday (Friday) and the holiness of the Sabbath (beginning at sunset on Friday). These are prayers—mostly taken from the biblical book of Psalms—of praise and thanksgiving to God.

מוסף   MUSAF

(literally, "additional") is the additional service, added to the *shacharit* service (and following the reading of the Torah) on Shabbat, the festivals, and Rosh Chodesh.

This service acknowledges the specialness of the Sabbath, the festivals, or Rosh Chodesh day, and reflects the additional sacrificial offerings that were brought on the Sabbath and festivals.

Since sacrificial worship has long passed into history, the Reform movement contends that there is no cogent reason to continually invoke its memory, and has eliminated recitation of the *musaf* service.

הלל   HALLEL

(literally, "praise") is the service consisting of psalms of praise to God that is recited following the *shacharit* service on the festivals of Pesach, Shavuot, and Succot. *Hallel* is also recited on Rosh Chodesh and on Chanukah.

The recitation of these psalms indicates the special joyful nature of the festival observance.

הבדלה   HAVDALAH

(literally, "separation") is the brief service, held just after sunset on Saturday evening (both at the synagogue and at home), separating the Sabbath from the rest of the week.

A modified *havdalah* service is also recited at the conclusion of each festival to mark the end of that festival.

THE SYNAGOGUE AND ITS RITUAL OBJECTS

8.   THE SYNAGOGUE

From its origins until today, the synagogue—a Greek word meaning "place of assembly/gathering/meeting"—has been the central communal institution of Jewish life, the space where the central public activities of Jewish life—including most public worship—take place.

There are three Hebrew name-designations for synagogue, each of which describes one function of its threefold purpose: בית הכנסת *Beit HaKnesset,* House of Gathering; בית התפלה *Beit HaTefilah,* House of Prayer; and בית המדרש *Beit HaMidrash,* House of Study/Learning. The synagogue is also sometimes called שול *shul,* a Yiddish word meaning "school." Since Jewish learning and worship most often take place within the same building—especially lessons for the children in a synagogue schoolroom—the name is most appropriate.

In modern times, especially in the Reform community, the synagogue is often called temple. This name has become a clear designation for a Jewish place of worship, but many Jews prefer not to call a modern synagogue a temple, contending that the name rightly and solely belongs to the Holy Temple in Jerusalem, which was destroyed in 70 C.E., at the time the Jews were sent into exile.

In modern times, some Jews gather to worship in smaller, more intimate settings than the formal, communal synagogue. These "alternative synagogues" are called חבורות *chavurot* (singular, חבורה *chavurah*) meaning "friendship groups" or "associations"; or alternately מנינים *minyanim* (singular, מנין *minyan*) from the word for "prayer quorum," meaning "prayer group."

The *chavurot* or *minyanim* are formed by people who find contemporary synagogues—some with 1,000 or more family members—to be too large and impersonal. These people want fully participatory—and, in most cases, fully egalitarian—worship services, intense study, and a close-knit groups of friends with whom to experience Jewish life and celebrate Jewish holidays.

The groups most often meet in private homes, or are sometimes invited to gather in the classroom, library, or basement of a synagogue building. A *chavurah* or *minyan* may have as few as ten to as many as sixty or eighty members—a small enough group so that each member, including all the children, can personally participate in all the services and activities, and so that close friendships can be formed.

Some contemporary Jews find the modern *chavurah* or *minyan* to be a viable companion or alternative to the modern synagogue—a place where personal involvement and the intimacy of community are the central commitments.

Jews can pray anywhere, but an ordinary building or room becomes a synagogue—a specially designated sacred space—through its special structures and ritual objects.

9. ספר תורה   SEFER TORAH

is the Torah Scroll, the handwritten parchment containing the text
of the Torah, the Five Books of Moses.

The Sefer Torah—containing God's word and will, the history and the laws of the Jewish People—is the primary and most sacred ritual object of Jewish life, indispensable for Jewish worship, and essential in establishing and maintaining a synagogue. It is kept in a place of honor in the synagogue, and is read on specific occasions during the worship services.

Every synagogue needs at least one Torah Scroll in order to function properly. Most synagogues try to have at least three Torah Scrolls, because at certain services, the ritual calls for reading from two different sections in the Torah; and at certain services, in certain years, the ritual calls for reading from three separate sections in the Torah. So, to avoid delay in the service while rolling the Torah scroll from section to section, two or three separate Torah Scrolls are used.

In Ashkenazic synagogues, the Sefer Torah is dressed in a beautiful velvet or silk covering, and is often decorated with a כתר *keter,* a crown, and a חושן *choshen,* a breastplate of silver or gold. In Sephardic synagogues, the Torah scroll is often kept in a decorative silver or gold cylindrical container.

10. יד YAD

(literally, "hand") is the Torah pointer.

It is custom not to touch the parchment of the Torah Scroll as it is being read. Yet the reader needs to follow along in the text to keep the correct place. The *yad* serves as the pointer, with which the reader can keep place and not falter in the reading of the Torah. Because it is shaped like a hand with a pointed finger the pointer is called the *yad,* which means "hand."

11. בימה   BIMAH

is the raised platform—the pulpit—in the synagogue,
where the Torah Scroll is kept.

The *bimah* is usually at the eastern wall of the synagogue because Jews face east at worship, toward Israel and Jerusalem. (Jews living in Israel worship facing toward Jerusalem.)

In Ashkenazic synagogues, the service is conducted from this *bimah* at the eastern wall. In Sephardic synagogues, there is a second *bimah,* in the center of the room, from which the service is conducted.

12. ארון הקודש   ARON HAKODESH

is the Holy Ark, which houses the Torah Scrolls in the synagogue.

When the Children of Israel received the Ten Commandments in the desert, they were commanded to make an ark in which to place the Tablets of the Law (Exodus 25:10). In this ark—sometimes called the Ark of the Covenant (Numbers 10:33) or the Ark of God (2 Samuel 5:3)—the Tablets were carried from place to place. Later, when the Holy Temple was built in Jerusalem, the Tablets in the ark became the centerpiece of the Holy of Holies, the most sacred spot in the Temple.

The modern version of this ancient ritual object is the *Aron HaKodesh,* the Holy Ark, on the *bimah* of the synagogue. In this Holy Ark, the Torah Scrolls are kept. The modern ark is a cabinet-like structure—sometimes built into the wall, sometimes freestanding. In many synagogues, the *Aron HaKodesh* is an extremely beautiful piece of decorative art that enhances the beauty and the sanctity of the synagogue.

13. פרכת   PAROCHET

is the curtain-covering of the ark, behind which the Torah Scrolls are kept.

In the Tabernacle in the desert, a veil of blue, purple, and scarlet linen separated the ark from the rest of the Tabernacle. It effectively separated the holy space of the sanctuary from the holiest space where the Tablets of the Law were kept (Exodus 26: 31).

The modern version of the ark covering is the *parochet,* which separates the holy space of the synagogue from the holiest space where the Torah Scrolls are kept in the Holy Ark.

The modern *parochet* is most often a very fine piece of cloth, velvet or silk, decorated in a beautiful way to bring honor through artistic beauty to the Torah Scrolls and the synagogue.

14. נר תמיד NER TAMID

is the Eternal Light, which hangs over (and in front of) the *Aron HaKodesh*, the Holy Ark.

The Tabernacle in the desert contained a "lamp to burn continually" as a physical symbol of the presence of God (Exodus 27:20). The modern version of the lamp is the *Ner Tamid*, the Eternal Light, which is continually illuminated over the Holy Ark in the synagogue.

Originally, the *Ner Tamid* burned oil. Now, however, it is most often powered by electricity. Yet its purpose is the same as in antiquity. It burns day and night, every day of the year, as a physical symbol of God's eternal spiritual presence.

15. עמוד AMUD

(literally, "pillar" or "standing-place") is the leader's lectern.

The prayer leader conducts the worship service from a specially designated lectern, an *amud*.

In Orthodox synagogues, the *amud* is placed facing toward the Holy Ark, so the prayer leader conducts the service facing the Torah Scrolls and facing east toward Israel. In liberal synagogues, the *amud* is most often placed stage-style, facing toward the congregation, so that the prayer leader conducts the service facing the worshipers.

Since the prayer leader stands at the *amud*, it supplies the central focus for the worship service. Thus, when inquiring as to who is leading the service, one commonly asks, "Who is *davening* for the *amud* today?"

16. שלחן SHULCHAN

(literally, "table") is the table or lectern from which the Torah is read.

In the Tabernacle in the desert was a table made of wood overlaid with gold. It was to hold the showbread, the loaves that were brought on the Sabbath and later eaten by the priests (Exodus 25:23). While the purpose of the showbread remains unclear, most understand it to be an expression of gratitude to God, who provides all that is necessary for sustenance.

The modern version of the Tabernacle table is a *shulchan,* the table that is on the *bimah.* During the service, when it is time for the scriptural reading, the Torah scroll is taken from the *Aron HaKodesh,* placed on the *shulchan,* unrolled, and read. The *shulchan* is usually covered with a fine piece of decorative silk or velvet cloth.

17. עזרת נשים   EZRAT NASHIM

(literally, "women's court[yard]") is the women's section
in the (Orthodox) synagogue.

When the Holy Temple existed, only men were obligated to bring and witness sacrificial offerings. However, there was a specially designated area called the *ezrat nashim,* the women's court(yard), where women could stand to observe the proceedings.

Later, when worship services took the place of sacrifices and the synagogue took the place of the Holy Temple, the separation of men and women during worship was extended to the synagogue.

Some explain that since men are obligated to worship and women are not, those with the obligation sit together and those without the obligation sit together— separately. Others explain that men were concerned that seeing beautiful women and hearing their beautiful voices during worship might cause distraction from the sacred task of prayer.

Based on either or both of these reasons, a separate section of the synagogue— an elevated section, a balcony, or a back or side room—was designated as the separate women's section—the place for women to worship without sitting with or being seen by the men. In buildings where constructing a distinctly separate section was not practical, a מחיצה *mechitza* (literally, "partition"), a wall or a curtain, was set up to separate the men from the women.

In contemporary times, the words *ezrat nashim* and *mechitza* are often used interchangeably, indicating and designating the separate seating of men and women during worship. In Orthodox synagogues, men and women continue to sit separately from each other during worship services. In all non-Orthodox synagogues—Reform, Conservative, and Reconstructionist—men and women sit together during worship.

SYNAGOGUE PEOPLE

18. רב   RAV

(literally, "master" or "teacher") is a rabbi.

A rabbi is a trained scholar in Judaica, a teacher of Jewish texts and traditions. He (and in modern times, in Reform, Reconstructionist, and Conservative Judaism, she) is an interpreter and decider of Jewish law.

As the preeminent Jewish authority in a particular congregation or community—whose legal rulings are to be accepted and applied—the rabbi is designated as the מרא דאתרא *mara d'atra* (Aramaic, meaning "master of the land or locale"). In modern times the role and responsibility of the rabbi has expanded. He or she is a pastor-counselor, a community organizer or leader, and a professionally trained leader of Jewish institutions.

The most visible role of the rabbi is as the leader of the synagogue worship service, although any learned and capable Jew can lead the worship. The contemporary rabbi also most often acts as the officiant at life-cycle ceremonies, such as circumcisions, baby namings, Bar and Bat Mitzvahs, weddings, and funerals.

Despite the rabbi's great responsibility and authority, he or she has no special powers or relationship with God. The rabbi learns and transmits God's word and will, attempting to inspire Jews to a relationship with God, to living a life committed to Jewish values and ethics, to observance of Jewish rituals, and to participation in the life of the Jewish community.

In modern times, calling a rabbi *Rav* or *HaRav* (*the* rabbi/master) usually implies that rabbi's status as an outstanding scholar and expert in matters of Jewish law.

Calling a rabbi *Rebbe* usually implies that the rabbi has status as a beloved and often charismatic spiritual guide.

19. שליח צבור   SHALIACH TZIBBUR

(literally, "messenger or agent of the community") is the prayer leader.

Any Jew (in Orthodoxy, only men) who is knowledgeable, trained, and capable can conduct and lead a worship service. The *shaliach tzibbur*—alternately called the בעל תפלה *ba'al tefilah* (literally, "master of prayer")—is the one who conducts the worship service, serving, as the name implies, as the prayer leader and messenger-agent of the community, standing before God to represent and offer the prayers of the community.

20. חזן CHAZZAN

is a cantor.

To enhance the beauty and artistry of the worship service, many synagogues have a *chazzan* who serves as the *shaliach tzibbur*.

The *chazzan* is a fine singer, especially trained in the music of the synagogue, who chants the worship service and leads the musical and vocal parts of the prayers. He (and in modern times, in Reform, Reconstructionist, and Conservative Judaism, she) uses music to inspire worshipers, and to lead all of the participants in the service closer to God.

21. בעל קורא BA'AL KORAY

(literally, "master of reading") is the Torah reader.

When the Torah is read during the synagogue service, it is chanted according to a series of musical notes and notations.

However, the musical notes do not appear in the Torah text that is in the hand-written parchment Torah Scroll. The notes are only annotated in books, in printed copies of the Torah.

It takes special knowledge, training, skill, and preparation to chant the Torah reading directly from the Torah Scroll. The *ba'al koray* is this specially trained Torah reader.

Any Jew (in Orthodoxy, only men) who possesses this knowledge and training can serve as the *ba'al koray*.

22. גבאי GABBAI

(literally, "collector") is the synagogue official.

Originally, the *gabbai* was the fiscal officer of the synagogue and community, collecting funds to maintain the ongoing functions of the synagogue, and collecting and distributing funds for the needing.

The *gabbai*—usually a learned and respected member of the congregation—now holds an honorary position.

The main role of the *gabbai* is to stand next to the *shulchan* during the Torah reading, following along in a printed text, and offering assistance or correction to the *ba'al koray,* should it be needed. The *gabbai* is often the one to select the members of the congregation who will be called to the Torah for an *aliyah* (the recitation of the blessings over the reading of a section of the Torah).

In most synagogue services when the Torah is read, there are two *gabbaim,* one standing on each side of the reading table.

In some synagogues, this role is played by a volunteer (or, sometimes, a synagogue employee) called the שמש *shammas* (literally, "servant.") In addition to distributing the honors and assisting the *ba'al koray,* the *shammas* often sees to the scheduling of services, the upkeep of the ritual objects, and all the other tasks that it takes to keep the synagogue functioning smoothly. The *shammas* is the "jack-of-all-trades," "the religious handyman."

WORSHIP PRACTICES

23. עליה ALIYAH

(literally, "to go up") is to go up (to the *bimah*) to recite
the blessings over the reading of the Torah.

At the services when the Torah is read (Monday, Thursday, and Saturday mornings, Saturday afternoon, festival mornings, Yom Kippur afternoon, and other fast day afternoons), that particular Torah portion-section is subdivided into a specific number of parts.

Each part is called an *aliyah* (meaning "to go up") because for each part, a member of the congregation is called up to the Torah to recite a blessing, both before and after that part is read.

Coming to the Torah to recite the blessings is called having an *aliyah.*

• On weekday mornings, Shabbat afternoon, Yom Kippur afternoon, and other fast day afternoons, there are three *aliyot* (plural of *aliyah.*)

• On Rosh Chodesh morning (the first day of the new Hebrew month) and on Chanukah mornings, there are four *aliyot.*

• On Rosh HaShanah and festival mornings, there are five *aliyot.*

• On Yom Kippur morning, there are six *aliyot.*

• On Shabbat morning, there are seven *aliyot.*

Traditionally, the first *aliyah* goes to a Kohen, a descendant of the Priestly tribe, and the second *aliyah* goes to a Levi, a descendant of the assistants to the priests. All the other *aliyot* go to a Yisrael, any member of the Jewish People who is neither a Kohen nor Levi.

24. מפטיר MAFTIR

(literally, "dismiss/discharge/conclude") is the final *aliyah*.

On Shabbat, Rosh HaShanah, Yom Kippur, and festival mornings, an additional *aliyah* is added to the normal number (a sixth on Rosh HaShanah and festivals, a seventh on Yom Kippur, an eighth on Shabbat). This additional, concluding *aliyah*, called *maftir,* is created by repeating the last several verses of the final *aliyah*.

Adding the *maftir aliyah* indicates the specialness of the day, and provides another opportunity for another member of the congregation to be honored with an *aliyah*.

The reading from the Prophets, the *haftarah,* which follows the Torah reading on Shabbat and festival mornings, is recited by the person who had the *maftir aliyah,* so the *haftarah* is sometimes also referred to as the *maftir*.

Since the Bar or Bat Mitzvah boy or girl most often has the *maftir aliyah,* and then recites the *haftarah,* the *maftir-haftarah* is closely identified with the Bar or Bat Mitzvah ceremony.

25. הגבה HAGBAH

(from the word meaning "to lift up") is the lifting of the Torah.

At the conclusion of the Torah reading, the *Sefer Torah,* the Torah Scroll, is lifted from the reading desk in a ceremonial manner, called *hagbah*.

The person honored with doing this task is called המגביה *hamagbiah* (literally, "the lifter"), and has the *hagbah aliyah*.

26. גלילה GELILAH

(from the word meaning "to roll") is the rolling and the binding of the Torah.

After the Torah Scroll has been lifted off the reading desk, it must be rolled back into scroll form, bound together with a binder/clasp, and dressed in its cover. This is done in a ceremonial manner called *gelilah*.

The person honored with doing this task is called הגולל *hagolayl* (literally, "the roller"), and has the *gelilah aliyah*.

27. נוסח NUSACH

is the melody of prayer.

The chant of each prayer service has its own unique modalities and melodies. Each service—daily, Shabbat, High Holiday, festival; morning and evening—is chanted according to its own *nusach*, its own prayer melody. The *nusach* sets the tone and the atmosphere for the service, and identifies each service through its music.

28. TROP

is the cantillation for the scriptural readings

When the Torah is read in the synagogue, it is chanted according to a set pattern of musical notes, known as the *trop*, or cantillation. The individual notes—called טעמים *ta'amim*, signs or accents—are notated in a series of symbols.

The *trop* provides not only a pleasant musical chant, but indicates the punctuation and sometimes the nuance of meaning of the Hebrew text.

There are separate *trops* for the Torah and for the *haftarah*. There is an another separate *trop* for the Torah reading for the High Holidays. In addition, each of the *megillot*—the five scrolls of the Bible that are read in the synagogue on specific holidays—has its own *trop*.

Although every scriptural reading has its own unique *trop* and its distinct music, the notation symbols for every *trop* are the same. It takes a highly trained and specialized musician to be able to prepare and chant each of the scriptural readings, and to clearly differentiate between the various *trops*.

To add to the difficulty in chanting the various *trops*, the notation symbols do not appear in the handwritten parchment texts of the Torah scroll, or in any handwritten parchment scroll of the Prophets or the *megillot*. The notation symbols appear only in books, in printed copies of the text. Therefore it takes great knowledge, training, skill, and preparation to chant directly from the handwritten scroll.

THE "UNIFORM" OF JEWISH PRAYER

29. כפה KEPAH

(Hebrew) also known as *yarmulka* יארמולקה (Yiddish) is a head-covering.

Judaism was born and grew up in the Eastern world, where a sign of respect to other people and certainly to God was—and still is—a covered head.

Though Judaism moved to the Western world—where the sign of respect is to uncover the head—it has maintained its original custom of the covered head as a sign of respect to God.

Reasoning that we are always in the presence of God, Orthodox Jews wear a *kepah* (or keep their heads covered with a hat) at all times. More liberal Jews wear a *kepah* for worship, study, and eating. Modern Reform Judaism adopted the custom of the West—showing respect with an uncovered head—and eliminated the use of the *kepah*. However, in the last few decades, many Reform Jews have returned to the custom of wearing a *kepah* for worship.

In addition to being a sign of respect to God, the wearing of the *kepah* today is a symbol and a statement of Jewish identity.

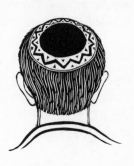

Until recent times, it was only men who wore a *kepah*. Now many women choose to wear a *kepah* also. In traditional Judaism, married women cover their heads with hats or scarves while attending worship services. Observant Orthodox Jewish women cover their heads at all times (or wear wigs) as a sign of sexual modesty.

30. טלית TALLIT

is a prayershawl.

The Torah commands: "Wear fringes on the corners of your garment, look at them, and remember all of God's commandments, and do them" (Numbers 15:39).

The fringes, called ציצת *tzitzit,* knotted in a certain way to symbolically represent the number 613—the number of commandments in the Torah—were originally worn on regular clothing.

The Torah commands that one thread of the *tzitzit* be made of blue. Originally, the blue dye was obtained from a snail-like animal from the Mediterranean Sea. Over

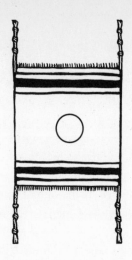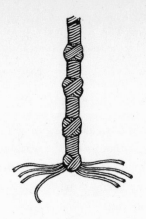

the years, the snails became scarce and—although other sources might have been used to make the dye—the blue thread is no longer part of the *tzitzit.*

As the commandment indicates, the *tzitziyot* (plural of *tzitzit,*) are not, by themselves, important. It is that they serve as a reminder of all of God's commands and of the obligation to fulfill them. Wearing *tzitzit* is somewhat like tying a string around a finger. The string serves as a reminder of the task or obligation that must be fulfilled; the *tzitziyot* are reminders of the commandments, which must be observed.

At the time in history when people began wearing clothing that did not have corners on which to tie the *tzitzit,* in order to fulfill the command, they began wearing a four-cornered undershirt-like garment called ארבע כנפות *arba kanfot* (literally, "four corners") or alternately, the טלית קטן *tallit katan* (literally, "the small prayer-shawl"). It has a hole in the center for the head, and drapes over the shoulders down the front and back. The *tzitziyot* are tied on the four corners.

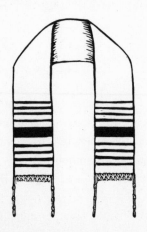

In modern times, Orthodox Jews wear the *arba kanfot/tallit katan* so that the commandment to wear the *tzitzit* can be fulfilled throughout the day. The garment itself is worn under regular clothing. Some men keep the *tzitziyot* under their clothing as well. Others keep the *tzitziyot* outside their clothing, in order to literally fulfill the command "to see" the *tzitzit.*

Liberal Jews do not wear the *arba kanfot/tallit katan* each day. However, at morning prayer, liberal Jews (except for some Reform Jews) along with traditional Jews wear a large shawl-like garment over their regular clothing. This prayershawl is called the טלית *tallit,* and it has *tzitzit* tied on its four corners.

The *tallit* is sometimes decorated with black stripes, which some say is a remembrance or memorial to the destruction of the Holy Temple and the exile. The modern *tallit* is sometimes made with colorful stripes and decorative neckbands, with many beautiful designs and colors woven into the fabric, making it an object of aesthetic beauty. But the kind of cloth, the colors and the decor of the *tallit,* make no difference. What makes a *tallit* a *tallit* are the *tzitziyot,* the fringes.

At its beginnings, modern Reform Judaism eliminated the use of the *tallit.* But in recent decades, many Reform Jews have returned to wearing one.

In some communities, young men begin wearing the *tallit* at the time of Bar Mitzvah. In other communities, a man does not wear a *tallit* until he is married. Historically, women have not worn a *tallit;* but in modern liberal Judaism, many women choose to do so.

The reason that the *tallit* is worn only at morning prayer—and not at afternoon or evening prayer—is that the command is "to see" the *tzitzit.* At the time when the *tallit* came into use—before electricity and light bulbs—it was reasoned that by the late afternoon and evening services, it was too dark "to see" the *tzitzit,* and therefore the command could only be properly performed at the morning service.

Nevertheless, it is the custom in many communities for the *shaliach tzibbur,* the prayer leader, to wear a *tallit* at the afternoon and evening services.

Once each year—at the *Kol Nidre* service, the evening when Yom Kippur begins—the *tallit* is worn during evening prayer by all the worshipers, because Yom Kippur is considered to be "one long, continual day."

The blessing on putting on the *tallit* thanks God for the command "to wrap oneself up in the fringes." Wrapping up in the tallit can be both a symbolic and deeply spiritual way for the worshiper to wrap up in the spirit of prayer, and to be enveloped in God's presence and love.

31. תפלין TEPHILLIN

are phylacteries.

The Bible commands: "You shall bind them (these words which I command you this day—to love the Lord your God) as a sign upon your hand and they shall be frontlets between your eyes" (Deuteronomy 6:8 and, in variation: Exodus 13:9; Exodus 13:16; and Deuteronomy 11:18).

The rabbis interpreted this command to mean that, somehow, they were to write and attach the words of God's commandments (the sections of the Torah that enjoin the binding) to their heads and to their arms or hands.

They wrote the words of the commandments onto a small parchment scroll, called a קלף *klaf,* rolled it up, and placed it inside small leather boxes—one for the hand, called the של יד *shel yad* (literally, "of the hand"), and one for the head, called the של ראש *shel rosh* (literally, "of the head"). They connected leather straps to the boxes, by which the boxes could be strapped onto the arm and hand and the head.

They called the boxes containing the parchment scrolls *tephillin.*

Each *tephillin* box—the one for the head and the one for the arm and hand—contains the four separate sections of Torah (Exodus 13:10 and 11–16, Deuteronomy 6:4–9, and 11:13–21) that give the instruction to bind God's commands on hand and head.

In the *tephillin* box for the hand, the four Torah sections are written on one piece of parchment and placed in the box. In the *tephillin* box for the head, the four Torah sections are written on four separate pieces of parchment and placed in the box into four separately divided sections.

The *shel rosh* is worn by use of a leather loop that fits onto the head. The *shel yad* is placed above the elbow of the left arm (the right arm for those who are left handed) and is attached by means of a loop, and

the wrapping of the leather straps seven times around the forearm. The *tephillin* straps are then wound around the hand in a specific configuration that creates, on the hand, in the leather strap, the Hebrew letter ש *shin,* standing for the word שדי *Shaddai,* one of the biblical names of God.

The *tephillin* are worn by men (and, in recent decades, by some liberal women) beginning at Bar Mitzvah (age thirteen), at the weekday morning prayer service.

Tephillin are not worn on Shabbat or festival mornings. Because the *tephillin* are considered a "sign" between God and the Jewish People, and since Shabbat is also called a "sign" (Exodus 31:17) of the covenantal relationship between God and the Jewish People, the sages decided that the additional "sign" of the *tephillin* was not necessary on Shabbat (and by extension, the festivals).

The *tephillin* are considered a sign and a symbol of love between God and the Jewish People. This love relationship is manifest when the worshiper puts on the *tephillin* each day and, while wrapping the strap around the hand, recites: "And I will betroth you to Me forever. I will betroth you to Me through righteousness and justice, through lovingkindness, mercy and faithfulness; and you shall know the Lord" (Hosea 2:21–22). The daily use of *tephillin* permits the worshiper to be "bound up" with God and His law and to be "wrapped up" in God's protection.

While today it is mostly Orthodox and some Conservative Jews who put on *tephillin* each weekday morning, the ritual remains one of Jewish identity, Jewish commitment, and a visible, dramatic connection to God and His commandments.

AN ESSAY ON PRAYER

The story is told of a faraway village where worshipers would gather every morning in the little *shul* to recite the morning prayers.

Each morning, when the townsmen arrived at their synagogue, their *rebbe* was always there, wrapped in his *tallit* and *tephillin,* standing against the eastern wall, swaying in prayer.

They began to wonder: Why did the *rebbe* come before all the others? Why was he in *shul* so early in the morning?

Each day, for a week, the worshipers came a few minutes earlier than the day before, but the *rebbe* was always there first.

Their curiosity fully aroused, they asked the *rebbe:* "Tell us, our master, why do you come to synagogue so early every day? The prayer service does not start for an hour or more. What are you doing here, and what are you saying before the worship begins?"

And the *rebbe* replied, "I am praying that I will be able to pray."

CONNECTING

For even the most pious, for even the most faithful, prayer is often very difficult.

In this modern age, when intellectual inquiry and rational discourse are celebrated as the highest good, when so many worship at the altars of secular universities and science laboratories, many contemporary Jews are embarrassed and uncomfortable talking *about* God, and do not have the language or the facility to talk *to* God.

Yet there is an inherent human hunger for the sacred, for the spiritual, for the eternal. There is a basic human desire to connect and communicate with the God who created us and our world. There is an intrinsic human longing to acknowledge and celebrate the awesome wonders of the universe, and to understand—or at least wrestle with—the mysterious, perplexing questions of existence. There is a compelling human yearning to be assured of God's interest and participation in our lives; to feel God's care, protection, and love.

How shall we seek and find God?

The Chasidic Rebbe Menachem Mendel of Kotzk put it this way: "God sends souls down to earth and brings them back by making them all climb ladders. Thus man's preoccupation: souls upon souls, all in pursuit of ladders."

The best-known and most popular "ladder," the most workable and successful vehicle for coming to God, is prayer.

Prayer, said Rav Avraham Kook, the first Chief Rabbi of Israel, is "the yearning of every human being to return to its source, to return to God, the craving for growth toward perfection, the soul song of existence."

In much more prosaic but equally profound terms, prayer is you talking to God, and listening as God talks to you.

THE INTENT

The ancient sages knew what prayer could accomplish. They called the intent, the purpose, the meaning of prayer כונה *kavanah* (literally, "intention")—the spiritual connection that is to be made, the spiritual uplift that is to be felt.

But the sages also recognized that a person might not feel the *kavanah* each time he or she wished to commune with God in prayer. And the sages were afraid that if a person did not regularly experience the *kavanah,* he or she might stop trying, and might stop worshiping God.

So the sages developed a fixed order or structure of prayer, the קבע *keva* (literally, "permanence").

Also known as the מטבע תפלה *matbe-a tefilah,* the form, the order of prayer, *keva* created a standard structure for each prayer service.

Each service—evening, morning, and afternoon—was fashioned with its own natural rhythms, its own natural ebb and flow, including its own "highs" and "lows," its moments of great drama, and of quiet meditation; its times of individual contemplation and of public participation.

Through *keva* the sages gave people something to say to God, even when they felt like saying nothing. With *keva* people continued coming to worship, assuring an ongoing communication with God, in an environment where *kavanah* might be experienced.

The sages were confident: Out of *keva* would come *kavanah.* Or, as the contemporary writer Lisa Grunwald puts it, "Out of repetition, sometimes magic is forced to rise."

THE STRUCTURE

The *matbe-ah tefilah* is the basic structure of the prayers, which the sages fixed for the two main worship services of the day—evening and morning (the afternoon service is an abbreviated version). It revolves around the recitation of two prayers.

The שמע ישראל *Sh'ma Yisrael* ("Hear, O Israel, the Lord is our God, the Lord is One") is both the declaration of faith and the prayer of connection to God. It has been described as the "Jewish mantra," the words of focus and concentration, the way to journey into the highest and deepest realms of the place where God dwells, the way to touch and be touched by God.

The עמידה *amidah* (literally, "standing," because it is recited standing up), also known as התפלה *hatefilah* (literally, "the prayer"), is the prayer of encountering God and communicating with God through meditation. All the other prayers of the service lead up to or away from these two central prayers.

The two major prayers leading up to the recitation of the *Sh'ma Yisrael* have as their themes creation and revelation. The one major prayer leading away from the *Sh'ma* and up to the *amidah* has as its theme redemption. These are the exact same three themes that summarize the Torah, and are repeated in the Jewish festival cycle. However, in the prayer service, the order of the themes was purposely changed from the Torah and the festival cycle, where the order is: creation, redemption, revelation.

Redemption has two meanings: It recalls the historical redemption of the Hebrew slaves from Egyptian bondage, and it foretells the ultimate redemption, when there will be an end to all the ills that beset the world, when peace will envelop the earth.

The sages who fixed the order of the service placed the prayer with the theme of redemption out of its regular order, placing it instead toward the end of the worship service. In this way, the worshiper would be reminded that ultimate redemption is yet to come, and as the service ends, will leave the quiet of the sanctuary to go back to the everyday, to continue working to bring about ultimate redemption.

So the *matbe-a tefilah,* the fixed order of the Jewish prayer service, looks like this:

Introductory, "warm-up" prayers
The formal call to worship
Creation
Revelation
Sh'ma
Redemption
Amidah
Concluding prayers

The *amidah* is also known as the שמונה עשרה *shemoneh esray* (literally, "eighteen") because it originally had eighteen separate blessings. A nineteenth blessing was added, but the name was not changed.

At every service—evening, morning, afternoon; daily, Shabbat or festival—the first three blessings and the last three blessings of the *amidah* are the same. (The very last blessing has a longer version for the morning service and a shorter version for the afternoon and evening services).

The weekday *amidah* has thirteen blessings in the middle, for a total of nineteen. The Shabbat *amidah* replaces the thirteen weekday middle blessings with one blessing, for a total of seven blessings on Shabbat—symbolic of the six days of creation and the seventh day of rest.

The Shabbat evening middle blessing has *creation* as its theme; the Shabbat morning middle blessing has *revelation* as its theme; the Shabbat afternoon middle blessing has *redemption* as its theme. The original order of the themes is reversed in the same way as it is in the prayer service so that the last part of the Shabbat observance will be a reminder and a challenge to go out to transform and perfect the world, to work to bring ultimate redemption.

Thus as small a scale as the three Shabbat *amidot* (plural of *amidah*) reflects the same themes—creation, redemption, and revelation—as the Torah, the festival cycle and the order of prayer.

When the sages reiterate Judaism's major themes—articulated on a grand scale in the Torah and the festival year—in as specific a place as the Shabbat *amidot,* they weave the many parts of Judaism into a unified, thematic whole.

Because the Jewish worship service follows this standard order of prayer, a Jew familiar with the service will be able to participate knowledgeably and comfortably in a worship service in almost any synagogue anywhere in the world.

THE PURPOSE OF PRAYER

Prayer is the personal journey that brings you to encounter God, the quest that takes you to both the depths and the heights of your emotions, the voyage that transcends time and place, and transforms the very essence of your being.

Prayer is your shout of joy, your cry of anguish, the intimate whisper of your heart and soul.

Prayer is the celebration of the triumphs and the joys that exalt you, the confrontation with the monsters of tragedy and sorrow that plague you.

Prayer is asking questions and hearing answers; being in distress and getting help; being afflicted and sensing deliverance; seeking guidance and receiving counsel; experiencing pain and feeling healing; needing solace and being wrapped in comfort.

Prayer is the mutual encounter of faith and love between you and God.

PRAYER IN COMMUNITY

Prayer is an intensely personal quest, and Judaism acknowledges and acclaims the individual prayers of the individual pray-er.

But much of Jewish prayer is public, communal, shared.

The sages who set the structure of prayer—and the generations of Jews who have affirmed their wisdom—realized that there are many great benefits in being part of the group that comes to recite the fixed order of prayers, of being part of a praying community.

In prayer-community, there is *history*.

Coming to say the same prayers that countless generations of Jews have recited, and that generations yet unborn will continue to recite, makes you part of the Jewish People, puts you on the continuum of Jewish history, gives you a place and entrusts you with a role in the continually unfolding process of Jewish life.

In prayer-community, there is *energy*.

In community, there is deeper joy, richer sharing, and more noble living. That is why we take some of our most personal moments and put them into the public arena.

What could be more personal than a wedding, when two people speak intimate words of love and commitment? Yet wedding ceremonies are conducted in the midst of the community, so that through their witness and participation, the members of the community can add their spirit and vitality, their public approval and support, to the couple's private affirmations.

What could be more personal than a burial, when a spouse says farewell to the intimate partner of a lifetime? Yet funerals are conducted in the midst of community, so that grief can be shared, the grieving can be embraced, and friendship and comfort can be offered.

When there is achievement to be celebrated, triumph to be heralded, joy to be expressed, it can be done alone. But it is that much richer, that much fuller, in community.

When the expressions of joy are spoken to God individually, they are worthy and good. When they are spoken by the collective whole, the pleasure and gladness seems deeper, the happiness more satisfying.

When danger lurks, it can be faced alone. But it feels that much safer, there is that much more hope, in community.

My father remembers a Yom Kippur eve in the early years of World War II. Parents had just sent their young sons off to war, to dangers unknown and fates unsure. When the cantor chanted the words of the traditional *Kol Nidre* prayer, "From this Yom Kippur until next Yom Kippur, may it be for us for good," a spontaneous, collective cry went up from the mothers and fathers standing in that synagogue. They did not know what the next year would bring to them and their precious sons, but being together in community gave them a sense of united purpose, shared commiseration, and collective strength.

When it comes time to pray for peace, it can be done personally and alone. But the collective voice of the community—and presumably the collective peaceful actions of those who pray for peace—denotes a larger sense of desire, a greater sense of commitment, and brings a better chance for reality.

What if everybody prayed for peace? Who would be left to make war?

In prayer-community, there is *friendship*.

The late writer and newspaper editor Harry Golden told the story of his father who was an avowed socialist and atheist. Yet every evening Mr. Golden would go to the synagogue to recite the evening prayers.

One day his son said to him, "Pa, I don't understand. You don't believe in God, you don't believe in prayer, you don't believe any of the words that are being said in *shul*. So why do you go?"

And the elder Mr. Golden replied, "You know my friend Ginsburg? Ginsburg goes to *shul* to talk to God. I go to *shul* to talk to Ginsburg."

In prayer-community, there is *responsibility*.

Many of the prayers of the worship service are spoken in the plural, "*We* praise You, Lord, *our* God . . ." "*We* have transgressed, *we* have made mistakes . . ." "May *our* eyes witness Your return to Zion." "Heal *us* . . . save *us* . . ." "Bless *us* . . ."

This design of communal prayer confirms the mandate in the Talmud (BT San. 27b and BT Shevuot 39a) that "All Israel is responsible, one for the other." It also recognizes the very real human factor that there is more gratification in sharing a collective obligation than in standing alone.

Yet it is more than prayer-words that create a sense of Jewish communal responsibility. The late sociologist Barbara Meyerhoff reported that the elderly Jews of Venice, California, who got up every morning to go to the synagogue to say prayers, lived longer than the Jews who did not go to the morning service.

Did their prayers to God make them healthier, grant them longer life?

Very possibly. But there is much more.

More likely, the men who got up each morning to go to the synagogue knew that others were waiting for them to make up the *minyan*. They couldn't sleep late, they couldn't let their little aches and pains keep them in bed, because others were counting on them. These men felt a sense of obligation and responsibility, a purpose and a mission, to the prayer community that was more important than their personal proclivities, that kept them feeling important and needed, that kept them alive.

In prayer-community, there is *power*.

By tradition, some of the prayers of the Jewish worship service cannot be recited alone; they must be said in public worship, as part of the community.

One of the most famous of these prayers is the *kaddish*—the doxology that lauds God—that is recited by mourners in the days and months following the death of a loved one. The *kaddish* does not speak about death, or mourning, or the soul of the deceased. It is a simple affirmation of faith that is spoken in the midst of community—that even in my grief and sorrow, I can still rise amongst my fellow Jews and praise God.

Many mourners find these words hard to recite. Even though prayer is not an intellectual exercise but an emotional outpouring, the words of praise may hurt, offend, or ring hollow in the face of painful loss and deep grief.

Yet the history of these words within the Jewish community, the connection of these words to the spiritual quest of the Jewish community, the support and love that these words engender for the mourner within the Jewish community, the very cadence and rhythm and sounds of these words themselves uttered within the Jewish community, bring comfort and healing. Words can work magic because words have a power all their own—a magical power that is affirmed within the Jewish community, which knows their potency and lives with their effect.

In prayer-community, there is *unity*.

God loves all people, but Jewish communal prayer is brought to God by the people of His covenant, His partners and stewards, His "treasure from among all peoples. . . . [His] kingdom of priests and holy nation" (Exodus 19:5–6).

God understands every language, but Jewish communal prayer is recited in Hebrew, because Hebrew taps into Jewish memory, and creates Jewish sound and rhythm and resonance. God hears every sweet melody, but Jewish communal prayer is chanted to Jewish music, because Jewish song resounds through the Jewish centuries, and is filled with Jewish laughter and tears, with Jewish struggles and rejoicings.

The Jewish prayer-community is physically scattered all over the globe, but is spiritually connected by the covenantal relationship with God, by the reverberation of language and the echoes of melody. Wherever a Jew goes to pray, the community is open and inviting, warm and accepting, safe and enveloping. Wherever Jews go to pray, they belong to the community, and the community belongs to them.

Every Jewish prayer-community is family.

Every Jewish prayer-community is home.

WHAT PRAYER CANNOT DO

For all its power and all its efficacy, however, there are some things prayer simply cannot accomplish.

The Mishnah (Berachot 9:3) teaches about prayers that are invalid and in vain.

If a woman is pregnant, it is useless for her husband to pray that the child will be a boy. Why? If the woman is already pregnant, the gender of the child is already determined, and God will not change that reality.

If a person hears cries of distress coming from the city, it is useless for him to pray that the lament is not coming from his house. Why? If the anguish has already befallen, and the grieving has already begun, God will not change that reality.

In modern terms, a child cannot ask God for a new red bicycle. God is not Santa Claus, and does not deal in retail toys. Parents, not God, give children new red bicycles.

A student cannot ask God for an "A" on a test. God doesn't do school homework. The student, not God, is responsible for studying and passing the exam.

This principle of invalid prayer means that you cannot come to God with a wish list that asks God to change the already established reality. And you cannot come to God to ask for things that are controlled solely in the human realm—things that God does not provide.

As the modern prayer-writer Rabbi Jack Riemer teaches, "We cannot merely pray to You, O God, to end war . . . to end starvation . . . to root out prejudice . . . to end despair . . . to end disease. . . . For You have made the world in such a way that we must find our own path to peace. . . . You have given us the resources to feed the entire world . . . to see the good in all people . . . to clear away the slums and give hope . . . to search out cures and healings. . . . Therefore, we pray 'to do' instead of only 'to pray.'"

Then there are the contradictory requests that God receives every moment.

Tomorrow is my day off, and I would like to take my family on a picnic. So I pray, "Please God, don't let it rain tomorrow." You are a farmer, and your crops are in need of water. So you pray, "Please God, send the rains tomorrow." On the sports field, opposing teams both pray to win. On the battlefield, opposing armies—each justifying its cause in the name of God—both pray for victory.

To whom shall God listen? Whose prayer is more reasonable, more valid, more sincere, more worthy—yours or mine?

In his splendid novel *The Last Temptation of Christ*, Nikos Kazantzakis deals with this dilemma in a lighthearted but wise manner: "Just think what poor God must go through. . . . He certainly got Himself in hot water when He created the world. The fish screams, 'Don't blind me Lord; don't let me enter the nets!' The fisherman screams, 'Blind the fish, Lord; make him enter the nets!' Which one is God supposed to listen to? Sometimes He listens to the fish, sometimes to the fisherman—and that's what makes the world go round!"

In reality, God does not choose between you or me, our teams or soldiers, rain or sun, fish or fisherman. Although the ancients believed otherwise, God does not want to be a heavenly weatherman, a tournament scorekeeper, a military strategist, or a tender of earthly schools of fish. God has neither time nor inclination to mediate conflicting requests to micromanage the world.

Perhaps, on a grand scale, our prayers can and do influence and affect God's cosmic design.

But God's plan for the world, God's established patterns for the world, God's process for the regular, everyday unfolding of the universe, are set and settled, and your plea or mine will not change the natural order. For neither you nor I can understand or know which of our competing claims is for the higher good, which of our desires best reflects the Divine blueprint.

As the late, great teacher Rabbi Abraham Joshua Heschel taught, "Man in prayer does not seek to impose his will upon God; he seeks to impose God's will and mercy upon himself."

WHAT PRAYER CAN DO

With all it *is not,* with all it *cannot do,* what *is* prayer?

What is prayer's real purpose, its real power?

What does prayer accomplish?

What is prayer's effect on God, on the universe, on you and me?

For all its seeming complexity, there are really only three categories of prayer: prayers of *praise,* prayers of *thanksgiving,* and prayers of *petition.*

Prayers of Praise and Thanksgiving

It is all too easy to take for granted the wonders of existence.

We listen, but do we really hear? Our eyes are open, but do we really see? Our hearts beat out the rhythm of life, but are we aware? Our entire beings are infused with the glories of the universe, but do we appreciate?

Words of real admiration and sincere appreciation are sometimes difficult to express. But prayer gives us the voice to praise and thank God for the bountiful gifts with which we have been blessed.

We praise You and we thank You, O God, for the beauty of creation; for the breath of life; for choosing us to be Your partners; for endowing us with the capacity to think and reason and remember, the potential to create and grow and choose; for teaching us the difference between right and wrong; for granting us the discernment to temper justice with compassion; for making us able to feel pain and failure, and bring hope and healing; for the extraordinary power to care and share and love; for the unique ability to make the life of another as precious as our own; for calling and challenging us to be human and humane, to do well and to be good.

I praise You, for I am grateful, O God, that I and the ones I love are healthy and well; that I have food to eat, a place to live, and clothes to wear; that today I was saved from accident and harm—that no errant car crashed into me, that no hurtful person attacked me, that no stray bullet found its way to me; that today I was spared from disaster and calamity—that an earthquake did not thrust up the ground under my feet, that flood did not submerge my land, that fire did not consume my house; that no evil has befallen me, and no pain has engulfed me.

I praise You and I thank You, O God, in the words of the poet Ruth Brin, "for the blessings You bestow openly, and for those You give in secret. . . . For the blessings I recognize and those I fail to recognize. . . . For the blessings that surround me on every side."

Your prayers of praise and thanksgiving are for God who delights in them. But they are as much—and more—for you. For in your prayer is your greatness and your humility.

It takes a great person to be able to say "Thank you; I appreciate you." It takes a humble person to know that he or she must.

Prayers of Petition

Prayers of petition—prayers of beseeching request and supplication—all begin from the same place: מן המצר *min hamatzar,* "from out of the depths." From out of the depths of my pain, my anguish, my loneliness, my despair, my transgression, my guilt, my lament, my fear, my deepest needs, קראתי יה *karatee Yah,* "I call out to God"(Psalm 118:5).

These heartfelt prayers of petition are far different from the invalid prayerful requests that ask God for things He does not provide, such as earthly material possessions; or to intervene in ways He never does, such as acting in exclusively human affairs. These are the prayers to which God listens and responds.

Like a loving parent, God loves you, and cares about you, and takes pride in your accomplishments, and rejoices in your happiness, and hurts when you are in pain, and wants only what is best for you.

Like a loving parent, God would always like to be able to say "Yes" to you, to give you what you want, to fulfill your heart's desire.

But like a loving parent, God cannot shield you from all harm, solve all your problems, take away all your pain.

And like a loving parent—whose choices you may not understand and whose reasons you may not always know—God may not be able to say "Yes." As much as He feels your disappointment and, perhaps, your rage, God—who knows the highest good, which may still be hidden from you—may not be able to answer your prayer in the way you would like.

When your prayers are not answered to your satisfaction; when your prayers seem to bring little relief from hurt, and do not help you avoid loss and grief; when

God seems to say "No" to your request; you can feel deep disillusionment and frustration, bitter anger and resentment, loss of faith, and even denial of God. "I prayed that my illness would be cured, but I am still so very sick." "I prayed that my suffering would ease, but I am still wracked with pain." "I prayed for an end to my despair, but I am still broken-hearted." "I prayed that my child would live, but he died anyway."

"How could God do this to me? Didn't God listen to my prayers? Weren't my prayers sincere enough, heartfelt enough, poignant enough? Am I not worthy of God's compassion? Is my child not innocent enough to deserve God's mercy? Have I done something so horrible that God ignores me or rebukes me? Are my neighbor's prayers more powerful, more acceptable, more commendable, than mine, so that her prayers are answered while mine are not?"

Yet whatever your prayer—spoken in faith and in assurance, or in doubt and uncertainty, or in anger and discontent—your prayer always, always brings you into God's presence.

You may come with shouts of jubilation, with cries of agony, with soft whispers of hope, even with "the sounds of silence."

And God will always, always listen.

And then God will always, always, answer.

LISTENING TO GOD

You must listen well.

For God speaks in many voices—in the clamor and the racket of the everyday, and, also in the "still small voice" (Job 4:16) of the darkest night.

And God wraps you in comfort and love; God offers you advice and counsel and guidance. When you pray, when you ask, God will give you a measure of His wisdom, Her insight, His courage, Her fortitude, His strength, and Her compassion.

And you must listen, also, to the sounds of your own voice, your own wisdom and good counsel, your own fullness of spirit.

The Hebrew word "to pray," פלל *pa-lal,* is translated "to entreat, to plea, to request." But it is always said in a reflexive grammatical construction that renders the meaning "to do to oneself." Thus להתפלל *lehitpallel,* "to pray," means to turn upward and outward—to address God with your petition. But it also means to turn inward—to talk to yourself, to seek your own understanding and growth, to hear your own response to your own needs.

Your prayer is to God; and at the very same time, your prayer is to yourself.

There is a moment, at the deepest level, when you and only you can bear witness.

The Bible teaches, "As a person thinks, so he is" (Proverbs 23:7). Modern medical science—operating under strict scientific research criteria—teaches that prayer works, that prayer can have as profound an effect on healing and cure as does surgery or medicine. There is an inextricable interconnectedness of attitude of mind and health of body.

As contemporary writer and thinker Norman Cousins explained, "The greatest force in the human body is the natural drive of the body to heal itself—but that force is not independent of the belief system, which can translate expectations into psychological change. Nothing is more wondrous about the 15 billion neurons in the human brain than their ability to convert thoughts, hopes, ideas and attitudes into chemical substances (which can cure the ailing body). Everything, therefore, begins with belief."

Your prayer can alter the state of your consciousness. Your prayer can change the biology of your body. Your prayer can create physical change, and bring healing.

Not only God, but you too, hear your prayer. And you are both moved to action.

WHEN GOD STILL SEEMS TO SAY "NO"

But what of the pious men and women who prayed sincerely and faithfully everyday for a lifetime, but who were still taken to the gas chambers of Auschwitz? What of the devoted husbands and fathers who still succumb to a savage heart attack, the loving mothers and wives who still die from ovarian cancer, the innocent and beautiful children who are still taken by the hideous ravages of childhood leukemia—despite their most ardent and passionate prayers, and the prayer-energy of their entire community of friends praying for them?

Has God abandoned them? Has God chosen to ignore them? Has God not been moved to saving or healing action through their fervent pleas?

No.

But even at His most merciful, even at His most compassionate, God never promised existence without suffering, a life without trial or pain. God never promised that no one will get sick, or that anyone will live forever. Pain and suffering—as bewildering and tormenting as they can be—are part of life.

So God endowed us with the capacity to meet trouble, and to overcome it. That is why Rabbi Zusya of Hanipol prayed, "Thank You, O Lord, for making me blind, so that I might be able to see the inner light."

Death, as mystifying and as frightening as it may seem, is the inexorable conclusion to life on this earth as we know it. Everyone who ever lives dies. No one, no matter how sincere and heartfelt his prayer or her plea, will escape the inevitability of death.

So of what use is prayer to the dying, if death is sure to come?

The martyrs who walked into the gas chambers with words of prayer on their lips knew that their prayers would not help them escape death. But they knew, just as assuredly, that their prayers would help them face death with faith, with trust, with confidence, with calm, with peace.

The High Holiday liturgy says that prayer can help avert not the "severe decree" of death, for that cannot be avoided, but רוע הגזרה *ro-a hag'zarah,* the "severity of the decree"—the fear, the anxiety, the dread of the letting go of this life, and the mystery of entering into the Great Beyond.

The prayer that is uttered over terminal disease or impending death invites God to accompany you on the journey—wherever it may lead, and help you with the transition from one life stage to another.

Faithful prayer brings faithful response from God, who watches over you and protects you and guards your soul throughout eternity—in this life here on earth and in life everlasting.

With prayer, you will not merely endure, you will prevail.

FINDING NEW PRAYER-MODES BY REDISCOVERING OLD FORMS

With all these profound life-enhancing and wondrous results of prayer, why do so many contemporary Jews still find it so hard to pray?

Some are not comfortable in the formal cathedral-like synagogues of Jewish suburbia. Some are unfamiliar with the structured prayer service, and find no meaning in reciting Hebrew words they do not understand. Some are uncomfortable with the formality of the worship service, and the collective—often rote—recitation of the prayers.

Yet many of these same contemporary Jews still want meaning, purpose, and direction in their lives through connection to that which is sacred and eternal.

In recent years, the organized Jewish community has watched in amazement as tens of thousands, perhaps hundreds of thousands, of Jews—young and old alike—have gone off seeking the sacred in other faith communities, and through the customs and practices of other religious and spiritual traditions.

For these Jews—and even for those Jews who are most familiar and comfortable with the traditional worship service, but who sometimes find the prayer-words empty and hollow—there are alternative Jewish ways to connect with God in the intimacy of soul-talk.

The late Rabbi Aryeh Kaplan, the great scholar and revered mystic, taught, "When I speak to young Jews and ask them why they are exploring other religions instead of their own, they answer that they know nothing deep or spiritually satisfying within Judaism.

"When I tell them that there is a strong tradition of meditation and mysticism, not only within Judaism, but in mainstream Judaism, they look at me askance.

"Until Jews become aware of the spiritual richness of their own tradition, it is understandable that they will seek other pastures.

"Although most seem to be aware that the mystical elements exist within Judaism, discussion is usually restricted to the kabbalah or the chasidic masters. . . . This is a serious oversight. Judaism produced one of the more important systems of meditation. . . . Meditative practices were widespread among Jews throughout Jewish history."

How did Moses first encounter God? For a long time, he stared and stared into a flame that burned and burned, but was not consumed. From out of that blazing light, he heard the voice of God.

How did God speak to His prophets Isaiah and Ezekiel and Jeremiah? Perhaps they were just walking down the street when God called out. But more likely, God appeared to them in a dream, or a dream-like state, when they were in a deeply meditative place, when they had focused their thoughts and concentrated their minds on being in the presence of God.

Meditation may sound to some like a very "new-age" word. It conjures up images of people in long beards and sandals, sitting cross-legged, wrapped in sheets. But meditation is a very old Jewish technique that can be used to lead the way toward finding the "holy sparks" that come from you reaching up to touch God, and God bending down to touch you.

Jewish prayer can take many forms—all equally valid and effective. For Jewish prayer is simply yet profoundly God waiting to answer when you call. Your call may come in *any* form, as long as—in the words of the old prayer—"your heart and soul swiftly take you to the place where the words of God are heard."

FINDING NEW PRAYER-LANGUAGE
BY RECAPTURING ANCIENT CONCEPTS

Some people have difficulty with contemporary prayer because of the language of prayer.

In recent years, feminists of both genders have made us sensitive to the almost exclusively male name-designations of God and the dominant male imagery of prayer.

For most Orthodox women, the clear and separate gender delineation in Jewish life—in role and participation—is natural and acceptable. But many other woman feel shut out from significant parts of ritual life by exclusive rather than inclusive language, and by lack of a Godly role model to whom to relate.

In response, the liberal community, slowly but dramatically, has eliminated some of the sexist language from prayer translations, and has added new words to some Hebrew texts.

Rather than saying "mankind," many now say "humankind." Rather than speaking of the "God of our fathers," many now speak of the "God of our ancestors." Rather than invoking only the memories of Abraham, Isaac, and Jacob, many now also remember Sarah, Rebecca, Rachel, and Leah.

Yet the limitations of vocabulary compound the problem, because in both Hebrew and English, the third-person pronoun is either masculine *or* feminine— "he" *or* "she." There is no one word that addresses a being of either gender, a being with no gender, or a being with both genders.

Some of the more ardent feminists contend that all masculine designations of God should be eliminated. God should no longer be referred to as "He" or "Him," but simply as "God" or "Adonai."

While this argument effectively addresses the female worshiper's problem of not being able to relate to a masculine image of God, it does not produce an alternative feminine image or model. By eliminating God's masculine designations, all that would be accomplished would be to neuter God.

What is really needed is a way to acknowledge both God's masculine and feminine attributes and characteristics.

The archetypes of ancient gods are both masculine and feminine; often a duality exists within the same deity. The masculine attributes are of power and rule. The feminine attributes are of fertility and nurturing. The clay figurines of ancient gods that have been uncovered by modern archaeology illustrate that the masculine god is a strong-muscled warrior with spear in hand, while the feminine god is the reproductive childbearer, big of breast, wide of hip.

Much later, Christianity understood the need for masculine and feminine aspects of God when it taught of God, the Father and Son, as well as the Madonna, Mother.

At its very beginnings—in order to firmly implant its unalterable core belief that God is one—Judaism moved away from any recognition of the dual aspect of God. Any notion of a duality of Godly attributes would have challenged Judaism's basic theology.

Judaism could have chosen *either* the masculine *or* the feminine characteristics of God as its one God-image. It most likely chose the masculine for two reasons: to clearly differentiate from the pagan goddess cults, and to reflect the male-dominated, patriarchal society into which it was born.

Yet Judaism has *always* acknowledged the masculine and the feminine aspects of God. We know God as Adonai and Elohim, the powerful Creator and Ruler of the universe. But we also know of God as Shechinah, the enveloping, caring, nurturing presence, who accompanied the Jewish People into exile and protected them "under her wings."

We know of God having two attributes: the masculine attribute of stern, strict justice, and the feminine attribute of tender, compassionate mercy. The very Hebrew word for compassion, רחמים *rachamim*, comes from the root word רחם *rechem*, which means "womb." God's attribute of compassion is instinctively connected to the female womb, the source of all life, the place of nurture and growth.

We know that when the sages of the Talmud called on God for direction and counsel, God often spoke to them בת קול *bat kol*, in "the heavenly voice/echo," the Divine voice of God in its feminine expression.

Over the years, Judaism's God concept grew further and further away from acknowledging and celebrating the masculine and feminine aspects of God—surely in response to Christianity's claim of trinity, later perhaps in response to the bawdiness of the Middle Ages, and later again in response to the rationality of the Enlightenment.

Whatever its reasons, Judaism lost much when it lost the continual recognition of God as both male *and* female, Father *and* Mother, ruler *and* nurturer. For when we rob God of His maleness and Her femaleness, we rob ourselves of a tremendously rich and deeply moving experience of a God who touches us at our own deepest places.

We are all human beings created from the dust of the same earth, from the same bone, from the same sinew. We are all human beings created בצלם אלהים *b'tzelem Elohim*, "in the image of God," (Genesis 1:27).

God could create both men and women in His/Her image, because God has both male and female characteristics.

And just as both masculine and feminine attributes reside within the same God, every human being has within both the masculine and the feminine. Every man has within him feminine attributes, and every woman has within her masculine attributes.

The great psychologist Carl Jung explained it this way: In the collective unconscious, there is an inheritance of our universal experience as human beings, encoded in a multitude of archetypes. Every archetype has its polarity, its opposite, so that in each of us there is both animus, the male, and anima, the female.

Thus as we acknowledge and get in touch with the masculine and feminine of God, at the same time we can acknowledge and get in touch with the masculine and feminine within us. Woman can touch their masculinity and become empowered. Men can touch their femininity and feel compassion.

Then, regardless of the limitations of language, we can all know that we are praying to God the Mother and God the Father. We are praying to God who will protect us and guide us with His strength and wisdom, and will envelop us and shelter us with Her compassion and love.

Then, prayer can help us find that most intimate and personal place within God and within ourselves—that deep place that makes us who and what we are, that sacred place that tells of what we are made, and calls us to what we might become.

CREATING A PERSONAL RELATIONSHIP WITH GOD

Still, the greatest reason that many contemporary Jews find it so difficult to pray is because they do not have a personal relationship with God. To whom do you pray if you do not know God? What words do you speak if you don't know how to talk to God?

In discomfort or embarrassment, it is easy to dismiss the need or the desire to communicate with God.

But wouldn't it be wonderful to have the place, to have the relationship, where you can come to God, where you can speak the passions of your heart, where you can pour out the yearnings of your soul?

How do you meet God if you don't know Him? How do you speak to God if you can't find God? How do you get faith if you don't have it?

Finding God Through Ritual

An old Jewish technique is to come to God not through belief, but through practice.

When the Children of Israel received God's laws at Sinai, they said, "*First*, we will do them, *then* we will come to understand them" (Exodus 24:7). And later, the sages of the Talmud taught that it is permissible to do something (good) for an ulterior motive, for, eventually, it may come to be done for its own sake (BT Pes. 50b).

If you observe the rituals and participate in the ceremonies of Jewish life, not out of any declaration of belief, but because they bring beauty or meaning to your existence, or because they link you to practices of your people and your history, the repeated performance of the rituals may, eventually, lead you to faith.

You will come to understand that the ritual serves no inherent purpose but to bring you into God's presence. The ritual helps you know God's word, and to fulfill God's will. The ritual gently guides you to speak first *about* God, and then, *to* God; to slowly develop a relationship and to, ultimately, forge your lasting commitment *with* God.

Finding God Through Study

Another time-honored Jewish way to God is through study.

When you learn sacred texts—in the quiet contemplation of intellectual inquiry—you come to comprehend God's word and will. As you engage in dialogue with the text, if you listen carefully enough, God will begin to speak to you. And in your internal discussion and debate, your newfound understanding and enlightenment, you can begin to speak to God.

Finding God By Finding Faith

If ritual practice and study do not work for you, do not speak to you as your path to God, then there is still a way to faith, there is still a way to God.

You get faith the same way you get thin and healthy.

I would like to be thin and in good physical shape. Most of the time, my overweight and out-of-shape body serves me well. I feel good, and I am in fairly good health. As long as I don't call on my body for any extraordinary physical exertion, I should be just fine.

So far, my body has gotten me through sitting at my desk in front of my computer, through the meetings and the classes and the working lunches.

But if one day soon I have to run down the airport corridor to catch the last plane out at night, I am sure that my breath will come fast, my heart will pound, my legs will probably give out, and the plane will take off without me. When I need my body—with its extra pounds and sedentary heart—to get me through a tough situation, it may not respond. It will be then that I learn the real consequences of too many hot fudge sundaes.

I would like to get thin by thinking "thin thoughts." I would like to get in shape by sitting on my couch watching workout videos.

But I know that there is only one way. I have to diet. I have to exercise. The principle is simple. If I take in fewer calories than I burn up, I'll lose weight. If I establish a workout routine and stick to it, I will get in shape.

But the everyday implementation is hard work. I must be really committed, I must have discipline and self-control.

I could probably turn away from the fattening desserts by myself, if I have enough desire. I could probably do sit-ups and push-ups alone in my room, if I have enough motivation. But it might be easier if I enroll in a diet program and go to the gym, where I know that others are struggling just as I am, where I will find a coach to direct me and a friend to encourage me.

If I have every good intention but never act on it, if I never try, or if I make constant excuses, I will remain fat and flabby. But if I diet and exercise regularly and faithfully, I will become healthier.

Not being in spiritual shape, not communicating with God, may make little difference to you, as long as your life is going well—as long as you sit comfortably at your spiritual desk or dinner table. But in times of difficulty or tragedy, at the times you need to call on your faith—when you have to run down the spiritual airport corridor—you may not have the spiritual ability or stamina to find your God.

Just as you cannot simply *hope* to be thin, you cannot simply *hope* that you will get faith. You cannot expect to sit at home—or even search in the beautiful rainbow or in the glorious sunset—and hope that faith will wash over you.

You need to work at getting faith, you need to struggle hard to develop a personal, intimate relationship with God.

If you are motivated enough, you could probably do it alone, in the quiet of your room—or at the seashore or from the mountaintop—but it may be easier if you come to the synagogue or prayer-group where people of faith come to express and celebrate their faith, to challenge and wrestle with their God.

And you need to work at it not just once in a while, not just when you feel like it, not just when the spirit moves you, but continually, everyday. Faith awakenings and commitments build slowly, day by day, year by year—first tentatively and haltingly, then more assuredly.

If you give up the diet because you didn't lose enough weight during the first week or month, then you give up the chance of ever being thin. If you give up the quest for God because you don't find Him immediately, you give up your chance to meet Him.

Begin to seek God, and never give up. And just as one day the scale will settle on the magic number, one day, you will find yourself having faith, knowing God.

THE REWARD

Why go through the struggle? Why go through the difficult, repetitious, lengthy, possibly painful process of seeking God?

Knowing God and having faith—being able to talk to God through the prayer of your personal relationship—means having a full measure of God's wisdom and strength, confidence and courage. It means joy and contentment, friendship and love.

Knowing God and having faith—being able to come to God in prayer in times of trauma or tragedy—means that you are never alone, that you will always have God's comfort and consolation, good counsel, and wise guidance.

Knowing God and having faith—being able to speak to God and to yourself in the honesty, the intimacy, and the power of prayer—means being able to tap into the unlimited possibility and potential within you. For when you have faith, together you and God can accomplish anything.

Prayer is your pathway to God.

Prayer is the way to encounter God, and be utterly transformed by the experience. באורך נראה אור *beorcha nir'eh or,* "In Your light, O God, we see light," (Psalms 36:10). Coming into God's presence, being bathed in God's splendor, you reflect God's being and God's reason for being.

Prayer is your channel to the universe.

Prayer is the way to transcend time and place—to reach backward through forever, and extend forward through infinity—and feel your ineffable connection to the wholeness of the universe, to the inextricable one-ness of everything and every one.

Prayer is your avenue to your soul.

Prayer is the way to touch the absolute core of your being, to know your source and your genesis, to meet yourself in yourself, to have the place to weep and laugh, to quietly contemplate and shout in ecstasy, to shape your destiny and assure your eternity.

"To pray," taught Abraham Joshua Heschel, "is to take notice of the wonder, to regain a sense of the mystery that animates all beings, the Divine margin in all attainments. Prayer is our humble answer to the inconceivable surprise of living."

Ultimately, for what shall you pray?

The modern Jewish thinker Albert Vorspan teaches, "Pray for a heart of flesh instead of stone; for the capacity to feel, to love, to grow; to celebrate the only life we've got; to have the faith to shape a better, more gentle world; to leave a sweet ripple in the lake of eternity."

And how shall you pray?

Pray carefully. Your prayers *will be* answered.

6

JEWISH LIVING

1. חנוכת הבית CHANUKAT HABAYIT

(literally, dedication of the house) is the dedication of a (new) home.

When a Jewish family (or an individual Jew) moves into a new dwelling place, that house or apartment is then consecrated and dedicated as a Jewish home.

A Jewish home has been described as a "miniature sanctuary," and the table from which food is eaten has been called a "miniature altar." For a Jewish home is to be not just a place where people live, but a place where people live according to the ideas and the ideals of the Jewish faith and the traditions and the values of the Jewish People.

The *chanukat habayit,* the dedication of the home, is the ceremony that formally marks the family's (the individual's) entry into the new home and consecrates the home to its sacred purposes. The central ritual of the *chanukat habayit* ceremony is the affixing of a *mezuzah* to the doorpost of the house.

2. מזוזה MEZUZAH

(plural: *mezuzot*) (literally, "doorpost") is the (decorative container and the) parchment inscribed with words from the Torah, placed on the doorpost of a Jewish home.

The Torah commands, "Hear O Israel, the Lord is our God, the Lord is One. You shall love the Lord your God with all your heart, with all your soul and with all your might . . ." (Deuteronomy 6:4–5).

The Torah then continues, "And these words [to love the Lord your God . . .] which I command you this day shall be in your heart. You shall teach them diligently to your children, speaking of them at home and away, morning and night. And you shall bind them as a sign upon your hand and between your eyes. And you shall write them on the doorposts of your house and on your gates" (Deuteronomy 6:6–9).

The commandment is clear: Write the words, "Hear O Israel. . . . You shall love the Lord your God . . ." on the *mezuzot,* the doorposts, of your house.

Why write sacred words on a doorpost of a house?

First, there is most likely a connection between this command to write God's words on the doorposts of a Jewish home and the command to the Hebrew slaves in Egypt to smear the blood of the paschal sacrifice on their doorposts so that the Angel of Death would "pass over" and protect their homes, permitting their firstborn sons to live, while the firstborn sons of the Egyptians died in the tenth plague (Exodus 12:21 ff). The words on the doorpost will serve as an everlasting remembrance of God's miraculous and providential care of the Jewish People, and of the sad fact that others suffered and died for Jewish freedom.

The commandment has a second, compelling purpose: The writing on the doorpost will be a constant reminder to you—every time you enter or leave your home—of your obligation to "love the Lord your God . . . [and follow all His commandments]."

Finally, the writing on the doorpost will identify this house as a Jewish household, a home where the *mitzvot,* the commandments of God, are loved and practiced.

When it became impractical to write Torah words directly onto the doorposts of houses (although a few very traditionally observant households in Israel today continue to follow the ancient injunction and write the words right on the doorpost), it became the custom to write the words on a piece of parchment, to roll up the parchment, and to place it into a small cylinder-like container that could easily be affixed to the doorpost.

The parchment is called a קלף *klaf.* It is handwritten, with quill and ink, by a סופר *sofer,* a scribe, the same highly trained scribal writer who writes the Torah scroll.

The *klaf* contains the Torah passage from Deuteronomy 6, which begins with the words, "Hear O Israel . . ." and contains the command to "write these words upon the doorpost of your house." The parchment is also inscribed with another Torah passage from Deuteronomy 11:21–31, beginning with the words, "And it shall come to pass, if you hearken diligently unto My commandments . . ."

The backside of the *klaf* is inscribed with one Hebrew word, שדי Shaddai, a biblical name of God.

The parchment is placed into the cylinder-like container, often a very lovely and decorative piece of art. Over the centuries, the container itself—rather than the doorpost—has come to be called the *mezuzah.*

The Hebrew name for God, שדי Shaddai, written on the backside of the parchment, often shows out through a small hole in the container. If the container is solid, it is often engraved with the Hebrew letter ש shin, standing for Shaddai.

Some suggest that, in addition to being a biblical name for God, the word שדי Shaddai is an acronym for three Hebrew words beginning with the three letters of the word שומר דלתות ישראל Shomer dalatot Yisrael, the Guardian of the doors of (the people of) Israel.

The *mezuzah* is affixed to the right doorpost, placed at an angle, with the top tilting inward toward the house. Some contend that the *mezuzah* is placed with an inward tilt to signify that God and God's word enters into this household. Others contend that the ancient rabbis and sages could not decide whether the *mezuzah* should be affixed vertically or horizontally, and compromised on the angled tilt.

In some traditional households, a *mezuzah* is placed not just on the doors to the outside, but on the doors to each room of the house (except the bathroom). When entering or leaving the house, traditional Jews kiss their fingertips and then reach up to touch the *mezuzah* as a sign of love for God and His commandments.

The placing of a *mezuzah* on the doorpost of a Jewish home is one of the rituals that has been continually observed by most Jews, for it is a simple yet profound statement of identity and commitment.

3. צדקה   TZEDAKAH

(literally, "justice" or "righteousness") is the Jewish concept of charity—the right, the just, the responsible way human beings care for each other.

Judaism has no word for "charity."

The English word charity comes from the Latin word *caritas,* which means "from the heart." And the English word "philanthropy" comes from the Greek words *philo,* which means "lover," and *anthropos,* which means "mankind."

Thus charity is something you give when you feel like it, when you are emotionally moved to do so, when you have some extra money, when your profit and loss statement looks good, or when your accountant tells you that you need a tax deduction because, as a philanthropist, you feel and express a certain love for your fellow human beings.

The Jewish concept of *tzedakah*—taken from the word meaning "just" and "righteous"—is not dependent on your feelings, your emotions of the moment, your whim, or your financial condition. *Tzedakah* is given because—as a human being, created in the image of God—you have the responsibility to take care of your fellow human beings who are in need. It is not an option, it is an obligation. It is not a matter of choice, it is a requirement, a command. It is the right, the just, thing to do.

The concept of *tzedakah* has its roots in the Torah, which teaches, "When you reap the harvest of your land, you shall not completely reap the corners of your field, nor shall you gather the gleanings of your vineyard, or gather the fallen fruit of your vineyard. You shall leave them for the poor and for the stranger" (Leviticus 19:9–10).

An owner of a field, a landlord, is only a temporary guardian of the land. The real owner, the real landlord, is *the Lord*—God, the *Lord* of all the *land*.

God does not care if a person is rich or poor—that is a temporal human condition, brought about not by the inherent worth of a human being, but by human circumstance and chance. God wants all His children—whether they are wealthy land owners or poor peasants—to eat and be satisfied.

In essence, God says to the land owner, "Remember, this land really belongs to Me. So when you plant your field and harvest your crop, the produce belongs to Me too.

"And since I want all My children to have enough to eat, when you harvest your field, leave the corners uncut. The corners do not belong to you, they belong to the poor and the needing in your midst. The poor do not have to come to you begging for a handout or asking for your generosity, because the produce of the corners is not yours. It is *theirs*.

"They can come in dignity and take what rightfully belongs to them.

"You have an absolute responsibility to provide for the poor and the stranger. It is not a matter of desire or choice. It is My requirement of you, and My command to you. You have an obligation to give to those in need because I, God, enjoin you to share what is yours—which is, really, ultimately, Mine—with all of My children."

This law is known as the law of פאה *pe'ah*, which means "corner." It is a law that assures human rights and human dignity for every person, and gives solemn responsibility to those who are more fortunate than others.

There is an interesting possibility that another Torah law is connected to this injunction of not reaping the corners of the land. The Torah commands, "You shall not round off the corners of your head . . ." (Leviticus 19:27). Those who follow this law do not cut the hair off the corner—the side—of their heads. When permitted to grow uncut, the hair of the side of the head becomes quite long and is often curly.

This hair is usually called "sidelocks," or in Hebrew, פאות *payot,* or *payes.* Today *payot* are seen most commonly on very Orthodox and chasidic Jews.

This is one of the laws for which the Torah gives no reason. It is an injunction that is to be followed simply because God commanded it. Some contend that the law was to distinguish Jews from pagans, who would often cut all the hair off their heads as a sign of mourning. But others speculate that this law may be another one of those rituals that leads to a specific ethical behavior.

By leaving the corner, the *pe'ah,* of the head uncut, it will serve as a constant visual reminder to leave the *pe'ah,* the corner of the field, uncut. With this ritual serving as a dramatic reminder, people will be more likely to remember the ethical proscription of providing for the poor and the needing.

In practical terms, giving *tzedakah* means giving money to any one of the myriad people and causes who need help and assistance. Unfortunately, in this world, there are so many people who are hurting and in need that the places to give *tzedakah* are almost limitless.

Most people give to and support the institutions, organizations, and agencies that help the people and causes that touch them most deeply. You can give to any charitable organization, support any cause, respond to any need, but you must give.

How much should you give? The Torah offers instruction: "You shall surely tithe . . ." (Deuteronomy 14:22). A tithe is 10 percent. So in modern terms, the Bible teaches, "From every (pretax) dollar you earn, give ten cents."

This 10 percent is, of course, a minimum, not a maximum. You can give more if you wish.

But what happens when your own financial circumstances do not permit you to give 10 percent of your income for *tzedakah?* What happens if you are "just getting by" yourself, and do not have any extra money to give away?

The law of *tzedakah* requires that you give *something.* If you cannot afford the full 10 percent, then give 8 percent or 6 percent or 2 percent. But you must give. And you must predetermine the amount you will give—either in a fixed percentage, or in a set amount of money—so that your giving is not left to whim or chance, but is the obligatory giving that *tzedakah* requires.

Thus no matter how little you may have, you must share with others who are in greater need. In biblical times, the Levites—those who served God by officiating at the Tabernacle in the desert, and later at the Holy Temple in Jerusalem—had no other job than Divine service. They were supported solely by the tithes that the people brought to the sanctuary. Nevertheless, God tells Moses to tell the Levites, "When you take from the Children of Israel the tithe which I have given you from them as your sustenance, then you shall set apart from it a gift to the Lord, a tithe of the tithe" (Numbers 18:26).

The sages of the Talmud (BT Gittin 7a) reiterate this concept by teaching, "Even a poor person living on *tzedakah* should give *tzedakah* from what he receives."

The medieval philosopher and legalist Moses Maimonides identified eight ways of giving *tzedakah* (MT Matenot Aniyim 10:7–14), each one higher than the previous one. These eight degrees of *tzedakah* (in ascending order) are:

8. The person who gives reluctantly.

7. The person who gives less than he or she should, but gives graciously.

6. The person who gives what he or she should, but only after being asked.

5. The person who gives before being asked.

4. The person who gives without knowing the recipient, but the recipient knows the giver.

3. The person who gives knowing the recipient, but without the recipient knowing the identity of the giver.

2. The person who gives completely anonymously: neither giver nor recipient knows the other.

1. The person who gives a gift or a loan or gives a job, or goes into a business partnership, so that the recipient becomes self-supporting, and no longer needs *tzedakah*.

Tzedakah given grudgingly, or because the donor wants recognition or thanks, still accomplishes its purpose of giving support to those who need it. But Maimonides' hierarchy of giving contends that it is much better—for both giver and receiver—to give with a full, open, and generous heart and spirit. The best *tzedakah*—from the time that the corners of the fields were left uncut until today—is *tzedakah* that celebrates and affirms human dignity and honor.

Most synagogues and many Jewish homes have a *tzedakah*-box called a פּושקה *pushke* (Yiddish for "box"). By putting a few coins into the *pushke,* either on a regular basis (right before Shabbat begins is a popular time) or as a prayerful act in times of concern or gratitude, people have and use a visible, constant reminder of the need to give *tzedakah.*

Giving *tzedakah* is one of the greatest of all *mitzvot,* for it is truly joining with God in working toward the sustenance and preservation of our world, and the dignity of each human being.

4. גמילות חסדים G'MELUT CHASADIM

(literally, "doing acts of lovingkindness/covenantal love")
is the doing of good deeds.

The *mitzvah* of caring for other human beings only begins with *tzedakah*—with giving money for food, shelter, clothing, and other needs. But giving money—in modern parlance, "just writing a check"—is not enough.

The *mitzvah* continues with personal service, with one human being reaching out to help another through acts of kindness.

The term *g'melut chasadim* comes from the Hebrew word חסד *chesed,* which is often translated as "lovingkindness" but more accurately means "covenantal love." In the Bible, God's unconditional, ultimate love for His people is called *chesed,* meaning that God will care for His people regardless of situation or circumstance.

Human beings—who are created in the image of God—are to imitate God by caring for any of God's children who are in want or need. By performing *g'melut chasadim,* acts of unconditional, convenantal love, people bring assistance and comfort to those in need; share with God in moving the world toward perfection; and bring *kedushah,* holiness, to their own lives.

There are so many people who need help, and so many needs to be met, that it sometimes seems an overwhelming task to offer aid and encouragement. But since the ways to help fellow human beings are endless, Jewish tradition beckons each person to perform *g'melut chasadim* and offers direction where to begin.

בקור חולים BIKKUR CHOLIM

is visiting the sick.

It is a great act of kindness and love to visit those who are ill, to offer comfort, encouragement, and support.

הכנסת אורחים HACHNASAT ORCHIM

(literally, "welcoming guests") is hospitality.

It is a great act of kindness and love to provide hospitality, food, and shelter for relatives, friends, and strangers, especially those on a journey. It is an especially great *mitzvah* to provide Shabbat meals for those who would not otherwise be able to celebrate the Sabbath in the proper fashion.

הכנסת כלה   HACHNASAT KALLAH

(literally, "welcoming the bride") is providing a dowry.

In the days when it was the custom for brides to bring a dowry into marriage, it was a great act of kindness and love to provide a dowry for a poor bride who could not otherwise afford it.

פדיון שבויים   PIDYON SHEVUIM

is freeing the captives.

It is a great act of kindness and love to work for freedom for any person who is held captive or imprisoned in political bondage. If a ransom is required, then it is a great *mitzvah* to pay the ransom to obtain the captive's freedom.

בית זקנים   BEIT Z'KENIM

(literally, "house of the elderly") is providing for the needs of the elderly.

It is a great act of kindness and love to care for the elderly—especially, but not only, grandparents and parents—with great respect and reverence. When the physical frailties of old age set in, it is a great *mitzvah* to provide for the material and physical needs of the elderly, and to accord them the honor that is duly theirs for their gift of life and nurture, and for their accumulated wisdom and experience.

הלוית המת   HALVAYAT HAMET

(literally, "escort/ accompany the dead") is attending
to the needs of the deceased.

It is a great act of kindness and love to assure the proper care and burial of the deceased, including caring for the dying, preparing the body for burial, placing the body in a proper coffin, accompanying the coffin to the cemetery, and burying the deceased in a proper grave. This is one of the highest of all *mitzvot,* because it is an act of kindness that can never be repaid. It is performed selflessly to honor the life of a cherished human being.

נחום אבלים   N'CHUM AVELIM

is comforting the mourners.

Just as it is a great act of kindness and love to attend to the needs of the dead, it is an equal act of kindness and love to comfort the mourner. It is a great *mitzvah* to visit the home of the mourner to share memories of the deceased and to offer solace and consolation in time of grief.

בית יתומים   BEIT YETOMIM

(literally, "house of the orphan") is providing for the orphan.

It is a great act of kindness and love to provide food, clothing, shelter, and education to children whose parents have died. Orphaned children are among the most vulnerable and most needing people in a community, so it is a great *mitzvah* to provide for their welfare.

צער בעלי חיים   TZA'AR BA'ALEI CHAIM

(literally, "pain of living creatures") is protection of animals.

It is a great act of kindness and love to protect all of God's creatures—including animals—from undue pain and harm. It is a great *mitzvah* to protect animals from danger—and extinction—to help heal wounded animals and, certainly, not to hunt and kill animals for sport.

בל תשחית   BAL TASHCHIT

(literally, "do not harm/ destroy") is protection of the environment.

It is a great act of kindness and love to protect the natural resources of the earth. A person may not wantonly destroy or pollute anything that may be of use to another—either practically or simply for its beauty. It is a great *mitzvah* to actively protect and preserve the wonders of God's creation.

הבאת שלום HAVA'AT SHALOM

is bringing peace.

It is a great act of kindness and love to bring harmony, tranquility, and peace to humankind. It is an especially great *mitzvah* to intercede between family members or friends who are in conflict and to help mediate peace.

Today, no less than in ancient days, the performance of *g'melut chasadim* brings help and healing to human ills, and enriches and ennobles human existence. Because the problems that beset humankind are vast, and the needs are greater than ever before, the members of the Jewish community often band together to perform *g'melut chasadim.*

Following the model of the קהלה *kehillah* (literally, "community")—the united Jewish community, which has assumed responsibility for Jewish communal needs throughout the ages—most American Jewish communities have formed federated organizations to make sure that financial and human resources are always available to the needing. Institutions such as a Jewish Community Center, a Board of Jewish Education, a Jewish Family Service, a Jewish Old Age Home, a Hebrew Free Loan Society, and a Jewish Burial Society, assure that a Jewish community meets its responsibilities to itself and to every single one of its members.

Since there are so many acts of kindness and love always waiting to be done, the ancient sage Rabbi Tarfon taught (Avot 2:21), "It is not your task to complete the work, but neither are you free to desist from it."

5.   כשרות   KASHRUT

(literally, "fitness") are the laws of keeping כשר   *kasher*
(kosher; literally, "fit/proper") the dietary laws.

The Jewish dietary laws are based in Torah law and have been clarified and expanded by the sages and rabbis throughout the millennia.

The laws of *kashrut* specify what kinds of foods may be eaten (כשר *kasher*, those that are fit, and thus permitted) and what foods are prohibited from being eaten, and how food is to be acquired and prepared.

THE LAWS OF KASHRUT

Basically, and briefly, the laws of *kashrut* are as follows:

1. *All vegetables, fruits, grains, and nuts are kosher.* This is based on God's statement, "Behold, I have given you every seed-bearing plant on the earth and every tree that has seed-bearing fruit; they shall be yours for food . . ." (Genesis 1:29).

2. *A kosher animal is one that both chews its cud and has a cloven (split) hoof* (Leviticus 11:3). Examples of kosher animals are cattle and sheep. If an animal neither chews its cud nor has a cloven hoof, or if it has one but not the other of these characteristics, it is not kosher and may not be eaten. Examples of nonkosher animals are pigs, dogs, rabbits, and horses.

In addition, in order to be kosher and permitted for consumption, a kosher animal must be slaughtered in a proscribed manner. שחיטה *shechitah,* the laws of ritual slaughter, are rooted in the Torah (Deuteronomy 20:21) and detailed by the rabbis. The basic tenet of *shechitah* is to provide the swiftest, most painless, most humane death for the animal.

Shechitah is performed by a שוחט *shochet,* a ritual slaughterer, a person highly trained and skilled in the art of *shechitah.*

The Torah enjoins that if death comes to the animal in any other manner—by natural causes, or by being "torn apart" by another animal—it may not be eaten (Leviticus 22:8). The Hebrew word for "torn apart" is טרפה *terefah.* While the word *terefah* has the specific meaning of "torn," and thus not permitted to be eaten, it—and its slightly shortened form טרף *tref*—has come to mean anything that is not kosher. So today all food is described as either *kasher,* kosher, or *tref,* not kosher.

Even after *shechitah,* two other steps must be taken for the meat of the animal to be declared kosher. Since blood is considered the symbol of life, the Torah commands, "You shall not eat any manner of blood, either from fowl or animal . . ." (Leviticus 7:26).

The blood of the animal is removed by a method known as "soaking and salting." The meat is first soaked in water, and then coarse salt is spread on it to draw up and drain away the remaining blood. With meat that has an excess of blood, such as liver, soaking and salting is not sufficient to remove all the blood. So in order to be permitted to be eaten, liver must be broiled, which removes all the blood.

In addition, excess fat must be removed from the meat. Based on the biblical command, "You shall not eat the fats of the ox, sheep, or goat" (Leviticus 7:23) (because the fat was used as part of the ancient sacrificial rite), the rabbis extended the prohibition to include the fat of cows as well. A precise butchering process assures modern fulfillment of this injunction.

There is still one more requirement for meat to be kosher. The Torah tells the story of the patriarch Jacob on his way back home to be confronted by his brother Esau, whom he had deceived for the birthright more than twenty years earlier. Faced with the demons of his past, Jacob spends the night alone, wrestling with God/an angel/himself. He prevails and is told, "Your name shall no longer be Jacob, but Israel, for you have wrestled with God and man and you have prevailed" (Genesis 32:29).

But Jacob was injured during the altercation, and he limped for the rest of his life. So the Torah commands, "Therefore the Children of Israel shall not eat of the thigh muscle, which is on the hollow of the thigh [probably meaning the hip socket] unto this day, because Jacob was injured at the thigh muscle" (Genesis 32:33).

Thus even if the animal is a permitted animal, and even if it is slaughtered according to the laws of *shechitah,* and even if the blood is properly drained and the fat removed, Jews are still prohibited from eating the hindquarter of the animal. This means that cuts of meat from the forequarter of the animal, such as shoulder steak and chuck steak, are kosher; but popular cuts of meat from the hindquarter, such as sirloin steak, porterhouse steak, T-bone steak, and filet mignon, are not kosher.

In Israel, where meat is scarce, the rabbis, ritual slaughterers, and *kashrut* supervisors have devised a method of removing the sciatic nerve (the major vein) from the hindquarter of the animal. Claiming that Torah law will be followed precisely, because the "thigh muscle (the sinew")" prohibited in the Torah will not be eaten, the rabbis declare the deveined meat to be kosher. Thus more—and better cuts of—meat are available in Israel. In countries outside the Land of Israel, the rabbis and ritual slaughterers contend that removing the sciatic nerve is too time consuming and costly, and the cuts of meat from the hindquarter of the animal are still considered nonkosher.

To be kosher, meat must satisfy *all* these requirements. Kosher meat is available only from kosher butcher shops (or frozen in a package that is certified as kosher) or from a kosher restaurant. Meat in the meat department of a regular supermarket is not kosher—even though it is from a permitted animal and is a permitted cut— because it was not slaughtered properly. A roast beef sandwich in a restaurant or a hamburger in a fast food restaurant is not kosher—even if the meat is from a permitted animal—because it may not be a permitted cut of meat and it was not slaughtered properly.

To determine whether a butcher shop, a restaurant, or a package of food is kosher, it is best to look for a certificate or seal of *kashrut* supervision, provided by a duly ordained and highly trained rabbi. *Kashrut* supervision is called השגחה *hash-gachah.* The supervisor is called a משגיח *mashgiach.*

A number of prominent American rabbis and well-known organizations—most notably the Union of Orthodox Jewish Congregations—provide *kashrut* supervision and place their distinctive symbols on commercial institutions and packaged foods. These visible and highly trusted symbols offer complete assurance that the product is unquestionably kosher.

3. *A kosher fowl is a domesticated bird, such as a chicken, turkey, tame duck, and goose.* A nonkosher fowl is a wild bird or bird of prey, such as a hawk, eagle, owl, or vulture (Leviticus 11:13 ff).

In order to be kosher and permitted for consumption, a bird must be slaughtered in the same ritually proscribed manner as an animal. A bird shot to death with an arrow or a bullet may not be eaten, even if it is a bird that would be permitted if it were slaughtered properly.

Eggs from kosher birds are kosher, and may be eaten. Eggs from nonkosher birds are not kosher, and may not be eaten.

4. *A kosher fish is one that has both fins and scales* (Leviticus 11:9). Examples of kosher fish are halibut, salmon, sea bass, pike, sole, haddock, tuna, and anchovy.

A fish that does not have both fins and scales, or has one but not the other, is not kosher (Leviticus 11:10–11). Examples of nonkosher fish are shark, whale, and porpoise. There is a dispute over whether or not swordfish is kosher, because it has scales when it is young but loses them as it gets older. Some consider swordfish kosher; others declare it nonkosher.

All shellfish are also nonkosher. Examples include lobster, shrimp, clams, and oysters.

In order to be kosher and permitted for consumption, a fish does not have to be slaughtered in a proscribed manner. It simply dies a "natural death" out of water.

The eggs (caviar) of kosher fish are considered kosher and may be eaten. The eggs of nonkosher fish are not kosher and may not be eaten.

To dispel a popular myth, there is no such fish as a *gefilte* fish. *Gefilte* (Yiddish, meaning "stuffed") fish—popular among Ashkenazic Jews—is a combination of chopped whitefish, pike, and carp, molded and cooked. It is most often eaten as an appetizer course, particularly with Sabbath evening and Passover meals. For many, *gefilte* fish is definitely an "acquired taste!"

5. *All insects—winged, swarming creatures that creep on four legs, and all creatures that crawl on the earth—are not kosher* (Leviticus 11:20 and 29 ff).

While the Torah (Leviticus 11:21–22) permits certain types of leg-jointed swarming creatures and several kinds of locust to be eaten, the rabbis, unable to identify the permitted types, eventually declared every kind of winged insect to be nonkosher.

6. *It is not permitted to eat together meat foods* (called in Hebrew בשר *basar,* and known in Yiddish as פלייישיג *fleshig,* or פלייישיק *fleshik,* from the word meaning "flesh" or "meat") *and dairy foods* (called in Hebrew חלב *chalav,* and known in Yiddish as מילכיג *milchig,* or מילכיק *milchik,* from the word meaning "milk").

This prohibition comes from a verse in the Torah that is repeated three times: "You shall not seethe (boil) a kid in its mother's milk." (Exodus 23:19, 34:26 and Deuteronomy 14:21). The sages did not really understand the intent or purpose of this law, so they reasoned that it was a law of compassion directed toward the mother goat. No one—not even an animal—should have to see her child boiled in her own milk.

Since it became impossible to tell which baby goat and which mother's milk were related, the law was extended to say that no animal (meat) should be cooked in any milk (dairy.) The law was extended even further to say that meat and dairy should not be eaten together. In time, the prohibition against mixing and eating milk and meat together became firmly implanted as one of the central laws of *kashrut.*

The prohibition was further extended to say that since dairy and meat products may not be eaten together, they may not be prepared together in the same pots, and may not even be eaten from the same plates or with the same utensils. Since the pots or tableware may be porous, the meat may leave behind a residue that would mix with dairy, or the dairy may leave behind a residue that would mix with meat, rendering the food unkosher.

Thus Jews who observe the laws of *kashrut* have two separate sets of pots and pans, two sets of dishes and plates, two sets of silverware—one for meat and the other for dairy. Only glass—which is considered nonporous—may be used for both meat and dairy.

The most observant Jews may have two stoves and ovens, two separate sinks, even two separate refrigerators, to make a complete separation between meat and dairy. In large public Jewish buildings, such as synagogues, catering halls, and Jewish camps, there may be two completely separate kitchens—one for meat, one for dairy.

Kashrut-observing Jews wait a predetermined amount of time between eating meat and dairy. The most strict observers wait six hours after eating meat before eating dairy. More lenient observers wait an hour or two. There is much less of a wait—up to a maximum of three hours—after eating dairy before eating meat because presumably it takes less time for the dairy to make its way through the digestive system.

For *kashrut*-observing Jews, the prohibition against eating meat and dairy together is usually fairly easy to observe because milk products and meat products are so easily distinguished from each other. There is little question that it is prohibited to eat a cheeseburger, to drink a milk shake while eating a steak, or to have ice cream for dessert after eating roast beef for dinner.

But it is not as easy to beware of "hidden dairy" in many commonly eaten foods. For example, many breads are made with milk or nonfat dry milk, or have whey solids as part of the recipe. The careful *kashrut*-eater must be sure not to eat a hot dog on a bun that contains dairy ingredients. This makes modern *kashrut*-observing Jews very cautious and precise "label readers," carefully checking to see if any of the ingredients in breads, rolls, cakes, and cookies that are to be eaten with meat contain any dairy product.

This meticulous label reading extends to looking for the type of shortening used in the recipes of commercial products. Many products still use animal shortening—sometimes beef shortening, but most often lard, which comes from a pig. The animal shortening is, undoubtedly, from a nonkosher animal (either a prohibited animal like a pig, or an animal that was not properly ritually slaughtered) and may not be eaten. The *kashrut*-observing Jew reads the label to make sure that pure vegetable shortening has been used in the preparation of the product.

To avoid any question, and to avoid making any error, many *kashrut*-observing Jews will buy baked goods only from a certified kosher bakery, and will eat only commercial products that have a seal of *hashgachah*, supervision, from a duly certified *mashgiach, kashrut* supervisor.

In modern times, clever food manufacturers have produced products that look and taste like dairy but in reality contain no dairy, and products that look and taste like meat but contain no meat. Products such as nondairy milk, butter, sour cream, cheese, ice cream, and vegetarian burgers—made with vegetables, soy beans, a combination of chemicals, or with the increasingly popular tofu—make it possible for *kashrut*-observers to eat combinations of food that had previously been forbidden. It may not be "the real thing," but these products, and the resulting recipes that can now be made, are deeply appreciated by *kashrut*-observing Jews.

Modern scholarship has finally uncovered the reason for the original Torah law prohibiting seething a kid in its mother's milk. Seemingly, boiling a baby goat in its mother's milk (or, at the very least, boiling meat in milk) was both a pagan form of hospitality and a pagan form of worship. The Torah is saying, "Do not behave or worship the Lord your God in the same way that the pagans behave or worship their pagan gods."

With this newfound understanding, it could be argued that there was never any Torah-based prohibition against eating meat and dairy together, and certainly no requirement to have separate sets of dishes and utensils. This contention could lead to the discarding of the laws of *basar v'chalav*, meat and milk. However—whatever their original intent—the laws prohibiting the eating of dairy and meat together have been observed by Jews for centuries, sanctified over time, and have taken on their own unique and distinctive Jewish characteristics and validity. They continue to be followed by Jews who are committed to *kashrut* observance.

7. *Some foods are considered neither dairy nor meat*. These foods are called פארווע *parve*, or *pareve* (from the Yiddish meaning "neutral"). These foods may be eaten either alone, or with either meat or dairy.

All fruits, vegetables, grains, and nuts are *parve*.

Fish is *parve*.

This may seem a strange designation, because fish is the flesh of a living creature, and it would seem likely that it would be considered meat, just as the flesh of an animal. However, the sages contended that the original Torah law prohibiting seething a kid in its mother's milk should be applied specifically and exclusively to animals, especially since there is no chance that a mother fish would ever see its baby boiled in its own milk.

Using the same reasoning, many Sephardic Jews from Spain and the Middle East contend that fowl is *parve*. Ashkenazic Jews consider fowl to be meat.

Eggs—even though they come from fowl—are *parve*. However, if an egg has a blood spot in it (blood may not be eaten because it is a symbol of life) the egg is no longer kosher and may not be eaten.

8. *Wine production must be certified and supervised to be kosher*. It might be presumed that all wine is kosher because wine is made of grapes or other fruits, which (like all vegetables and fruits) are kosher. But the *kashrut* of wine is not determined from its ingredients, but by how its production is supervised and certified.

In ancient days, wine was used by pagans in libation rituals.

Judaism wanted to be sure that any wine used for Jewish ritual purposes was never used or tainted by pagan worshipers. So Judaism required that its ritual wine be carefully supervised in all phases: the planting of the vines, the growing of the grapes, the harvest, the winemaking, the barreling, the bottling, and finally, the pouring. All of these tasks had to be performed by Jews, and supervised and certified by rabbinic authorities. Today this entire process of thorough supervision is still required in order for a wine to be certified as kosher.

Traditional Jews drink only kosher wine, both for ritual purposes and as a beverage, and still insist that the wine be poured from bottle to glass by a Jew.

In contemporary days, some commercial wine companies put certain chemicals into their wines as preservatives. Often, one or more of these chemicals is derived from a dairy product. So a *kashrut*-observing Jew would not drink a wine containing this dairy-based chemical additive with a meat meal.

In contemporary Jewish life, there is a wide variety of *kashrut* observance. Orthodox and many Conservative and Reconstructionist Jews eat only kosher food. At its beginnings, the Reform movement rejected the laws of *kashrut* as binding; but in recent years, a number of Reform Jews have returned to observing *kashrut.*

Many American Jews adhere to the spirit of *kashrut,* but not to all of its laws. Some maintain a strictly kosher home, but eat nonkosher foods in restaurants. Some buy kosher meats and foods for their homes, but do not have two sets of dishes. Some eat nonkosher meat, but do not eat milk and meat together. Some avoid eating the biblically prohibited foods such as bacon, ham, and shellfish. Some do not observe the laws of *kashrut* at all, arguing that eating or not eating certain kinds of food has nothing to do with personal religious feelings or commitments.

Some would like to "keep kosher," or to increase the level of their *kashrut* observance, but find it difficult because the price of kosher foods, particularly kosher meats, is so high—especially in comparison to the prices of nonkosher food and meat. Because of all the special steps that must be taken in its production and supervision, and because there is a relatively small market for kosher foods, the prices that are charged are certainly higher than for mass-produced, mass-market food and meat.

Those who are deeply committed to *kashrut* observance argue that there can be no price tag on fulfilling the *mitzvah* of *kashrut,* so they pay whatever price they must. However, there is little question that lower *kashrut* prices would make *kashrut* observance easier for those who already keep kosher, and more palatable for those considering becoming *kashrut*-observant.

American Jews who keep kosher exercise constant awareness and caution to make sure that the integrity of their personal *kashrut* is maintained. For example, the popular commercial designation "kosher style" is often used to describe food like hot dogs, corned beef sandwiches, and chicken soup. "Kosher style" food is *not kosher.* It may look and taste like kosher food. It might have been kosher meat if it had been properly ritually slaughtered and supervised. But it is not kosher food, and no one who wants to observe *kashrut* should be confused or fooled by the designation. In New York—where there is an extremely large Jewish population—food stores are required to post a sign that says, "Kosher and Nonkosher food sold here," so that there will be no doubt in the mind of the consumer.

Contrary to one of the most popular of all misconceptions about *kashrut,* there is no such thing as a "kosher pickle." Actually, all pickles are kosher because all fruits and vegetables are kosher. The pickles that are called "kosher pickles" are simply pickles that are cured in dill and garlic, and with seasonings that are popular among Jews of Russian or Polish descent. Since most American Jews come from Russian or eastern European backgrounds, and since they often eat this particular kind of pickle with their kosher meals, the pickle came to be known as a "kosher pickle." It may be an especially delicious pickle, but it is not specifically kosher.

For some *kashrut*-observing Jews, the basic laws of *kashrut* are enhanced by even *stricter* observance.

For these Jews, regular *shechitah*, ritual slaughter, is not enough. The law requires that after the animal is slaughtered, it must be carefully inspected to determine that it is a healthy animal, fit for human consumption. The law permits certain deficiencies in the animal. For example, the lungs of the animal may have certain lesions that have been determined to be harmless. However, the strictest *kashrut*-observing Jews declare as kosher only an animal with smooth, lesion-free lungs, and with no questions or doubts about its physical worthiness. This super-inspected meat is called גלאט *glatt* kosher—from the Yiddish word for "smooth"—and Jews who eat only this meat are said to eat only *glatt*.

Since *glatt* refers to meat, it cannot be used to describe dairy products, and contrary to some commercial designations, there can be no such thing as "*glatt* dairy." However, the strictest *kashrut*-observing Jews also have special requirements for the dairy products they eat.

All milk—and products made from milk—is carefully watched and supervised from the time of milking until the time that it is made commercially available to insure that it never comes into contact with any meat or meat products. The very, very strictest *kashrut*-observers go a step further and make sure that the milk-producing cow is watched so that she never eats any nonkosher food, or has her milk mixed with any other nonkosher milk.

The production of cheese is also rigidly supervised. Most hard cheeses are made through a process that includes curdling or coagulating milk in rennet, the lining membrane of the stomach of a calf. Unless the process is strictly supervised, the assumption is that the stomach lining of a nonkosher animal was used in the production, making the cheese nonkosher. Strict *kashrut* supervision assures that the rennet comes from a kosher animal—one that was properly ritually slaughtered, and whose stomach was properly prepared and thoroughly dried—so that the cheese will be kosher.

Recently, a process has been developed by which cheese can be made using no rennet at all. This rennetless cheese has been embraced as the highest standard of kosher cheese, because now no part of the cow—no matter how meticulously supervised—has to be used in making a dairy product.

This most strict dairy supervision is called חלב ישראל *chalav Yisrael*, the milk of Israel (the Jewish People). The designation of a dairy product as *chalav Yisrael* is assurance that its production has followed the strictest standards of *kashrut*.

More liberal Jews, who are nevertheless deeply committed to the observance of *kashrut,* reject the demand for *glatt* kosher meat and *chalav Yisrael* dairy. They argue that, in regard to meat, the original standards of ritual slaughter and inspection are rigid enough, and that no higher standard is warranted or needed.

In regard to dairy, they argue first that modern standards of production coupled with government regulation assure that there is no possibility that milk and meat will be accidentally mixed. And in regard to cheese, they argue that since the stomach lining of the animal is thoroughly dried, it has entirely ceased to be food, and therefore there should be no concern over whether or not the original source was a kosher or nonkosher animal.

These differences of opinion and practice are between those who are committed to the observance of *kashrut,* and are to be respected as varying degrees of the performance of the same *mitzvah.* The only problems arise when the more strict observers demand that community stores, institutions, and public events use and sell only *glatt* kosher meat and only *chalav Yisrael* dairy products, effectively controlling everyone's level of observance and making already high *kashrut* prices even higher. This is one of the areas of contemporary Jewish life that calls for understanding, respect, and mutual accommodation.

THE PURPOSE OF KASHRUT

What is the purpose, the reason, for *kashrut?*

A popular notion is that the laws of *kashrut* are laws of cleanliness, laws of health and hygiene. The contention is that by observing the laws of *kashrut*—not eating pork (which uncooked or undercooked can cause serious illness) and not mixing milk and meat (which may easily spoil and cause sickness)—Jews will be assured of good health.

Today there is medical evidence of the effects that eating, or avoiding, certain foods have on health. A kosher diet—with its unlimited portions of fruits and vegetables, its limit on certain cuts of red meat, its requirement to eliminate as much fat as possible, and its focus on chicken and fish—may very well contribute to good health.

But in biblical times, it is highly unlikely that the Jews would have discovered that eating pig can cause illness, without the rest of the other Semitic tribes finding out. The ancient Middle East was just too small for the word not to spread. It would be as if the residents of Manhattan made a very important medical discovery and—even without the benefit of technological communication—the residents of Brooklyn never hear about it. If the ancient Jews possessed important health-related knowledge concerning food, everyone else would have learned it and used it, and all the ancient Semitic tribes would have observed some form of *kashrut.*

It is much too expedient and convenient—and too simplistic—to attribute the laws of *kashrut* to health and hygiene. The real reasons for *kashrut* have ancient validity and equally modern value.

1. *Compromise.*

There are two ways to view God's instructions to humankind about food.

Some contend that God intended human beings to eat both plants and the meat of animals, birds, and fish. This opinion is based on two Torah verses. One verse says, "Behold I have given you every herb-yielding seed . . . and every tree which is the fruit of a tree-yielding seed for food" (Genesis 1:29). The other verse says, "and let them [people] have dominion over [rule over] the fish of the sea, and the fowl of the air, and over the cattle, and over all the earth, and over every creeping thing that creeps on the earth" (Genesis 1:26). According to this viewpoint, since humankind is given dominion over all the animals, and since the Torah later outlines a complete set of rules for which animals, fish, and fowl may be eaten and which may not, and how the animals are to be slaughtered, there is no question that animals may be used for food, just as plants and fruits are used for food.

Others contend that explicit permission is given in the Torah for using plants and fruits for food, but *not* for using animals. For having dominion—being given the right and the power to rule over the animals—is not permission to eat them. According to this viewpoint, *every* living being—human beings *and* animals, fish, and fowl—is a sacred creation of God, so animals should not be killed to be used for food.

According to this theory, the laws of *kashrut* serve as a compromise, a way of reconciling the use of a living creature as food. By permitting some animals and prohibiting others, by requiring the most humane manner of slaughter, by draining the blood, the laws of *kashrut* impose discernment and discrimination.

A human being cannot kill—even an animal—casually or easily. A person who is going to eat an animal must think carefully about which animal to choose, and how to take its life.

According to this viewpoint, in a more perfect world, everyone would be a vegetarian, and no one would kill a living creature for food. But until that more perfect world comes, *kashrut* requires awareness, sensitivity, prudence, and choice.

2. *Identity.*

In biblical times, the observance of *kashrut* had the effect of keeping the Jews separate and distinct from their pagan neighbors.

One of the most intimate acts of human existence is sharing food and eating a meal with another person. The biblical insistence that Jews eat in a specific, prescribed manner made it virtually impossible for them to share meals with their pagan neighbors—who were, of course, not eating kosher food—where they might be influenced to adopt pagan beliefs and customs. As Judaism emerged out of the pagan world, *kashrut* was one of the ways to help Jews become distinct and distinguished as followers of the one Lord God.

In modern times, observing *kashrut* is a constant, three-or-more-times-a-day reminder of being Jewish. Every time a Jew eats, the requirement to eat kosher food—and to not eat nonkosher food, which is so readily available in contemporary society—serves as a dramatic reminder of membership in the Jewish People and of the commitment to serve God and fulfill all the *mitzvot*.

The observance of *kashrut* helps define who is a Jew.

3. *Humanity.*

Observing *kashrut* is one of the ways to be constantly reminded of humankind's status as children of God, as human beings elevated far higher than any other of God's creations—given the power to think, reason, remember, and decide.

Animals eat anything. They simply respond to the physical demand of hunger, and they eat whatever food is available to them. Human beings can rise above the animals, by being discriminating and exercising choice.

Choosing to eat kosher food is a continuing celebration of humanity.

4. *Humility.*

While pausing long enough to select or reject certain kinds of food, the *kashrut*-observing Jew can also pause long enough to remember and acknowledge the source of food.

In this technological and scientific age, human beings seemingly have almost unlimited power and mastery. With control over so much, it is easy for powerful people to forget that all power is not ultimately theirs.

Regarding food—produced with human ingenuity and labor—it is easy to forget that oranges do not originally come a dozen to a plastic bag, and that bread does not originally come in cellophane wrappers, neatly lined up on a supermarket shelf.

Eating kosher food—being acutely aware of what goes into the mouth—is an every-meal reminder that the ultimate power of the universe, the ultimate origin of the spark of life that creates food, the ultimate source that provides food, is not human beings, but God.

Life-sustaining nourishment is never to be taken for granted, never to be unappreciated. So before eating a meal, a Jew pauses to recite a blessing, acknowledging the source of the life and expressing thanks and gratitude to God for food.

Kashrut helps define humankind's place and purpose in the universe.

5. *Ethical behavior.*

Most importantly, *kashrut* is a *ritual observance that leads to ethical behavior.*

While the Torah gives the basic rules of *kashrut,* it does not explain *why* some animals, fish, and fowl are permitted to be eaten and why others are not. It simply permits halibut but prohibits lobster; permits beef steak but prohibits bacon.

The laws of *kashrut* are to be followed not for any articulated reason, but simply and solely because they come from God. Obeying a law of God—especially without knowing the rationale behind the law—helps develop a sense of discipline and self-control.

A person learns this process:

Even though those pork chops look and smell delicious, I do not eat them *because God said so.* Even though I am famished, I do not eat that ham sandwich *because God said so.* By observing the ritual laws of *kashrut*—not for any particular rational or logical reason, but because this is God's law for me—I am trained in the human skill of self-discipline.

Having developed this sense of self-control through the observance of a ritual law—just as I said "no" to the pork chops and ham sandwich because *God said so*—I have presumably developed the same skills of discipline and self-control that I can call on when facing an ethical dilemma.

Even though I am experiencing great financial hardship, even though I desperately need it and would very much like to have it, I do not take that pile of money over there that does not belong to me, *because God said so.* Even though I am greatly attracted to that beautiful woman, who is someone else's wife, I do not approach her, *because God said so.*

With the very same human skills of discipline and self-control developed through ritual behavior, I am able to confront any ethical situation and say "no" when I must—not necessarily because I am not sorely tempted, but because I have learned to obey God's law.

The observance of the ritual of *kashrut* helps develop the human skills necessary to uphold ethical principle.

For all its elaborate laws and meticulous rules, in the final analysis, *kashrut is far less about eating than it is about behaving.*

Kashrut is one of the central observances of traditional Judaism.

In contemporary times, there are widely differing allegiances to *kashrut* observance and a wide variety of *kashrut* practices. Yet hallowed through the centuries, and preserved and fostered in modernity, *kashrut* still clearly marks and distinguishes a Jew, and is a uniquely defining characteristic of Jewish life and lifestyle.

6. מקוה MIKVEH

(literally, "collection" [of water]) is the ritual pool or bath.

There are two kinds of cleanliness.

One—well-known in contemporary society—is physical cleanliness, required to keep a person's physical body clean and hygienic.

The other—rooted in the antiquity of Torah times—is ritual cleanliness, required to keep or put a person in a state of ritual purity for the purpose of performing *mitzvot*.

The Torah specifies a number of instances in which a person comes into a state of ritual impurity. These circumstances all revolve around *loss*—loss of bodily fluid, loss of potential life, loss of life itself. In a state of loss, a person was not considered whole, and thus was not able to participate in ritual observances (in those days, the bringing of sacrifices to the sanctuary) with a full and complete heart.

Examples include the person who has leprosy (Leviticus 13:3 ff), because the physical disease was considered a manifestation of some kind of spiritual defect; a person who has any discharge from the body (Leviticus 15:2 ff), because this was also considered a manifestation of spiritual defect; a man who has a discharge of semen (Leviticus 15:16 ff), because this was treated as a loss of the potential for the creation of life; a menstruating woman (Leviticus 15:19), because this too was treated as a loss of the potential for the creation of life; a woman following childbirth (Leviticus 12:2 ff), because immediately following childbirth a woman cannot conceive, and— even with the new life that has just been born—there is, for a short time, the loss of potential for any new life being conceived; a person who comes in contact with a corpse (Numbers 19:11 ff), because a dead person cannot perform *mitzvot* and participate in ritual observances.

The Torah enjoins that in order to reenter a state of ritual purity, to be eligible to participate in the ritual rites, a person is to bathe—to immerse in natural, flowing water as a symbolic act of purification (Leviticus 14:8; 15:5; 15:9; 22:6; and Deuteronomy 23:12). The act of immersion is called טבילה *tevilah*.

The waters are not used to remove any physical uncleanliness, but rather serve as a symbolic rebirth, an emergence from the purified, cleansing waters of new beginnings. The immersion removes any ritual impurity and the person is considered ritually pure—eligible to participate in the ritual life of the Jewish People.

Ritual immersion was also performed by the priests, as part of their consecration for office (Exodus 29:4 and Leviticus 8:6) and in preparation for officiating at the Yom Kippur rituals (Leviticus 16:4). Here too the cleanliness is not physical, but an act of symbolic purification—moving from a secular role to the position of priest, and moving from the ordinary tasks of the year to the holy tasks of the Yom Kippur rituals.

In every instance, the ritual immersion symbolizes moving from one state to another—from ritually impure to ritually pure, or from temporal to holy.

The required place for ritual immersion is a natural body of water—a river, stream, pond, lake, or ocean.

However, when Jews live in a locale where there is no natural body of flowing water, or in climates where the waters are frozen over for part of the year, an alternative place of immersion must be found.

To meet this need, a *mikveh* is built.

A *mikveh* is a pool-like structure, built to collect natural water from rain or snow. A building is constructed over the pool, which is called a בור *bor*. Enough water must go into the *bor* so that a person can completely immerse.

In warm climates, where there is never enough rain or snow to collect sufficient water to have the necessary amount of water in the *bor* for a person to immerse, an adjoining pool is built that is filled with regular water. A plug between the *bor* and the adjoining pool is opened to permit the collected water and the regular water to mix or "kiss," creating the legal fiction that the entire amount of water in the pool is collected natural water.

In addition to the requirement that the *mikveh* be large enough for complete immersion, the tradition is to build the *mikveh* with seven steps—representing the six days of creation and the Sabbath—leading down into the pool.

The building is constructed over the *mikveh* not only to protect from the elements, but to protect the modesty of the one immersing, because immersion in the *mikveh* is done completely naked, so that the waters can touch every part of the body.

A person immersing in the *mikveh* removes not only all clothes, but also all jewelry, makeup, nail polish, bandages, or anything else that might obstruct the waters from touching the entire body.

The person takes a bath or a shower before entering the *mikveh,* to indicate, both literally and symbolically, that the immersion is not done for physical cleanliness, but for ritual purity.

A *mikveh* is a vital component of every Jewish community. There are *mikvaot* (plural of *mikveh*) in Europe dating back many hundreds of years. One of the most stunning finds in the archaeological dig at Masada (the mountaintop fortress where the Jews of Israel made their last stand against the Roman conquerors in 73 C.E.) was a *mikveh,* hewn out of the rocks, meeting the exact legal specifications for water capacity. In very recent years, a series of *mikvaot* from the Second Temple era have been unearthed very near the Temple Mount in Jerusalem, undoubtedly used by Jewish pilgrims before bringing their sacrificial offerings to the Holy Temple.

Today *mikvaot*—which are often described as looking like large spas or jacuzzis—are built according to ancient specifications, and furbished and maintained according to the highest standards of modern sensibility.

The waters of the *mikveh* are called מים חיים *mayim chayim*, the waters of life, for *tevilah*, immersion in a *mikveh*, engenders feelings of spiritual rebirth and rejuvenation.

In modern times, the *mikveh* is sometimes used for immersion by people before performing a sacred task, for example by a *sofer*, a scribe, before writing a Torah Scroll.

The *mikveh* is often used by Orthodox men before the Sabbath to dramatically indicate the transition between the secular week and the holy Sabbath day.

In the Orthodox community—and in growing numbers in the Conservative, Reform, and Reconstructionist communities—grooms, and particularly brides, immerse in the *mikveh* prior to their wedding, as a symbolic act of purification and renewal.

But the two main uses of the *mikveh* in the contemporary Jewish world mirror its two main uses throughout the Jewish centuries. Immersion in the *mikveh* is done by *gerut*, people converting to Judaism, and by women observing the laws of *taharat hamishpacha*, the laws of family purity.

7. טהרת המשפחה   TAHARAT HAMISHPACHA

(literally, "purity of the family") are the laws of family purity.

The Torah instructs: "And you shall not approach a woman to uncover her nakedness [meaning: to have sexual intercourse with her] during her period of [ritual] uncleanliness" (Leviticus 18:19). Since a menstruating woman is considered ritually impure (Leviticus 15:19) because of the loss of potential life, this Torah-law forbids normal marital sexual relations during the time of the impurity.

When the monthly menstrual flow begins, a woman becomes a נדה *niddah* (literally, "remove/separate.") She begins a period of sexual separation from her husband that lasts for the five days of the menstrual period, plus another seven "clean" or bloodless days following, for a total of twelve days.

During these twelve days, husbands and wives who observe this law not only do not have sexual intercourse, but do not kiss or even touch each other. Since affectionate touching can be the prelude to sexual intercourse, this more stringent observance aids in maintaining the sexual abstinence.

The most observant couples have separate beds, and during the twelve days will not even allow casual touching. For example, instead of saying, "Please pass the salt," one will set the salt shaker down and the other will pick it up. In this way, nothing that might lead to passionate sexual expression is allowed.

It is this rule that forbids touching a *niddah,* a menstruating woman, that has led to the custom-with-the-force-of-law that many Orthodox men do not touch their wives in public (for protection of her privacy and modesty, by not indicating whether or not she is a *niddah* at the moment) or shake hands with any woman (not knowing whether or not she is a *niddah*). This is also why men and women do not dance together in public, or if they do, grasp a handkerchief between them rather than holding hands. (Remember the dance scenes in *Fiddler on the Roof?*)

On the evening of the completion of the twelfth day (assuming there has been no bleeding during any of the seven days following the five days of menstrual flow, for if there is, the count of seven days must begin again from that time), the woman goes to the *mikveh* to immerse as an act of symbolic ritual purification.

This is the most prominent and important use of the *mikveh,* and the reason why every Jewish community must have one.

Following the immersion, normal marital sexual relations are resumed.

These laws of sexual abstinence for a *niddah,* followed by ritual purification in a *mikveh,* are called *taharat hamishpacha,* the laws of family purity, for they are intended to elevate the relationship between husband and wife to a level of sacred holiness.

The Torah makes clear that sexual abstinence with a menstruating woman has nothing to do with physical cleanliness or hygiene. Menstruation is not "dirty," and a menstruating woman is not "unclean."

As with all other instances of ritual impurity, the reason for a menstruating woman being ritually impure—ineligible to participate in the ritual observances (in ancient days, the bringing of sacrifices to the sanctuary) of the Jewish People—is because she is experiencing the loss of both bodily fluids, and most important, the loss of potential life. She is therefore unable to participate in the ritual observances with a full and complete heart.

So the "uncleanness" or "impurity" is not at all physical, but is wholly ritual.

Husbands and wives who observe the laws of *taharat hamishpacha* affirm that the sexual relationship between them need not be left unregulated, where it has the potential of being reduced to the most basic animalistic needs and demands. In this most intimate of all human relationships, there can and must be care, consideration, respect, and above all, self-control. *Taharat hamishpacha* proves that human beings have the ability to control their passions, and to restrain even their most primitive instincts.

Through the laws of *taharat hamishpacha,* one of the most basic of all human behaviors—sexual intercourse—becomes a holy act.

Husbands and wives who observe the laws of *taharat hamishpacha* report that their marriages retain a "freshness" and a vitality. Each person has his or her own monthly "space" and time of privacy. And together, the couple renews the sexual relationship each month with an eagerness and a passion that is reminiscent of their honeymoon.

There is one more reason for the laws of *taharat hamishpacha* that the Torah and the sages do not relate, for it is the hidden—and perhaps most important—reason. *Taharat hamishpacha* is Jewish birth control—in reverse.

If a couple must abstain from sexual intercourse for twelve days, and then is permitted to resume normal sexual relations on the evening of the twelfth day after the woman immerses in the *mikveh,* there is little chance that the couple will not have intercourse that night—and most likely, on the following few nights also.

In a normal menstrual cycle, a woman is able to conceive in the middle of the cycle—the thirteenth, fourteenth, and fifteenth days of the twenty-eight-day cycle. It is virtually certain that after twelve days of sexual abstinence, the *taharat hamishpacha*-observing couple will have intercourse on the very days of the menstrual cycle on which the woman is most likely to conceive. *Taharat hamishpacha* is a Jewish ritual that assures the continuity of the Jewish People, by making sure that as many Jewish babies as possible are conceived and born!

In a time of sexual freedom—when so many young people are sexually active at such young ages, and when so many are sexually active outside of marriage—*taharat hamishpacha,* the laws of family purity, may seem quaint and outmoded.

Yet not only Orthodox couples, but a growing number of young couples from the more liberal denominations of contemporary Judaism, are embracing the laws of *taharat hamishpacha* and enhancing their lives through them.

Couples who observe *taharat hamishpacha* describe how these laws enrich their marital relationship, deepen their love and commitment, and ennoble their human spirit.

Women who observe the laws of *taharat hamishpacha* tell of feeling validated and valuable as women, respected and cherished as human beings. They feel nurtured and sustained by the enveloping, protective, womb-like waters of the *mikveh,* which offer monthly rebirth and renewal.

Even in this permissive world—how much the more so *because of* this permissive world—the laws of *taharat hamishpacha* affirm, support, and strengthen the institution and sanctity of marriage, confirm the value and worth of each and every human being, and bring God-like holiness to the most intimate of human relationships and moments.

8. בית דין BEIT DIN

(literally, "house of judgment") is a rabbinic court.

A *beit din* is a Jewish religious court.

The *beit din* is known as the rabbinic court because it is comprised of rabbis—usually three—who are highly trained and skilled in matters of Jewish law. The *beit din* adjudicates Jewish legal questions and disputes that need interpretation or decision.

In times and places where the countries in which Jews lived left disputed issues between Jews to be settled by Jews, the *beit din* had far-ranging authority—not only over religious issues, but also over everyday matters of commerce and interpersonal relationships.

Today, when most Jews live in countries that retain civil jurisdiction over all their citizens, the *beit din* has three main functions:

1. The *beit din* convenes to question the sincerity and knowledge of a prospective convert to Judaism, and certifies his or her acceptance as a member of the Jewish People.

2. The *beit din* also convenes to grant Jewish divorces, and oversees the writing and delivery of divorce documents.

3. Sometimes Jews who have disputes with other Jews and wish to avoid a civil court trial, will bring their disputes to a *beit din* for resolution. They call upon the *beit din* to convene a דין תורה *din Torah* (literally, "Torah judgment"), which is a hearing or trial conducted according to, and decided by, Torah law.

Sometimes these are disputes over matters of interpersonal relationships, or disagreement in business dealings. Just as often, they are issues of conflict within the Jewish community, or matters of personal honor.

In these types of disputes, the parties agree beforehand that the decision of the *beit din* will be binding upon them. In matters that rightly belong in a civil court, if the parties agree beforehand to abide by the decision of the *beit din*, then they also promise not to seek further recourse in the civil court.

Of course, the defeated party may choose to violate the prior agreement, and file suit in a civil court anyway, rendering the decision of the *beit din* moot. However, in a few jurisdictions, the civil court has recognized the validity and the wisdom of the *beit din*, and refuses to accept cases where the disputing parties had come before the *beit din* with a prior agreement to abide by its decision. In these cases, the decision of the *beit din* has the full force and effect of the civil court.

In Israel—which essentially functions as a theocratic democracy—the state has given full authority to the religious courts—Jewish, Christian, Muslim, and Druze—in all matters of personal status. So in Israel the *beit din* has both its own religious power, coupled with the authority of the state, to render all decisions concerning marriage, divorce (and the financial settlements of divorce), and conversion to Judaism, and—with the prior agreement of both parties to abide by its decision— certain civil disputes.

In all its functions, the *beit din* is a court of honor in which matters of dispute are settled with the wisdom, fairness, and compassion of Jewish law.

9.   JEWISH SYMBOLS

מגן דוד   MAGEN DAVID

(literally, "shield of David") is the Star of David, also known as the Jewish star.

The *magen David* is the best known, most popular modern symbol of Judaism.

 The six-pointed star was not created by the Jews, but was—like many geometric shapes—a common and often used design in the ancient world.

Some ancients attributed special "magical" powers of protection to the six-pointed star, because its shape points to and encompasses the entire universe.

According to legend, the star was on the shields of King David's warriors and soldiers—because they wanted their armaments marked with the symbol of God's protection.

Thus the six-pointed star is known as the Star of David.

A Jewish tombstone from the third century in southern Italy is marked with the Star of David—a sign of protection for the soul.

The Talmud (BT Pes. 117b) teaches that *magen David* should be used as concluding words of the *haftarah* blessings—the Sabbath and festival scriptural reading from the Prophets—as a sign of protection for the departing worshipers.

A twelfth-century manuscript indicates that a *magen David* is placed next to the *mezuzah* on the door of a Jewish home—as a sign of added protection.

The Star of David has been used to symbolize the Jewish community—on the flag of the Jewish community of Prague in the fourteenth century; as a seal of the Viennese Jewish community in the seventeenth century; on the coat of arms of the Rothschild family in the nineteenth century.

The six-pointed star became so well-known as a Jewish symbol that during the Nazi Holocaust, European Jews were forced to wear a star made of yellow cloth as identification.

Since 1948, the Star of David has been the symbol that is on the flag of the State of Israel.

Today, the six-pointed star is used throughout the world as the clear and unique identifying symbol of Jews and Judaism.

מנורה   MENORAH

(literally, "candelabrum") is the seven-branched candleholder.

Though not as well-known or as popular as the *magen David*, the seven-branched *menorah* is a much older and more authentic Jewish symbol.

The *menorah* is one of the ritual objects described in the Torah, constructed and used in the sanctuary in the desert.

When the Holy Temple was built in Jerusalem, the *menorah* took its rightful place as a central ritual object. When the Second Holy Temple was destroyed by the Romans in 70 C.E., the *menorah* was carried off in triumph to Rome, as a spoil of war. Depiction of the Second Temple *menorah* can be seen today in bas relief on the Arch of Titus in Rome, built to celebrate Rome's victory over Jerusalem.

In modern times, most people are much more familiar with the nine-branched *menorah*, which is used in celebration of the holiday of Chanukah. But it is this seven-branched *menorah*—one branch for each of the six days of creation, and one for the Sabbath of rest—that is the ancient and authentic Jewish symbol.

Today, the seven-branched menorah is used as the logo of the State of Israel and the Israeli government.

לוחות   LUCHOT

(literally, "tablets") are the Tablets of the Law (of the Ten Commandments).

When Moses came down the mountain carrying the Ten Commandments, they were engraved on two stone tablets.

The Tablets of the Law were kept in the most honored position in the Ark of the Covenant—first in the Tabernacle in the desert, then in the Holy Temple in Jerusalem.

The Tablets—though not as widely used as other symbols—are a popular and well-known symbol of Jews and Judaism. They are often used as symbols in synagogue architecture, particularly on or around the Holy Ark, where the Torah Scrolls are kept.

The Tablets are used by the United States Military as the insignia worn by Jewish chaplains serving in the Armed Forces.

LIONS OF JUDAH

are the symbol of Jewish strength.

Since the lion was the original symbol of the tribe of Judah—the largest tribe, after

which the southern kingdom was named—and because the lion is an animal of power and strength, the "king of the beasts," lions—known as the Lions of Judah—have become a symbol of Judaism.

The symbol of lions often decorates ritual objects—especially surrounding the Holy Ark in the synagogue where the Torah Scrolls are kept, on the curtain that covers the ark, and on covers in which Torah Scrolls are dressed.

מזרח MIZRACH

(literally, "sunrise/east") is a decorative plaque placed on the eastern wall of synagogues and homes.

Jewish custom and tradition requires that Jews face eastward—toward Israel and Jerusalem—when praying.

That is why a seat at the eastern wall of the synagogue is considered the most prestigious place of honor. (Remember Tevye in *Fiddler on the Roof,* singing, "If I were a rich man

... I'd have the time that I lack to sit in the synagogue and pray, and maybe even have a seat by the eastern wall.")

To mark and distinguish the eastern wall of synagogues and homes, a plaque with the word *mizrach,* east, is often placed on the wall. The *mizrach* plaque is most often a beautifully illustrated and illuminated piece of art, which adds aesthetic beauty to the wall.

חי CHAI

(literally, "life") is the Jewish symbol of life.

The Hebrew word *chai* means "life." Used as a symbol, the Hebrew חי expresses the hope and prayer for life, health, and prosperity.

The best wish one can offer another—and the salutation used before having a drink—is לחיים *L'chayim!* "To Life!"

The word *chai* is also used as part of a well-known rallying cry of faith and trust in the history and the destiny of Judaism and the Jewish People—עם ישראל חי *"Am Yisrael chai!"* "The Jewish People lives!"

Each Hebrew letter represents a numerical equivalent (as if, in English, A equals 1 and B equals 2 . . . and so on). In Hebrew ח *chet* is 8, and י *yud* is 10. So *chai* (*chet* and *yud* added together) is 18.

Modern Jews often make contributions to worthy causes or give gifts of 18 dollars, or multiples of 18——36, 54, 72, 180, 1,800——so that, as well as good wishes, the gift or contribution represents the prayer for life.

10. POPULAR HEBREW WORDS AND PHRASES

מזל טוב MAZAL TOV

(literally, "good star/constellation") means good luck or congratulations.

The original meaning of the well-known and popular Hebrew phrase expressing congratulations conveys the idea that the ancients felt that luck or good fortune was somehow influenced by the alignment of the stars.

Though not many modern Jews give credence to the principles of astrology, the ancients surely did—and perhaps their notions are worthy of thoughtful consideration.

Whatever its origin, the phrase *mazal tov* is used to express congratulations for achievement, or at a time of celebration.

At the birth of a baby, for a Bar or Bat Mitzvah, at a wedding, for a birthday or anniversary, at any time of accomplishment or life-triumph, the expression of congratulations is *"Mazal tov!"*

שמחה SIMCHAH

(literally, "joy") is a joyous occasion.

Any happy, joyous occasion in the life of a Jew—a Bar or Bat Mitzvah, a wedding, a significant birthday, anniversary, graduation—is called a *simchah*.

At such a time, the wish that is extended is, *"Mazal tov* on your *simchah!"*

ברכה והצלחה BERACHAH V'HATZLACHAH

(literally, "blessing and luck") means blessing
and good luck/good fortune/success.

When a person is about to do something that requires a successful outcome (take a test in school, have medical testing done, negotiate a business deal, move to a new home), good wishes are expressed with *"Berachah v'hatzlachah"*—"You should be blessed (by God) and have good fortune."

With a handshake, the recitation of the phrase seals a business deal with confidence and trust.

ישר כח YASHER KOACH

(literally, "straight strength," meaning, "May your strength be increased")
means congratulations—job well done.

Congratulations—conveying, at the same time, the sense of "good job" or "job well done"—is expressed in the phrase *yasher koach*.

Yasher koach is most often used to extend congratulations and good wishes acknowledging participation in a ritual event, such as having come to the Torah to recite the blessings.

ברוך תהיה   BARUCH TIHYEH

means "May you be blessed."

When a person is wished *"Yasher koach"* for a job well done, rather than just saying "Thank you," the greeting is returned with an equal wish, *"Baruch tihyeh"* (*beruchah tihyee* to a woman), meaning "May you be blessed."

ברוך השם   BARUCH HASHEM

(literally, "blessed is the Name") means "Thank God."

A Jew recognizes and acknowledges God as the source of all blessings and gracious favor. The phrase *baruch HaShem* is used to express gratitude to God for all goodness. "How are you today?" *"Baruch HaShem"* (meaning "Thank God, I'm fine.") "I was just in a horrible automobile accident, but *baruch HaShem,* no one was hurt."

בעזרת השם   B'EZRAT HASHEM

(literally, "with the help of the Name") means with God's help.

Jews acknowledge God as an intimate partner in all of life's quests. Many Jews feel that God assists them in every aspect of life, so they often say that they will succeed *b'ezrat HaShem,* "with God's help." "Will you be coming to visit next week?" *"B'ezrat HaShem*—with God's help—I'll be there."

Many Jews will put the Hebrew letters ב"ה *bet, hay,* an abbreviation for *b'ezrat HaShem*—with God's help—in the top right corner of any written paper or document.

אם ירצה השם   IM YIRTZEH HASHEM

(literally, "if the Name wants it") means God willing.

Jews who view God as a constant participant in every phase of human life will often speak of plans for the future being fulfilled, *im yirtzeh HaShem,* "God willing." "I'll be celebrating my birthday next week, *im yirtzeh HaShem*—God willing."

ברוך הוא וברוך שמו   BARUCH HU U'VARUCH SH'MO

means "Blessed is He (God) and blessed is His name."

Anyone who hears the name of God uttered aloud—especially in the traditional formula of blessing: *"Baruch Atah Adonai . . ."* "Praised are You, O Lord our God . . . ,"—acknowledges the Divine name and the invocation of the Divine presence by responding *"Baruch Hu uvaruch sh'mo,"* "Blessed is God and blessed is His name." This phrase is heard most often during worship services, when the formula of blessing is recited over and over again.

אמן   AMEN

(literally, "so be it") means I agree/affirm.

After a blessing has been recited, it is customary for those who have heard the blessing to say, "Amen." By uttering this word of agreement, the listener associates with the prayer or blessing that has been said and confirms his or her participation, consent, and affirmation of the praise or petition of the blessing.

Even if a person does not recite the blessing, by saying "Amen" it is as if the blessing were personally said.

The Talmud (BT San. 111a) suggests that the word *amen* comes from the first letters of the words אל מלך נאמן *Eyl melech ne'eman,* meaning "God is a faithful King." Thus in responding "Amen," a person not only affirms a blessing that has been recited, but at the same time affirms the majesty and the greatness of God.

מי שברך   ME SHEBAYRACH

(literally, "He who blessed") is a prayer that means "May God Who blessed . . . (X also bless Y)"; also used to mean endorsement; recommendation.

A fixed rubric of a long-established Jewish prayer begins with the words *me shebayrach,* "May He [God] who blessed our ancestors, Abraham, Isaac, and Jacob, Sarah, Rebecca, Rachel, and Leah, also bless. . . ." The prayer is recited on behalf of one who has participated in a public Jewish ritual, such as being called to the Torah to recite the blessings over the reading. It is also used to ask God's blessing for a newborn child, a couple about to be married, or a person who is ill. The *me shebayrach* asks for God's blessings, approval, and assistance.

Today it has also come to mean a personal endorsement, recommendation, or testimonial, given by one person on behalf of another. "When I apply for this job, will you give me a *me shebayrach?*"

נסיעה טובה   N'SSEEAH TOVAH

(literally, "good journey") means "Have a good journey."

ברוך הבא   BARUCH HABA

means "Blessed is the one who comes—welcome."

When a person arrives at a destination, the greeting is *"Baruch haba"* (*B'ruchah haba-ah* to a woman; *B'ruchim habaim* to more than one person), which means, "You are blessed in coming/being here—welcome."

ברוך הנמצא   BARUCH HANE'EM'TZA

(literally, "blessed is the one who is found")
means "Blessed is the one who is here."

When greeted with *"Baruch habah,"* the reply is *"Baruch hane'em'tza* (*B'ruchah hane'em'tzet* to a woman; *B'ruchim hane'em'tzaim* to more than one person), meaning, "You are blessed in being here."

לבריאות   LABRIUT

(literally, "to health") means "To your health."

When a person sneezes or coughs, or is not feeling well, the salutation and wish is "To your health," *"Labriut."*

רפואה שלמה   R'FUAH SH'LAYMAH

(literally, "complete health") means speedy and complete recovery.

A person who is ill is wished *r'fuah sh'laymah,* a speedy and complete recovery.

דרך ארץ   DERECH ERETZ

(literally, "the way of the land") means proper behavior.

Having *derech eretz* means to exhibit proper conduct—to behave politely, with courtesy and respect.

By reflecting God's standards for ethical behavior, a person brings decency and dignity to every word and deed, to each moment of life.

Jewish parents always urge their children to have *derech eretz*—to do what is right and what is good, to behave with suitable propriety, and to act with honor.

עד מאה ועשרים   AD MAYAH V'ESREEM (HEBREW); BIZ AHUNDRET UNTZVANTZIG (YIDDISH)

(literally, "until one hundred-twenty")
means "May you live until the age of 120."

According to the Torah, Moses, the greatest leader of the Jewish People, lived until he was 120 years old. Even then, "His eyes were not dim and his natural strength was not abated" (Deuteronomy 34:7).

This is the wish for every person: *"Ad mayah v'esreem,"* "Until 120——like Moses, may you live until 120, in health and vigor."

עין הרע   AIN HARA OR   עין הרעה   AIN HARA-AH (LITERALLY, "THE EVIL EYE"); YIDDISHIZED TO KINNA HORA

means keep evil away.

In the Bible, the "evil eye" denotes greed, jealousy, envy, or ill will (Proverbs 23:6–7). In the Mishnah (Avot 2:16), Rabbi Joshua teaches "the evil eye and the evil inclination and hatred of his fellow creatures drive a man out of the world. The Talmud (BT Bava Metziah 107b) states that "ninety-nine out of a hundred die of an evil eye."

It became common belief that all evil comes upon a person who is greedy, jealous, or envious; who creates ill will between people. So people began to say, "Don't give an evil eye"—that is, don't act in such a way that evil will befall you. Later, a touch of superstition was added to the formula—that evil could come not just through the overt acts of people, but on its own. People began to say, "Don't give it an evil eye"—that is, don't let evil come anywhere near me for any reason.

The Yiddishized pronunciation of the Hebrew—*kinna hora*—is now used as a popular expression to ward off evil from any and every situation: "How are you today?" "*Kinna hora,* I'm fine." "I just bought a new car." "Drive it safely, *kinna hora.*" "My daughter, *kinna hora,* is getting married next week."

Also, when something is about to happen where the outcome is not yet assured, people will say, "Don't give it a *kinna hora*"—that is, don't bring the evil eye upon it; don't spoil or ruin it. "He's taking his final exams next week. Don't give it a *kinna hora.*" "Your baby is growing so fast." "Don't give it a *kinna hora.*"

Affirming that *kinna hora* is as much superstition as it is practical, many people tie a *kinna hora bendle,* a red ribbon, onto a new home, a new car, or a baby stroller to—*kinna hora*—keep away the "evil eye."

שלום SHALOM

means hello/goodbye/peace.

The Hebrew greeting *shalom* is used to say both "Hello" and "Goodbye," for its central meaning is "peace"—which should be part of every arrival and departure.

The word *shalom* comes from the root word שלם *shalem,* which means "whole/complete." Peace comes when there is wholeness, completeness, unity.

Often a person will greet another by saying, שלום עליכם "*Shalom aleychem,*" "Peace be upon you." The response is עליכם שלום "*Aleychem shalom,*" "To you, peace."

The eternal Jewish prayer is in the perpetual Hebrew greeting—*shalom*—peace in the world, peace between people, inner peace and harmony.

7

JEWISH LIFE CYCLE

BIRTH

1. ברית מילה   BRIT MILAH

(literally, "covenant of circumcision") popularly known as *brit* or *bris,*
and also as *milah,* is ritual circumcision.

When Abraham declared his belief in the One Lord God, he was commanded by God to circumcise himself (remove the foreskin of his penis) as a physical sign of the spiritual covenant (Genesis 17:10 ff). In affirmation of the covenant between God and Abraham—and thus between God and the Jewish People in every succeeding generation—every Jewish male is circumcised on the eighth day of his life.

Wherever Jews have been—during times of peace and prosperity, or during times of torment and persecution, when circumcision had to be done in secret or in hiding—this ritual ceremony has been performed by the Jewish People, virtually unchanged, for almost 4,000 years.

Today, when so many male children, Jewish or not, are medically circumcised—often in the hospital, a day or two after birth—circumcision is not considered very unusual. But throughout the last four millennia, when circumcision was almost uniquely a Jewish ritual, a circumcised male was distinct and distinguished from the other men around him. Circumcision was a clear, visible, permanent, identifying mark; a statement literally "cut into the flesh" that this person is a member of the Jewish People, in covenant with God.

The Jews did not invent circumcision. It was a ritual practiced by many of the ancient Semitic nations.

Originally, a number of pagan tribes sacrificed firstborn males in the hope that if the firstborn son were offered as a sacrifice to the gods, then the gods would be satisfied and would permit all subsequently born sons to live full lives.

Eventually, human sacrifice was stopped; and instead of offering up a whole body to the gods, a small body part was offered—the tip of the finger or the foreskin of the penis.

Other Semitic tribes used circumcision as a rite of sexual initiation when a boy reached puberty.

Judaism took this popular folk ritual and internalized it, Judaized it, sanctified it, and gave it new meaning and new purpose. Circumcision became and endures as the sign of the covenant between God and the Jewish People.

The circumcision takes place on the eighth day of a boy's life, counting the day of birth as day one. Thus, for example, if a child is born on a Tuesday before sundown, the *brit milah* takes place on the following Tuesday. If, however, the birth takes place on Tuesday evening after sundown—which is the next Jewish day—then the *brit milah* takes place on the following Wednesday.

The *brit milah* is so important, so central to Jewish life, that it takes precedence over everything else—including Shabbat and even Yom Kippur. If the eighth day of a child's life falls on Shabbat or Yom Kippur, that is when the *brit milah* takes place.

However, medical consideration always supersedes religious law. If the health or safety of the baby would be in any way jeopardized by having the circumcision on the eighth day, the *brit milah* is postponed until a physician certifies that the baby is healthy enough for the procedure.

The Torah gives no reason for the choice of the eighth day of a child's life for the *brit milah*. Some scholars speculate that Judaism simply used the same day for the circumcision as did the pagan tribes. According to this theory, the pagans chose the eighth day of a child's life for the sacrificial offering to appease the gods because, they reasoned, if the gods permitted the child to live for a full week, it was most likely that the child would be protected from harm or death. The circumcision-offering on the eighth day—after one full week of life had passed—was the final act of supplication and appeasement in order to assure a child's life and health.

Since there is no real evidence to support this theory, it remains only speculation, and the eighth day seems to be an arbitrary choice for the *brit milah*.

Yet modern medical science has taught that there is a sound medical reason for the choice of the eighth day: In a newborn, there is a factor in the blood that gives the blood the ability to coagulate and clot, and which does not mature until approximately the eighth day of life. Babies who are cut or who bleed before the eighth day might very well bleed to death. Only after the eighth day of life has this factor in the blood developed enough so that proper clotting takes place if bleeding occurs. Thus the ancients must have learned—through painful trial and error—exactly when the circumcision procedure could take place without jeopardizing the life of the baby.

Modern medicine has also learned that vitamin K is responsible for the clotting factor. Thus, newborns who must undergo any kind of surgical procedure (including non-Jewish babies who are circumcised before the eighth day) are given an injection of vitamin K, which results in the blood being able to clot.

The *brit milah* most often takes place in the morning, observing the custom to "arise (get up early) to do (eagerly perform) a *mitzvah.*"

The *mitzvah* of circumcising his son is to be performed by the father. However, most fathers do not have the expert medical knowledge or skill necessary to be a competent circumciser.

So certain men (and in modern times, in liberal Judaism, some women as well) train to become a highly skilled expert in the art of ritual circumcision. This expert is called a מוהל *mohel,* a ritual circumciser. The father appoints the *mohel* as his agent, to circumcise his son and to recite the proper prayers and blessings.

Today, when a *mohel* is not available, liberal Judaism permits a Jewish physician—who is familiar with the ritual as well as the medical aspects of circumcision, and is an observant Jew—to perform the *brit milah.*

Assisting the *mohel* at the *brit milah* is the סנדק *sandak,* who holds the baby during the circumcision. The special honor of being the *sandak* is usually given to the baby's grandfather, uncle, or a close friend of the family.

Although it is not a Jewish requirement to have godparents for the baby, many families choose to honor a close relative or friend with the designation. The godfather and godmother—called *kvater* and *kvaterin* (from the German/Yiddish)—participate in the *brit milah* by carrying the child into the room where the ceremony will take place.

At the *brit milah* ceremony, it is custom to set aside a special chair, which remains empty. This chair is known as כסא של אליהו *keesay shel Eliyahu,* the Chair of Elijah. By setting aside this special chair, the prophet Elijah is, symbolically, invited to the *brit milah*—just as he is to the Passover *seder.*

Two explanations are given for this quaint custom. Some say that Elijah is invited to the *brit milah* since he was a fiery prophet—always chastising the people for forsaking God's *mitzvot.* Here he is called to witness and be heartened that God's people are continuing to fulfill God's commands.

Others contend that the birth of this baby—representing hope and faith in the future—is evidence that the world is moving closer and closer toward perfection, toward messianic times. Since Elijah will be the one to announce the coming of the messiah, he is invited to the *brit milah* to witness the ongoing progress toward the transformation and perfection of the world.

Prayers and blessings are recited as part of the circumcision ceremony, indicating that this circumcision is taking place not merely as a surgical procedure, but for the purpose of entrance into the covenant with God.

Immediately following the procedure, announcement is made—with appropriate prayers and blessings—of the child's Hebrew name, the identity by which he will be known among the Jewish People. According to the Torah, originally, Abraham was called אברם Avram, and his wife, Sarah, was called שרי Sarai. With the establishment of the covenant and the *brit milah,* they were given their new names—אברהם Avraham and שרה Sarah—new identities as partners in the covenant (Genesis 17:1–16). By giving children their Hebrew names as part of the *brit milah* ritual, modern Jews continue this custom of affirming Jewish identity as covenant partners.

The *brit milah* is often followed by a festive meal. Family and friends congratulate the newborn baby and his parents, and rejoice in the continuation of the age-old covenant, originally made between God and Abraham and renewed in each Jewish generation.

Under certain circumstances, ritual circumcisions do not take place in the usual way.

These instances might include: (1) Babies who are born without a foreskin (highly unusual but nevertheless possible); (2) babies who were medically circumcised before the eighth day, or without the proper prayers and blessings; and (3) older children and adult men who convert to Judaism and must be circumcised as part of the conversion ritual, but who were medically circumcised as babies. In these circumstances, the circumcision has taken place (either naturally or medically) but the procedure was not done for the purpose of entering into the covenant.

Jewish law provides a way to turn a medical circumcision into a proper ritual circumcision called הטפת דם *hatafat dam,* (literally, "drawing of a drop of blood"). A drop of blood is drawn from the skin behind the head of the penis, and the proper blessings are recited.

In this way, the circumcision is no longer considered simply medical, but meets the ritual requirements of a proper *brit milah,* done for the purpose of entering into the covenant.

2.   BABY NAMING CEREMONY

Boys are given their Hebrew names at the time of the *brit milah.*

Since there is no circumcision ceremony for girls, traditionally, girls are given their Hebrew names at a synagogue service on a day when the Torah is read (Monday, Thursday, or Shabbat morning, Shabbat afternoon, or a festival morning). The father is called to the Torah to recite the blessings, and the rabbi recites special prayers, naming the newborn baby girl. In modern times, in liberal Judaism, the mother comes with the father to the Torah and often the baby is brought, so that she can be blessed as part of the naming ceremony.

As an alternative, many liberal Jews are now having "at-home" naming ceremonies for girls. Reasoning that there should be no inequality in the celebrations for newborn baby boys and newborn baby girls, many parents are opting to have large celebratory ceremonies in their homes for the naming of their daughters, just as they have large celebratory ceremonies for the naming of their sons at the times of the *brit milah.*

A number of very beautiful ritual ceremonies for the naming of a baby girl have been written in recent years. In this way, girls and boys are welcomed into the covenant with the same sense of privilege, responsibility, and joy.

3.   NAMING A JEWISH CHILD

At the *brit milah* or baby naming ceremony, a Jewish child is given a name, known as a Jewish or a Hebrew name—the identity by which he or she will be known in the Jewish community.

At one time, the Hebrew name was the only name a Jewish person ever had. Today, however, it is customary for a Jewish person to have a secular name as well.

For the past several hundred years, a secular name usually includes a first name, often a second or "middle" name, and a "family" or last name.

A Hebrew name includes a first name, sometimes a second or "middle" name, and the designation "son of" or "daughter of" the father (and in modern times, liberal Judaism, the mother as well). Thus a typical Hebrew name for a boy would be יצחק Yitzchak (Isaac) בן ben (son of) אברהם Avraham (Abraham) (and, in modern times, in liberal Judaism, ושרה v'Sarah [and Sarah]). For a girl, a typical Hebrew name would be רבקה Rivkah (Rebecca) בת bat (daughter of) אברהם Avraham (Abraham) (in modern times, in liberal Judaism, ושרה v'Sarah [and Sarah]).

Some children are given Hebrew names (most often taken from the Bible) that also serve as their secular names, such as שרה Sarah or דוד David. In Israel, a Jewish child is given one name that serves both in the religious and the secular communities, although, in these modern times, an Israeli name also includes a last or "family" name.

The Hebrew name is used during religious ceremonies and rituals—at the time of birth and naming, on being called to the Torah for an *aliyah,* on the marriage document, and at the time of death as part of a special memorial prayer. Then the Hebrew name is engraved on the gravestone, marking a person's final resting place.

There is no Jewish law about choosing a name for a child, but there are differing customs among Ashkenazic and Sephardic Jews.

Sephardic Jews most often name children after a living relative. So, if a child's grandfather, יעקב Ya'akov, Jacob, is still alive when he is born, the child will be named יעקב Ya'akov. Following the Hebrew name formula, he will be called יעקב בן Ya'akov ben (son of) שלמה Shlomo (Solomon), his own father. Ya'akov's fondest hope is that when he grows up, his own father, Shlomo, will still be alive when his grandson, Ya'akov's own son, is born. Then Ya'akov will name his son Shlomo (honoring his father, the baby's grandfather) ben Ya'akov (his own name as the baby's father).

Ashkenazic Jews most often name children after a deceased relative. If the child's grandparent, aunt, uncle, or other relative, or a close friend, dies before the child is born, the memory of that relative is honored by giving the newborn child that relative's Hebrew name. If Grandpa's name was שמואל Shmuel (Samuel), the child is given the name שמואל Shmuel.

Normally, that would be sufficient to honor Grandpa's memory; but many parents want to also give their children a secular name that is somewhat similar to the Hebrew name. The perfect solution, in this case, would be to give the child the secular name Samuel, a direct translation of the Hebrew name Shmuel.

But some parents may think that Samuel is an "old-fashioned" name, and so they try to find secular a name that "sounds like" or "begins with the same first letter as" the Hebrew name. Thus a generation ago, a child given the Hebrew name Shmuel might be given the secular name Stanley, and in this generation he might be named Shawn.

Some may wonder, "What kind of Jewish name is Shawn?"—or Amber, or Kimberly, or Christopher, or the many other very secular, "non-Jewish-sounding" names that Jewish children have been given in recent years. Yet when the giving of names to Jewish children is by custom, not by law, it is understandable that some parents want to reflect the society in which they live. They choose secular names that they feel will help their children fit comfortably into their everyday world.

This is not a new phenomenon in Jewish life. One of the sages quoted in Mishnaic tractate Pirkae Avot is Antigonos of Socho, who lived in the first half of the third century before the common era. His name clearly reflects the influence of Hellenism and Greek culture on his parents, who named him.

It is never an easy task to choose a name for a newborn child, for there are so many (sometimes conflicting) needs to be met—Jewish custom, the desires of the parents, the sensibilities of two families, and the expectations of many assorted relatives.

Yet the giving of a Hebrew name is cause for great joy and happiness, because it means that another precious child has been born into the Jewish community and has entered into the sacred covenant with God.

4. פדיון הבן PIDYON HABEN

is the redemption of the (firstborn) son.

The release of the Hebrew slaves—the Children of Israel—from Egyptian bondage came, finally, as the result of the tenth plague—the death of all the firstborn Egyptian males. Though that plague was necessary to secure the freedom of the Hebrew slaves, there is no rejoicing in the knowledge that others suffered and died.

As eternal remembrance and atonement for the death of the firstborn Egyptian males, God decreed that all firstborn Jewish males, in every generation, would be designated for Divine service, for working in and for the sanctuary and in the religious life of the Jewish People (Exodus 13:15).

According to the story, when Moses was atop Mt. Sinai receiving God's law, the people—feeling abandoned and alone—lost faith in their leader and in their God. They prevailed on Aaron, the High Priest, to build an idol, a golden calf, which they could see and worship (Exodus 32).

God saw that all the people—including the firstborn of all the tribes—participated in the worship of the golden calf, and He decided that He could not have as His servants those who lost faith so quickly. God also saw that only the members of the tribe of Levi refrained from worshiping the golden calf.

So God decided to make a trade (Numbers 3:11 ff): God told Moses that it would be the Levites, instead of the firstborn of all the tribes, who would be sanctified to Divine service.

God told Moses to count up the number of firstborn and the number of Levites. According to the count, there were 22,273 firstborn, but only 22,000 Levites (Numbers 3:44 and 39). Thus there were not enough Levites for an even trade, so the extra 273 firstborn had to be somehow redeemed from the obligation to Divine service, since they were "left over" from the trade.

God commanded the firstborn to make monetary compensation to the Levites to balance the trade, using money to make up for the fewer number of people. The money would serve to equalize the trade, and all the firstborn would be released from their obligation to Divine service. The price was set at five *shekalim* (the plural of *shekel*, the monetary unit of the time) for each of the 273 extra firstborn (Numbers 3:47). The money was given to Aaron, the High Priest, the head of the tribe of Levi.

Though the reason, setting, and obligation of the firstborn or the Levites to a life of Divine service has long since passed into history, the ceremony of redeeming the firstborn from Divine service—called *pidyon haben*—is still practiced by traditional Jews today.

On the thirtieth day of his life, or any time thereafter, parents bring their first-born son to a Kohen or Levi (the modern descendants of the ancient tribe of Levi) to redeem him. The reason that the thirtieth day of life or later was designated is that the rabbis decided that after thirty days, the infant mortality rate declined enough so that the child had a good chance of surviving.

The Kohen or Levi asks the parents if they wish to give over their son to Divine service, or if they wish to redeem him. To redeem him, the parents give the Kohen or Levi five *shekalim*, the redemption price set in the Torah. In the United States, parents used to use five silver dollars. But since real silver dollars have become so rare, and since the monetary unit of the modern State of Israel is now the *shekel*, many parents now obtain five Israeli *shekalim* for the *pidyon haben* ceremony. If *shekalim* or silver dollars are not available, other coins are used.

With the acceptance of the coins by the Kohen or Levi (which he may keep, give back to the parents or child, or give to *tzedakah*), and with appropriate prayers and blessings, the redemption ceremony is complete.

In actual practice, very few parents and children participate in the *pidyon haben* ceremony because the requirements for those who must be redeemed are very narrow and limited. The ceremony takes place only for a child whose mother or father is neither a Kohen or a Levi. The child must be male, and must be "the first issue of the womb" (Numbers 3:12), meaning that the ceremony does not take place if a girl is the firstborn and a boy is born later. It also does not take place if the mother had a miscarriage or an abortion before the first birth, or if the child is born by Caesarean section.

Yet for those who are obligated to be redeemed, the ceremony is considered important enough that if parents forget to redeem their son at the proper age, they are to do so as soon as they become aware that the child is not yet redeemed. And if parents never redeem their son, he is obligated to redeem himself, as soon as he learns that he was not redeemed as an infant.

While many consider this *pidyon haben* ceremony to be outmoded—especially since children are no longer mandated to Divine service—this ceremony serves to link modern Jews to the beginnings of the Jewish People, when the Children of Israel came out of Egypt. It also reminds us of our continual obligation to serve God with a full heart. It is a ceremony of history and of humility.

COMING OF AGE

5. בר מצוה AND בת מצוה BAR MITZVAH
AND BAT (OR BAS) MITZVAH

(literally, "son or daughter of the commandments"); practically:
one who is part of the community obligated to fulfill the privileges
and responsibilities of the commandments of God.

The Talmud states that at the age of thirteen and one day, a Jew (meaning, in those days, a male Jew) becomes obligated to observe the commandments (which, until that age, he is not required to observe) (Avot 5:1; BT Yoma 82a; BT Baba Metziah 96a). Before age thirteen, he is considered a "minor"; but at age thirteen, he reaches Jewish "majority" and takes on both the privileges and responsibilities of fulfilling the *mitzvot*.

Not only does he become personally responsible for his own conduct in fulfilling the ethical commands, but he assumes responsibility for fulfilling the ritual commandments—such as being counted in the *minyan*, being able to be called to the Torah for an *aliyah*, putting on *tephillin* for the weekday morning service, and fasting on Yom Kippur.

On reaching the age of thirteen, the young man automatically becomes a Bar Mitzvah. Whether or not he exercises them, the privileges and responsibilities of Jewish adulthood are his.

It is much the same as when young people in the United States reach the age of majority and are no longer minors. Whether they exercise them or not, they now have the privileges and the responsibilities of adulthood—being able to vote, being able to buy liquor, and being able to sign a binding contract. In American society, the first public act marking reaching the age of majority is usually going into a bar or restaurant to order a drink, or going into a voting booth to cast a ballot. In Judaism the first public act marking reaching the age of majority is the Bar Mitzvah ceremony.

The Bar Mitzvah ceremony, as it is known today, came into Judaism in the Middle Ages. The central act is being called to the Torah for an *aliyah*. Thus a Bar Mitzvah can take place any time the Torah is read—on Monday, Thursday, or Shabbat morning, Shabbat afternoon, or any festival morning. In practice, most Bar Mitzvah ceremonies today take place on Saturday morning, during the regular Shabbat morning service.

Usually, the Bar Mitzvah is called to the Torah for the final *aliyah,* the *maftir aliyah.* Since it is customary for the one who recites the blessings for the *maftir aliyah* to also recite the blessings for and chant the *haftarah*—the scriptural reading from the Prophets—the Bar Mitzvah usually chants the *haftarah.* In addition, he often leads parts of the worship service, reads directly from the Torah, and gives a short speech, commenting on the Torah or *haftarah* lesson and expressing his own personal feelings.

The age of Jewish majority for a girl is twelve years and one day (BT Kid. 16b and MT Ishut 2:9–10), for it was assumed that girls matured physically and emotionally earlier than boys. In traditional Judaism—where women do not have the same ritual obligations as men—there is no need for a Bat Mitzvah ceremony because women do not have the responsibility or the privilege of being counted in the *minyan* or being called to the Torah.

In recent times, however—recognizing the coequal education of girls and recognizing women's increasingly expanded role in society—many Orthodox and traditional synagogues have devised Bat Mitzvah-like ceremonies for young women that take place on Friday night, on Saturday night, or on Sunday afternoon.

In the liberal branches of Judaism, the historical roots of Bat Mitzvah go back to nineteenth-century Europe, where liberal Judaism was born. In America's non-Orthodox movements—where coequal education has been the norm for decades, and where women have had full religious and ritual equality throughout the history of the movement (Reform and Reconstructionist) and surely within the last decades (Conservative)—the Bat Mitzvah ceremony has been part of American Judaism since at least 1922. Most agree that the first American Bat Mitzvah was Judith Kaplan Eisenstein, daughter of Rabbi Mordecai Kaplan, the founder of Reconstructionist Judaism. In these branches of Judaism, the Bat Mitzvah ceremony for young women—and the level of the young woman's participation in the service and her assumption of the privileges and responsibilities of fulfilling the *mitzvot*—is the same as the Bar Mitzvah ceremony for young men.

The Bar/Bat Mitzvah ceremony is a time for celebration and rejoicing, with family and friends often traveling long distances to be present for the Bar/Bat Mitzvah service. The service is usually followed by a celebration (most often a *kiddush* or luncheon immediately following the morning service; sometimes a dinner on Saturday or Sunday evening) with food, drink, and sometimes dancing and entertainment. In recent times, some Bar/Bat Mitzvah celebrations have suffered from lack of taste and excessive expenditure. But most celebrations reflect the occasion—honoring a thirteen year old who has just participated in a sacred religious ceremony.

The Bar/Bat Mitzvah ceremony—public recognition of a young person's new status within the Jewish community—can serve not only to mark the assumption of the obligation to fulfill the *mitzvot*, but also as a catalyst in a young person's life—a time for grappling with identity and ideas. It can be the beginning of a time of growth and enrichment for the young man or woman, his or her parents, and his or her entire family. It can be a moment of deep meaning, high significance, and everlasting commitment—a vital part of a young person's development as a Jew and as a human being.

This, then, is what the Bar/Bat Mitzvah was intended to be and remains until this day: a time to recognize growth, evolving maturity and newfound potential of a young man or woman; a time to assume responsibility and to chart the future.

MARRIAGE

6. חתן CHATAN

is a groom.

7. כלה KALLAH

is a bride.

8. אויפרוף AUFRUF

(Yiddish; literally, "to call up") is an *aliyah* and blessing for a groom (and bride) prior to the wedding.

On the Shabbat preceding a wedding, the groom (Orthodox) or the bride and groom (Conservative, Reconstructionist, Reform) are called up to the Torah for an *aliyah*. Following their recitation of the Torah blessings, the rabbi recites a special prayer, asking God's blessings on their upcoming wedding and on their marriage.

In some communities, at the conclusion of the *aufruf,* it is customary to throw (to "shower with") candies and raisins at the bride and groom, symbolically wishing them a sweet and good life together.

9. קדושין KIDDUSHIN

(literally, "holiness") is the marriage ceremony (also, popularly known as
חתונה *chatunah* or *chusunah*, from the word חתן *chatan*, groom).

The modern-day Jewish wedding ceremony is a combination of two ancient ceremonies blended into one.

Originally, a bride and groom were betrothed to each other in a ceremony called אירוסין *erusin*, meaning "forbidden." This ceremony indicated that the man and woman were now "forbidden" to any other than the betrothed, and that their marriage is one that is "permitted," rather than one that would be, by Jewish law, "forbidden" (such as an incestuous marriage). This ceremony is alternately known as תנאים *tena'im*, meaning "conditions" or "terms."

The ceremony consisted of three elements: (1) the signing of a document of agreement; (2) the presentation by the groom to the bride of an item of value (a coin or, later, a ring) while reciting the marriage declaration to her (and her acceptance of the item); and (3) the recitation of a blessing over a cup of wine. The couple would be legally married, except that they would not consummate the marriage sexually, and would not yet live together.

Sometime later (often as much as up to a year) the groom would come to the bride's (father's) house and, in a festive ceremony, escort the bride to his house. This ceremony was called נשואין *nissuin*, meaning "carrying" or "taking." Blessings would be recited over a cup of wine, the couple would consummate the marriage sexually, and they would live together as husband and wife.

Sometime during the Middle Ages, these two ceremonies came closer and closer together in time until they were combined into one ceremony—the Jewish marriage ceremony as it is known today. The contemporary ceremony—which can be held at any time, except on Shabbat or on the festivals—contains elements of both the ancient ceremonies.

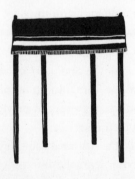

The marriage ceremony takes place under a חופה *chuppah*, a canopy. The canopy has four sides, or poles, and a roof-like covering. The *chuppah* symbolizes a house—the house to which the groom brought his bride in the ancient ceremony, and the new house that the bride and groom are about to create.

The wedding prayer is that theirs will be a "faithful home in Israel," a home where the values and the traditions of Judaism and the Jewish People will be lived, loved, and taught.

Shortly before the ceremony begins, it is customary for the groom to place the veil over the bride's face, in a rite called באדעקן *badeken* (literally, "cover" or, alternately, "examine"). The supposed origin of this custom is the biblical story of the deception of Jacob, who expected to marry Rachel but was given Leah as a bride instead (Genesis 29:16 ff). To make sure that the "right bride" is under the veil, the groom now places the veil himself.

The ceremony begins with the ברכת אירוסין *bircat erusin*, the betrothal blessing, belonging to the original betrothal ceremony.

This blessing praises God, who permits proper marriages and prohibits certain other (specifically, incestuous) marriages and sanctifies the Jewish People by means of marriage. This blessing is recited over a cup of wine (the first cup that will be drunk during the ceremony, corresponding to the cup of wine that was used during the ancient betrothal ceremony). Both groom and bride drink from the first cup of wine. Some modern Reform wedding ceremonies eliminate this first blessing accompanied by the first cup of wine, and include only the blessings over the second cup of wine (which thus becomes the only cup of wine in these Reform ceremonies) later in the ceremony.

The second ritual of the modern-day wedding ceremony is the presentation of the item of value, from groom to bride, while he recites the marriage declaration.

In the Middle Ages, it became customary to use a ring as the item of value, although any item of value still meets the legal requirement. The ring must be owned by the groom (it cannot be the property of anyone else), it must be a solid band, and it must be made of gold. Rings with precious jewels are not permitted to be used as the wedding ring, in order to avoid the possibility of fraud.

If, for example, a woman agreed to marry a man *on the condition* that the wedding ring be made of expensive diamonds, and if the ring were found to be made of inexpensive glass, it could be claimed that the marriage was based on a fraudulent declaration (that the jewels were real) and subject to nullification. Since few people are expert in the evaluation and worth of precious gems, and since most people are generally aware of the relative price of a ring of gold, the rabbinic authorities declared that if a ring is to be presented by the groom to the bride as the item of value, then it must be a gold ring, unadorned with any precious jewels.

The groom places the ring on the first finger of the bride's right hand and speaks the marriage declaration to her in Hebrew. In translation, the marriage declaration says, "With this ring, you are consecrated (made holy, sanctified) (meaning separate and unique from any other woman) to me, according to the law of Moses and Israel." With the groom's presentation and declaration, and the bride's acceptance—in the presence of two qualified witnesses—the act of Jewish marriage takes place.

Today many brides also present a ring to the groom. Since this is a new custom and not law, there is no need for the legal declaration to be recited. However, most brides choose to recite some form of marriage declaration to the groom.

The next ritual of the marriage ceremony is the reading of the כתובה *ketubah* (literally, "[the] written [document]"), the marriage document.

Originally, brides were sold and bought through a marriage contract, setting the "bride price" to be paid by the groom to the bride's father. This "bride price" was considered fair compensation to the father in exchange for losing a productive member of his household, his daughter.

Some 2,000 years ago, while most of the rest of the world continued to sell and buy brides, Judaism made a tremendous advancement in human rights and human dignity. Judaism created the *ketubah*, the first document in the history of the world to protect the rights of women.

Traditionally, women did not have any property or inheritance rights. If a man were to die, or if a man were to divorce his wife, all his property automatically passed to his sons. His wife inherited nothing, and could be left destitute, or dependent on her children for her sustenance and support.

The *ketubah* changed all that.

The *ketubah* set aside a certain amount of money as the wife's separate and sole property. If the husband were to die, or if he wished to divorce his wife, then that money would go directly to her as her inheritance or her alimony. Through the *ketubah*, a woman would no longer be left without her husband, and without any financial support. She would have money and resources of her own.

Some grooms, however, were too poor to set aside the money required by the *ketubah*. Yet without the *ketubah* money, the marriage could not take place. So some brides agreed to take a lien against the *ketubah*, agreeing that the money would not be set aside before the marriage, but that if a husband were to die, or wished to divorce his wife, then she would have first claim on his assets, up to the amount provided to her in the *ketubah*.

If he were to die without having accumulated the *ketubah*-guaranteed amount of money, the issue of inheritance would be moot anyway. If, however, he wished to divorce her, he had to come up with the *ketubah*-guaranteed amount of money. Since, for so many centuries, many Jews were so poor—and never accumulated the amount of money required by the *ketubah*—many of these marriages were probably saved from divorce because the lien on the *ketubah* could never be fulfilled.

The *ketubah* is a contract with only one copy, for it is not a contract of mutual benefit, but a contract of sole benefit for the woman.

Immediately before the ceremony, the *ketubah* is signed by two qualified witnesses, who attest to the promises made by the groom to the bride.

The signing of the *ketubah* is a legal transaction, where authority is acquired from the groom to formalize a legally binding agreement. As a sign of "acquisition" of the authority, the groom—in the presence of the witnesses—is asked by the officiant at the ceremony to validate the transaction by holding on to a handkerchief that is extended to him. This symbolic act is called קבלת קנין *kabbalat kinyan*, the "receiving of acquisition/possession," or simply *kinyan*, "acquisition," where the groom agrees to be bound by all the conditions stated in the *ketubah*.

During the wedding ceremony, the *ketubah* is read and then presented to the bride.

In modern times, the *ketubah* may seem antiquated and quaint—especially because there are so many women of independent means, and because civil laws in many states guarantee equality in inheritance and division of community property.

Many Reform, Reconstructionist, and some Conservative wedding ceremonies do not use the *ketubah,* reasoning that its original purposes no longer apply. Instead of a *ketubah,* the bride and groom in many liberal wedding ceremonies are given a Certificate of Marriage.

In recent years, a number of more egalitarian versions of the *ketubah* have been written, and a number of Reform, Reconstructionist, and Conservative wedding ceremonies now use a contemporary egalitarian *ketubah.*

However, the *ketubah* is still an integral part of traditional wedding ceremonies for two reasons: First, it links the groom and bride to every Jewish couple, in every generation, who has been married according to Jewish law. Second, it reminds the groom and bride, in this generation, to protect each other—with insurance, wills, trusts, and other documents of financial security—in the same way that grooms and brides of past generations protected themselves in the best way they knew how.

The *ketubah* is a document of history, practicality, and security.

The next ritual of the wedding ceremony is the recitation of the שבע ברכות *sheva b'rachot* (literally, "seven blessings"), the seven wedding benedictions.

These blessings, recited over a cup of wine, belong to the ancient *nissuin* nuptial ceremony (in which the groom would bring the bride to his house for the conclusion of the wedding rites). This is the second cup of wine of the wedding ceremony.

These seven blessings praise God for His acts of creation, and for granting joy to the bride and groom. All the good that bride and groom—and those who love them—wish for each other is contained in these blessings.

As the concluding ritual of the wedding ceremony (there by custom, not by law) the groom breaks a glass by stepping on it. Many explanations have been offered for this custom, the most accepted of which is זכר לחרבן *zecher l'churban,* remembrance of the destruction of the Holy Temple.

Even at the moments of greatest and most supreme joy, Jews remember that they are a people whose Holy Temple was destroyed and who were sent into exile to wander the earth. The joy of the wedding ceremony was traditionally tempered with the recognition that the bride and groom were part of a People whose homeland was still not their own (before the establishment of the modern State of Israel in 1948).

Yet the breaking of the glass—especially by grooms today—also implies the hope that the new generation that will be created through the bride and groom will be the generation that is restored to a free, independent, and completely peaceful Land of Israel, so that in the words of the final blessing of the *sheva b'rachot,* "It may soon be heard, in the cities of Judah and in the streets of Jerusalem, the voices of joy and gladness, the voices of the groom and the bride."

10. יחוד YICHUD

(literally, "alone" or "seclusion") is the private time spent together by bride
and groom immediately following the wedding ceremony.

In ancient times, following the nuptials, the bride and groom would be left alone to sexually consummate the marriage.

Today, reminiscent of this ancient intimacy, the bride and groom spend a few private moments alone together immediately following the wedding ceremony, before joining with family and friends in celebration of their marriage.

DIVORCE

11. גרושין GERUSHIN

(literally, "expulsion" or "banishment") is divorce.

While Judaism reveres and cherishes the institution of marriage, it also recognizes that some marriages break down and fail. Therefore Judaism accepts and provides for divorce, when a marriage is no longer viable.

The *ketubah,* marriage document, came into Judaism approximately 2,000 years ago, but a document of divorce is described in the Torah (Deuteronomy 24:1), from a time more than 1,000 years earlier.

Until Jews lived in countries that claimed jurisdiction over divorce in civil courts, a Jewish couple seeking a divorce would come before a *beit din,* a rabbinic court. The rabbis of the *beit din* would carefully question the couple and try to affect a reconciliation. When reconciliation was not possible, the *beit din* would grant a divorce.

12.   גט   GET

(literally, "legal document"; known in Torah times as a
ספר כריתות *Sefer Keretut* [literally, "a letter/document of cutting off"])
is the document of divorce.

Before the members of the *beit din,* the husband would recite a formula requesting that a *get,* the document of divorce, be written. Under the direction of the *beit din,* a *sofer,* a scribe, would handwrite the *get,* a carefully formulated twelve-line document.

The document is written in twelve lines because the letters that spell the Hebrew word גט *get* represent the number twelve; the ג *gimel* represents the number 3; and the ט *tet* represents the number 9. Because 3 + 9 = 12, the *get* document is written in twelve lines.

Under the supervision of the *beit din,* the husband or his agent/representative would deliver the *get* to the wife—by dropping the document into her hands—while reciting a formula terminating the marriage.

The wife, or her agent/representative, would accept the *get* by holding on to it, and by walking a few steps with it, in order to indicate her possession of the document. The wife would then return the *get* to the members of the *beit din,* who would cut it, so that particular document could never be used again (for example, by another couple with similar names who were seeking a divorce but wanted to avoid an appearance before the *beit din*).

Both husband and wife were issued a פטור *p'tur,* a release, stating that their marriage is terminated and that each is free to marry again. The husband could marry immediately. The wife could marry only after ninety days. The waiting period is in case of pregnancy. By waiting the ninety days before remarriage, it would be clear whether the divorced husband or the new husband is the father of the baby. This knowledge is necessary for the legal issues of inheritance.

In modern-day Israel—for matters of personal status, such as marriage and divorce—there is no civil court. The state, which in many ways functions as a theocratic democracy, has given jurisdiction in all matters of personal status to the religious courts—Jewish, Christian, Moslem, and Druze. Thus in Israel, where there is no civil marriage or civil divorce but only religious marriage and divorce, the granting of a divorce is presided over by one of the religious courts.

The United States, and most other countries of the world, retains civil jurisdiction over divorce. A Jewish marriage must first be terminated in a civil court, which terminates the civil aspect of the marriage. However, a civil court cannot terminate the Jewish aspect of the marriage, so even after a civil divorce, the Jewish aspect of the marriage is still intact.

A Jewish couple who have been divorced in a civil court must still come to a *beit din,* the Jewish religious court, to terminate the Jewish aspect of the marriage.

The contemporary *beit din* follows the same time-honored procedures for granting, writing, and delivering the divorce as have been in effect for centuries. With the writing, delivering, and acceptance of the *get,* the Jewish marriage is terminated, and the parties each receive a *p'tur* and are free to remarry.

Since Judaism's origins are in a patriarchal society, Jewish law provides that only the husband can institute Jewish divorce proceedings. In modern times, this often poses a problem because, following the civil divorce, some men—acting out of spite—refuse to give their wives a Jewish divorce. This means that according to Jewish law, the couple is still married, and the wife becomes known as an עגונה *agunah* (literally, "deserted/abandoned"). If she wishes to remarry, she cannot do so under Jewish law and in a Jewish ceremony. A woman is also an *agunah* and ineligible to remarry if her husband disappears. Unless there are two eyewitnesses to his death, he is considered to be alive and the marriage still intact.

In Israel, where the decision of the rabbinic court in matters of personal status has force of civil law, a recalcitrant husband who refuses to grant a Jewish divorce to his wife can be sent to jail until he agrees to grant the divorce. In places such as the United States, where civil and rabbinic courts are separate, the same recourse is not available. So in recent years, a number of ways of dealing with the problem of the recalcitrant husband have been proposed.

Some couples sign a prenuptial agreement or have a clause written into the *ketubah* stating that if the marriage ends in divorce, the husband promises to grant his wife a Jewish divorce within a certain time after the civil divorce decree. If he refuses, or fails to do so, the *beit din* will act on his behalf to grant the divorce, citing his agreement to the prenuptial agreement or to the *ketubah*-clause as his agreement to the divorce.

For couples who do not have this kind of prenuptial agreement or *ketubah*-clause, it is suggested that a clause be included in the civil divorce settlement and decree stating that the husband agrees to grant his wife a Jewish divorce within six months of the civil divorce decree. If he fails to do so, he can be held in contempt of the civil court, just as if he failed to fulfill any other requirement (such as paying child or spousal support) of the civil divorce settlement and decree.

Without a Jewish divorce, no person who has been previously married can be married again with an Orthodox or Conservative rabbi officiating. For without a Jewish divorce, according to Jewish law, a person married a second time would be a bigamist—married to two people at the same time. In addition, the Jewish legal status of any child born of the second marriage is in very serious jeopardy.

The Reform movement does not require a *get* in order to terminate a Jewish marriage, contending that the divorce decree of the civil court is sufficient; thus many Reform rabbis will officiate at a second marriage of a person who does not have a Jewish divorce from the first marriage.

While this position is widely accepted within the Reform movement, it causes problems throughout many parts of the Jewish world where these marriages are not recognized as valid Jewish marriages, and where the legal status of the children born of these marriages is in serious question.

Jewish marriages are created and sanctified "according to the law of Moses and Israel." The issuance of the *get,* the Jewish divorce document, is the way to terminate Jewish marriages, according to Jewish law, with the same dignity and the same sanctity.

DEATH

13.   חברה קדישא   CHEVRAH KADESHA

(literally, "holy society") is the holy burial society.

When a Jew dies, Jewish law and tradition require that the funeral and burial of the deceased take place as soon after death as possible—ideally within twenty-four hours, but certainly within forty-eight hours.

The funeral and burial are held so soon after death to emphasize the Jewish belief that the soul—wherein is the spark of life—immediately returns to God who gave it; so the body—which is the earthly abode of the soul—should be returned, with the same immediacy, to the dust from whence it came. Since the body is but the container-dwelling of the soul—and not life itself—it should not become the object of mournful veneration, but should be swiftly returned to its source, the dust of God's earth.

Exceptions to this rule can be made if it will take a close relative slightly longer to travel to the site of the funeral in order to honor the deceased, or if Shabbat or a

Jewish holiday (on which funerals do not take place) intervenes, or if a delay is ordered by government requirement.

The body is honored as the holy vessel that contained the soul, so it is treated with the utmost reverence and respect.

That is why traditional Judaism requires ground burial and prohibits mausoleum interment or cremation (although some modern denominations do permit cremation or the use of a mausoleum.) Reverence for the body means returning it to God in the way that God gave it—fashioned out of the dust of the earth (Genesis 2:7; 3:19; Job 10:9). Mausoleum interment does not return the body to the earth, and cremation destroys the body—a right not given to humankind. Today, after the Nazis burned up so many Jewish bodies in crematoria, it seems to many particularly inappropriate for Jews to choose cremation as the method for disposing of the deceased.

The members of the *chevrah kadesha* care for the body from as soon as possible after death until burial. They remove the body from the place of death, prepare it for burial according to the proscribed rituals, place it in the coffin, watch over it until the time of the funeral, accompany it to the grave, and assure proper burial.

In modern times, the professional mortuary has often taken over the role of the *chevrah kadesha,* but in many communities, it is still only the *chevrah kadesha* that assumes this role; and in other communities, the *chevrah kadesha* works along with the professional mortuary.

The members of the *chevrah kadesha* perform one of Judaism's highest *mitzvot*—a *mitzvah* that can never be acknowledged or returned by its recipient—the caring for and burying of the dead with honor and dignity.

14.   טהרה   TAHARAH

(literally, "purification") is the ritual purification (of the deceased).

The main ritual performed by the members of the *chevrah kadeshah* in the preparation of the body for burial is *taharah,* the ritual purification.

First, the body is washed in a proscribed manner, as physical cleansing. Appropriate prayers and blessings are recited.

Then a specific measure of water (equivalent to approximately twenty-four quarts) is poured over the body. This is the *ritual* purification, distinct and different from the hygienic cleansing that has just taken place.

Since the body has already been physically cleaned, this pouring of water has no practical purpose, but is clearly the *symbolic* purification of a person passing from one state to another—from life to death. Just as a human being enters life from the waters of the womb, he or she departs life in the waters of *taharah.*

15. תכריכין TACHRICHIN

are shrouds.

The deceased is dressed by the members of the *chevrah kadesha* in *tachrichin*, shrouds made of white linen. (Some liberal denominations of modern Judaism permit the deceased to be dressed in regular clothes.)

The *tachrichin* consist of: a head dress; trousers; a chemise covering the entire body; a *kittel* (a robe-like upper garment); a belt; and a linen sheet. Men have their *tallit* (prayershawl) draped over their shoulders, with one of the *tzitzit* (fringes) cut, indicating that the deceased is no longer obligated to fulfill the *mitzvot*.

The *kittel* is the same type of garment that is worn by traditional men on Yom Kippur and at the Pesach *seder*. Some men are buried in the very *kittel* they wore during their lifetime.

None of the garments of the *tachrichin* have pockets, because "You can't take it with you."

When the body, dressed in the *tachrichin*, is placed into the casket, it is customary to put earth or sand from the Land of Israel (according to some traditions, wrapped in a linen bag; according to other traditions, sprinkled) into the casket with it.

The pure white of the *tachrichin* is symbolic of the purity of the soul. And because the shrouds are exactly the same for all people, the use of the shrouds demonstrates the uniformity, egalitarianism, and equality in death. The rich are not dressed in fancy garb; the poor are not forced to wear threadbare clothes. All are dressed in simplicity and in equality.

16. ארון ARON

is the casket.

The casket is to be made entirely of wood. It can have no nails, no metal, or any other kind of decor.

There are two reasons for the of requirement of a simple wooden casket. First, wood decomposes much more rapidly than metal. Since the body is to "return to the dust" as quickly as possible, a metal casket, or a wooden casket with metal parts, would impede the process of the body's return to the dust. The wooden casket decomposes and, along with the body, returns naturally to dust.

The second reason is that the use of a wooden casket (any wood is permitted, but the simplest—and most preferred—wooden caskets are made of pine) is a statement of equality in death. The rich cannot make displays of their wealth by burying their deceased in fancy, expensive coffins, and the poor need not be embarrassed burying their dead in simple, inexpensive coffins. The wooden casket reflects the reality that in death all are equal.

In addition to eliminating the competition among the survivors over whose loved one is given the finest casket, the use of the wooden casket restricts unnecessary spending to provide a fancy casket—or feeling any guilt for not doing so.

17. לויה LEVAYAH

(literally, "escort," "accompany") is the funeral.

The Jewish funeral service is simple, dignified, and concise.

It begins with the recitation of biblical psalms, and concludes with the recitation of the prayer אל מלא רחמים *Eyl malay rachamim,* "God, full of mercy, . . ." asking God to receive this soul and grant it eternal rest in His sheltering presence.

The centerpiece of the funeral service is the הספד *hesped,* the eulogy. The deceased is remembered in love and reverence and is praised for his or her deeds.

Most often, the rabbi delivers the *hesped* on behalf of all the mourners and the community.

Today, in some communities, because many Jews do not belong to a synagogue or do not have a personal relationship with a rabbi, family members and close friends of the deceased also offer words of remembrance and tribute.

18. אנינות AND אבלות ANINUT AND AVELUT

(literally, "delicate" or "sensitive"; and "lament" or "mourn")
are states of mourning.

Death brings sadness and grief to almost everyone who knew the deceased, but there are seven categories of relationships for which one becomes an "official" mourner, one who follows the laws, customs, and procedures of Jewish mourning.

One becomes a mourner for a (1) father, (2) mother, (3) sister, (4) brother, (5) son, (6) daughter, or (7) spouse.

In the period between the time of death and the funeral, the relative of the deceased is in a state of *aninut,* a time of intense grief. He or she is exempt from the performance of all ritual *mitzvot* because the shock of the news and the depth of sadness is so great, and the need for making funeral arrangements is so immediate.

Immediately following the funeral, the state of *avelut* begins, when the mourner is "in mourning" and mourning practices are observed.

19. קריעה KERI'AH

(literally, "tearing" or "rending") is the torn garment of the mourner.

Immediately upon hearing of the death of a relative for whom one is obligated to mourn (the seven relatives), or (in modern times) at the time of the funeral, the mourner tears a garment that he or she is wearing.

Today, in some communities, instead of tearing clothing, the mourner is given a black ribbon that is attached to a garment and then torn.

The torn garment is the physical sign of the grief—the "torn" heart and spirit—of the mourner.

20. קדיש KADDISH

(literally, "holy") is the prayer recited by the mourner.

Beginning at the funeral and continuing for eleven months, the mourner recites the *kaddish.*

The *kaddish* is not a prayer for or about the dead. It is a doxology: a prayer of praise to God.

The mourner recites this prayer as an expression of faith in God, even in the midst of tragedy and grief.

Traditional Jews recite the *kaddish* at each of the three worship services, each and every day during the eleven-month period.

In modern times, when most Jews do not worship three times a day, some come to the synagogue for one of the daily services to recite the *kaddish.* Others recite the *kaddish* weekly, attending a service on Shabbat—Friday evening and/or Saturday morning.

According to a Jewish legend, the *kaddish* is recited for eleven months because a soul that does not have enough of its own merit to enter into heavenly reward has one year to "earn" eternity. According to this legend, each time a mourner recites *kaddish* for the deceased, the soul "earns points" in its heavenly quest. Yet, the legend goes, no person could be so bad, have so little personal merit, that he or she needs a full year of "*kaddish* points." Thus the *kaddish* is recited for only eleven months—not for a full year—following the death.

A more plausible explanation is that reciting *kaddish* for the eleven months following death is part of a mourner's "grief work," a ritual that helps the mourner slowly but assuredly accept the reality of the death, go through the mourning process, and heal. The one-month break between the completion of the recitation of *kaddish* and the first anniversary of the death permits the mourner to "let go" of mourning and return to a more normal existence.

21. שבעה SHIVAH

(literally, "seven") is the seven-day period of mourning
(following the funeral).

Beginning immediately after the funeral, and continuing for seven days (counting the day of the funeral as day one), the mourner enters a period known as *shivah*. This is a time when grief and sadness are great, and so the mourner is sheltered from and relieved of everyday concerns and obligations.

Immediately on returning from the cemetery—the beginning of the *shivah* period—a candle—known as the *shivah* candle—is lit in the home. The Bible teaches that "the candle [the flame, the light, the spirit] of God is the soul of humankind" (Proverbs 20:27). The *shivah* candle is therefore symbolic of the soul of the deceased.

After lighting the *shivah* candle, the mourners are required to eat a small meal, known as the meal of consolation, prepared for them by neighbors and friends. Although grief is great, the meal symbolizes the need to continue living and to begin the healing process. While the desire may be to shun food, shut out the world, and grieve in private, the *shivah* meal—being a ritual required of the mourner—forces life to go on and the healing to begin.

Traditionally, during this seven-day period, the mourner does not leave the house, so friends and relatives come to visit, to express sympathy, and to speak of the deceased. So that the mourner does not have to be bothered with or involved in the details of everyday existence, friends and relatives prepare food and bring it to the house. Since the mourner must recite *kaddish*, but cannot leave the house, a *minyan*—a prayer service with the minimum quorum of ten worshipers—is held in the home each morning and (afternoon and) evening, giving the mourner the opportunity to worship within a community and to say *kaddish*.

Shivah is suspended over Shabbat, because Shabbat is a time not of mourning, but of joy. Shabbat still counts as one of the seven days of *shivah,* but the mourning customs are not observed. The mourner leaves the house to go to the synagogue to worship and recite *kaddish* within the synagogue community.

In modern times, many people cannot afford to leave their jobs for the full seven-day period of *shivah.* In the liberal communities, some modify the *shivah* period to three days, or the days from the day of the funeral until Shabbat begins.

During *shivah,* it is customary for the mourner to sit on the floor or on a low stool or bench. This is a symbol of "being brought low" in grief, as well as a symbol of submission to the will of God. This custom recalls ancient days, when mourners would sit on the ground, in sackcloth and ashes, to symbolize grief. Sitting on the floor or on low furniture is such an integral part of the *shivah* ritual that a mourner is said to be "sitting *shivah.*"

Other customs for the mourner during the *shivah* period include not bathing or cutting hair or beard, a sign of vanity; and not wearing leather belts or shoes, a sign (in ancient times) of comfort and luxury.

In some homes, the mirrors are covered. Some say that this custom is because of a superstition that the Angel of Death has already visited this household, and that the mourner might see the "reflection" of the Angel of Death in the mirror and die also. A more plausible explanation for the covering of the mirrors is that looking in the mirror is another sign of vanity, to be avoided during mourning.

Shivah concludes on the morning of the seventh day, following the morning service. The mourner leaves the house and takes a walk around the block, symbolic of reentry into some of the normalcy of life.

The ancient Jews who developed *shivah* understood what modern psychology has begun to teach in the last few decades: that mourning is a process of "grief work" that must take place systematically over a prolonged period of time.

In the period of time between the death and the funeral, *aninut,* no real mourning can take place because the grief is so fresh and so raw. The Mishnah understood this when it taught: "Do not comfort the bereaved while their dead are still (lying) before them" (Avot 4:23).

But the mourning—and the healing—begins with the funeral service. The *keri'ah,* the sound of the tearing cloth, is symbolic of the torn and stricken spirit. The sound of the dirt falling on the casket in the grave is the heart-rending reality of the finality of death.

Then the *shivah* period is a time of intense but sheltered and controlled grief. It begins with the requirement to eat—a life-affirming act. It shelters the mourner from everyday activities—the need to go outside the home, to conduct business, and even to be concerned about appearance. It provides the time to remember the deceased, to tell—through recollections and reminiscences, and in modern times, with pictures, movies, audiotapes, and videotapes—the story of his or her life. It surrounds the mourner with caring, comforting friends.

The *shivah* period leads the mourner on a slow but steady return up from out of the depths of grief, toward a level of sadness that is far from gone but that permits the mourner to reenter the world and function in daily life. *Shivah* is the Jewish law and *ritual* that regulates the conduct of the mourner and (as modern psychology now understands) leads the mourner to psychological grief work and through the process of healing.

22. שלושים SHLOSHIM

(literally, "thirty") is the thirty-day mourning period.

Following the *shivah* is another period of less intense but nevertheless serious mourning, called *shloshim,* which takes place during the twenty-three days following the *shivah.* With the seven days of *shivah,* this totals thirty days of mourning.

While the mourner leaves the house and returns to work, many other activities—such as attending celebrations, weddings, and being in places where there will be music or dancing—are prohibited. Some mourners continue to wear the rent garment, and some continue not to cut hair or shave during *shloshim.*

During *shloshim,* it is also prohibited to go to the cemetery to visit the grave of the deceased.

Shloshim is the next phase of the grieving process—the return to the everyday world, with some signs of mourning still visible, and with activities inappropriate to mourning still prohibited. At the same time, *shloshim* limits mourning by not permitting the mourner to visit the grave, keeping him or her from excessive expressions of grief.

In some communities, some mourners—especially those who are in mourning for a parent—do not attend celebrations—especially where there will be music or dancing—for a full year following the death.

23. מצבה MATZEVAH

is the gravestone/ tombstone.

The grave is marked with a stone in which is carved the name of the deceased (in both Hebrew and English) and the date (according to both the Hebrew and the secular calendars) of birth and death. Sometimes expressions of affection and love, and sometimes a tribute in Hebrew verses, are also carved into the stone.

The top of the stone often has the Hebrew letters נ פ *pay* and *nun* standing for the phrase פה נטמן *poh nitman,* "Here lies buried," or פה נקבר *poh nikbar,* "Here is interred." The bottom of the stone often has the Hebrew letters ה ב צ נ ת, *tav, nun, tzadee, bet,* and *hay,* standing for the phrase תהי נשמתו (נשמתה) צרורה בצרור החיים, *T'hi nishmato (nishmatah) tzrurah b'tzror hachayim,* "May his (her) soul be bound up in the bond of life eternal."

In Israel it is the custom to place and dedicate the *matzevah* soon after the *shloshim* period is over. In the United States, it is the custom to place and dedicate the *matzevah* sometime around the first anniversary of the death (weather conditions permitting). The ceremony of dedicating the *matzevah* is often called an unveiling, for the *matzevah* is "unveiled" by removing a covering or cloth.

When visiting the cemetery, it is customary to place a small stone on top of the *matzevah,* to indicate that the grave has been visited and that the deceased is lovingly remembered.

24. יאהרצייט YAHRZEIT

(Yiddish; literally, "a year's time") is the anniversary of death.

Each year, the anniversary of the death of a loved one (according to the Hebrew calendar) is commemorated. On the first anniversary following the death, the *yahrzeit* is commemorated on the anniversary of the day of the funeral. From then on, it is observed on the anniversary of the day of death.

A *yahrzeit* candle is lit in the home, symbolic of the soul and the spirit of the deceased. (Remember: "The candle [flame, light, spirit] of God is the soul of humankind.")

The relative goes to the synagogue for each of the three daily services (evening, morning, and afternoon, or in modern times, some go to the synagogue on the Shabbat closest to the *yahrzeit*) to recite the *kaddish.* If possible, the grave is visited on the *yahrzeit.*

The commemoration of the first *yahrzeit,* the first anniversary of the death, is a vital part of the mourning process. It signifies "closure," the ending of the mourning period. While the deceased will always be remembered and loved, the mourner must finish mourning and fully return to life. The *yahrzeit* symbolizes that the healing process can now be complete.

That is why, in the United States, the placement and dedication of the *matzevah,* the gravestone, often takes place on or around the time of the first *yahrzeit.* Along with going to the synagogue to say *kaddish,* the dedication of the gravestone is another dramatic ceremony of closure.

Other cultures commemorate the birthdays of the deceased—for example, Washington's birthday, Lincoln's birthday, Martin Luther King's birthday. But a birthday—literally, the day a person was born—really only marks that person's *potential,* what he or she may become from the day of birth onward. By commemorating the anniversary of the day of death, Judaism celebrates a life fulfilled. It is a different and unique way of looking at the world, and at the life and death of each human being.

Each year, when *yahrzeit* is observed and *kaddish* is recited, the life and deeds of the deceased live on in the memory of those commemorating the *yahrzeit. Yahrzeit* is a yearly tribute of remembrance and love.

25. יזכור   YIZKOR

(literally, "remember") is the memorial service.

Four times each year—on Yom Kippur, and on the last days of the three pilgrimage festivals, Succot, Pesach, and Shavuot—the entire community joins together in reciting memorial prayers in memory of all the deceased.

Inserted into the festival morning service (and at mid-afternoon during Yom Kippur day) the *Yizkor* prayers include both communal and individual prayers of memory. The central prayer calls on God to "remember" the souls of the deceased.

In recent years, prayers for those who perished in the Holocaust and for those who died defending the Land of Israel have been added to the *Yizkor* services in many synagogues.

Yizkor is the public, communal expression of both communal and private memory and tribute.

When referring to someone who is deceased, many people say the name of the deceased, followed by the phrase עליו השלום *"Alav hashalom,"* for a man, or עליה השלום *"Alehah hashalom,"* for a woman (literally, "On him [her] peace"), "May he (she) rest in peace." Sometimes, when it is written, the named of the deceased person is followed by the Hebrew letters ע"ה *ayin* and *hay,* standing for the phrase *"Alav (alehah) hashalom,"* "May he (she) rest in peace." Another custom is to follow the name of the deceased with the Hebrew letters ז"ל *zayin* and *lamed,* which stand for the phrase זכרונו לברכה *"Zichrono levracha,"* for a man, or זכרונה לברכה *"Zechronah levracha,"* for a woman, meaning, "May his (her) memory be for a blessing." Both these phrases are used to distinguish the dead from the living, and to demonstrate respect, reverence, and affection for the deceased.

AN ESSAY ON LIFE AND DEATH

The greatest human fear is the fear of death, because death is the ultimate unknown.

Since the dawn of human history, spiritual traditions and philosophical and religious systems have tried to grapple with this most perplexing and frightening of all of life's mysteries: What happens to me after I die?

Most faith communities have shaped and settled on an answer for themselves, which brings their faithful adherents a measure of certainty, confidence, and comfort.

But Judaism has no one singular response.

Much like its ever-evolving ideas of God, its continually developing system of law, and its ever-present delicate balance between the worlds of law and spirit, Judaism has no absolute definitive dogma about what happens after death.

Instead, Judaism offers a number of different viewpoints of life and death—each born out of particular historical, political, social, or theological circumstance, each an intellectual or spiritual—if not entirely emotionally comforting—attempt to answer life's last and most puzzling question.

VARIETIES OF THOUGHT AND BELIEF

In biblical times, Judaism's main emphasis was on life not death. Judaism was born into a world that worshiped and glorified death. A primary sacred document of the ancient Egyptians was *The Book of the Dead,* chronicling and extolling the journey to eternity. Egyptian slaves spent entire lifetimes building elaborate burial tombs to shelter their kings and nobles in death, surrounded by the finest of life's material goods—gold, silver, precious jewels, delicate fabrics, fine foods, companion animals, and even clay figurines of entire armies.

To counter this preoccupation with death, the Hebrew Bible teaches nothing of an afterlife. According to the Bible, immortality was achieved by living a good, worthy, meaningful, productive life on this earth, and by leaving progeny—children who would carry on the good deeds and the good name of their parents.

Yet the Bible does not teach that death means complete oblivion. It implies an eternity of the soul—the unique God-given spark of life that makes the material body into a living, breathing human being—when God tells Abram, "As for you, you shall *go to your fathers* in peace; you shall be buried at a ripe old age (Genesis 15:15). When Abraham (remember, his name was changed at the time of the covenant of circumcision) dies, the Bible describes his death by saying, "And Abraham breathed his last, dying at a good, ripe age, old and content, and *he was gathered to his people. . . .* " (Genesis 25:8).

While it does not define it in any clear way, the Bible describes a place called שאול *sheol,* a netherworld to which souls descend at the time of death.

The Bible thus implies that death means the end of physical existence, but does not mean a total cessation of being. Rather, there is an eternity to the soul, which will somehow "live on" and be reunited with the souls of ancestors who have previously died.

As the Bible teaches, "the dust returns to the earth that it was, but the spirit returns to God who gave it" (Ecclesiastes 12:7).

In the early Rabbinic Period (200 B.C.E.–200 C.E.), reflecting growing human awareness, and in response to the political and theological crisis they were facing, the rabbis and sages introduced a brand new concept into Judaism: the idea of life after death, with reward for good behavior during life on earth.

Far more sophisticated and enlightened than their biblical ancestors, the people began to understand some of the mysteries of the world in which they lived. Their view would not be limited to the world they could see and experience, but could begin to include other elements of the entirety of God's universe. This expanding human consciousness led the rabbis and sages to reveal some of the secrets, to introduce the people to metaphysical truths that, until this time, had remained hidden.

At the very same time, the people—oppressed and persecuted by the Greeks and then the Romans—came to the sages in theological revolt. Why, they asked, should the Romans, who seemed subject to no higher authority than laws of their own invention, enjoy a life of freedom and frolic? And why should they, Jews loyal to God, continue to observe the *mitzvot,* to follow God's sometimes restrictive commands, when their only reward seemed to be a life of hardship and suffering?

Faced with a Jewish populace that seemed ready to hear timeless truths, and yet was also on the brink of forsaking many of God's laws, the sages revealed some of the secrets and, at the same time, quelled the rebellion by asserting that there are really two interconnected worlds.

If reward for following the *mitzvot* did not come in העולם הזה *haolam hazeh,* in "this earthly world," then it would surely come in העולם הבא *haolam haba,* in "the world to come," the afterlife, the world after death in this lifetime.

God, the sages insisted, watches and knows how each and every person behaves. For following the *mitzvot,* for faithfully observing God's commands here in this lifetime on earth, God will give eternal heavenly reward in the world to come.

As the talmudic sage Yose ben Abin taught (JT Yeb 15.2), "The day of death is when two worlds meet with a kiss; this world going out, the future world coming in."

At the very same time, the sages introduced another related theological concept.

The collective Jewish longing for national redemption—introduced some 1,000 years earlier at the time of the death of King Solomon—was never stronger.

The oppressed and persecuted Jewish People wanted their משיח *masheach*, their messiah, anointed one, who would unite the broken monarchy and bring back the time of harmony, tranquility, and peace that marked the reign of King Solomon.

Yet here too the people worried. What if *masheach* comes a day after I die? I understand that I will be rewarded in God's heavenly realm for my good deeds here on earth. But that is not enough. I do not want to miss the moment of national redemption, the time when peace comes to this world. It is not fair that I have suffered the indignities of oppression all through my lifetime, and, yet, I might not be here for the moment of glory, the coming of *masheach*.

The sages responded by giving assurance: When *masheach* comes, they taught, everyone who has ever lived will be physically resurrected, and will return to Jerusalem in triumph and celebration. As the Talmud taught (BT San 91a), "If a glass vessel which is fashioned by the breath of man can be restored again after it is once broken, how much the more so can the soul of man be restored, seeing that it has been fashioned by the breath of God."

In a theological instant, Judaism—which had accepted the biblical viewpoint about life and death for close to two millennia—now had two new and stunningly distinct assertions about life and death: There is an afterlife, a world to come, where people are rewarded for earthy conduct; and there will be physical resurrection of the dead when the messiah comes.

Yet just as afterlife and resurrection were being made central to Jewish theology, newly forming Christianity made these concepts basic tenets of its religious beliefs. To emphasize the differences between the two faiths, Judaism never made afterlife and resurrection into absolute dogma. Instead they became part of Jewish consciousness about life and death, alongside the long-held biblical views.

Nevertheless, the idea of afterlife with reward and eventual resurrection became a popular—and comforting—Jewish belief, and has endured throughout the generations.

The prayers of the era, and prayers composed throughout the Jewish centuries reflect this belief.

The morning prayer says, "The soul You placed in me O God, is pure. You created it, You fashioned it, You breathed it into me, and, eventually, You will take it from me, but You will restore it to me in future time to come. . . . Blessed are You, O God, who restores souls to dead bodies." And the *amidah* says, "He . . . maintains faith with those who sleep in the dust." "Blessed are You, O Lord, who resurrects the dead."

The Talmud and the Midrash offer many stories and legends about the eternity of the soul, and its place and purpose.

High Holiday liturgy composed in the Middle Ages sets the metaphoric scene of God sitting on His Throne of Judgment, reviewing the words and deeds of each person, writing in His Book of Life "who shall live and who shall die," and who shall receive heavenly reward.

The Yiddish writers of the nineteenth and twentieth centuries—particularly Y. L. Peretz and Nobel Laureate Isaac Bashevis Singer—spun fanciful tales of the heavenly realm, of the prosecuting and defending angels arguing the merit of each life before the heavenly tribunal, of the rewards or punishments of eternity, of the roles and missions of each soul.

The Talmud (Derech Eretz) sums it up: "If you fulfilled My commandments joyfully, My Divine attendants will come out to meet you, and I, Myself, will bid you welcome."

The Kabbalists—beginning in the thirteenth century, and continuing through the seventeenth century—added an even broader perspective to the eternity of the soul.

The mystical Kabbalists taught of גלגול הנפש *gilgool hanefesh*, "the rolling or the transmigration of the soul," commonly known as reincarnation.

Not only does every soul have eternity, but each soul can return to earth, housed in a different body. Each soul has eternal memory, so that implanted within each soul is the complete memory of everything that has ever happened to it, and to every other soul with which it has ever had contact. Each soul also knows the secrets of the universe, revealed to souls in the heavenly realm but not remembered when the soul returns to an earthly body.

It does not matter if the soul returns to earth in a male or female body, because the body is only the earthly housing for a particular lifetime. The soul—created in the image of God—has both masculine and feminine attributes, just as God does. So the soul does not depend on earthly gender in fulfilling its eternal mission.

Some souls return to earth to continue work from a previous lifetime. Some souls return to earth to make up for transgressions and mistakes of a previous lifetime. Some souls return to earth to add to the work and the progress of the world, helping it move forward toward balance and perfection. Some souls return to earth to learn new lessons that will help them achieve "soul-perfection," when they can join the "soul hall of fame" and will not need to return to earthly existence again.

Souls that have been together in one lifetime often return to earth together in one or more future lifetimes—playing out their relationships, correcting and healing past wrongdoing, enhancing past opportunities, learning and growing.

When people who have never met before feel an immediate affinity and intimacy, when lovers—who have been searching all their lives—finally find their "soul mate," it is no accident. Souls that were together in previous lifetimes have been reincarnated and reunited in this lifetime.

Rav Kook taught, "The soul sings all the time."

In the modern era, in response to the hugely intellectual, strictly logical thinking that characterizes so much of contemporary life, Jewish thought about death has become highly rational.

Since there is no scientifically provable evidence of what happens after death, modern rational discourse dismisses all previous attempts to describe after-death experience as mere speculation.

Death, the modern rationalists insist, is death. The "invention" of an afterlife by the Rabbinic sages, and the Kabbalists' assertion of reincarnation, are nothing more than emotionally comforting attempts to confront—and perhaps defy—physical reality.

The political thinker Karl Marx went even further, arguing that religion is nothing more than "the opiate of the masses," allowing people to suffer horrible indignities in this lifetime, in anticipation of an eternal reward in the life to come. Marx contended that rather than being deceived and deluded by religious fantasy, rational, thinking people should take responsibility for improving their lives here on earth.

The rational thinkers of most recent times reject the reported descriptions of "near-death" experiences, contending that "near-death" is not death, and that those who relate such episodes are not "coming back from the dead" with factual information, but have simply been involved in similar experiences, induced by the trauma of being close to physical death.

Modern rational thinkers agree with the medieval thinker Ibn Zabara, who taught, "What is the cause of death? Life." And they affirm Ben Sirah, who taught in the Apocrypha, "Fear not death, for it is your destiny."

Since there has been no one, singular Jewish belief and no one continually accepted tenet, each different viewpoint has enjoyed varying degrees of popularity and allegiance. Sometimes the strands of various thought have been intertwined, producing an even wider spectrum of choice and sentiment.

CONTEMPORARY RESPONSES

How, then, is a modern Jew to answer the age-old question, What happens to me after I die?

There are a number of possibilities, each with its own unique advantages and disadvantages.

Nothing.

This is the "dead is dead" theory of modern intellectual rationalism. This belief has its share of disadvantages. First, in asserting that death leads to nothing but complete oblivion, the great fear of the unknown that death invokes is not conquered. It also inspires deeper questions: What is the purpose of life? What is the purpose of existence, if it is only these few short years here on earth? Am I not part of a greater plan, a grander design, than my own personal life encompasses?

This belief can easily lead to a life of hedonism: If this is the only life I am ever going to have, why should I bother to lead a good life—a life that will surely include tragedy and suffering—if righteousness does not ultimately triumph over evil—even in the world to come? I might as well just enjoy life completely, unconcerned with anything but my own pleasure.

Yet this belief has the advantage of being intellectually honest, and calls a person to live this life on earth—the only life he or she will ever know—to the fullest. Since a person lives to live, and not because of a possible reward in an afterlife, this life should embrace and affirm every possibility for meaning, worth, and goodness.

As the Midrash teaches (Tanchuma Kedoshim), "The day of death is concealed so that man will build and plant."

Living on through memory.

This belief affirms that death is death, but celebrates the meaning and purpose of each individual life, which lives on through the memory of those still alive.

The measure, the lasting value of a person's life is what he or she accomplished in work and in love.

A person's tangible works remain—the business he built, the book she wrote, the picture he painted, the tree she planted.

The works of a person's passions and commitments remain—the cause she championed, the community he forged, the organization she founded, the ideals he professed.

The words a person speaks remain—echoing into eternity, influencing and inspiring those who heard them.

A person's children remain—embodying the love, the lessons, and the legacy that a parent leaves, continuing on a parent's good deeds and good name into yet another generation.

This belief has its disadvantages, for unless a person achieves enduring greatness, how long will the memory of his or her life last?

Great countries and political systems—and their leaders—fall and are forgotten. Buildings crumble, books gather dust, trees get chopped down. Causes go out of fashion, ideals tarnish, organizations change, communities move on. Even if the accomplishments of a Shakespeare or a Beethoven or a Da Vinci remain, the persona fades in a generation or two. After I die, my life will be reduced to but a few stories told to my great-grandchildren who stand at my grave.

Yet the belief in living on through memory offers a taste of immortality. It inspires worthy living, and gives direction to life, and ultimate purpose to existence.

The late Rabbi Morris Adler prayed, "We thank Thee, O God of life and love, for the resurrecting gift of memory, which endows Thy children fashioned in Thine image, with the God-like sovereign power, to give immortality through love."

Eternity of the soul.

With no exact vision of an afterlife, this belief affirms the everlasting, eternal existence of the soul, the Divine spark of life.

What makes the lump of clay that is the human body into a living, breathing human being? The source of life is the soul, and the source of the soul is God.

I—the vessel that housed the God-given soul for these years on earth—am precious to God: I am one of God's children, created from a tiny spark of God's being.

If I believe that God cares enough about me to place a soul into my body, and to breathe Divine spirit into me giving me life, then, I equally believe that when God takes back my soul and I die, God will not abandon my soul at the grave. God will somehow protect and watch over my soul, for it is not an independent being, but it is a part of God.

This belief has its disadvantages, for so much of it is so ambiguous. What is the nature and the form of the soul? Does the soul have ultimate knowledge? Does it have human awareness? Does the human awareness disappear at death or does it continue on? Where—and how—does the soul spend eternity?

Yet this belief in the eternity of the soul assures immortality, if not in physical, earthly form, then surely in eternal, spiritual form.

As the modern prayerbook (UPB I) puts it, "Death is not the end; the earthly body vanishes, the immortal spirit lives with God."

Reward or punishment in a world to come.

Reflecting the concept introduced by the Rabbinic sages, this belief teaches that for following God's commands here on earth and exhibiting good, decent, ethical behavior, God offers an eternity of reward. For transgressing God's commands, and violating standards of decency and goodness, God metes out an eternity of punishment.

Despite the many and varied descriptions of heavenly paradise and wretched hell that theologians, writers, artists, and storytellers have envisioned in the last two millennia, this belief has a number of disadvantages—most of which revolve around the unknown.

If the sages "invented" the concept of the world to come in response to a particular earthly circumstance, does it really exist or is it just the product of human imagination?

What is heaven? What is hell? What is the nature of God's reward, of God's punishment?

Do I enter heaven or hell in my human form? Do I remain that way throughout eternity? Do I retain human awareness? Will I meet relatives and friends who have already died? Will my grandmother still be old and sick, as she was when she died? Will she recognize me, since she died when I was twelve and now, when I die, I am eighty-seven? Will my friend who withered away from cancer or was crushed in an automobile accident be restored to healthy form?

Do I enter a paradise of eternal pleasure? Do I enter a fiery inferno of eternal pain and suffering?

What if I weren't good enough, what if I didn't behave well enough, to merit heavenly reward?

Will my parents, my spouse, my children merit heaven? If not, will I ever see them again? How can I spend eternity without them?

The unknown nature of reward and punishment in an afterlife—with so much at stake—is very scary, and may make me even more afraid of death.

Yet this belief has many advantages. It makes life's purpose obvious: to lead a life worthy of eternal reward. It satisfies the human demand for justice: There *is* reward for the righteous, no matter how much they suffer in this lifetime. And, for many, it lessens the fear of death, because it offers assurance that death means not oblivion, but life everlasting. Even if the details of heavenly reward are not well-defined, the promise of eternity with God is enough.

As the Midrash teaches (Ecc. Rab. 5.14), "If a man sought the best course in life, reward awaits him beyond the grave . . . that will last through eternity."

Reincarnation.

This belief affirms the teachings of the kabbalists and the chasidim that souls have not only everlasting, but independent, existence and return to earth in human form in succeeding lifetimes.

Like God, souls are eternal and dwell in the heavenly realm, in the world of the spirit. There they are endowed by God with ultimate and universal knowledge.

The medieval philosopher Saadya Gaon put it this way: "Even though man's body is of small dimension, his soul is more extensive than heaven and earth, because its knowledge embraces all that they contain."

Now and then, souls come to earth housed in a human body, and exist in the material realm for a period of time. When in an earthly incarnation, the souls' ultimate knowledge is hidden from them, for no human being can exist on the earthly plane with ultimate knowledge.

When their sojourn in a particular earthly body is complete, the souls leave the earthly plane and "pass over" or "pass away" into the spiritual plane once again. There they rest and are cleansed of imperfections that may have attached during the earthbound journey, incorporate the lessons they learned, add their earthly experiences to their soul-memory, reenergize, and prepare for another earth-journey.

For some, belief in reincarnation demands the suspension of all rational thinking. For others, it is the most logical, natural, and irrefutable explanation of the mysteries of the universe.

For those who find the idea appealing, but whose logical minds foster doubt and skepticism, there are questions to ask:

A dog hears the sound a of dog whistle that is inaudible to the human ear. Does that mean that the sound does not exist? Of course not. The human sense of hearing is simply not developed enough to hear it.

An AM radio can only receive AM signals. Does that mean that FM signals are not there? Of course not. The AM radio simply does not have the capacity to receive them.

A camera captures a picture that the lens is open enough to see. Does that mean that anything outside the lens's view isn't there? Of course not. The camera simply does not have the capability to record it.

Are we to think that there is no more to this world than that which we can see and hear and experience at this moment?

Since the beginning of time, God has guided the universe to unfold bit by bit, divulging its secrets, revealing its mysteries, bringing us closer and closer to understanding God's will, to knowing God's plan.

The universe continues to unfold, and each day, each moment, new realities, new truths are revealed—things that were there all the time, but which we had not yet developed the capacity to perceive.

To many, the belief in *gilgool hanefesh*, reincarnation, makes perfect sense as the affirmation that souls are eternal, as the obvious answer to the meaning and purpose of earthly existence, as the logical response to the demand for justice in life, and as the ultimate answer to the mystery of death—that there is little distinction between life and death, for both life and death are part of the continual flow of the wholeness of the universe.

As the chasidic Rebbe Menachem Mendel of Kotzk, paraphrasing the holy Baal Shem Tov, taught, "Fear not death. It is just a matter of going from one room to the other."

THE CHOICE

It would be assuring and comforting to have a definitive answer to the ever-enduring question, What happens to me after I die?

But in having a variety of responses, in leaving the choice of belief to each individual, Judaism insists that each person come into personal encounter with God, that each person enter into personal dialogue with God—exploring, probing, wrestling with life's ultimate question.

In this way, Judaism challenges each human being to focus not just on the destination that comes with death, but on the journey that is life.

THE JOURNEY

Physical death is certain.

There is "a time to be born, and a time to die" (Ecclesiastes 3:2).

But the spiritual mysteries of life and death are only mysteries when they are clouded by the limitations of earthbound existence and earthbound knowledge.

For at its deepest and most hidden place, each God-created transcendent soul—each human being—knows its origins, its pathways, and its destinations:

From God.

To God.

In the light of God.

The circle is never-ending. The circle continues still.

"Blessed are you in your coming in. Blessed are you in your going out. Blessed are you in your coming in. Blessed are you in your Going out. Blessed are you . . ." (after Deuteronomy 28:6).

8

THE JEWISH LAND

1. ארץ ישראל ERETZ YISRAEL

is the Land of Israel.

Eretz Yisrael, the Land of Israel, has been central to Judaism since its very beginnings.

The covenant that God made with Abraham included the promise of land—which would eventually come to be known as Israel—as an everlasting homeland for the Jewish People: "Unto your seed I will give this land" (Genesis 12:7). "Lift up your eyes and look from the place where you are, northward and southward, eastward and westward. All the land which you see, I will give to you and your seed forever. . . . Arise, walk through the land, its length and its breadth, for I will give it unto you" (Genesis 13:14–15, 17). "I am the Lord who brought you out of Ur of Chaldees to give you this land to inherit it" (Genesis 15:7). "And I will give to you, and to your seed after you, the land of your sojournings, all the land of Canaan, for an everlasting possession" (Genesis 17:8).

When God told Moses to go to Pharaoh to tell him to release the Hebrew slaves, it is so that God would be able to fulfill His original promise to Abraham. "I have come down to deliver them out of the hands of the Egyptians, and to bring them up out of that land unto a good and large land, a land flowing with milk and honey, unto the place of the Canaanite . . ." (Exodus 3:8).

The journey of the Children of Israel through the desert has a clear destination. Joshua, the successor of Moses, is told by God, "Prepare to cross the Jordan [river] together with all this people, into the land which I am giving to the Children of Israel" (Joshua 1:2).

There is no doubt as to where the land is. In speaking to Moses (Exodus 3:8), God lists all the tribal inhabitants of the land. In precise detail, the borders of the land—north, south, east, and west—are described by God to Moses (Numbers

34:2–12). When God charges Joshua with the responsibility of bringing the people into the Promised Land, He carefully sets out the boundaries (Joshua 1:4–5).

From the moment, in approximately 1200 B.C.E., that "Joshua fought the battle of Jericho" and the Children of Israel entered the land God had promised to their progenitor Abraham, Jewish history unfolds in that place.

A loose confederation of Judges ruled until approximately 1030 B.C.E., when the monarchy was established and Saul was anointed king. In approximately 1010 B.C.E., King David established Jerusalem as the political and spiritual capital of the land.

In 950 B.C.E. King Solomon built and dedicated the בית המקדש *Beit HaMik-dash,* the Holy Temple, as the centralized locale for worshiping God through the sacrificial rite.

The Land of Israel was often the target of foreign invaders. In 722 B.C.E., the Assyrians destroyed the Kingdom of Israel, leaving only the small Kingdom of Judah as the independent Jewish homeland.

Other countries used Eretz Yisrael as the bridge—from east to west, and from west to east—as they tried to conquer other nations and dominate the world.

Despite its political woes, the Land of Israel was the place where the prophets (750–450 B.C.E.) taught the enduring values of spiritual faithfulness and social justice.

In 586 B.C.E. the mighty Babylonians conquered the land, destroyed the *Beit HaMikdash,* ended Jewish independence, and sent the people into exile.

Yet it was an exile that would not last long. In 538 B.C.E. the Persians defeated the Babylonians and permitted the Jews to return to Eretz Yisrael. There the *Beit HaMikdash* was rebuilt, and religious reformation took place, and sovereignty was eventually reestablished.

As the Greek world spread its influence throughout the ancient Middle East, Israel came under Hellenistic and then Roman domination and rule. In 70 C.E. the Romans conquered the land, destroyed the *Beit HaMikdash,* and sent the people into another exile—one that, this time, would last almost 1,900 years.

During those almost two millennia, Israel was ruled by the Roman and Byzantine Empires (586 B.C.E–614 C.E.); the Persians (614–629); the Byzantines again (629–638); the Moslem Arabs (638–1099); the Crusaders (1099–1291); the Moslem Arabs again (1291–1517); the Ottomans (1517–1917); and the British (1917–1948). Yet there was never one moment when some Jews did not live in the land. They were not independent, they had no self-determination, they were subject to the laws of the ruling power, but they were there: Jews in the Jewish land.

The Jews outside the land lived in what they termed גלות *galut,* exile, or diaspora. No matter where they lived, what language they spoke, what king of flesh and blood ruled over them, whether they were oppressed or comfortable in the lands in which they lived, the exiled Jews—and their descendants for more than nineteen Jewish centuries—never gave up the hope and the desire to return from exile to a restored and reestablished Jewish homeland in Israel.

They were never really at home anywhere else. In reality and in spirit, they were always in exile from their rightful homeland. Not for one moment did the thought of Eretz Yisrael leave the mind of any Jew.

Wherever Jews lived, they prayed facing east—toward Israel and Jerusalem. Three times each day, Jews prayed for an end to the exile: "Sound the great *shofar* proclaiming our freedom. Raise the banner to assemble our exiles and gather us from the four corners of the earth." "O gather us in peace from the four corners of the earth and restore us triumphantly to our homeland. . . ." "O may our eyes witness Your return to Zion." "Return in mercy to Jerusalem Your city and dwell in it as You have promised. Rebuild it in our day as an everlasting habitation, and speedily set up the (continuation of) the throne of David."

For almost 1,900 years, at the end of every Passover *seder* and the end of the Yom Kippur prayers, Jews cried out, "Next year in Jerusalem!"

No matter how long the exile stretched on, Jews were always confident of eventual restoration and return, for together with God and Torah, Eretz Yisrael—the Promised Land of Israel—forms the essential foundation of Judaism and the Jewish People.

2.   כותל המערבי   KOTEL HAMA'ARAVI

is the Western Wall, the last remnant of the Holy Temple.

When the Romans destroyed the *Beit HaMikdash,* the Holy Temple, in Jerusalem in 70 C.E., they utterly devastated the entire building and almost all of its surrounding structures.

The only remnant of the Temple that was left standing was a wall—not part of the Temple itself, but a portion of the western retaining wall that had been built by Herod (the Roman-appointed king of Israel, 37–4 B.C.E.) surrounding the Temple Mount.

This wall—called the *Kotel HaMa'aravi,* the Western Wall, or simply the *Kotel,* the Wall—became an important symbol for the Jewish People for a number of reasons.

If it were not part of the Temple itself, at least it was closely associated with the Temple, so the *Kotel* became a holy place for Jews—the last vestige of the spot where the Holy Temple once stood.

It also became a place for mourning and weeping over the destruction of the Temple and the exile of the people. That is why the Western Wall is sometimes known as the "Wailing Wall," for in their despair over the events that had befallen the Jewish People and the Jewish Land, Jews would come to the *Kotel* and weep and wail.

Yet the *Kotel* also became a symbol for the hope of restoration and return—that one day Israel would be reestablished as an independent Jewish homeland, and God could once again be worshiped at the site of the Holy Temple.

Whenever Jews could come to Jerusalem—the few Jews who still lived in the land, and the few Jews who were able to visit there throughout the centuries—they would come to the *Kotel* to pray.

There is a Jewish legend that if a person places a letter or a note of prayer directly into one of the cracks between the stones of the *Kotel,* the prayer goes straight to God. It was customary for Jews from around the world to send prayer notes to Israel to be placed in the *Kotel.*

When the modern State of Israel was established in 1948, all of Jerusalem was supposed to be open and accessible to all peoples. However, the Arab nations cut off East Jerusalem—the site of the Holy Temple—from Jewish access. Jews could not visit the *Kotel* or worship there.

In 1967, during the Six Day War, Israel captured all of Jerusalem. Since that time, Jews—as well as peoples of all faiths and nations—have been able to come to the *Kotel,* which now has become a symbol of Jewish return and restoration.

3.   ציונות   TZIYONUT

is Zionism.

ציון Tzion, Zion, is a biblical synonym for Jerusalem, and by extension all of Israel.

The love of Zion, the yearning for return to Zion, permeated Jewish thought, life, and literature throughout the centuries of diaspora.

Modern Zionism—the political movement to secure Jewish return to the Land of Israel—was born in Europe in the last years of the nineteenth century.

It began in France in 1894, when Alfred Dreyfus, a Jew, was falsely accused of treason. Even though the Jews had enjoyed political equality in France for more than a century, French citizens were quick to condemn Dreyfus, blaming his disloyalty on his being Jewish. Dreyfus was finally released from prison when the popular French writer Emile Zola took up his cause.

The Dreyfus case dramatically reminded many Jews that even in a nation where Jews had been granted political freedom and equality, a Jew is never safe from unjust accusation by a society looking for a scapegoat.

In response to the Dreyfus case, Theodor Herzl, a secular Jewish journalist from Budapest and Vienna, wrote *Der Judenstaat, The Jewish State,* advocating the creation of a free and independent Jewish state in Palestine.

Herzl's writing struck deep into the Jewish consciousness, and the millennia-old yearning for return to Eretz Yisrael was keenly felt throughout much of the Jewish world.

Some Jews opposed any move toward the establishment of a modern Jewish state, reasoning that as citizens of the world, as citizens of countries where they enjoyed political equality, there was no need to differentiate or separate themselves from their fellow citizens.

But those in opposition were in the distinct minority.

In 1897 Herzl convened the First Zionist Conference in Basel, Switzerland. It attracted more than 200 delegates from nineteen countries, who demonstrated strong support for the establishment of a Jewish state and effectively gave birth to modern Zionism as a political movement.

The hope for the creation of a modern Jewish state was given greater impetus when Great Britain defeated the Ottomans and took control of Palestine in 1917.

The British issued the Balfour Declaration—named for Britain's Foreign Secretary Lord Balfour—which stated that the British Government "views with favor the establishment in Palestine of a national home for the Jewish People."

However, Great Britain's early support and enthusiasm was to be tragically reversed.

In 1939—in an apparent attempt to appease both the Arabs and the Nazis—Great Britain issued a White Paper stating that it was no longer British policy to support the creation of a Jewish state in Palestine. At the same time, Britain limited immigration into Palestine to no more than 15,000 Jews a year, giving the Jews fleeing Nazi Europe no place to go, and effectively aiding Hitler's plan to exterminate the Jews.

The horrific death of millions of Jews in the Nazi Holocaust emphasized more than ever the need for a safe, secure, free, and independent Jewish homeland.

Immediately following World War II, with the evidence of the Nazi destruction being slowly etched into the consciousness and the conscience of the world, the Zionist cause—its need and its right—was magnified, and the work of political Zionism intensified.

Zionists were largely responsible for rallying public opinion and creating the political atmosphere that moved the world toward the Zionist cause and moved the United Nations toward the vote that set the stage for the establishment of the modern State of Israel.

Since the creation of the State of Israel in 1948, Zionism has been under constant attack from those peoples and countries that oppose the existence of the independent nation-state of Israel. Claiming no opposition to Jews or Judaism, and vehemently denying any anti-Semitism, the anti-Zionists nevertheless object to contemporary Jews establishing a modern Jewish state in the ancient ancestral Jewish homeland.

Zionism and Zionists have become the target of hatemongers and terrorists, as well as reasonable people with differing political agendas. The Zionist cause has been subjected to great hardship and hostility, conflict and confrontation, constant political wrangling, and more than sporadic acts of terrorism.

But secure in their principles and convictions and confident in their historical and contemporary rights, Zionists continue to support, build up, and nurture the State of Israel, knowing that the destiny of the Jewish People is inextricably intertwined with the destiny of the Jewish Land.

4. מדינת ישראל   M'DINAT YISRAEL

is the State of Israel.

On November 29, 1947, the United Nations voted for the partitioning of Palestine, which effectively created the possibility for the establishment of both Jewish and Arab states in Palestine.

On May 14, 1948—corresponding to 5 Iyar, in the year 5708 of the Jewish calendar—Israel declared independence, creating the Third Jewish Commonwealth, the modern State of Israel.

The Jewish People was restored to the Jewish Land!

After almost 1,900 years of exile and wandering, the Jews, once again, had their free and independent homeland in the biblically Promised Land.

Since that time, Israel has existed as a nation-state of the world—the physical homeland for millions of Jews, and the spiritual homeland of every Jew.

5. THE GEOGRAPHY OF ISRAEL

The territory of modern-day Israel is considerably smaller than the Promised Land defined in the Bible (Numbers 34:2–12 and Joshua 1:4–5).

The 1948 borders were originally set by complex international political maneuverings, and finalized through the realities of military conquest during the War of Independence.

As a result of that war, Israel gained more territory than the mapmakers had originally designated. But the Arab nations captured portions of Jerusalem—which was supposed to be an international city—and cut off Jewish access to East Jerusalem and its holy sites.

Pre-1967 Israel contained 7,992 square miles, roughly the size of the state of New Jersey. From its northern tip to its southern tip, it was no more than 400 miles. At its narrowest, it was but twelve miles from Arab-held territory to the Mediterranean Sea.

Israel is bordered by the Mediterranean to the west, by Lebanon to the northwest, and Syria to the northeast and east, by the Sea of Galilee, Jordan, the Dead Sea, and Saudi Arabia to the east, and by the Red Sea and Egypt to the south and southwest.

During the 1967 Six Day War, Israel captured and later annexed the Golan Heights overlooking Israel from Syria. Israel also captured and occupied a large portion of the Sinai desert, the Gaza Strip, and the West Bank—known in the Bible as Judea and Samaria.

In 1979, when Israel and Egypt signed the Camp David Peace Accords, Israel returned the Sinai desert to Egypt.

As a result of the mutual recognition by Israel and the Palestine Liberation Organization in 1993, Israel permitted limited Palestinian self-determination in Gaza and in the city of Jericho on the West Bank—paving the way for further steps toward peace between Israel, the Palestinians, and the neighboring Arab countries.

The north of Israel is called גליל Galeel, (literally, "district"), the Galilee. The Galilee is a fertile region, characterized by its lush vegetation and fields. The area's most notable feature is ים כנרת Yam Kinneret, Lake Kinneret, also known as Lake Tiberias, or the Sea of Galilee. The lake is called *kinneret,* which means "violin," because it is shaped like that graceful musical instrument.

During biblical times, the Galilee is said to have contained more than 200 towns and villages, with a population of close to 3 million. Today it contains many agricultural settlements, especially in the עמק יזרעאל Emek Yezre'el, the Jezreel Valley, commonly known simply as the Emek. The Galilee's best-known towns are מטולה, Metullah, Israel's northernmost city; צפת Tz'fat, Safed, a city made holy by the sixteenth-century kabbalistic mystics; and טבריה Tvaryah, Tiberias, on the shores of Lake Kinneret.

On the western coast of Israel is the beautiful hillside city of חיפה, Haifa, often compared to San Francisco and Naples. Down the coast is the biblical port of יפו Yaffo, Jaffa, right alongside the modern cosmopolitan city of תל אביב, Tel Aviv, sometimes called "the Paris of the Middle East," carved out of the seaside sand dunes by a small group of settlers, beginning in 1909.

The south of Israel, called נגב, the Negev, is characterized by its hot, barren desert landscape. The "capital" of the Negev is the biblical town of באר שבע, Be'er Sheva. The southernmost city is אילת, Eilat, most notable as a modern tourist town with its clear-water swimming and diving in the Gulf of Eilat. In the Negev's northeast is ים המלח Yam HaMelach (literally, "the salt sea"), the Dead Sea. At the tip of the sea is the biblical city of סדום S'dom, Sodom, close by to the caves of Qumran, the site where the Dead Sea Scrolls were discovered in 1947. Also near the Dead Sea is the mountaintop fortress of מצדה Matzadah, Masada, where the Jewish zealots mounted their last stand against the Roman conquerors in 73 C.E.

Since 1967 Israel has occupied and governed what is commonly known as the West Bank—the biblical area of יהודה ושומרון Yehudah v'Shomron, Judea and Samaria. This territory includes the biblical cities of יריחו Yerecho, Jericho, where the Children of Israel entered the Promised Land; חברון Chevron, Hebron, the ancient burial site of Abraham, Isaac, and Jacob, and Sarah, Rebecca, and Leah, and also the site of Rachel's Tomb, on the road to Bethlehem. The rights to and control of this territory is a highly disputed and deeply emotional contemporary political issue for Israel and the neighboring Arab states.

6. ירושלים YERUSHALAYIM

is Jerusalem.

Near the geographical center of Israel—and certainly at the heart of Jewish life and experience—is the capital city, the holy city of Jerusalem.

King David established Jerusalem as Israel's capital in 1010 B.C.E. It is the site of both Holy Temples, and the place where Jewish pilgrims came at least three times each year to celebrate the festival days and to offer sacrifices to God.

Jerusalem is so much at the core of Jewish existence that for all the centuries of exile, Jews dispersed throughout the world echoed the words of the biblical psalmist, "If I forget you, O Jerusalem, let my right hand forget its cunning, let my tongue cleave to the roof of my mouth, if I cease to think of you, if I do not keep Jerusalem in memory, even at my happiest hour" (Psalms 137:5–6).

Modern Jerusalem has three main sectors. העיר העתיקה HaEir Ha'Atikah, The Old City, is the ancient city enclosed by the walls built during the Ottoman period. The walled city has eight entry gates, and contains the Christian Quarter, the Armenian Quarter, the Moslem Quarter, and the Jewish Quarter, as well as the Temple Mount, the site of the Holy Temples.

To the north of the Old City, East Jerusalem is the predominately Arab section of the city. The New City, or West Jerusalem, was begun in 1860, when the British philanthropist Sir Moses Montefiore constructed the first buildings outside the walled city. West Jerusalem is the predominately Jewish section of the city.

Jerusalem is the capital of the modern State of Israel, and since 1967 it has been united under Jewish control. Its sites—holy to Jews, Christians, and Moslems—are visited by peoples of all faiths.

7. קבוץ KIBBUTZ

(literally, "gathering") is a collective farm.

Rather than living in cities and towns, some Israeli Jews live and work in agricultural settlements.

Some of Israel's farming and agricultural settlements are privately owned, but many others are arranged in a unique way. The most notable of these special structures is called a *kibbutz* (plural, *kibbutzim*) a farming community where the members of the community personally own nothing, but where, together, all the members of the community own everything.

A *kibbutz* is socialism at its finest: "From everyone according to his ability; to everyone according to his need." Each member of the *kibbutz* works to produce income for the *kibbutz* by doing his or her share of the work necessary to produce the *kibbutz's* product. In turn, the *kibbutz* provides for all the needs of its members— housing, food, clothes, health care, recreation, entertainment, education for the children, lifetime retirement care.

In most *kibbutzim*, each family is given a house in which to live, But in some *kibbutzim*, the children live separately from the parents in special children's dormitories. While they spend time with their parents each day, the children are cared for by specially trained *kibbutz* caretakers and educators. Most *kibbutzim* have a communal dining room, where all members of the *kibbutz* eat together.

In a *kibbutz*, all major decisions are made through the democratic process, with each member having equal voice and vote. Most every *kibbutz* handles its day-to-day affairs through a group of committees elected by the members.

In the early years, the major industry of most *kibbutzim* was agriculture. Today almost most every *kibbutz* combines farming with one or more other light industries as additional—and steady—sources of income.

To people used to the free enterprise system and financial success achieved through personal ambition and initiative, the *kibbutz* may seem like a strange way of life. But to people who want to feel a sense of communal belonging and responsibility, to people who want their work to be part of a greater whole, to people whose basic life commitment is to collective rather than individual achievement, to people who want deep and lifelong friendships and partnerships, the *kibbutz* is the perfect place to live, to work, and to grow.

Israel also has a number of variations on the *kibbutz* structure. The מושב *moshav* (literally, "dwelling") is a smallholder's settlement, where the members live separately and work on land leased to them, but pool their resources to buy their supplies and sell their products.

A מושב שתופי *moshav shitufee* (literally, "a cooperative/participatory dwelling") combines the privately owned housing of the *moshav* with the collective farming of the *kibbutz*. Members live in separate family homes, but they own land and equipment collectively and share work and profits.

To the contemporary Jew, no less than to the Jews of ancient times, life within Israel's borders—in her farms, villages, towns, and cities—is everyday evidence of the fulfillment of God's promise, "I will bring you to the land which I swore to give to Abraham, Isaac and Jacob, and I will give it to you for a possession . . ." (Exodus 6:8).

8. צה"ל   TZAHAL

is the acronym for צבא הגנה לישראל *Tzvah Haganah L'Yisrael*
the Israeli Defense Forces (IDF)—the Israeli Army.

When the United Nations voted partition in Palestine, and when Israel declared independence, not everyone was as happy as was world Jewry.

The united Arab nations immediately declared war against the new state and amassed a powerful army to destroy Israel before she ever had a chance to really exist.

With little more than sheer *chutzpah*—bold nerve and moxie—raw courage, and the passionate will to survive, the rag-tag band of citizen soldiers and sailors who formed Israel's first army crushed the mighty Arab forces. Israel's existence was confirmed on the bloody but victorious battlefields of the War of Independence.

Every eighteen-year-old Israeli citizen—except those exempt for religious reasons—is drafted into the Israeli army. Men serve for three years, women for two.

Until age fifty-five, men are on reserve duty, called מילואים *meluim* (from the Hebrew word meaning: "fill" or "full"). *Meluim* service is at least thirty days of active duty each year.

The Israeli army is forced to draft every citizen and to keep men on active reserve duty for decades because not during the War of Independence alone was Israel forced to defend her right to exist and protect her lands, homes, and children from annihilation.

In 1956 Israel and Egypt went to war in what is now known as the Sinai Campaign. Israel prevailed.

In 1967, Israel was challenged on three sides: the Egyptians from the south, the Jordanians from the east, the Syrians from the north. In a stunning display of military prowess, Israel defeated all three aggressors in a series of battles that lasted only six days. Israel captured territory from all three countries: the Sinai desert from Egypt, the Golan Heights from Syria, and the West Bank and all of Jerusalem from Jordan. This Six Day War permanently erased the long-held world perception of the Jew as weak victim. As exemplified by the Israeli soldier, Jews were now considered strong, brave, bold defenders of their faith and their land.

In 1973, in an unprovoked sneak attack that took place on Judaism's holiest day of the year, Egypt and Syria invaded Israel. Eventually, Israel prevailed in what came to be called the Yom Kippur War, but the military might of the attackers, the slow response of the Israeli political and military leadership, and the many casualties suffered by Israel took a deep national psychological toll. The entire country underwent a severe crisis of confidence and a long period of soul searching. It took many years before Israel and her army regained pride, self-esteem, and renewed confidence.

The 1979 peace treaty with Egypt took some day-to-day pressures off the army. But because all the other neighboring nations continued their state of war with Israel, the military had to remain constantly prepared and on alert.

In 1982, when Lebanon's complicated political situation made attempts at political negotiation almost impossible, the Israeli army invaded southern Lebanon in an attempt to rid Lebanon of terrorists who randomly attacked inside of Israel. The strong-willed Lebanese people—particularly the terrorists—resisted Israel's military might, frustrating Israel's hopes for quick victory. A series of Israeli political and military miscalculations and mistakes turned what should have been a swift military mission into a long-term involvement. Once again, Israel was forced into a national soul searching to justify this military operation.

Beginning in 1987, Palestinians began a series of random terrorist attacks and civilian uprisings centered in the Gaza Strip and the West Bank. Through their actions—which they called an *intifada,* a rebellion—the Palestinians hoped to press their cause for self-determination and independence. To maintain order and security, the Israeli army stopped civil disobedience whenever it arose. The *intifada* went on for years, in a war of nerves, determination, and persistence between the terrorists and the Israeli government and army.

The issue of the Palestinians remains one of Israel's most vexing political problems and a dilemma that poses a great and ongoing military challenge. Unlike a neighboring government—a structured nation-state with internationally recognized status—the Palestinians are not a single entity but loosely confederated groups with differing agendas and competing leadership. The emotional charges and counter-charges between Israelis and Palestinians over history, just claims, and perceived and real offense, has made finding a negotiated settlement very difficult.

The 1993 mutual recognition pact between Israel and the Palestine Liberation Organization was intended, in great part, to move beyond the rhetoric and reality of terrorism and military occupation. If the fringe fanatics who sabotage the process can be controlled, the pact can be a large step toward assuring Israel's right to exist within secure and defensible borders, while at the same time affirming the Palestinian right to self-determination and self-rule.

The 1994 peace treaty with Jordan brought Israel and the Arab world one step closer to a comprehensive and lasting peace, but the unwillingness of some nations—particularly Syria and Syria's puppet government in Lebanon—to join in making peace left Israel still vulnerable to terrorist attack and threat of war.

The army remains ever-vigilant in the protection of the land and the people, and ever-hopeful that complete and enduring peace will come.

When a country—and the life of every one of her men, women and children—is constantly under threat and at risk, she must defend herself and her very existence. Out of necessity, the Israeli army has become one of the finest fighting forces in the world.

Yet there is no one in Israel—from the citizen on the street, to the highest-ranking general, to the Prime Minister—who does not long for the day when God's ancient promise will be fulfilled: "I will bring peace to the land, and you shall lie down and no one shall terrify you. I will rid the land of vicious beasts, and it shall not be ravaged by war" (Leviticus 26:6).

On that day, Israel and her neighbors will be able to enact the fervent hope of the ancient prophet, "They shall beat their swords into ploughshares and their spears into pruning hooks. Nation shall not lift up sword against nation. And they shall never again know war" (Isaiah 2:4).

9. THE ISRAELI FLAG

Like every other nation state in the world, the newly established State of Israel had to create and adopt symbols and instruments of government.

The flag of the modern State of Israel has its origins in a similar design suggested by Theodor Herzl and the early Zionists.

The flag is a white rectangle, with two blue horizontal stripes—one near the bottom and one near the top. In the center of the flag is a blue, six-pointed star, the *magen David,* the Shield, or Star, of David.

The designer explained that the stripes on the solid background are to make the Israeli flag look like a *tallit*, the Jewish prayershawl—the traditional "flag" of the Jewish People.

The six-pointed star is a millennia-old Jewish symbol, originally used on the shields of King David's soldiers and recognized as the most identifiable and popular sign of Jews and Judaism.

The colors white and blue were derived from an 1860 poem by A. L. Frankl, "All that is sacred will appear in these colors: white—as the radiance of great faith; blue—like the appearance of the firmament."

A prototype of this flag was first flown by early Zionists in Israel in 1885. It was adopted as the official flag of the Zionist Movement by the 18th Zionist Conference in 1933.

Soon after Israeli independence was declared in 1948, this flag was adopted as the official flag of the modern State of Israel.

10.   THE EMBLEM OF THE STATE OF ISRAEL

The emblem of the State of Israel is the seven-branched candelabrum, the *menorah,* surrounded by olive branches that entwine the word ישראל Yisrael, Israel. The *menorah* is the oldest and most authentic Jewish symbol: It is described in the Bible, and was used as a ritual object in the Tabernacle in the desert and in the Holy Temples in Jerusalem.

The emblem of the modern State of Israel combines the *menorah,* the symbol of light, with olive branches, the symbol of peace.

11.   התקוה   "HATIKVAH"

(literally, "the hope") is the Israeli national anthem.

Although it has never been officially proclaimed, popular sentiment and acclamation has made the song *"Hatikvah"* Israel's national anthem.

The words were written by Naphtali Herz Imber in 1887, in the form of a poem called *"Tikvatanu,"* "Our Hope." In the same year, Samuel Cohen put the words to the melody of an old Moldavian-Romanian folk song called *"Carul cu Boi,"* "Cart and Ox." The classic Czech composer Bedrich Smetana (1824–84) had used the same melody for his piece *"Moldau,"* which is part of his suite "My Fatherland."

"Hatikvah" was sung at successive Zionist Conferences until 1905, when its powerful words and melody moved the delegates to adopt it as the unofficial anthem of the Zionist Movement. In 1933, at the 18th Zionist Conference—the same Conference that adopted the official flag—*"Hatikvah"* was adopted as the official anthem of the Zionist Movement.

At the moment Israel was declared a state in 1948, *"Hatikvah"* was played and sung, and has been the anthem of the state ever since.

The simple poem is a powerful and moving statement of the Zionist dream: "As long as deep in the heart, the soul of a Jew yearns, so long as the eye looks eastward, looking toward Zion, our hope is not lost—the two thousand year hope, to be a free people in our land, the land of Zion and Jerusalem."

It was this hope that motivated the leaders of the Zionist Movement to work for the establishment of the modern Jewish state. And it is the fulfillment of this hope that the citizens of the State of Israel—and the Jews of the world with them—celebrate every day.

12.   כנסת   KNESSET

(literally, "gathering") is the Israeli Parliament.

The Israeli Knesset is a unicameral (one-house) legislature, with 120 seats.

Elections for the Knesset are held every four years. Every citizen of the state—including every Arab citizen—has one vote.

Rather than voting for individual candidates, Israelis cast votes for the political party that best represents their views.

Each party receives a proportional number of seats in the Knesset, according to the percentage of votes it receives in the election.

The individual representatives of each party become members of the Knesset based on a list the party has prepared. If the proportional vote a party receives entitles it to forty seats in the Knesset, the first forty people on the party's list become members of the Knesset.

The party with the majority of members elected to the Knesset is asked by the president of Israel (a Knesset-appointed ceremonial position) to form a Government. The leader of the party becomes Israel's prime minister, and the leading members assume cabinet posts, such as foreign minister, minister of defense, or minister of education.

Israel has more than twenty political parties vying for adherents and for votes for seats in the Knesset.

From the inception of the state, the two major parties have been Labor and Herut. Herut has now merged with other like-minded parties into the contemporary party called Likud.

The more liberal Labor party—and its well-known members such as David Ben Gurion, Levi Eshkol, Abba Eban, Moshe Dayan, Golda Meir, Shimon Peres, and Yitzchak Rabin—dominated much of Israel's early political history.

Beginning in the late 1970s, the more conservative Likud party—led by Menachem Begin, and later by Yitzchak Shamir—prevailed in the elections and set the tone for government.

The problem with Israel's electoral system is that in the entire history of modern Israel, no one party has received enough votes to give it the plurality of sixty-one seats in the Knesset.

The party with the most seats—usually between thirty-five and fifty—must go to the smaller parties—each with two or six or eleven seats—and invite them to form a coalition Government.

For joining the Government—and thus permitting the majority party to form a Government and govern—the smaller parties exact high prices: positions in the cabinet; controlling the ministries they deem most important to their political cause; and demanding that policy set by the Government reflects their own—sometimes narrow—position.

Since the majority party has always been forced to turn to the smaller parties to join in a coalition to form a Government, these smaller parties hold much greater influence than their electoral support and few Knesset seats would otherwise merit.

Most notably, the religious parties—the strongest of which usually wins between eight and fifteen seats, with the smaller ones garnering two or three seats each—have demanded, as their price for joining the coalitions, that the Government closely abide by their very conservative and strict religious principles.

Thus the religious parties have made Israel into a de facto theocratic democracy.

In matters of personal status—in particular, for marriage—there are no civil courts in Israel. All matters of personal status are adjudicated by a religious court—Jewish, Christian, Moslem, or Druze. Thus there is no civil marriage, and effectively no interfaith marriage, in Israel.

The religious parties have shaped government policy about what is publicly permitted or prohibited on the Sabbath and festivals. They have demanded and received government subsidy for religious schools equal to that of public schools. They have arranged for exemptions from military service on religious grounds.

The majority party must usually meet the policy demands of its coalition partners because—like the British system—the Government is, at any time, subject to a "no-confidence" vote of the Knesset. If the Government were to alienate its coalition partners and lose a "no-confidence" vote, the Government would fall and new elections would have to be called.

Clearly, Israel is in need of electoral reform that will create a system to stabilize the governing power of the majority party and reduce the undue influence of the smaller parties. The direct election of the prime minister will be a step in the right direction.

As in most every political system, however, sweeping change is unlikely to come swiftly. For Israel's political parties are highly motivated by self-interest, and are not ready to vote for reforms that would reduce their power or threaten their survival.

In the few short decades of modern Israel's existence, the Knesset has been faced with incredible challenges: assuring the very survival of the country by defending it against mighty foreign armies; using the natural resources of the country—and finding additional resources—to make the desert bloom, to turn swamp land into farm land, to build up the villages, towns and cities; absorbing and integrating the hundreds of thousands of immigrants to the state; providing for the education of every child, the health and welfare of every citizen; mixing the diverse religious, ethnic, and cultural differences of the citizenry—including its Arab population—into a unified whole; occupying and governing the territories; attempting to make peace with Arab neighbors.

All of this takes a tremendous amount of effort—and money. Israel has been blessed with good friends in the world community who help with grants and loans. But the Israeli citizens—fewer than 4 million people—are required to support the needs of the state, which are so many and so expensive. As a result, Israeli citizens pay some of the highest taxes in the world.

The building in which the Knesset meets is also called the Knesset. It is located in a beautiful setting in the hills of West Jerusalem, not far from the Israel Museum and the Shrine of the Book, the military cemeteries of Mt. Herzl, and the Holocaust Memorial, Yad V'Shem.

Whatever the shortcomings, whatever the problems, whatever the challenges, the Israeli Knesset is an age-old dream come true. For the first time in almost 1,900 years, free and independent Jews, in the free and independent Jewish land, meet to govern themselves and control their own destiny.

The Knesset is a modern miracle at work every day.

13. עליה ALIYAH

(literally, "to go up") means to go up to live permanently in Israel.

Immigration—individually or as part of a group—to Israel is called *aliyah,* which means "to go up"—because coming to live permanently in Israel is like making ascent to a place of spiritual holiness.

Even though Israel was not under Jewish control from 70 C.E. until 1948, a few Jews always made their way to come to live in Israel.

In the mid-1700s, there were no more 10,000 Jews in Jerusalem. Throughout the rest of that century, and continuing until the late 1800s, Jews came to Israel when they could—from Turkey, from eastern Europe, from Germany, and from the Asian countries.

The modern-era *aliyah* to Israel—the coming of the people who would form the nucleus of the Jewish population in anticipation of the establishment of the modern state—began in response to the Russian pogroms of the 1880s. Between 1881 and 1903, some 25,000 eastern European Jews came to Palestine, in what would later be known as the First Aliyah, as part of a group that called itself BILU, an acronym for the Hebrew phrase בית יעקב לכו ונלכה *beit Ya'akov l'chu v'nelcha,* "O house of Jacob (Jewish People) come and let us go (to the mountain of the Lord)" (Isaiah 2:5).

The Second Aliyah (1904–1914) brought 40,000 Jews; the Third Aliyah (1919-1923) brought another 35,000.

The Second and Third Aliyot were characterized by the presence of immigrants who called themselves חלוצים *chalutzim* (singular, *chalutz*), pioneers. They came to use their physical strength to work the land, to turn wasteland into productive agricultural settlements. They transformed the image of the Jew as pious students, small merchants, and shopkeepers into the new reality of the Jew as tough, strong, physical laborers. Their pioneering spirit captured the imagination of the nation, and set the tone for Israel's future growth and development.

The *chalutzim* inspired the native-born Israelis to take renewed pride in the designation they had given themselves—סברה *sabra,* from the Aramaic word meaning "cactus." Native-born Israelis—then and now—see themselves as a cactus—tough and prickly on the outside; sweet and tender on the inside.

The Fourth Aliyah (1924–28) brought a record number 67,000 people to Israel. And the Fifth Aliyah (1929–39), when Hitler's shadow had already begun to cast its way across Europe, brought more than 250,000 Jews who were saved from sure death at the hands of the Nazis.

During this period—beginning in 1933—a special Youth *Aliyah* was developed, so that even if adults could not get out of Nazi Europe, their children could be sent to Israel, to be saved and cared for by social service agencies.

During and just after World War II, another 100,000 Jews made their way to Israel. These were the fortunate ones who could escape the Nazi terror, and the tiny remnant who had survived in the forests, the underground, the ghettos, and the concentration camps.

After Israel was declared a state in 1948, another 250,000 survivors of the Holocaust made their way to the Jewish homeland, and "Operation Flying Carpet" brought thousands of Jews living in the Arab lands to the Jewish state.

The repopulation of the free and independent Jewish state, the modern State of Israel, had begun.

Throughout the existence of modern Israel, more than 1.5 million Jews have come from all over the world to "make *aliyah*," to come to live in the ancient and renewed Jewish land.

In very recent years, political situations across the globe have made new *aliyah* possible:

• In 1984 "Operation Moses" rescued thousands of Jews from political and economic hardship in Ethiopia and brought them to Israel.

• Beginning in 1990, with the collapse of the Soviet Union, a massive *aliyah* of Soviet Jews, called "Operation Exodus," began, bringing the first of what could eventually number 1 million Russian Jews to Israel.

• In 1991 the last of the Ethiopian Jews were brought to Israel in a stunning twenty-four-hour airlift dubbed "Operation Solomon."

Yet all is not perfect in modern Israel. For a variety of reasons—economic, political, cultural, social—some Israelis have chosen to leave Israel, and to live in other countries.

Just as coming to live in Israel is called *aliyah*, "to go up," leaving Israel to live permanently in another place is called ירידה *yeradah*, "to go down." Israelis who leave Israel permanently—although most contend that living in another country is just temporary, even if "temporary" means twenty or thirty years or more—are called יורדים *yordim*, "descenders."

Those who "make *aliyah*" join native-born Israelis in creating the population and the citizenry of the modern State of Israel. Under the Law of Return, any Jew, from anywhere in the world, can come to Israel and claim citizenship in the state.

It has been—and continues to be—no easy task to meld Jews from such wide varieties of backgrounds and cultures—especially the sometimes stark differences between Ashkenazic, Sephardic, and Edot HaMizrach Jews—into one modern nation-state.

Since the inception of the state, many Sephardic and Edot HaMizrach Jews have felt that they are the "underclass" of Israeli society—politically, economically, and socially. But the army, in which almost every eighteen year old serves, is the great leveler; and in recent years, old class barriers have been breaking down. With new awareness and sensitivity, old cultural distinctions are being erased, creating equal status and equal opportunity for all.

It is no easy life in Israel—having to build up a country; being under continual threat of foreign assault; serving in the army in order to defend home and family; being constantly on the alert for terrorist attack; paying high and heavy taxes.

Yet Israel is the Jewish homeland reborn in this generation, and those who live there rejoice in her existence and feel the great privilege of being her citizens.

The contemporary citizens of the modern State of Israel—like every Jew who has ever made *aliyah*—joyfully say, in the words of the old Israeli folk song, "We have come to the land to build her, and to be built by her."

They say, paraphrasing the psalmist of old, "May the Lord bless us in Zion, and may we share the prosperity of Jerusalem all the days of our lives. May we live to see our children's children. May there be peace for all of Israel." (Psalms 128:5–6).

AN ESSAY ON ISRAEL

The Talmud claims, "Ten measures of beauty were given to the world. Nine were taken by Jerusalem; one by the rest of the world" (BT Kid. 49a)

The Talmud must have been speaking metaphorically; because physically, except for a few rare and stunning vistas, Jerusalem—and all of Israel—is far from beautiful.

Unless it is well tended, the north can be insect-infested swamp land. The south is dry, barren desert. The winds off the sea swirl sand onto the coastal plains. Jerusalem herself is isolated and remote—hilly and rocky, with no natural source of water.

The old joke is that if Moses had only turned left instead of right, rather than being in this desolate land, we'd all be on the French Riviera!

Yet anyone who has ever been to Jerusalem knows that the Talmud is right. For Israel and Jerusalem possess an inherent beauty, an innate splendor.

In Israel the sky seems bluer, the water tastes sweeter, the air feels purer than anywhere else. The sun splays its brilliant rays against the ancient stones and bathes them in gold.

Israel is alluring, enthralling, bewitching.

Jerusalem is a city of magic.

In the words of the Midrash, "The Land of Israel is the holiest of all lands" (Nu. R. 7.8). And in the heart of the psalmist, Jerusalem is "the joy of all the earth" (Psalms 48:3).

THE JEWISH PEOPLE AND THE JEWISH LAND

The Jewish attachment to Israel and Jerusalem is strong and deep:

It is the land God promised to Abraham and to his descendants in every generation.

It is the land of destination and destiny. The Children of the People of Israel journeyed through the desert to become the Children of the Land of Israel.

It is the land where the kings of Israel built a nation, a "kingdom of priests and a holy nation" (Exodus 19:6).

It is the land where God's holy people built God's holy sanctuary, so that God's glory could dwell in their midst.

It is the land where the prophets walked, cajoling and inspiring, demanding justice and expecting compassion, calling for decency and goodness from God's precious but sometimes stubborn children.

It is the land that was devastated and destroyed by the enemy, sundering the people from their place, imposing painful and lonely exile on the people ripped from their home.

It is the land where the sages taught, bringing down God's word once again, as it had once been brought down from Sinai, to instruct and guide God's chosen people.

It is the land that was devastated and destroyed a second time, wrenching God's people away from God's holy land, condemned to wander the earth, bereft and homeless.

It is the land for which Jews yearned and prayed for almost 1,900 years of dispersion. Jews were in the west, said the medieval poet Yehudah HaLevi, but our hearts were in the east—longing for Jerusalem. Every day—three times a day—the pleas bombarded the heavens: "Return us; restore our land. Bring us home; reestablish Your kingdom. Sound the call of our freedom; gather us from the four corners. Next year in Jerusalem. Next year in Jerusalem. Next year in Jerusalem."

It is the land to which Jews finally, finally came home.

Through all the ages, I dreamt to behold you. I yearned and yearned for the light of your splendor. Jerusalem, O Jerusalem, shine forth, for your exiles return. Jerusalem, O Jerusalem, your ruins I shall soon rebuild.

FOLKSONG

I rejoiced when they said to me, "Let us go to the House of the Lord." Our feet stood inside your gates, O Jerusalem.

PSALM 122:1—2

How fortunate are we. How good is our portion. How pleasant our lot. How beautiful our heritage.

MORNING PRAYER

Of all the generations of Jews scattered and dispersed, of all the generations of Jews who have longed and hoped, of all the generations of Jews whose suffering was intense and whose need was great, of all the generations of Jews who have cried out, "How long, O Lord, how long?" it is this—our generation—that bears witness to the miracle.

We thank You and we praise You, O Lord our God, for bringing us to this moment—the promise, long delayed, once again fulfilled: the Jewish People in the Jewish Land.

THE CHOSEN GENERATION

Who are we—especially those of us who have lived in safe and secure homes all our lives—to know of exile and wandering and suffering?

Who are we—especially those of us not old enough to remember a world without the modern State of Israel—to speak of restoration and return?

Who are we—especially those of us who have not risked our lives for Israel's survival, and not given our children to her defense—to triumph in her existence?

In God's vast and, to us, unknown plan, we have been chosen from amongst the Chosen People to be given the gift of Israel reborn in our time.

Those who live in the land, and those who are bonded to the land through spirit, accept the privilege and the responsibility of inheriting the land, with joy, with thanksgiving, and with humility.

And we feel the gentle arms of the past hugging us in triumph, and the eager hands of destiny pointing us toward the future.

OF SEWERS AND SOLDIERS—WITNESS TO FREEDOM

I first went to Israel in 1965, when I was a teenager.

I felt the excitement of a country in its youth—overcoming adversity, proud and a bit arrogant, exuding confidence, earnest and ambitious. And I felt the frustration of peering though the barbed wire, forbidden from going to the holy sites of Jerusalem, by politics and guns.

This may seem silly, but of all the incredible historical, military, and religious sights I saw that summer, the most awesome to me were the sewer covers in the streets of Jerusalem.

For the sewer covers were emblazoned with the symbol of the Lions of Judah, and with the Hebrew word ירושלים Yerushalayim: Jerusalem.

In their pedestrian simplicity, those sewer covers made a profound statement. For there is no greater evidence of the true independence of a country than when its sewer covers carry its national symbol and its name.

After almost 1,900 years of foreign occupation, the Jewish land could cast its own sewer covers and shout out its freedom.

Five years later, in 1970, I returned—this time in the midst of my studies.

On the ninth day of the Hebrew month of Av—which that year fell on August 11—I walked down the valley and up the hill toward the Temple Mount in the Old City of Jerusalem, three years in Jewish hands.

In my mind's eye, I saw the scene of exactly 1,900 years before.

On the ninth day of the Hebrew month of Av in that year—70 of the Common Era—Jews were not walking toward the Temple Mount, but were running the other way—fleeing in terror. For at that very moment, Romans soldiers were utterly destroying the city. The Holy Temple was in flames. Men, women, and little children were being slaughtered. Blood flowed ankle-deep in the streets. Jerusalem was being laid waste.

But on *this* day, Jews were coming back, gathering at the holy wall—the last vestige of the Temple Mount.

The Temple itself was long gone. Yet the Jews remain to worship God.

The powerful Romans were long gone. Yet the Jews remain to tell the story.

The enemy soldiers, who brought destruction and death, were long gone. Yet the Jewish soldiers remain, to provide protection and security.

Exactly 1,900 years after the Jews were murdered by the foreign soldiers invading their land, Jewish soldiers stood guard in the restored and independent Jewish land, assuring Jewish freedom, guaranteeing Jewish safety.

Sewers and soldiers—the symbols and the certainty of Israel reborn.

THE MODERN NATION-STATE

The Third Jewish Commonwealth, the modern State of Israel, is home to millions of Jews.

Some are descendants of Jews rooted in the land for generations; some came during the periods of *aliyah,* the prestate times of both legal and illicit immigration. Some came barely alive—the battered and broken remnants of the horrors of Hitler's hell. Some came in swift migration from the countries of the east; some have come throughout the years from lands of freedom and in freedom newly gained.

The Jews of modern Israel have built a country and a society, deeply rooted in ancient values, tempered by all the realities of contemporary life. They are the modern inhabitants of an ancient land, the contemporary stewards of antiquity's promise.

For the contemporary Jew living outside the land, the Jewish People living in the Jewish land have, in the words of the modern prayer, "nurtured our pride and renewed our hopes. They have gathered in our homeless and healed the bruised and broken. Their struggles have strengthened us; their sacrifices have humbled us. Their victories have exalted us; their achievements have enriched us."

Since that glorious day in 1948 when modern Israel came into being, we have lived with her; shared her struggles; rejoiced with her and cried with her; built her with our hands; supported her with our dollars; and visited her time and time again.

We love Israel because she is, for us, spiritual, holy.

But we have learned that we must deal with her too, in the stark terms of international realpolitik: as one nation-state among many; as a country judged by others not for her moral mandate, but for her political savvy; as a public entity often splintered by partisan factionalism; as a bureaucracy often caught up in its own disarray; as a government that tries and fails and tries again, that makes mistakes and pays the price, that wants only to improve the lot of its citizens, even if the public good is sometimes elusive and hard to know.

HEROIC ISRAEL

At first, our pride and our exultation knew no bounds.

We were amazed at how that little band of citizen-soldiers—underarmed, unequipped, untrained—defeated the massive Arab armies to assure the survival of the newly independent state.

We knew that it could only be their spirit and their resolve that brought them victory—especially when we heard this jocular story that Israelis tell on themselves:

There was, so the story goes, a border *kibbutz* that was being shelled by the enemy. At any moment, the invaders could come to overrun the settlement and kill the men, women, and children.

But there were only a few guns and no more ammunition. Yet something had to be done to protect the *kibbutz.* So as night fell, they sent Chaim out on guard duty and gave him a broomstick. "Put this on your shoulder," they said, "and pretend that it is a gun. If intruders come in the darkness, perhaps they will see the shadow of the broomstick on your shoulder, think it is a rifle, and be scared away."

So Chaim went out to guard the *kibbutz,* marching back and forth, broomstick on his shoulder. All of a sudden, he heard footsteps coming from the woods. He took his broomstick off his shoulder, pointed it into the woods, and called out, "Halt, or I'll shoot." The footsteps kept coming. "Halt, halt, or I'll shoot," he demanded. But the footsteps kept coming. "Halt or I'll shoot," he yelled, with much more bravado than he felt, pointing his broomstick menacingly toward the woods. But the footsteps kept coming.

All of a sudden, Chaim saw a face emerging from the woods. He looked carefully—and he saw his own brother, Moshe. "Moshe, Moshe," he cried. "What's wrong with you? Why didn't you stop when I yelled 'Halt'? You didn't know that this is only a broomstick. I might have shot you and killed you."

And Moshe looked at Chaim, stood straight up, puffed up his chest, and said, "You can't hurt me. I'm a tank!"

We were awestruck when the people in the land fulfilled the vision of the ancient prophet: "They shall rebuild the ruined cities and inhabit them; they shall plant vineyards and drink their wine; they shall till gardens and eat their fruits" (Amos 9:4).

We looked on in wonder as, in the words of the modern prayer, "They made the wilderness like Eden, and the desert like the garden of the Lord."

In 1967, with Israel's stunning and complete victory in the Six Day War, every Jew in the world shared a new measure of confidence, of esteem, of glory. Not only was Israel's military triumph extraordinary, but her moral courage was exceptional.

After that war, a book entitled *The Seventh Day* was published, recording the experiences of some of the Israeli soldiers.

One soldier related, "When we got to the base (in Jenin on the West Bank) we found the storemen and the cooks absolutely rolling in the things they had looted from the village. . . . Then I remember, the CO got all the company together in a semi-circle and stuck the storemen and the cooks in the middle along with their loot. Then he started quoting them chapter and verse of the Bible: 'Thou shalt not plunder! Thou shalt not . . . ! Thou shalt not . . . !' It was really impressive.

"After he had finished, one of the storemen got up and asked, 'What about that bit in the Bible, "And when Jehosophat and his men came to take away the spoil," what do you make of that?' So the CO began to explain that Rashi commenting on the verse says that it should be taken to mean that a conquering army takes only what it needs during the fighting. . . . I stood in a corner and I thought to myself, 'What a peculiar army this is. . . . ' But there was really something in it.

"After that, there was no more looting in our company."

That is the kind of Israel we all respect and love—an Israel where a commanding officer of an army unit quotes Bible to teach his soldiers ethical conduct, where the soldiers are steeped enough in learning to be able to counter with another verse, and where the issue is resolved through an interpretation from a medieval biblical commentator.

The Israel of the Six Day War understood the teaching of the prophet, speaking in the name of God: "Not by might, nor by power, by My spirit said the Lord of Hosts" (Zecariah 4:6).

That was an Israel that lived the vision of its first prime minister, David Ben Gurion, who taught, "The State of Israel will prove itself not by material wealth, not by military might or technical achievement, but by its moral character and its human values."

Yet victory is not always as sweet as it first seems.

Israel—praised and celebrated for her military prowess and her manifest spirit—was left to govern the territories she had captured, left to deal with the people she had conquered, left to engage a world that was little used to Jewish parity.

In the beginning, Israel was hailed. She brought electricity and running water and toilets and roads and schools to people who had been suppressed and oppressed by their own governments for the nineteen years between 1948 and 1967.

But the inherent human craving for self-determination and independence was more powerful than physical amenities.

Soon, Syria—which, for nineteen years, had used the Golan Heights for nothing more than to shoot rockets down into Israel's border *kibbutzim*—claimed that the empty hills were her mother earth.

Soon, Egypt—which, for nineteen years, had used the Sinai desert for nothing more than war games—claimed that the barren sand dunes were holy land.

Soon, there was an outcry for an independent Palestinian state in the West Bank.

It was a curious demand, for who had heard a word about Palestinian self-determination for the nineteen years that Jordan had used people as political fodder, keeping them in squalid refugee camps, rather than integrating them into society?

Who had heard of the desire for a Palestinian state in the nineteen years that Jordan controlled the West Bank?

Who, for that matter, had heard much of people or a political entity called Palestinians?

In a historical second, almost the entire world joined the Arab world in making a new demand on Israel: If you want peace with us, you must give back the land which you took from us when we went to war against you.

Israel was issued a unique and unbelievable ultimatum, never before given to any country in the recorded history of the world: In order to have peace, the victor must return land to the vanquished.

The occupation became a burden, an albatross, a quagmire of conflicting interests.

The military victory of the Yom Kippur War of 1973 exacted its psychic toll.

The ongoing war of attrition, the random terrorists attacks, the boggled incursion into Lebanon, the civil disobedience of the *intifada*, the killings—defensive and offensive—continued to shake Israel at her very roots, and cut deep into the national conscience.

Everyone agreed: Israel must be able to survive and flourish in secure and defensible borders; Israel must find her way to peace with her neighbors. But few In Israel could agree on how to best achieve her goals.

The daily battle—liberally tempered with both self-doubt and self-confidence—was between resistance and accommodation.

Israeli society—and Jews living around the world—split in two: the hard-liner hawks and the conciliator doves.

Israelis—and Jews living around the world—were confused, pained, and deeply saddened, and began asking hard, probing questions:

Is this the people and the land that were called by God to be "a light unto the nations?" (after Isaiah 42:6 and 49:6).

Is this land God gave to us as an everlasting possession ours only through force and intimidation?

Is this land that God promised us best secured by building instant settlements?

Is this land best protected by bombing villages to root out suspected terrorists?

Is this the much-lauded Israeli army shooting into crowds of children?

Question and criticize we can and must—lovingly, yet forcefully—for our moral sensibilities are sorely tested; our sense of justice, of fairness, of right and wrong, severely challenged.

The Arabs want what we Jews have always wanted—freedom and independence, self-determination and self-rule, in their own land. Arab mothers want their children to grow up—safe and secure, in a place of peace.

We—who have been oppressed for so long—have become, for many, the oppressors.

Have we lost our direction, our focus? Have we forgotten our moral mandate, our eternal mission?

Israelis agonize over the dilemma. Fiercely determined to safeguard their own people and land against all danger and peril, at the same time they affirm human dignity and rights for all peoples. Wanting to recapture the spirit and vision of its beginnings, Israel valiantly seeks a just solution that will satisfy everyone—Israelis of every political persuasion, Arab governments, the Palestinians, world Jewry, the nations of the world, and world public opinion.

The Jews of the world share Israel's quandary, but the stakes are not the same. Our sense of morality and justice may be challenged, but it is not our sons and daughters who daily defend the land with their lives.

So how can we ever know the pressures and the tensions of assuring daily survival? How can we question Israel's means of protecting herself in the best way she knows how? Why do we still sit here—in relative comfort and safety—while our brothers and sisters build the land and fend off the danger?

Our doubts or ambivalence fade when we remember Golda Meir's warning: "The Arabs can lose a thousand times, but we can lose only once."

So we say to Israel: We will continue to question and criticize and call you to moral account. But here are our hearts and our hands. We are your partners in building up and sustaining our homeland. We share with you in your struggles. We offer you our knowledge, our skills, our participation, our commitment, our love.

We are inextricably bound together. What happens to any Jew happens to every Jew. What happens to the Land of Israel happens to all the People of Israel.

We know that together we can overcome any obstacle, meet the emerging challenges, and forge a secure, peaceful, worthy future for the Jewish people in the Jewish land.

For we know that there is so much at stake.

We know, with the first Chief Rabbi of Israel, Rav Kook, that "It is in the Holy Land that the spirit of our people will develop, and they will become (again) a light for the world."

So we yearn for the day when God will, in the words of the evening prayer, "spread over us the tabernacle of peace—over us and over Jerusalem." And we yearn for a just and a lasting peace for Israel and her neighbors—open boundaries for travel and trade and cultural exchange; life without the constantly lurking shadow of attack and destruction; the end of violence; new security and safety.

We yearn for the day when the lion and lamb will lie down together, when in Israel—and across her borders—air raid shelters will be turned into nursery school rooms, and military bunkers will become playgrounds.

And with the psalmist, we "Pray for the peace of Jerusalem. May those who love you be at peace. May there be well-being within your walls, peace within your citadels. For the sake of my kin and my friends, I say now, 'Peace unto you.' For the sake of the Lord our God, I seek your good" (Psalm 122:6–9).

DESTINY AWAITS: THE QUESTION

Even as we pray for peace for the land and the people of Israel, we who live outside the land have our own peace disturbed by a question that nags at us and haunts us.

For 1,900 years, Jews who wandered from land to land, Jews who lived as guests in host countries, Jews who suffered and died at the hands of the persecutors and the tyrants, would have crawled on hands and knees if only they had the opportunity to end the exile, and come home to the Jewish land.

Now, for the first time in 1,900 years, nothing stands in our way. The land is there, the gates are wide open, the gleaming El Al jet is poised on the runway.

Yet we who could return to our homeland do not.

Instead, we remain in the country of our birth, or the country of our sojourn, the countries of our comfort and convenience.

What, we wonder, will history say of us—what do we say of ourselves—the first Jewish generation in 1,900 years that can finally return to a free and independent Land of Israel but chooses not to do so?

What will history say of us—what do we say of ourselves—the voluntary exiles, the Jews of the diaspora who choose to remain in the diaspora, even though our ancestral homeland beckons, welcomes, and needs us?

I cannot answer the question myself, for after all, I am the question.

So I took my question to Jerusalem, where—for you and for me—I asked my friends.

I asked Carmi, who owns a jewelry store on Ben Yehudah Street. I asked Olga and her son Yigal, who own a bakery in the center of town. I asked Shaike, who guides tourists throughout the land. I asked Elie, who drives a bus but still goes off to the army to maneuver tanks for at least thirty days a year. I asked David and Rita, Jonny and Deena, Moshe and Margery, John and Natalie, Jerry and Maggie—American colleagues and friends who have made *aliyah*. I asked hotel clerks and university professors and government officials. I asked lifelong Israelis and new immigrants. I asked anyone and everyone who would listen to my question and respond with a thoughtful answer.

DESTINY UNFOLDS: THE ANSWER

I had anticipated some of the replies: "Come here. Be with us. We need you. Your people need you; your land needs you. The only place for a Jew to be is in Israel. How can you live anywhere else? How can you even consider staying in America, when Israel needs every Jew she can get? In America you do nothing that is really important. In Israel you will add Jewish strength to the Jewish land. If you do not come, Jewish history will belittle you and condemn you. Jewish history will never forgive you for not coming to join your people when you had the chance."

While I expected an answer like this, it was nevertheless chilling to hear. Am I really forsaking my people by not returning to Eretz Yisrael? Have I sold out to the comforts and luxuries of America when my people need me? Have my prayers to God been hollow, and my commitment to Jewish unity empty?

While my soul struggled with these stark questions, I heard another answer to my query from many of the people I questioned. It was a very different answer, but it was equally nagging and challenging.

"No," I was told, "Jewish history will not condemn you for not coming to live in Israel. History will understand that for one of the rare and precious times in 1,900 years, there are two great centers of Jewish life and Jewish creativity—Israel and the United States.

"We have our job here. We build and defend the land.

"You have your job there. You support us, and give us courage and love, and you create a dynamic Jewish life for yourselves and for us.

"The two jobs are very different, but they are equally important. It takes both of us to keep Jewish life strong. We, here in Israel, keep the homeland secure. You keep the American Jewish community vibrant. In your strength, we are strengthened, and Jews, Judaism, and the Jewish land all prosper.

"But," my friends warned, "Jewish history will condemn you if you do not do your job well.

"We have the Jewish land on which to live Jewish lives: rhythmed by the Jewish calendar, marking the Jewish holidays, walking the paths of Jewish history, speaking the Jewish language, reading Jewish literature. Even if we are not religiously observant, we are immersed every day in the continually unfolding Jewish experience.

"But you. Why have so many Jews forsaken God? Why do so few Jews in America attend synagogue? Why do so few Jewish children get a decent Jewish education? Why can't Jews read the Jewish Book in the Jewish language? Why have so many assimilated? Why have so many intermarried? Why are you having so few Jewish babies? How can America be a center for Jewish creativity if America's Jews are not committed to leading Jewish lives?

"You need not come to live in Israel to fulfill your role as a Jew in the modern world," I was told. "But if you remain in America, then you all must be serious, committed, involved Jews there. You must participate in Jewish ceremonies and rituals, celebrate Jewish holidays, give money to Jewish causes, marry Jewish men and women, have lots of Jewish babies. That is the way for you to meet your Jewish obligations.

"We will send our sons to defend the land. You send your sons and daughters to good Jewish schools, and bring them up in good Jewish homes. We will keep the land strong. You keep the faith strong.

"Together we will meet history's questions, and together we will give history a resoundingly affirmative answer of Jewish unity and Jewish affirmation."

So there is the answer. Some Israelis want us there to build, defend, and strengthen the land. Others are perfectly willing to have us stay in America, as long as we build, defend, and strengthen the faith.

Some of us will choose to go to Israel; others will choose to remain in America. But with either choice—both, we now know, valid and worthy—we are to be not passive observers, but active participants in building up and sustaining the Jewish people, the Jewish land, the Jewish heritage.

Then history will not have to question us. History will be very proud of us.

A PLACE LIKE NO OTHER

For all their earthly reality and worldly concerns, Israel is a land alone, and Jerusalem is a city like no other.

A Midrash (Tanchuma, Lev., Kedoshim 10) teaches, "Just as the navel is placed in the center of the human body, the Land of Israel is placed at the center of the world. . . . Israel is the center of the world, Jerusalem is the center of Israel, and the Temple is the center of Jerusalem. In the Holy of Holies, there was a stone—the foundation-stone of the world."

A 1581 woodcut map by the cartographer Heinrich Buenting has the world in the shape of a three-leafed clover. Europe, Asia, and Africa are each a leaf, spread out from the center circle, which is Jerusalem.

The modern writer Israel Zangwill taught that "Jerusalem is more a state of mind than a place."

And Elie Wiesel captured her essence—for himself and for us—when he was asked, "You were born in Transylvania; you have apartments in New York and Paris; you teach in Boston. Where is your home?" Replied Wiesel, "Jerusalem—when I am not there."

The Talmud put it most succinctly: "Jerusalem is eternity" (BT Ber. 58a).

The great dramas of existence will be played out in her.

Her very name embodies the eternal quest, for she is called עיר שלום, *eir shalom,* "the city of peace," ירושלים Yerushalayim, Jerusalem.

Her very being bespeaks the eternal mission. "It shall come to pass in the days to come that the mountain of the house of the Lord will be established as the highest of mountains, and shall be raised above the hills. And all the nations shall come and say, 'Come let us go up to the mountain of the Lord, to the house of Jacob; that He may teach us His ways, and that we may walk in His paths.' For from out of Zion shall go forth the law, and the word of the Lord from Jerusalem" (Isaiah 2:2–3).

Her very presence evokes the eternal vision of the long-awaited moment of ultimate redemption. "At that time, Jerusalem will be called the 'Throne of the Lord,' and all nations shall assemble there in the presence of the Lord, in Jerusalem . . ." (Jeremiah 3:17).

That is why tradition teaches that when the world has been perfected under the Kingdom of God, when *masheach,* the messiah, comes, he will enter into the gates of

Jerusalem. Within her holy walls, the celebration of joy and thanksgiving will begin, and everyone who has ever lived will return to that sacred place.

HEAVENLY JERUSALEM

Yet with all her earthly tasks, it is not enough for Jerusalem to be only ירושלים של מטה *Yerushalayim shel matah*, the "Jerusalem below."

Jerusalem is more.

For, according to the Midrash (Tanchuma, Ex.. Pikuday 1), out of His great love for the Jerusalem below, God made another Jerusalem in the highest heavens.

It was not enough for His children to dwell in the earthly Jerusalem. God Himself wanted Jerusalem as His own heavenly abode. So He made ירושלים של מעלה *Yerushalayim shel ma'alah,* "the Jerusalem above."

Thus the eternal connection: the earthly Jerusalem as the inspiration for the heavenly Jerusalem; the heavenly Jerusalem as the ideal for the earthly Jerusalem—interwoven, inseparable—timeless, limitless, never-ending.

CONNECTING HEAVEN AND EARTH

But it is not even enough to have two Jerusalems—one in the heavens and one on earth.

The Midrash (Pesikta de Rav Kahana 143b) teaches in the name of Rabbi Eliezer ben Yaakov, "Jerusalem is destined to be elevated, and rise up until she touches the 'Throne of Glory.'"

Jerusalem is the mystical place where heaven and earth meet—where the glory of God and the greatness of God's children become one.

Jerusalem is the heart of the Jewish People, the soul of humankind, the spirit of God.

ISRAEL AND JERUSALEM: NOW AND FOREVER

Israel and Jerusalem—enduring reality, eternal symbol, life-breath itself.

The *reality* of the Jewish people in the Jewish land—once, again, and forever.

The *symbol* of the long-awaited perfection of the world; the end of days at God's holy mountain; the coming of *masheach;* the ultimate redemption.

The very *life-breath* of existence—"O, Israel," sang the poet, "the very life of souls is in your land."

"Rejoice with Jerusalem and be glad for her, all you that love her" (Isaiah 66:10).

"And give Him no rest, until He establishes Jerusalem, and makes her praised on earth" (Isaiah 62: 7).

"For Zion's sake, I will not be silent, for the sake of Jerusalem, I will not be still, until her triumph emerges radiant, and her deliverance like a flaming torch" (Isaiah 62:1).

The fervent prayer for the Jewish People and the Jewish Land is recited time after time, day after day. It is a prayer to which all people of peace and good will can add a heartfelt, "Amen."

"As God establishes peace in the highest heavens, so may He establish peace for us, for the People and the Land of Israel, and for all humankind"—now and forevermore.

9

HIGHLIGHTS OF JEWISH HISTORY

The history of Judaism is long and proud.

Through more than 3,800 years of the Jewish experience, there have been times of great discovery, unlimited creativity, and soaring achievement, mixed liberally with times of deep despair, painful suffering, and broken dreams. Centuries of freedom and independence gave way to millennia of exile and wandering. More than once—more than ten times—acceptance, admiration, and honor were shattered by tyranny, persecution, and—all too often—death.

Through it all, Jews and Judaism survived, prevailed, and flourished because of an enduring belief in God, a commitment to fulfill God's *mitzvot,* abiding faith in community, and unbounded hope and trust in the future.

To fully understand Judaism, it is necessary to have a broad perspective of Jewish history—to put the development of Jewish beliefs and practices into historical context.

There are many fine books that can and should be consulted and studied in order to gain an understanding and a mastery of the scope of Jewish history.

What is given here is a reference, an outline of Jewish history—first a concise timeline, then a complete annotated listing of events.

These are the most important events, the events that have had the greatest impact on Jewish life.

Here is the way to understand the historical setting, the philosophical and political environment, the times, people, and ideas that influenced, shaped, and formed Judaism and the Jewish People.

Here are the events—great and small—that make up Jewish history.

THE CONCISE TIMELINE OF
JEWISH HISTORY

BEFORE THE COMMON ERA

ca. 1800	Abraham declares belief in the One Lord God
ca. 1250	The exodus from Egypt and the giving of Torah at Mt. Sinai
ca. 1200	Entry into the Promised Land of Israel
1030	The Israelite monarchy is established
950	The Holy Temple is built
931	The Kingdom splits into two, Israel and Judah
750–450	The age of the prophets
722	The Kingdom of Israel is destroyed; only Judah remains
586	The Holy Temple is destroyed by the Babylonians and the people sent into exile
538	Permission to return from exile
520	The Second Holy Temple is built
200	The Rabbinic Period begins

THE COMMON ERA

1	The birth of Jesus
70	The Second Holy Temple is destroyed by the Romans, and the people sent into exile
600	The Talmud is completed and the Rabbinic Period ends
632	The death of Mohammed and the beginnings of Islam
THE MIDDLE AGES	Continued development of Jewish law and theology; expulsions from many lands; the beginning of the kabbalah, the mystical tradition; the "Golden Age" in Spain; the Reformation of Martin Luther; the publication of the Shulchan Aruch
1654	First Jews come to North America
MID-1700S	The *Haskalah*, the Enlightenment,
1791	The Emancipation—France grants full political rights to the Jews
1939—45	The Holocaust
1948	The modern State of Israel established

THE HIGHLIGHTS OF JEWISH HISTORY

ca. 1800   *The Covenant between God and Abraham*
Abraham's declaration in his belief in the One Lord God; the beginning of Judaism.

ca. 1700   *The Hebrews Migrate to Egypt*
The sons of Jacob begin a 450-year sojourn in Egypt.

ca. 1250   *The Exodus*
Moses leads the Children of Israel out of Egyptian slavery.

ca. 1250   *The Revelation at Mt. Sinai*
God gives His commandments to the Children of Israel.

ca. 1200   *The Conquest of Canaan*
Joshua leads the Children of Israel into the Promised Land.

ca. 1200–
    1030   *The Period of the Judges*
The Tribes settle into the land; a time of unrest and strife; attacks from surrounding nations; the civil rule of a succession of judges.

    1030   *Saul Anointed King*
The establishment of the monarchy.

    1010   *The Reign of King David*
The warrior-poet-king establishes Jerusalem as the capital and centralizes sacrificial worship there.

    970   *The Reign of King Solomon*
The wise, peaceful king brings a period of stability and harmony to the land and the people.

    950   *The Holy Temple Is Built*
The centralization of the worship of God into the magnificent Temple in Jerusalem; the unity of the political and religious life of the land and the people.

    931   *The Split of the Kingdom*
Following the death of Solomon, the united kingdom splits into two—the ten tribes of Israel, led by Jeroboam, and the two tribes of Judah, led by Rechoboam.

750–450   *The Age of the Prophets*
God's message of obedience to the *mitzvot* and social justice; punishment for transgression; repentance, forgiveness, and restoration—all
taught by God's messengers, the prophets.

> The date given for each prophet is the approximate date of the beginning
> of his prophecy. Some of the prophets continued to prophesy for many
> years:
> 750 Amos
> 745 Hosea
> 740 Micah, Isaiah
> 700 Jonah
> 650 Nachum
> 625 Jeremiah, Zephaniah
> 605 Habakkuk
> 590 Ezekiel
> 520 Zechariah, Haggai
> 450 Obadiah, Joel, Malachi

722   *The Assyrian Defeat of the Kingdom of Israel*
The kingdom of Israel is destroyed and vanishes forever, leading to the
designation of the "ten lost tribes."

622   *The Reformation of King Josiah*
Religious renewal and a national commitment to following God's law.

600   *The Beginning of the Babylonian Domination*
Religious and political oppression and persecution from the foreign
invader and occupier.

586   *The Fall of Jerusalem, the Destruction of the Holy Temple, and the Exile*
The land plundered and overrun by the Babylonians; the end of sacrificial worship at the Holy Temple; the end of political independence and
sovereignty.

586   *Babylonian Exile*
Jewish existence without the Holy Temple; the beginning of the formulation of prayers as worship; Jewish existence as inhabitants in a host
country.

538   *King Cyrus of Persia Grants Permission to Return to the Land of Israel*
Persia defeats Babylonia and permits the Jewish People to return to
Israel.

ca. 520   *The Rebuilding of the Holy Temple*
Sacrificial worship in the centralized Sanctuary in Jerusalem resumes.

| ca. 450 | *The Events of Purim* |
| | In Persia, the plot to wipe out the Jewish People is foiled by the beautiful Queen Esther. |

| 450 | *Religious Reformation Led by Ezra* |
| | The establishment of the synagogue as a permanent institution; the establishment of a regular cycle of reading the Torah and hearing God's law; a stringent prohibition against intermarriage. |

| 450–330 | *The Men of the Great Assembly* |
| | A loose confederation of rabbinic sages gives religious (and some political) leadership to the people. |

| 336–323 | *The Reign and Conquests of Alexander the Great* |
| | The Greek world spreads its influence; Hellenistic dominance begins in the Land of Israel. |

| 250 | *The Beginnings of the Pharisees* |
| | The development of the Oral Law and the growth of the leadership of the Rabbinic sages. The development of the sects opposing the Pharisees—the Sadducees and the Essenes. |

| 200 | *The Political Dominance of Antiochus of Syria* |
| | Representing the Greeks, Antiochus imposes a series of political and religious restrictions on the Jewish People. |

| 165 | *The Maccabeean Revolt* |
| | The Maccabees lead a military uprising for religious freedom, defeat the army of Antiochus, recapture and rededicate the Holy Temple. These are the events that lead to the establishment of the festival of Chanukah. |

| 140 | *The Establishment of the Second Jewish Commonwealth* |
| | The Hasmonean Dynasty (the Maccabees) wins political independence from Syria and reestablishes a free and independent Jewish State, inaugurating a period of great geographical expansion, population growth, and religious, cultural, and social reform and development. |

| 63 | *Pompey Captures Jerusalem* |
| | The beginning of Roman rule, with its political and religious restrictions. |

| 37 | *The End of the Hasmonean Dynasty and the Beginning of the Rule of Herod* |
| | Internal strife leads to the invitation to the Romans to govern Israel; the rule of the cruel Herod the Great begins. |

1   *The Birth of Jesus*
Originally a traveling Jewish preacher, Jesus later becomes the central
figure in the establishment of a new religion.

> The year 1 is the popular designation used to mark the birth of Jesus
> and the beginning of the Common Era. According to the Gospel
> accounts, the actual birth of could have been as early as 4 B.C.E. or as
> late as 6 C.E.

36   *Jesus Is Crucified*
The death of Jesus is the catalyst for the formation of a new religion—
Christianity.

70   *The Fall of Jerusalem, the Destruction of the Second Holy Temple, and the
Exile*
The land plundered and overrun by the Romans; the end of sacrificial
worship at the Holy Temple; the end of any hope for the restoration of
political independence and sovereignty; exile.

70   *The Establishment of the Academy at Yavneh*
Rabbi Yochanan ben Zakkai sneaks out of a besieged Jerusalem and
obtains permission from the Roman general to establish a center of
Jewish learning and the seat of the Sanhedrin (the Jewish court) in the
outlying town of Yavneh. Judaism survives the destruction of Jerusalem
and the Holy Temple through this new center, where Jewish learning
and the religious authority of the rabbis is supreme.

73   *The Fall of Masada*
The last stronghold of Jewish resistance to the Romans falls and the
destruction of Jewish independence is complete.

ca. 90–100   *The Bible Is Canonized*
The sages make the final decisions as to which books are included in or
excluded from the Bible. (Some scholars contend that the final canonization was not complete until ca. 250–300 C.E.)

132–35   *The Bar Kochba Rebellion*
Another uprising against the Roman Emperor Hadrian fails; the final
attempt by the Jews of Israel to regain the land by military force is
crushed.

ca. 200   *The Mishnah Is Codified*
The first formal compilation of the Oral Law (the teachings and legal decisions of the rabbis in the period 200 B.C.E.–200 C.E.) is completed by the editor, Rabbi Yehuda HaNasi.

312   *Christianity Is Recognized as the Official Religion of Rome*
The Emperor Constantine spreads Christianity throughout the vast Roman Empire.

325   *The Council of Nicaea*
The emerging Christian Church changes the Sabbath from Saturday to Sunday, fixes the date of Easter, and restricts religious and political rights of Jews, thus formalizing the theological split between Judaism and Christianity.

359   *The Jewish Calendar Is Fixed*
The sage Hillel institutes calendar reform and fixes the dates of Jewish observances.

ca. 500   *The Jerusalem Talmud Is Completed*
The sages remaining in the Land of Israel extend the Oral Law of the Mishnah, adding their own teachings (called the Gemara). The Jerusalem Talmud (combination of the Mishnah and the Gemara) focuses on issues of law for those who are still living within the (non-independent) Land of Israel.

ca. 600   *The Babylonian Talmud Is Completed*
The sages living in exile (centered in Babylonia) extend the Oral Law of the Mishnah, adding their own teachings (called the Gemara). The Babylonian Talmud (combination of the Mishnah and the Gemara) focuses on issues of law for those who are living in the diaspora.

614   *The Persians Capture Jerusalem*
For the first time in 500 years, Jews are permitted to settle in Jerusalem.

629   *The Byzantine Empire (Rome) Recaptures Jerusalem*
The Jewish settlement in Jerusalem is short-lived. Roman rule is reestablished and new restrictions are imposed upon the Jews.

> By the seventh century, Jews continue to live in Babylonia and throughout Arabia, and, Jews also live in many lands in Europe, including northern Italy, Spain and the Franco-German realm. In all these countries, various restrictions are placed upon the Jews; in no country do Jews have full political rights.

632   *The Death of Mohammed*
The new-found religion of Islam is established and spreads throughout the Arab world. Many Jews live in countries now dominated by Moslem rule.

638   *Omar Conquers Jerusalem*
The successor to Mohammed spreads the Moslem influence into the Land of Israel. Jerusalem grows and flourishes under Moslem rule.

> The Moslem influence spreads throughout the Arab world and Europe. Islam comes into serious conflict with Christianity for adherents and supremacy. In some places, Jews are caught up in the conflict and suffer; in other places (particularly Spain) Judaism is allowed to thrive. The "Golden Age" in Spain (ca. 950–1200) is a time of great Jewish scholarship, creativity, and flourishing culture.

ca. 760   *The Karaites Split from Mainline Judaism*
The Karaite sect rejects the authority of the Oral Law, and accepts only Torah Law as binding.

870   *First Prayerbook Is Outlined*
In Babylonia, Amram ben Sheshna Gaon systematically outlines the first prayerbook.

940   *Prayerbook Outline Is Formalized*
In Babylonia, Saadya Gaon compiles a more complete, more logical, better organized prayerbook that serves as the basic prayerbook model from then until modern times.

1040–1105   *The Life of Rashi*
Rabbi Shlomo ben Yitzchak (Rashi) of France is the greatest commentator on the Bible and the Talmud. His commentaries form the basis for all future commentators and remain paramount biblical and talmudic commentaries.

1066   *Jews Settle in England*
Following the Norman Conquest, Jews are permitted to live in England.

1086–1142   *The Life of Yehuda HaLevi*
The poet-philosopher wrote the *Kuzari*, a work strongly advocating the supremacy of Judaism over all other religions.

1096   *The First Crusades*
The Christian Crusaders murder tens of thousands of Jews in their quest to spread Christian supremacy throughout Europe.

1099   *The Crusaders Capture Jerusalem*
        Once again, Jerusalem comes under Christian rule.

1135–1204   *The Life of Maimonides*
        Moses Maimonides (known as the Rambam) authors a code of Jewish
        law, the *Mishnah Torah,* and a philosophical work, *The Guide to the
        Perplexed.*

1215   *The Lateran Council*
        Under Pope Innocent III, severe restrictions are placed on the Jews
        (including the requirement of wearing a yellow identification badge).

1250–1305   *The Life of Moses de Leon*
        De Leon of Spain authors the *Zohar, The Book of Splendor,* mystical
        interpretations of the Torah, thus beginning the period of the kabbalah,
        spiritual and mystical teachings of the hidden meaning of the text, lead-
        ing toward the highest awareness of the purposes of human existence.

1290   *The Jews Are Expelled from England*
        The first countrywide expulsion of Jews for religious/economic reasons.

1291   *Moslems Recapture the Land of Israel*
        Ousting the Crusaders, Moslems—centered in Cairo—once again rule
        Israel, beginning what is known as the Mamluk Period.

1394   *The Jews Are Expelled from France*
        Again, Jews are expelled from a country for religious/economic reasons.

1492   *The Jews Are Expelled from Spain*
        Following the Inquisition, where thousands of Jews were tortured and
        murdered, the Jews are expelled from Spain, bringing to an end the Jew-
        ish "Golden Age" of Spain.

ca. 1500   *The Jews Are Expelled from Portugal and from German Cities*
        The continuing expulsion of Jews from European cities.
        The Jews expelled from Spain relocate to Holland, Turkey, the Arab
        lands, some to the Land of Israel, and some eventually to South America
        and Central America. The Jews expelled from central and western
        Europe make their way to eastern Europe and Russia. Old centers of Jew-
        ish life are repopulated; new centers grow up: some flourish; others lead
        to lives of struggle and hardship.

1517   *The Ottoman Empire Conquers the Land of Israel*
        Once again, Israel comes under the domination of yet another new
        ruler—this time the Ottoman Turks.

1534–1572	*The Life of Isaac Luria*

Known as the Ari, Luria is the central figure of the kabbalists, the mystics of Safed, in the north of Israel.

1544	*The Reformation of Martin Luther*

In addition to demanding reform in the Church, which will lead to the establishment of Protestantism, Luther (of Germany) writes virulent anti-Jewish propaganda.

1555	*The Establishment of Ghettos*

Pope Paul IV orders Jews to live in segregated areas throughout Italy.

1567	*The Publication of the Shulchan Aruch*

Joseph Karo authors a new code of Jewish law, the Shulchan Aruch, intended as a popular and concise guide to Jewish law.

1626–1676	*The Life of Shabati Zevi*

Responding to the dire conditions in which many Jews live, Zevi declares himself to be the messiah. His claims are rejected and, in despair, he converts to Islam.

1648	*The Chmielnitzki Massacres*

The Ukranian Cossack Bogdon Chmielnitzki leads a massacre of Polish Jewry that leaves more than 100,000 Jews dead.

1654	*The First Jews Come to North America*

Seventeen Jews, sailing from Brazil, land in New Amsterdam, beginning the Jewish sojourn in North America and in what will become the United States.

1655	*The Jews Are Readmitted to England*

Under Oliver Cromwell, Jews are permitted to return to England.

1656	*Baruch Spinoza Is Excommunicated*

For his radical theological views, Baruch Spinoza of Amsterdam is excommunicated from the Jewish community.

1700–60	*The Life of Israel Ba'al Shem Tov*

In response to oppressive living conditions for Jews in much of Europe, Israel ben Eliezer, taking on the name Ba'al Shem Tov (Master of the Good Name) founds Chasidism, a way to approach God spiritually with both contemplative meditation and fervent joy. Chasidism attracts many followers, who establish Chasidic centers in many towns. The vocal opponents of the Chasidim are known as the Mitnagdim, who maintain the rational, scholarly approach to Jewish thought and observance.

1720–97   *The Life of the Vilna Gaon*
Rabbi Elijah of Vilna represents the epitome of rabbinic learning and scholarship. His genius and his devotion to Jewish learning and law spreads his reputation throughout the Jewish world. He is a strong opponent of the Chasidim.

1729–1786   *The Life of Moses Mendelssohn*
An observant Jew and a passionate German national, Mendelssohn urges Jewish entrance into the modern world. He inspires a movement called the *Haskalah,* the Enlightenment.

1790   *President Washington Sends a Letter to the Jews*
In a letter to the Jews of the Synagogue in Newport, Rhode Island, United States President George Washington writes that he envisions a country "which gives bigotry no sanction . . . persecution no assistance." For the first time in history, Jews live in a country where they enjoy full and equal human and political rights—as a birthright of citizenship.

1791   *France Grants Full Rights to the Jews*
Jews are granted full religious and political rights in a "host country." This emancipation, coupled with the enlightenment advocated by the *Haskalah* movement brings Judaism fully into the modern world.

ca. 1800   *Russia Creates the Pale of Settlement*
Severe restrictions against the Jews are established in Russia. At least one-third of Russia's Jews are ordered to live in the isolated, barren, brutally cold Pale of Settlement.

1807   *Napoleon's Sanhedrin*
Napoleon, Emperor of France, convenes a meeting of Jewish leaders to determine Jewish loyalty as French citizens. While he finds satisfactory response to most issues, the reality of Judaism as a distinct faith community remains.

ca. 1818   *Reform Judaism Founded in Germany*
In response to the Enlightenment and the emancipation, a group of German Jews begins a reform of Jewish belief and practice. In light of modern scholarship, they deny the Divine authorship of Torah, declaring Torah to be written by Divinely inspired human beings. They declare only the ethical law binding; ritual law is but instructive and inspirational. They reform the worship service, reflecting many of the customs of their non-Jewish neighbors. Judaism, they declare, is a religion like all other religions, and its adherents can be loyal, participating citizens of

their country of residence, without any conflict over their membership in Judaism as a Peoplehood.

1820–1880   *German Immigration to the United States*
In this sixty-year period, more than a half-million German Jews migrate to the United States, bringing with them new-found Reform Judaism. They quickly integrate into American life and enjoy great success in business, industry, academia, and government.

ca. 1840   *Judaism Regarded as a Science*
Leopold Zunz of Germany claims that Judaism can be studied in a scholarly way, just as any other science. Removing Judaism from the realm of faith and entering it into the realm of scientific study subjects Judaism to the scrutiny of critical thinking and scholarly analysis. There is violent opposition to Zunz's theory from traditional Jews.

ca. 1840   *The Rise of Neo-Orthodoxy*
Rabbi Samson Raphael Hirsch of Germany attempts to reconcile traditional Judaism with the modern age. While insisting on strict adherence to Jewish beliefs and observances, he permits secular study and limited integration into the non-Jewish community.

ca. 1848   *Musar Movement Is Founded*
Rabbi Israel Salanter dismisses current philosophical debate and advocates the ethical teachings and ethical behavior as the essence of Judaism.

1853   *Conservative Seminary Founded in Germany*
Zachariah Frankel attempts to bridge the differences between Orthodoxy and Reform by establishing a rabbinical seminary dedicated to modern, scientific study, while *conserving* many of the traditional elements of Jewish belief and practice that Reform had discarded.

1875   *Reform Seminary Established in the United States*
Rabbi Isaac Mayer Wise establishes the Hebrew Union College in Cincinnati, for the training of American Reform Rabbis. Eventually, branch schools are located in New York, Los Angeles, and Jerusalem.

1881–84; 1903–6; 1918–20
Pogroms Against the Jews
A series of three violent attacks, sanctioned by the Government, against the Jews of Russia. Tens of thousands die; hundreds of thousands flee the country.

1881   *Aliyah to the Land of Israel*
        In response to the Russian pogroms, the BILU movement forms to
        encourage immigration to the Land of Israel. Known as the First Aliyah,
        some 25,000 Jews come to Palestine from eastern Europe from 1881 until
        1903. This immigration sets the stage for subsequent Jewish migration to
        Palestine from Europe: the Second Aliyah (1904–14; 40,000 people); the
        Third Aliyah (1919–23; 35,000); the Fourth Aliyah (1924–28; 67,000); and
        the Fifth Aliyah (1929–39; 250,000.) During and just after World War II
        (1940–48), another 100,000 people come to Palestine.

1880–1920 *Russian Immigration to the United States*
        In this forty-year period, more than 2 million Russian Jews migrate to
        the United States, bringing with them their Yiddish language, their rela-
        tive poverty, much of their Russian culture, and their Orthodoxy (much
        of which is quickly lost). Because of their lack of secular education and
        sophistication, they are not warmly welcomed by the German Jews who
        preceded them to America. Their full integration into America takes
        a generation. Their children and grandchildren live the "American
        dream" in the "golden land" and attain education, affluence, and wide
        acceptance.

1885   *The Pittsburgh Platform Is Written*
        At a convention in Pittsburgh, Pennsylvania, the American Reform rab-
        binate articulates the guiding principles of American Reform Judaism.
        In 1937, in Columbus, Ohio, another platform of principles is articu-
        lated. This one returns Reform Judaism to somewhat more traditional
        beliefs and practices.

1894   *The Dreyfus Affair*
        In France, Alfred Dreyfus, a Jew, is falsely accused of treason. Though
        Jews enjoyed political equality in France for more than a century, the
        country is quick to use this innocent Jew as a scapegoat. Dreyfus is
        released from his imprisonment when French writer Émile Zola takes up
        his cause. The Dreyfus case suggests to many Jews that even in a nation
        where Jews have been granted political freedom, a Jew is never safe from
        unjust accusation and persecution.

1897   *The First Zionist Congress Meets*
        In response to the Dreyfus Affair, journalist Theodor Herzl, of Budapest
        and Vienna, writes *Der Judenstaat (The Jewish State),* advocating the
        creation of a free and independent Jewish state in Israel. More than 200
        delegates from nineteen countries attend the First Zionist Congress in

Basel, Switzerland, to garner ongoing support for a Jewish state. Through the work of Herzl and the Zionist Congress, modern Zionism is born as a political movement.

1902   *The Jewish Theological Seminary Is Established in the United States*
Under the leadership of Solomon Schechter, the reorganized Jewish Theological Seminary is established in New York (it had originally opened in 1887) as a seminary for the training of American Conservative rabbis. Eventually, branch schools are located in Los Angeles and Jerusalem.

1915   *Orthodox College/Seminary Is Established in the United States*
Yeshiva College (later, University) and its Rabbi Isaac Elchanan Rabbinical Seminary is established in New York for secular undergraduate studies in an Orthodox milieu, and for the training of American Orthodox rabbis. Eventually, a branch school is located in Los Angeles. A number of other smaller but influential Orthodox seminaries are also established throughout the country, most notably in greater New York, Baltimore, Chicago, and Lakewood, New Jersey.

1917   *British Defeat Turks, Capture Jerusalem, and Issue the Balfour Declaration*
The British defeat the Turks, and once again, Israel is controlled by yet another foreign power. But the British issue the Balfour Declaration (named for the foreign secretary, Lord Balfour) which states that the British Government "views with favor the establishment in Palestine of a national home for the Jewish People."

1917   *The Russian Revolution*
With the defeat of the Czar and the establishment of a Communist government, Jews are granted political equality in Russia. However, the 1920 publication of *The Protocols of the Elders of Zion,* a forged document allegedly written by Jews, describing their plan to take over the world economically and politically, greatly increases international anti-Semitic sentiment.

1933   *Adolf Hitler Comes to Power in Germany*
Adolf Hitler, whose published book, *Mein Kampf,* is a blueprint for the extermination of the Jews, is elected Chancellor of Germany in free and open elections.

1934   *The Publication of* Judaism as a Civilization
Rabbi Mordecai Kaplan's controversial book claims that Judaism is not only a religion but a peoplehood. The principle is denounced by Ortho-

dox Jewry, but eventually will be widely accepted by the majority of Jews, and leads to the formation of the Reconstructionist movement.

1938   *Kristallnacht*
The Nazi plot to destroy the Jews turns violent as, in one night, most German synagogues and hundreds of Jewish-owned German businesses are destroyed. Almost 100 Jews are killed; more than 30,000 are arrested and sent to concentration camps.

1939   *The British White Paper Is Issued*
In a dramatic turnabout, Great Britain reverses the position of the Balfour Declaration, declaring instead that it is no longer British policy to support the creation of a Jewish state in Palestine. At the same time, it limits immigration into Palestine to no more than 15,000 Jews a year—giving Jews attempting to flee Nazi Europe no place to go and effectively aiding the Nazis in their program of eliminating the Jews.

1939–45 *The Holocaust*
Under the leadership of Adolf Hitler, the Nazis murder 6 million Jews (and millions of others) in a systematic attempt to wipe every Jew off the face of the earth.

1947   *United Nations Votes Partition in Palestine*
On November 29 the United Nations votes partition in Palestine, paving the way for the creation of an independent Jewish state.

1948   *The State of Israel Is Declared*
On May 14, in response to the United Nations vote, Israel declares independence. The Third Jewish Commonwealth is born, and for the first time in almost 1,900 years, the Jews have a free and independent homeland.

1948   *Israel's War of Independence*
In response to Israel's Declaration of Independence, the combined armies of the Arab nations invade Israel. Against all odds, Israel prevails. However, following the cease-fire, Jerusalem is divided and part of it (including the site of the Holy Temples) comes under Arab control.

1948–49 *Jews Return to the Jewish State*
Almost 250,000 Holocaust survivors make their way to Israel. In "Operation Magic Carpet," thousands of Jews living in the Yemen are brought to Israel. The repopulation of the Jewish state has begun.

1956   *The Sinai Campaign in Israel*
Egypt and Israel go to war. Israel prevails.

1967   *The Six Day War in Israel*
Egypt, Syria, and Jordan go to war against Israel. In a stunning victory,
Israel defeats the aggressors and captures large amounts of territory—all
in just six days.

1967   *The Reunification of Jerusalem*
The greatest achievement of the Six Day War is the capture of Jerusalem
and the reunification of the Holy City as the capital of Israel.

1968   *The Reconstructionist Rabbinical College Is Established in the United
States*
The Reconstructionist Rabbinical College is established in Philadelphia
to train American Reconstructionist rabbis.

1972   *First Woman Rabbi Ordained*
At the Hebrew Union College, the Reform seminary, Sally Priesand is
ordained as the first woman rabbi in history. The Reconstructionist and
Conservative seminaries follow, affirming full gender equality in every
aspect of Jewish life in Judaism's liberal movements.

1973   *The Yom Kippur War in Israel*
Egypt and Syria invade Israel on the holiest day of the Jewish calendar.
Israel will eventually prevail, but the unprovoked sneak attack and the
military might of the attackers take their toll. Israel suffers many casualties, and a deep psychological blow.

1979   *The Camp David Peace Accords*
Israel and Egypt sign a peace treaty, following intense negotiations led by
United States President Jimmy Carter at the presidential retreat, Camp
David.

1982   *Israel Invades Lebanon*
In an attempt to rid Lebanon of terrorists who randomly and frequently
attack inside Israel, the Israeli military begins a limited action. The
strong will of the Lebanese people—loyal to many different religious
and political leaders—and the very complicated Lebanese political situation turns a simple military exercise into a quagmire of miscalculations
and mistakes. Israel has a hard time extricating itself and undergoes a
deep soul-searching in justifying this operation.

1984   *Operation Moses Brings Ethiopian Jews to Israel*
Thousands of Ethiopian Jews are rescued from political and economic hardship and are brought to Israel.

1987   *The Intifada Begins in Israel*
Arab terrorist attacks and civilian uprisings are met with Israeli military action. The conflict—which is really an Arab bid for self-determination and independence and an Israeli insistence on security and protection—goes on for years.

1990   *Operation Exodus Brings Soviet Jews to Israel*
In the mid-1960s, the world became aware of the plight of almost 3 million Russian Jews held, against their will, in the Soviet Union. Despite worldwide protests, only a few thousand Soviet Jews were permitted to leave each year. Now the political climate changes, and hundreds of thousands of Soviet Jews come to Israel.

1991   *Operation Solomon Brings Ethiopian Jews to Israel*
The last of the Ethiopian Jews are permitted to leave and come to Israel in a stunning twenty-four-hour airlift.

1991   *Israeli-Arab Peace Talks Begin*
Under the sponsorship of the United States and other nations of the world, peace talks are held between Israel, Arab countries, and representatives of the Palestinian people, giving rise to the hope that peace can eventually come to Israel and her neighbors.

1993   *Israel and the Palestine Liberation Organization Sign Mutual Recognition Pact*
After decades of antagonism and terrorism, the PLO recognizes Israel's right to exist, and Israel grants Palestinians limited autonomy in the West Bank, paving the way for continuing peace talks between Israel, Palestinians, and Arab governments.

1994   *Israel and Jordan Sign Peace Treaty*
After being in an official "state of war" since the establishment of the Jewish state, Israel and Jordan agree to a peace treaty—full mutual recognition, diplomatic relations, open borders, and free trade—another dramatic step toward full peace between Israel and all her Arab neighbors.

In the post-World War II world, there have been three great centers of Jewish population—the United States, Israel, and the former Soviet Union. As more and more Russian Jews are permitted to leave that country, diminishing its Jewish population, the centers of Jewish life are now concentrated in Israel and the United States.

In both Israel and the United States, Jewish life is thriving, marking one of the only times in Jewish history in which Jewish life is simultaneously ever-growing, creative, and innovative in two widely separated geographical locales.

There are also significant Jewish communities in other parts of the world, most notably in Canada, Australia, Europe (particularly in England and France), South America (particularly in Argentina and Brazil), and parts of the Arab world. With the fall of communism in the former Soviet-bloc countries, small but newly revitalized Jewish communities are taking new root in eastern Europe.

Great challenges remain as the future unfolds: For Israel, peace with Arab neighbors is still elusive. The need to secure and defend the country takes great resources and energy that could otherwise be used to improve and enhance the everyday life of the country and its people. In the United States, a declining Jewish birthrate, an increasing interfaith marriage rate, apathy, and assimilation, threaten the vitality and the very future of the Jewish community.

Yet, at the very same time, in both Israel and America, there is great Jewish creativity, scholarship, and learning; deep commitment to Jewish causes; spirited Jewish renewal; and an abiding faith in the resiliency, strength, and survival of the Jewish People.

There is much of Jewish history still to be lived and written, and a great awareness that Jewish history now belongs to this generation of Jews to shape and mold. So, connected to past Jewish generations by faith, practice, tradition, and collective consciousness, and with enduring belief in its own abilities, virtues, and vision, this generation of Jews looks to the Jewish future with hope and determination.

THE LAST (BUT REALLY THE FIRST) JEWISH WORD

One final old Jewish legend:

Just like God, every eternal soul has all knowledge of the universe. Yet when a soul comes to earth and is placed in a physical body, it cannot bring with it the totality of knowledge; for on earth the soul must be delimited by the boundaries of human existence.

Just before a soul, now in the body of a baby in the womb, emerges into human life, an angel taps the baby on the upper lip—creating that little indentation right under the nose—and in so doing takes away the entirety of knowledge.

The soul, now a human being, lives its earthborn existence. But no matter how pleasing and satisfying its human sojourn, the soul—at its deepest and most hidden place—always feels a tinge of emptiness, a tinge of sadness. For at the core of its being, the soul sees tiny glimpses of all it once knew, and it sees momentary flashes of what it can know—and be—again.

That is why the soul-voyage of earthly existence is, at the same time, a journey back to the source, back to ultimate origin, back to infinite knowledge, back to God.

The angel—who feels bad for having taken away soul-knowledge—becomes a life guide.

And God—to whom each and every soul is a precious, eternal partner—gently shows the soul the way back to what it once had and what it will have again.

On earth—as they are through eternity—God's directions for the journey, the pathways back to all knowledge, are in the life-gift of Torah. Torah, and the Jewish teachings, traditions, and faith community that come from it, is the earthly bridge to the soul-world of spirit.

That is why the sage Yochanan ben Bag Bag taught, "Turn Torah, and turn it over again, for everything is in it; constantly contemplate it, grow old and gray over it, and do not swerve from it; for there is nothing more excellent than it" (Avot 5:25).

From ancient and ever-evolving Jewish teachings, you can learn enduring truths, and you can infuse your soul with ever-emerging heavenly wisdom.

On earth—as it is through eternity—God's presence shimmers in the light of divine being.

"God will be your everlasting light" (Isaiah 60:19).

You can be bathed in God's brilliance, so that your being continually reflects God; and your soul, which is a tiny spark of the Divine light, can grow in ever-evolving awareness.

On earth—as you will through eternity—you can journey happily and courageously.

"The whole world—here and there," taught the Chasidic Rebbe Nachman of Bratslav, "is a narrow bridge. But the main thing is not to be afraid."

On earth—as you will through eternity—you can humbly yet joyfully ask God for the greatest of all soul-gifts: that "goodness and covenantal love may be with you always; that you may dwell in God's house forever" (Psalms 23:6); and that "an ever-renewing light will shine upon you, and that it may be your blessing to see its splendor" (after *Or Chadash,* from the morning prayer, *L'Eyl Baruch*).

On earth—and through eternity—the Talmud's benediction (BT Berachot 17a) can be your most precious desire and most fervent prayer: "That your cherished hopes be fulfilled in your lifetime, and that your destiny be for worlds still to come; that your eyes shine with the light of holy words, and that your face always reflects the radiance of God."

INDEX

Ethical *mitzvot*, 33, 36–37
Ethical monotheism, 35–36
Ethical ritualism, 36–37
Evil/suffering: of each generation, 39–40; God's
    role with, 27–29; human, 20, 22–25; of "nat-
    ural disaster," 20–22; random-chance, 25–27.
    See also Holocaust
Exodus (Sh'mot), 73
Ezekiel, 76–77
Ezra, 80
Ezrat nashim (women's section), 215

Family purity (laws), 271–73
First Zionist Conference (1897), 327
Five Books of Moses, 73. *See also* Torah (law)
"Footprints" (Powers), 27
Forgiveness, 139–45
Four Questions (Passover), 171
Frankel, Victor, 188
Frankl, A. L., 335
Freedom Haggadah, 168
Free will, 20
Friday evening services, 128

Gabbai (synagogue official), 217–18
Galilee, 329
Galut (exile), 324–25
Ganzfried, Rabbi Solomon, 102
Gaon, Rabbi Saadya, 116, 202, 320
Gedaliah, governor of Judea, 198
Gefilte fish, 259
Gelilah (rolling of Torah Scroll), 219–20
Gemara, 97–98
Genesis (Bereshit), 73
Geonim, 99
Germany, 189–91
Ger tzedek (righteous proselyte), 65
Gerut (conversion), 65–71
Get (divorce document), 301–3
Gibbon, Edward, 189
Ginsburg, Asher, 130
Glueck, Nelson, 18
G'melut chasadim (good deeds), 253, 256
God: as author of Torah, 83–84; belief in one,
    4–5, 35–36; commandments of, 31–35;
    covenant with Jewish People, 17–19; evil
    and, 20–29; forgiveness from, 143–45; Jewish
    belief in, 1, 7–8, 11–16; listening to, 236–37;
    love of, 18–19; masculine/feminine aspects

of, 9, 240–41; names of, 8–9, 248–49; nega-
    tive answers from, 237–38; personal rela-
    tionship with, 242–45; Reconstructionist
    view of, 63; relationship with Jewish People,
    9–10, 17; will of, 13. *See also* Prayers
God is dead, 15
Golden, Harry, 231
Graf, Karl Heinrich, 83
Great Midrash, The, 114
"Great Purim Debate," 161

Habakkuk, 77
Hachnasat kallah (dowry), 254
Hachnasat orchim (hospitality), 253–54
Hadassah Hospital (Jerusalem), 58
Haftarah (reading from Prophets), 78, 209
Hagbah (lifting of Torah Scroll), 219
Haggadah (legend), 118, 167–68, 171
Haggai, 77
Haifa, 329
Halachah (Jewish law), 97, 104, 114
Halachic Midrashim, 114
HaLevi, Yehuda, 12–13
Hallel (praise), 210
Halvayat hamet (escorting the dead), 254–55
Haman, 158–61
Hamotzi (blessing for bread), 204
Hashgachah (*kashrut* supervision), 258, 261
Hasmonean Dynasty, 95
Hatafat dam (drawing of blood), 69, 288
HaTefilah (prayer), 228
Hatikvah (national anthem), 335–36
Hava'at shalom (bringing peace), 256
Havdalah (separation), 210
Hebrew Bible, 81
Hebrew language, 51–52
Hebrew name, 289–90
Hebron, 330
Herzl, Theodor, 327, 334
Heschel, Rabbi Abraham Joshua, 14–15, 139, 142,
    234, 245
Hesed in the Bible (Glueck), 18
High Holidays, 124, 138
"Historical revisionists," 192
Hitler, Adolph, 54, 64, 181, 183, 187–89
Holiness, 30–31
Holocaust: the affirmation, 193–94; description
    of, 183–86; explanations for, 188–91; impact
    on Jewish People, 181–82, 191–93; magnitude

61–62, 103; as peoplehood, 6, 54; personal responsibility within, 139–42; quest for the messiah, 43–50; Rabbinic, 95–96; on random suffering/evil, 26–27; Reconstructionist, 56–57, 63–64, 104; as religion of law, 106–13; as shared cultural experience, 51–54. *See also* Jewish worship; Reform Judaism

Judges, 75

Jung, Carl, 241

Kabbalah (mysticism), 115–16, 316–17
Kabbalat Shabbat (welcoming Sabbath), 209
Kabbalists, 13, 14, 110, 178, 316–17, 320, 366
Kaddish (doxology), 231–32, 307–8
Kallah (bride), 295
Kaplan, Rabbi Aryeh, 238
Kaplan, Rabbi Mordecai, 14, 63
Karo, Rabbi Joseph, 102, 106, 116
Kashrut (dietary laws): laws of, 257–65; purpose of, 265–68
Kavanah (spiritual intent), 227
Kazantzakis, Nikos, 233
Kedushah (holiness), 30–31
Keesay shel Eliyahu (Chair of Elijah), 287
Kehillah (community), 256
Kepah (head-covering), 221
Keri'ah (rending of garment), 307
Keriat hatorah (Torah reading), 208–9
Ketubah (marriage document), 298–99, 302
Ketuvim (writings), 78–81
Keva (order of prayer), 227
Kibbutz (collective farm), 331–32, 346
Kiddushin (marriage ceremony), 296–300
Kiddush (prayer for wine), 204
Kingdom of Israel, 45–46, 55–56, 58. *See also Eretz Yisrael* (Land of Israel)
Kingdom of Judah, 46, 55–56, 58
Kings, 75
Kinna hora (evil eye), 283–84
Kitzur Shulchan Aruch, 102
Klaf (parchment), 248
Klal Yisrael (unity of Jewish People), 64
Knesset (Israeli Parliament), 336–38
Kohen, 59, 292
Kol Nidre service, 135–36
Kook, Rav Avraham, 227, 350
Kosher food, 257–68
Kotel HaMa'aravi (Western Wall), 198–99, 325–26

Kushner, Harold, 15, 25
Kuzari (HaLevi), 12
Kvater (godfather), 287
Kvaterin (godmother), 287

Labriut (to your health), 282
Ladino, 52–53
Lag B'Omer, 175
Lamentations, 80, 196–98
Last Temptation of Christ, The (Kazantzakis), 233
Latter Prophets, 76–78
Law: Arba'ah Turim compilation of, 101–2; Conservative Judaism practice of, 62–63; evolution of Jewish, 106–13; Mishnah (Oral Law), 96–97; Mishnah Torah (code), 101; Orthodox Judaism practice of, 61; protecting converted Jew, 70–71; rabbinic court to administer, 274–75, 337; Reconstructionist Judaism practice of, 64; Reform Judaism practice of, 62; Shulchan Aruch compilation of, 102; Torah vs. natural, 13. *See also* Torah (law)
Law of Return, 340
Laws between God/humankind, 32
Laws between people, 32
L'chayim (To Life!), 278
Levayah (funeral), 306
Levi, 59, 291–92
Levi, Rabbi Joshua ben, 49
Leviticus (Vayikra), 73
Lions of Judah, 277
Liquor, 160–61
Lord, 7
"*L'shanah ha'ba-ah b'Yerushalayim*" (Next year in Jerusalem), 172–73
Lubavitch Chasidim, 62
Luchot (tablets of the Law), 276–77
Luria, Rabbi Isaac, 116

Ma'ariv (evening service), 207
Maccabees, 95, 152–53
Machzor (festival prayerbook), 117
Machzor Vitry, 117
Machzor Yannai, 117
Maftir (final *aliyah*), 219
Magen David (Star of David), 275–76, 334–35
Maimonides, Moses, 13, 101, 252
Major Prophets, 76–77
Malachi, 77

Palestine, 327, 348–49. *See also* Israel (modern state)

Palestine Liberation Organization, 334

Palestinian *intifada,* 333

Palestinian Talmud, 98

PARDES, 100

Parochet (covering of ark), 213–14

Parve food, 262

Path of Life, The, 101

Patrilineal descent, 56–57

Payot (sidelocks), 251

Pe'ah (corner), 250–51

People of Israel. *See* Jewish People

Peretz, Y. L., 52, 316

Personal responsibility, 139–42

Perushim, 100–101

"Pesach dishes," 164

Pesach l'atid (Passover of the Future), 174

Pesach (Passover), 123–24, 157, 162–74

Pesach "spring cleaning," 164–65

Philo, 12

Pidyon haben ceremony (redemption), 291–92

Pidyon shevuim (freedom for captives), 254

Powers, Margaret Fishback, 27

Prager, Dennis, 64

Prayer: community, 229–32; connecting through, 226–27; gender language of, 239–42; intent/structure/purpose of, 227–29; *kaddish* mourning, 231–32, 307–8; limitations of, 232–34; negative answers to, 237–38; new/old forms of, 238–39; possibilities of, 234–35; rewards of, 244–45; *yizkor* memorial, 177, 312. *See also* God

Prayer services, 202–6, 220. *See also* Jewish worship

Prayers of petition, 235–36

Proverbs, 79

Psalms, 79

P'tur (divorce grant), 301–2

Purim, 80, 124

Pushke (*tzedakah*-box), 252

"Questions and Answers" system, 103–4

Rabbinic Period: afterlife introduced during, 43–45, 314–16; Bible canonized during, 92; idea of God during, 11–12; law interpretation during, 108; *mitzvot* expounded dur-

ing, 33; political/social upheavals during, 95–96; use of Aramaic language during, 52

Random-chance evil, 25–27

Rashi, 100

Rav ("teacher"), 216

Rechoboam (son of Solomon), 45–46

Reconstructionist Judaism, 56–57, 63–64, 104

Redemption, 74

Reform Judaism: binding ritual law rejected by, 103–4; challenges to Judaism by, 14; Confirmation ceremony of, 178–79; Jewish definition under, 56–57; modern practice of, 62; *musaf* service eliminated by, 210

Reincarnation, 320–21

Repentance, 139, 145–46

Resurrection, 46–47, 315

Revelation, 74

R'fuah sh'laymah (speedy recovery), 282

"Righteous Gentiles," 186

Rishonim (the First Ones), 101

Ritual *mitzvot,* 33, 36–37

Ritual objects, 210–15

Roosevelt, Franklin, 187

Rosenzweig, Franz, 34

Rosh Chodesh (first day of month), 122–23

Rosh HaShanah (New Year), 119–20, 123–25, 130–34

Ruth, 65, 178

Ruth (Book of), 79

Saadya Gaon, 12

Sabra (native Israeli), 339

Sacrifice, 201–2

St. Louis (ship), 186

Samuel, 75

Sandak (assists circumcision), 287

Schachter-Shalomi, Rabbi Zalman, 15, 63

Schulweis, Rabbi Harold, 111

Sdom, 330

Second Holy Temple, 6, 196–99, 202, 324, 345. *See also* Holy Temples

Secular humanism, 15, 26

Seder (ritual meal), 167–68, 170–73

Sefer Torah, 74, 211–12. *See also* Torah (law)

Sefirat HaOmer (Counting of the *Omer*), 174–76

Sefirot, 13

Selichot service, 131

Sephardic Hebrew, 52

"Ten lost tribes," 45–46, 56, 58

Tephillin (phylacteries), 198, 223–25

Third Jewish Commonwealth. *See* Israel (modern state)

Tikkun Layl Shavuot (text study on the night of Shavuot), 178, 180

Tikkun olam (repairing the world), 37–42, 48

Tishah B'Av (destruction of Temple), 196–99

Torah (law): authorship of, 83–84; commandments of the, 31–35; constitutional basis of, 103; covenant legislated through, 18; cultural significance of, 5–6; described, 73–74; *keriat HaTorah* reading of, 208–9; modern neglect of, 179–80; natural law vs. law of, 13; Oral, 93–96; proof of, 86–87; purpose of, 89–90, 108; references to God in, 8; regarding *brit milah*, 286; regarding divorce, 300–303; response to skepticism in, 87–88; worship practices using the, 218–20; Written, 81–84. *See also* Law; *Sefer Torah*

Torah reading, 78

Torah *Sheb'al Peh* (Oral Torah), 93–96

Torah *Shebichtav* (Written Torah), 81–84

Tosaphot (The Additions), 100

Tribes of Israel, 57–59

Trop (cantillation), 220

T'shuvah (repentance), 139

T'shuvot (answers), 103

Tu B'Shevat (birthday of the trees), 155–56

Tur (The Four Rows), 101–2

Twelve tribes, 57–59

Tza'ar ba'alei chaim (protecting animals), 255

Tzahal (Israeli Army), 332–34

Tzedakah (justice), 249–52

Tziyonut (Zionism), 326–28

Union of Orthodox Jewish Congregations, 259

United Jewish Appeal, 64

Vatican II (1962–65), 190

Vatke, Wilhelm, 83

Vital, Rabbi Chaim, 116

Vorspan, Albert, 245

"Wailing Wall," 326

Warsaw Ghetto uprising, 182

Wellhausen, Julius, 83–84

West Bank, 330

Western Wall, 198–99, 325–26

White Paper (1939), 327

Wiesel, Elie, 17, 191, 353

Wine production, 252

Wisdom of Ben Sirah, 92

Wolf, Rabbi Arnold Jacob, 34

Women's Haggadah, 168

Worship services, 207–10

Written Torah, 81–84

Yaakov, Rabbi Eliezer ben, 354

Yad (Torah pointer), 212

Yahrzeit (anniversary of death), 311–12

Yamim Noraim (Days of Awe), 124

Yasher koach (congratulations), 279

Yehudah (Judah), 55

Yerushalayim. See Jerusalem

Yetze'at Mitzraim (Exodus from Egypt), 163

YHWH, 7–8

Yichud (following wedding ceremony), 300

Yiddish language, 52–53

Yisrael, 59

Yitzchak, Rabbi Shlomo ben, 100

Yizkor memorial prayers, 177, 312

Yom HaAtzmaut (Israeli Independence Day), 124, 195–96

Yom HaShoah (Holocaust Remembrance Day), 124, 181–82

Yom HaZikaron (Day of Remembrance), 195–96

Yom Kippur (Day of Atonement), 123–25, 130, 132, 134–38

Yom Kippur War (1973), 348

Yom Tov (holiday), 123–126

Youth *Aliyah,* 340

Zakkai, Yochanan ben, 49

Zangwill, Israel, 353

Zechariah, 78

Zecher l'churban (remembrance of the destruction), 300

Zephaniah, 77

Zionism, 326–28, 336

Zionist Conference (1933), 336

Z'man Matan Toratanu (time of the giving of our Torah), 177

Zohar (The Book of Splendor), 115

Zola, Émile, 326

Zusya, Rabbi, 237